THE COMPLETE BOOK OF BUSINESS PLANS

THE
COMPLETE
BOOK
OF
BUSINESS
PLANS

Simple Steps to Writing Powerful Business Plans

SECOND EDITION

JOSEPH A. COVELLO AND BRIAN J. HAZELGREN

SOURCEBOOKS, INC.®
NAPERVILLE, ILLINOIS

Published by Sourcebooks, Inc.
P.O. Box 4410, Naperville, Illinois   60567-4410
(630) 961-3900
Fax: (630) 961-2168
www.sourcebooks.com

Originally published in 1995

Library of Congress Cataloging-in-Publication Data

Covello, Joseph A.
  The complete book of business plans : simple steps to writing powerful business plans / Joseph Covello and Brian Hazelgren. -- 2nd ed.
    p. cm.
  Includes index.
  ISBN-13: 978-1-4022-0763-1
  ISBN-10: 1-4022-0763-8
  1. New business enterprises--Planning. 2. New business enterprises--Finance. 3. Proposal writing in business. I. Hazelgren, Brian J., 1961- II. Title.

HD62.5.C68 2006
658.4'012--dc22

2006026987

Printed and bound in Canada.
WC 10 9 8 7

CONTENTS

INTRODUCTION

Business planning, believe it or not, is a powerful tool that can help you achieve your highest and loftiest goals, as well as your wildest dreams. The act of researching, writing, creating, and expanding on your business idea can be an exhilarating experience as long as you have the proper tools at your disposal. *The Complete Book of Business Plans* is one of the tools that will help you get there in a much easier fashion.

You will find *The Complete Book of Business Plans* user-friendly and easy to follow. We use familiar words and phrases, and we're mindful that your time is valuable, so we get right to the point. This book will assist you in developing a world-class business plan that gets you the results you are looking for. It has been written and formatted in a way that will lead you along the planning path with less resistance and will assist you in cutting through the commerce forest with a professionally honed and sharpened blade.

How will you accomplish this? Simple: by following the lessons we have learned over the last twenty years. We have personally written over two hundred business plans; we have authored six books on the subject of planning; we both teach—or have taught—at colleges and a major university; one of us is a judge for one of the country's top annual business plan writing contests; and most important, we both have had to learn in the trenches on the front lines of small, medium, and large business on how to properly research, write, and craft a winning business plan.

As with any business management tool, business planning can be used for multiple purposes such as starting a new business, raising capital, launching a new line of products or services, expanding business facilities, selling an existing business, or gaining a better focus of an existing enterprise. Whatever your reasons, we are here to help you, and as long as you follow the simple advice, ideas, and format presented in *The Complete Book of Business Plans*, you will be well on your way to crafting a highly successful plan of your own.

We will be providing you with guidelines for successful business planning and real-life examples of what has worked and what has not worked in the planning process. Yes, there is a *science* to writing business plans, but it is the *art* that will take center stage. You are crafting a document that will serve as a foundation for your business quest. Our job is to help you focus your energy and balance your enthusiasm with a little bit of reality.

We have learned a lot during our years in business, and we'll share these lessons with you along the way. Learn from our experiences, both good and bad, as well others as you journey throughout the book and apply them to your situation. This is *art* at its finest form.

Although business planning is a disciplined effort to produce fundamental decisions and actions that shape and guide what you want to accomplish, the process must still have some elements of fun and reward. But, make no mistake, you will not be able to just snap your fingers, buy some software, push a few buttons, and call it good. Based on the complexity of your business model, plan on spending about fifty to one hundred fifty hours of researching, writing, rewriting, thinking, strategizing, and crafting a blueprint for your next successful venture.

The process is certainly about *planning* because it involves intentionally setting goals, choosing a desired future, and developing an approach to achieving those goals. You have to be disciplined in order to keep yourself focused and productive. The process of planning pushes entrepreneurs, business owners, and business managers to examine experience, test assumptions, gather and incorporate information about the present, and anticipate the environment in which the business will be working in the future.

Think of your business plan as a rolling ninety-day plan that plugs into the overall strategy and allows for a tactical focus, while you are ramping up the long-range plan. Your business plan is ultimately no more and no less than a set of decisions about what to do, why to do it, what resources to involve, and how to do it.

The following list highlights the importance of having a written business plan. We offer them here as a way to approach this important work of proper planning. Successful business planning:
- leads to action
- builds a shared vision
- is an inclusive and participatory process in which the team can claim ownership
- holds individuals accountable to the organization and stakeholders
- is both externally and internally focused and sensitive to the organization's environment
- is based on quality data
- requires openness to questioning the status quo
- is a key part of effective management

Many business managers feel that they can keep track of everything without the need to write it down. They figure a written plan is really just the representation of internal planning that every business manager does anyway. So what justifies the additional time and energy they will spend creating a written plan that presents a blueprint of their business or business idea? Well, the structure that a written plan provides makes it more likely that you will consider all relevant factors and that nothing important will slip through the cracks. Put simply, a written business plan increases your chance for success. Every successful team has some sort of game plan that they follow and update as they go forward. More specifically, a plan can be:
- a reality check that forces you to consider all relevant factors when you first examine the feasibility of your business idea
- your business's résumé, which will be vital in dealing with lenders and outside investors, and an important tool in negotiating with vendors and attracting employees
- a timetable for operations, helping you to coordinate all the diverse activities that go into running your own business
- a modeling tool that helps you evaluate the variables that affect your business, so you can better prepare to deal with situations that may arise as conditions change

- a way to track the progress of your business
- a blueprint against which you can adjust operations in order to achieve your goals
- a starting point for future planning
- the foundation for raising capital

The business planning process can be complex, challenging, sometimes overwhelming, and even chaotic, but it can also be a lot of fun. Take advantage of tools like this book and learn from the mistakes and successes of others. Our simple, easy-to-understand process can show you how to write a winning business plan that may save you time and money—an incredibly valuable proposition!

Well, then, sit back, roll up your sleeves, and prepare to be amazed at how much you will learn and how much fun you will have as you watch your dreams unfold. Develop your own road map for the greatest journey you could possibly imagine. Today's planning determines tomorrow's victories. Now is the time to start planning for a tomorrow filled with success and prosperity.

SECTION 1

Getting Ready to Write Your Winning Business Plan

CHAPTER 1

Evaluating You and Your Business Idea

A Few Facts

It is estimated that over one million new businesses are started in America each year, from small-scale home-based businesses to large corporate enterprises requiring many millions of dollars of start-up capital. Of all of these new businesses, it is anticipated that only one in five will make it to their fifth anniversary and will be achieving the results they originally forecasted at start-up.

That is an alarming statistic! Why in the world would only one out of five businesses in the "Land of Opportunity" survive, even for a relatively short period of time? There are several reasons why, yet the most common reason just happens to be the most controllable. The bottom line is that there is no magic equation for success; however, one basic rule holds true: "A business owner or business manager who fails to plan, plans to fail."

A business plan helps entrepreneurs and managers think through their strategies, balance their enthusiasm with facts, and recognize their limitations. It will help you avoid potentially disastrous errors like undercapitalizing, creating negative cash flow, hiring the wrong people, selecting the wrong location, underestimating your competition, and pursuing the wrong market.

A winning business plan requires time. Plan to spend fifty to one hundred fifty hours crafting a complete and comprehensive business plan, including research, documentation, analysis, and review. Entrepreneurs should really start planning at least six months before they intend to open or expand their business or begin raising capital. Most entrepreneurs will need to devote time to the start-up while still working another job, or if they are expanding an existing business, they need to continue to run the day-to-day operations. Six months gives you time to sharpen and focus your business ideas and concepts while you are testing your assumptions.

The Journey Begins with You

Many opportunities exist for each of us for going into business for ourselves. The opportunities are immense and can range from the thousands of home-based businesses available to the array of small-, medium-, and large-sized businesses in the manufacturing, distribution, retail, and service arenas. It is estimated that the largest corporations only account for 20 percent of the jobs in the United States. The remaining workforce is mainly employed by local, city, state, and federal governments; nonprofit organizations; and entrepreneurs, like yourself, who are willing to go out into the marketplace and take a huge risk in order to create their own journey and live life on their terms.

Writing a comprehensive and complete business plan will help you get your journey started on the right foot and avoid some of the pitfalls that plague entrepreneurs because they are shooting from the hip and banking on assumptions that are misleading, incomplete, or just flat-out incorrect. Over the years, we have had many individuals come to us with ideas, concepts, and inventions that they felt were surefire winners. Upon thoroughly researching what they wanted to do as part of the business planning process, they discovered for one reason or another—whether it was undercapitalization, wrong market timing, inadequate market size, poor management or people skills, or poor products or services—that their "surefire winner" was nothing more than pie in the sky.

Before you set off on this journey, there are certain issues and questions you should first consider that will be helpful in determining whether what you are planning to do is actually right for you and right for the marketplace.

First, consider what impact a start-up may have on you, your family, and other relationships:

- Your income will suffer.
- Your work hours will multiply.
- Your family relationships will be strained.
- You will expend your personal cash or be in debt.
- You will sometimes feel like you are running behind.
- You may become more irritable or critical with people around you.
- You will see less of your friends and family.
- You may get more headaches, backaches, or stomachaches.
- You will feel guilty at times if you are not working.
- Your life, for a time, may seem like all work and no play.

Second, ask yourself the following questions:

- How much money do I have to invest?
- Can I attract other investors?
- What amount of return do I want?
- What do I do well?
- What do I like to do the most and what do I have the most fun with?
- Will I be committed to working harder and longer hours?
- How do I make up for my shortcomings?
- Will I devote time to continuous personal development?

Whoa! That may seem overwhelming, but do not despair because these feelings and circumstances are a normal part of starting a business or embarking on a new project. We just want to make you aware of some of the challenges you will be facing. During your journey there will be a lot of traffic and a lot of obstacles in your way and when it comes time to cross the street, we want to make sure you look both ways and back again so you have a successful and efficient crossing. The worst thing you can do is go into your business blind. The second worst thing you can do is give up. As Robert Donovan once said, "Giving up is the ultimate tragedy."

Roles You'll Be Expected to Play

If you're currently employed, you have firsthand knowledge of what it's like to be an employee. If you think going into business for yourself will mostly mean doing the same thing but for yourself, you're in for a surprise. If you are writing your business plan to launch a small business, you should know that small-business owners are responsible for the entire business, which involves a lot more than just providing goods or services. It's likely that all the administrative and managerial duties currently performed by your employer will fall on your shoulders after you create your new business.

To evaluate your own aptitude for business ownership, at a minimum you need to understand the responsibilities of ownership. This includes what is involved in owning a business and what roles you will have to play if you own one. This is a good place to start if you're considering starting your own business but haven't owned one before. Ask yourself, what is really involved in running a successful enterprise? Do you possess the right skills to carry it out? We've all heard of the stressed executive who complains that he is overworked because he has to wear two or three hats at his company. Most small business owners would give anything to wear *only* two or three hats!

Sales taxes and payroll or self-employment taxes have to be collected, forms need to be completed, and payments need to be made. Accounts receivable must be collected, deposits must be made to the bank, and accounts payable will have to be paid in a timely manner. Providing customer service, keeping the appropriate equipment and supplies in stock, and tracking and maintaining inventory and work in progress are activities vital to most businesses. You'll be doing all these things *in addition to* the activities that directly relate to providing goods or services to your customers.

Here is a look at some of the roles you can expect to play when owning your own business:

- Business Planner: As you run your business, you will inevitably want to make changes, perhaps to expand the business or add a new product line. If you want to make a change, it will be your responsibility to actually do it. You will have to plan it and execute it, and you will have to consider all of the ramifications of your decision.

- Market Researcher: Before you start or expand your business, you will have to find out who your customers are and where they're located. You may also have to conduct market research at various times during the life of your business, such as when you are considering introducing a new product.

- Sales/Marketing/Advertising Executive: In addition to having to plan your marketing or advertising campaign, you will have to carry it out. You may write advertising copy, do some preliminary market research, visit potential customers, and make sure existing customers stay happy. Depending upon the type of business you own, you may have to join business groups; attend various breakfasts, lunches, and dinners; and generally network with anyone who could help your business prosper.

- Accountant: Even if you have an accountant, you will have to know a lot about accounting, including which records to keep and how to organize them. If you don't have an accountant, you will also have to prepare all of your tax forms and you will have to know how to prepare and interpret all of your own financial statements.

- Tax Collector: If you sell goods at the retail level, you are responsible for collecting a sales tax for various government entities. If you have employees, you are responsible for collecting payroll taxes from them as well as filing monthly and quarterly forms to the applicable government agency.

- Bill Collector: When customers don't pay, it will be up to you to collect from them. You will have to know what you can and can't do when collecting monies owed you, and you will have to decide how best to collect them and when to give up.

- Human Resource Manager: If you have employees, you will be responsible for all the human resources-related functions, including recruiting, hiring, firing, and keeping track of all the employee benefits information. You will also be the one filling out all the insurance forms, answering employee questions and complaints, and making the decisions about whether you should change the benefits package you offer your employees.

- Lawyer: Even if you have a lawyer, you will have to know a lot about the law. If you choose not to have a lawyer, you will have to prepare all of your own contracts and other documents and understand all of the employment laws if you have employees or want to hire someone.

- Technology Expert: As a business owner, you will probably come to depend upon your computer and you will have to load software, install upgrades, and fix the computer when it breaks. You will also have to keep up with the newest products and the latest changes in technology.

- Clerk/Receptionist/Typist/Secretary: Even if you have clerical help, you'll inevitably do some filing, typing, mailing, and telephone answering. You'll have to know how to handle a variety of tasks so that when you hire help, you can teach them what to do.

It is critical to review this list of the important responsibilities involved in running a business so you can realistically start to appraise your chances for success. Obviously, much of your time will be spent on handling the responsibilities imposed on you as a business owner. If you're going to succeed, you'll have to do so in the time that remains.

Don't make the mistake of underestimating the cost, in hours, of being in business for yourself. A person who spends forty hours a week focused on his work will have to work a lot more hours as a business owner to get in forty hours of activity directly related to providing customers with goods or services. During the start-up period, you'll probably be the busiest you've ever been in your life.

Starting a business takes a lot of courage. But as they say, courage doesn't pay the bills. To stay in business and be successful, you need more than courage. You need a combination of hard work, skill, perseverance, proper planning, and sometimes old-fashioned luck.

What do you want from your business? If you want to succeed, how will you know when you get there? Knowing what you want from your business permeates all of the other decisions you will have to make in starting a new business. It will affect which business you choose, how you evaluate your chances for success, and how you determine if you have the right skills. Before you begin this new venture, find out if you have the right stuff.

Can You Handle the Impact on Your Life?

As we continue our discussion of being a business owner, you should realize that it is fundamentally different from being an employee. The distinction between work time and personal time can get a little blurry. If a problem arises with the business, it's *your* problem, and it won't go away merely because you've closed the doors for the day.

Decisions you make regarding the business will have a direct and immediate impact on your personal life. For example, if you're in retail and decide to remain open evenings, it's your time that's affected. And you're likely to be on call twenty-four hours a day in the event that an emergency arises regarding your business. We have been called in the middle of the night because our building was broken into, and of course, we had to travel to the office to investigate the problem.

The impact is even greater if your business involves working out of your home. You may experience conflicts over the use of space for business or personal purposes. The distinction between your personal life and business life is even further attenuated. Even when you're at home, you're also physically at work. On the upside, there's no commute and you can eat more cheaply at home.

If you have a family, it's important to measure the impact that opening a new business will have on them. It's best to discuss this as soon as you seriously start to consider the idea. Both you and your family must be willing to put up with the changes in your lives that owning a business will bring. Some people experience emotional and physical strain from being in their own business and working the hours it takes to make it successful.

The following aspects of day-to-day living may seriously be affected by your decision to open your own business:

- Security and source of income: One of the biggest differences between being a business owner and being a full-time or salaried employee is the source of your income. Full-time or salaried employees can generally expect to receive a paycheck for a known amount at fixed intervals.

    As the owner of a new business, you will be paid only when and if the business generates enough money. Even successful businesses rarely generate a profit in the beginning stages of operation. You will have to be prepared for a period of time during which your expenses will exceed any income derived from the new business.

- Health insurance: Although employees are being called upon to pay an increasingly larger share of health insurance costs, it's even tougher for a business owner. There is no employer to pick up some portion of the premium cost. There's no pool of employees that would allow you to negotiate a more favorable rate than you can get on an individual policy. On the other hand, you may be able to join an association of other businesses so you can take advantage of less expensive group insurance rates.

    For those covered under employer-provided health care plans who leave to start a business, check with your employer to see if you have the option of continuing coverage under the COBRA law (Consolidated Omnibus Budget Reconciliation Act). If so, you will be responsible for the full cost of premiums since the employer is not responsible for contributing anything for you. Also, you're entitled to continued coverage for a limited period of time, as little as eighteen months or as long as thirty-six months, depending on the circumstances. You might be able to get better coverage for the same cost elsewhere. If you are married and your spouse has insurance through an employer plan, consider coverage through that plan.

- Retirement savings: Retirement savings are a little different from health insurance. If you don't have health insurance and experience a catastrophic injury or disease, you may be wiped out. The impact of failing to save for your retirement can be even more damaging, but people tend to minimize the risk because "retirement is such a long way off."

It is no surprise that the saving rate is higher among employees than newer business owners. Employer-sponsored plans provide a convenient and painless way to set aside a portion of each paycheck. A business owner has to make a conscious decision to save, outside the framework of a plan administered by someone else. That decision can often be deferred or forgotten when you feel the cash coming in has to be put right back into the business.

So, Do You Have the Right Stuff?

If asked whether they had the "right stuff" to run a business, most people who are interested in starting a new business would answer with a resounding "yes." But the purpose of this evaluation is not just to arrive at a yes or no answer. The purpose is to help you assess your strengths and weaknesses so that you will be in a better position to make certain decisions before you start a new business.

Do your best to gauge the scope of activities that make up the business you have in mind. Be particularly careful not to overlook the less enjoyable aspects of the business—every business has a few. Regardless of your desire to go into business for yourself, if you lack necessary skills, it's unlikely you will succeed unless you find a way to compensate.

Should you take on partners? Should you hire an accountant or a lawyer? Should you hire a store manager if you're opening a retail business? Should you work from home? Your answers to these questions and many others will depend in large part upon which skills you have and which skills you lack.

To begin the process of examining your strengths and weaknesses, complete the following steps:

- Assess your strengths and weaknesses.
- Examine the personality traits of a successful owner.
- Compare the two lists and determine what the areas are in which you need to improve, or hire people or outside consultants to assist you.

If you already feel that you know your strengths and weaknesses, you can move straight to evaluating your chances for success, which is an evaluation of your business idea, as opposed to an evaluation of yourself.

What Are Your Goals?

Why is it that you want to start a business? Money? Fame? Personal freedom? Ego gratification? Retirement income? Uncertainty about getting rehired or retrained? Discomfort with larger organizations? If someone were to ask you why you're going into business for yourself, what would you say? It is very important that you know your reason why, because it will be your "why" that drives you to be successful.

For many people, it helps to translate their expectations and desires into concrete terms by setting long- and short-term goals. When you have a solid mix of long- and short-term goals, you create a balance that can be implemented into a solid plan of action.

Long-term goals for the entrepreneur typically fall into one of the following three broad categories:

- Economic goals: For many entrepreneurs, this is a strong inducement. The opportunity to increase personal earnings and achieve their financial potential is often a powerful motivation in starting a business.
- Personal Goals: Unlike money, many of these factors can't be quantified but are important nevertheless. For many people, the chance to build something of their own, according to their own vision, is what drives them to start a business.
- Retirement Goals: It's vital for everyone, employee and entrepreneur alike, to recognize that there will come a time when they want to kick back and enjoy the fruits of their labors. In this time of growing concern over the continued viability of the Social Security system, any goal setting you do should involve consideration of your needs *after* you've built and run your business.

Short-term goals are vital in your journey. They will fill you with a sense of accomplishment as you complete each one and will provide hope and energy as you progress toward meeting your long-term goals. Your short-term goals should be realistic and achievable. Your short-term goals may include selecting a name for the business that you're happy with, obtaining a business license in a timely manner, finding a good business lawyer, or establishing a business credit card account. It will be important psychologically in those chaotic first months to be able to feel that you're making some progress. Short-term goals can help you achieve those small but crucial victories.

Why Goals Are Important

Goals are important because they will affect just about everything you do as you plan and operate your business. Goals are not just the destination you're driving toward, but they're also the painted white lines that keep you on the road.

Let's say you have a job that pays you $35,000. You hate your job and yearn to leave. You have an idea for a small business that involves servicing a small niche market, and you set a goal of being recognized as the expert in that niche area within five years.

You analyze your idea and discover that while no one else is servicing that market, it's a small market, and you're not likely to make more than $32,000 for at least the first three years. Yet you also discover that because your business is unique and your chances of reaching your goals and becoming a recognized expert are good, you'll have much greater income potential after the first three years. Despite the cut in income for three years, you decide the risks are worth it and that you'll start the new business.

Of course, goals won't just determine whether you start a business; they'll also play a prominent role in just about every decision you make along the way, from how you structure your business planning to whether you hire employees to how you sell and market your product or services.

Once you have some idea of what your general goals are, the next step is to make those goals concrete by quantifying them. It's not enough just to say, for example, that you want to change professions or that you want to be your own boss. You'll need to develop specific targets by quantifying your goals.

How to Quantify Your Goals

Quantifying your goals can be a long process. You'll have to gather a lot more information before you're ready to set specific targets that you'll incorporate into your business plan. But before we move on to the process of getting that information, let's take a look at some of the guidelines you should follow when quantifying your goals:

- Be specific: Establish targets that can be easily measured, and use numbers as targets whenever possible. For example, you may set a goal of selling your goods or services across a particular number of counties or states, having a certain number of employees, or reaching a particular level of sales. Set measurable objectives such as sales or sales growth, profitability or profit growth, market share as published by an objective and accessible source, and gross margin as percent of sales, for example.

    Avoid setting vague goals that can't be tracked. Where general or intangible goals are important to your business, find a way to make them specific. For example, if customer satisfaction is a priority, put your objectives in terms of percent of returns, specific numbers of complaints or letters of praise, or some other measure related to satisfaction. If image or awareness is a priority, include a survey that allows you to obtain information on how people feel about your products or services and how knowledgeable they are about them. You can build a customer satisfaction survey into your plan, set the sample size and satisfaction scores you want to achieve, then carry out the survey to check on success.

    In addition to setting these specific goals, tie those numbers to specific periods such as within six months, within two years, within ten years, etc. Making your goals concrete is the best way—possibly the only way—to tell when you've achieved them. Tracking your progress toward your goals with measured results is critical.

- Be realistic: Having high expectations is great, but make sure that you establish targets that are reasonable and achievable. If you're opening a fast-food restaurant, to say that you want to be bigger than McDonald's within six months is not realistic.

- Be aggressive: You can be realistic and still aim high. Don't set goals that are too easily achieved and make sure you also set both short- and long-term goals. If after six months in business you accomplish all of your goals, then what? Don't sell yourself short. If you want to be bigger than McDonald's within twenty years, go for it.

- Be consistent: Beware of inadvertently setting inconsistent goals. For example, a goal of growing fast enough to have three employees within two years might be inconsistent with a goal of earning a particular amount of money if the cost of adding the employees ends up temporarily reducing your income below the target level. There is nothing wrong with having both goals. Just be aware that potential conflict exists and you should establish priorities among your goals so that you'll know which ones are most important to you.

Develop a Foundation—Set Your Goals and Objectives

When developing your goals and objectives, generate a numbered list of a few selected objectives. Then pare this list to about ten goals, because a shorter list will make it easier to focus.

Some people have a hard time setting goals because they just don't know where to start. If this applies to you, try this simple exercise designed to help you get focused on your goals and objectives.

Start with an easily quantifiable goal. Then list the amount of money you'll need to earn in order to cover your living expenses and to run the business since, no matter what, you'll need to make enough to make ends meet. Quantify when you will achieve your goal of earning enough money to make ends meet.

Sample Goals for Your Business Plan

Below are a few examples of goals from actual business plans that received funding and became ventures. In the beginning, these goals served as a foundation for the rest of the business plan. This first example illustrates the top nine goals of a training and consulting firm:

1. Secure funding by October 2004
2. Train 100 executives by January 2005
3. Train 400 executives by May 2005
4. Train 2,000 executives by March 2006
5. Train 15,000 executives by the conclusion of fiscal year 2009
6. Expand 12-month Executive Training Series to three markets by October 2005
7. Select a company to develop and host web-based version of The Enterprise Assessment Tool by October 2005
8. Launch web-based version of Enterprise Assessment Tool in March 2006
9. Capture 1% of the outplacement services market by year five

This example is a list of goals developed for a manufacturing company that makes personal care products:

1. Achieve a 10% response rate on our direct mail and email campaigns
2. Convert 10% of the responses for the first six months after funding and bump this number to 12% thereafter
3. Operate a highly successful enterprise that continues to provide superior products
4. Achieve the sales projections previously outlined
5. Borrow $500,000 for the expansion of the enterprise and new products, as well as have commitments for capital for acquisitions
6. Provide an exit strategy for any stakeholders after 2006
7. Continue to develop new products that enhance the lifestyle of our customers
8. Build a successful distributor channel with worldwide presence
9. Achieve a gross profit margin of 55% or greater
10. Have the products in 5,000 retail outlets by year five of this business plan
11. Create jobs in rural areas close to the manufacturing and sales facilities

Your business plan will probably require different criteria in establishing and meeting goals that make sense for your set of circumstances. The key thing to remember is that in order to meet your goals, you must first establish and write logical, realistic, and attainable goals and establish a time frame within which you will achieve them.

Involving an External Coach

We have thrown a lot at you so far and you may be saying to yourself, "Wow! There is a whole lot more to it than I originally thought. How will I get it all done?" Well, hang in there! For an organization with little or no experience in planning, an external coach or consultant can enhance the planning process by providing the following services:

- Facilitating retreats, meetings, and the planning process as a whole: The use of a consultant to serve as the "conversation traffic cop" is one method of ensuring that good ideas do not get lost in the process as emotions run high or personalities clash. A consultant can work with an organization to minimize planning barriers that impact effectiveness, using his experience as a source of tried-and-true techniques.

- Training in planning information and processes: It is critical for everyone involved in the planning process to speak the same language and use the same planning tools. External consultants can provide that conduit of information flow and education.

- Providing an objective and different perspective in the process: As an outsider to the organization, the consultant can ask questions and challenge existing traditions, assumptions, and routines more objectively than staff and board members. Often planners do not realize that they are using jargon or have made certain assumptions about their constituency. Having an outside consultant participate in the planning process helps ensure that organizations stay true to a key feature of the planning process—a willingness to question the status quo.

- The process expert role: A consultant who has facilitated and conducted many strategic planning sessions can provide significant information and advice on tools and procedures that can help you best accomplish your process and content goals.

When looking to hire external coaches and consultants, ask for quality referrals from people or organizations you trust, like your family and friends, your local chamber of commerce, your law firm, and your accounting firm. Before hiring or retaining anyone or any firm, make certain that you meet with them, learn exactly what they do, and what services they feel they can provide that would be beneficial for you and your business. Also, ask them for contact information on clients they currently work with and get a general description of what industry these clients are in, along with how they have helped them improve their business. You can use this information to check references and choose the right external coaches or consultants for your business.

Self-Development and Self-Improvement

As you journey through your personal and business life, we highly suggest that you never make the mistake of thinking that you know enough. We personally feel that none of us do. There are many personal development books, how-to books, DVDs, CDs, magazines, newspapers, college courses, and governmental programs available that will help us to continually grow. Remember, if you keep on learning, you will keep on churning. The following is a brief list of self-development books available that may help transform your life and your business.

- *Think and Grow Rich*, Napoleon Hill
- *The 7 Habits of Highly Effective People*, Stephen R. Covey
- *The 8th Habit: From Effectiveness to Greatness*, Stephen R. Covey
- *The One-Minute Manager*, Kenneth Blanchard, PhD, and Spencer Johnson, MD
- *The 21 Irrefutable Laws of Leadership*, John C. Maxwell
- *True Leadership*, Jan Ruhe
- *Seven Strategies for Wealth and Happiness*, Jim Rohn
- *The Power of Positive Thinking*, Dr. Norman Vincent Peale
- *You Can If You Think You Can*, Dr. Norman Vincent Peale
- *Rich Dad, Poor Dad*, Robert T. Kiyosaki and Sharon L. Lechter
- *Cashflow Quadrant: Rich Dad's Guide to Financial Freedom*, Robert T. Kiyosaki and Sharon L. Lechter
- *Secrets of the Millionaire Mind*, T. Harv Eker
- *Conversations with Millionaires*, Mike Litman, Jason Oman, et al.
- *The Millionaire Next Door*, Thomas J. Stanley and William D. Danko
- *21 Success Secrets of Self-Made Millionaires*, Brian Tracy
- *Nuts!*, Kevin Freiberg and Jackie Freiberg
- *As a Man Thinketh*, James Allen
- *Acres of Diamonds*, Russell H. Conwell
- *The Power of Focus*, Jack Canfield, Mark Victor Hansen, and Les Hewitt
- *Dare to Win*, Jack Canfield and Mark Victor Hansen
- *Untapped Potential: Turning Ordinary People into Extraordinary Performers*, Jack Lannom

This is just a brief list to get you started. Take time to go to a bookstore or library to see what other books, magazines, and periodicals are available to you that will enlighten—and enrich—your life. And don't forget, check for college courses and government-sponsored programs that will help you grow in your personal and professional life.

The Journey Continues with Your Business Idea

You may be chomping at the bit to get started on your business idea; you may be pondering different ideas trying to decide which one will be fun to do or most rewarding; or you may have no idea at all what business you would like to start, but you do know that it is time to stop working for someone else. No matter what stage you are in regarding your business idea, the Free Enterprise Model developed by Brian Hazelgren will be helpful to you in evaluating your business idea and determining if it is actually viable as a product or service.

The following is quoted from "Understanding the Free Enterprise Model," a paper written and published by Hazelgren:

FREE ENTERPRISE MODEL

As I have worked with hundreds of companies over the years, there exists a certain model of basic entrepreneurship, or free enterprise. It consists of three basic principles, with a few subsets, or elements that drive the model. In fact, whether you own a business or you are a manager of an enterprise, small, medium and larger enterprises can use this model as a valuable tool in moving an idea forward. This model is universal and allows all types of managers in all types of industries to work with an idea and bring it to fruition or ban the idea.

First, begin with an IDEA that moves the manager to some form of action. The idea begins to take shape as the opportunity is sized up and analyzed. The manager then begins to communicate his or her idea to others, and conducts further analysis of the OPPORTUNITY. This analysis is required to realize just how viable the opportunity may or may not be.

Once it is determined that there exists a fairly practical OPPORTUNITY, the manager then begins to design a plan for gathering the proper RESOURCES, those elements that are needed to turn an opportunity into a reality. The resources required may vary from organization to organization, but there are a few basic resources to consider: Tools, Technology, Capital, Industry Best Practices, Partners, Suppliers, Value Added Resellers (VARs), and most important People, or staff, not just the management team. (We will discuss the TEAM in just a moment.) Resources are vastly important in the overall success of making the opportunity a reality.

After the Resources have been identified and even allocated, the next step is to formulate the TEAM that will be responsible for driving the entire concept into a formidable, moneymaking opportunity. The team is made up of individuals who will be held responsible for the success (or heaven forbid, failure) of the opportunity.

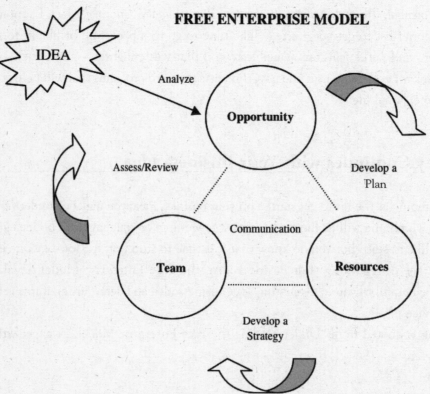

As you go through the exercises of sizing up an opportunity, gathering the proper resources, and assembling the best management team, let's not forget that there are four very important elements which should not be overlooked as the process continues as follows:

- Communication
- Plan of Action
- Strategy
- Assessment/Review

Communication is paramount throughout the entire process. If communication breaks down, then the process breaks down and will ultimately fail. Communication is the foundation of all successful planning operations. Pay close attention to the communication between members of the planning committee and management. Keep a close watch that someone is driving the process forward and that no backbiting or undermining is occurring.

Develop a **Plan of Action** and see the fruits of your planning labors. This is where you will actually begin to implement what you have designed. Your Action Plan is your Implementation Strategy.

How will you put into practice what you have committed to writing? Although the Strategic Plan itself is a call to multiple forms of action, a succinct Plan of Action to get things moving is also required. It will include an outline of the steps you will be taking, the milestones you and your team will be achieving, defining who is responsible for the completion of the milestone, determining the start and end dates, and a budget for each element.

In the Merriam-Webster's Dictionary, **Strategy** is defined as **1 a (1):** the science and art of employing the political, economic, psychological, and military forces of a nation or group of nations to afford the maximum support to adopted policies in peace or war **(2):** the science and art of military command exercised to meet the enemy in combat under advantageous conditions **b:** a variety of or instance of the use of strategy **2 a:** a careful plan or method: a clever stratagem **b:** the art of devising or employing plans or stratagems toward a goal **3:** an adaptation or complex of adaptations (as of behavior, metabolism, or structure) that serves or appears to serve an important function in achieving evolutionary success

And **Stratagem** is defined as **1 a:** an artifice or trick in war for deceiving and outwitting the enemy **b:** a cleverly contrived trick or scheme for gaining an end

Whether it comes down to war, winning a game, or beating your competition, formulating a strategy is the first step to achieving success.

Assessment and Reviews should occur after you have implemented your plan. You will need to assess how well your plan is working. You should review with your team which things are working and which things are not. Has the plan been implemented? What are the bumps in the road that have occurred? What changes should you make? Who should you reward if things are going well? (Don't forget this item. People like to be recognized for doing a good job.)

The key to the Free Enterprise Model is to evaluate an idea as best you can instead of blindly running with it. Too often, we have seen entrepreneurs put good money into bad ideas. Not only did they lose significant money assets, but they also lost a huge amount of their time and created stress and health issues in their lives. Don't let this be you.

Years back, we were hired by a law firm in Southern California to review one of their client's business plans. The law firm felt strongly that the business venture he wanted to go into was a long shot and they tried everything they could to talk him out of it, but he wasn't budging. Concerned about him losing everything he had on this venture (around $12 million), they contacted us for help.

Upon our initial review of the plan, we felt the law firm was justified in being concerned. After several discussions with the client and the law firm, along with independent research on our part, we concluded that the risk of going into this venture far exceeded the potential return. Our advice did not help. Again, because the client was so passionate and so intent on doing the venture, he still wouldn't budge and he set his eyes on getting things going.

Fortunately, through the law firm's persistence, the client agreed to meet with us to review and brainstorm the strengths and weaknesses of his plan. After many grueling hours and many painstaking debates, their client broke down in tears and admitted that we were right and the chances of his venture being successful were slim. He was heartbroken because he was passionate about it, but he did understand the reality of the situation—it was a long shot.

For most new business owners, $12 million is not at stake; nevertheless, we are talking about putting up a significant amount of money that took years to earn and save, and that is why it is critical to evaluate your business idea and not go into it with blinders on. You worked so hard for what you have, but it can be so easy to lose.

Remember, it is estimated that only 20 percent of businesses make it to their fifth anniversary! Increase your chances of being a successful business that makes it. Do your due diligence. Make sure you properly evaluate your business idea.

CHAPTER 2

Powerful Guidelines for Writing a Winning Business Plan

Ready, Set, Almost Go

We are sure by now that you are chomping at the bit to start writing your business plan, but the question is, are you really ready to get started? For some of you, maybe so; however, for most, our system will be of immeasurable value since it has been successfully used by many entrepreneurs and business plan writers to help them write and compile winning business plans.

Now that you have evaluated yourself and your business idea, our goals over the next three chapters are to educate you about what is generally included in a business plan, to provide you with practical tips and insights, and to stimulate your thought process by taking you through over one hundred important questions for business plan writers. Finally, you will read and review a sample business plan.

After you have completed these chapters, you will be ready to begin writing your own winning business plan.

Your Heart and Soul

By now you should be convinced that proper business planning is an absolute necessity. *Your business plan is the heart and soul of your operation and the most important set of documents you will provide to any lending institution or potential investor.* The business plan is the road map to success for your business. It explains all the financing you need to make it to your destination, and most important, it gives you insight into what you need to do to reach your goals and make your company one of the ones that makes it to its fifth anniversary with success and prosperity.

A comprehensive and realistic business plan will help you accomplish many essential objectives, including the following:

- Taking charge of your entrepreneurial life. The business plan is evidence of your initiative. It shows that you have the discipline to focus your energies on an important project and that you understand how to achieve progress and growth, solve problems along the way, and achieve ultimate goals. The business plan is the foundation of your vision and will allow you to structure your ideas into reality.

- Laying out a master blueprint. The business plan is to the entrepreneur what a set of detailed architectural drawings are to the builder. It details how you are going to reach your objectives, showing you every step of the way and where you plan to go in relation to where you actually are. It will also help you plan or pursue an alternate and possibly better route. The business plan is a powerful management tool.

- Communicating your master plan to members of your team. The business plan constitutes a concrete statement of purpose that allows you to communicate to your colleagues a step-by-step agenda for reaching your goals. Some portions of the business plan can also be used in training and coordinating meetings, as well as teaching staff persons what their role and accountability will be in making your business function successfully.

- Attracting money to your project. Potential suppliers of capital and other needed resources—bankers, brokers, investors, future partners, etc.—will place great value on your business plan as they decide whether to participate.

Your business plan will be your initial selling tool, your business résumé, your heart and soul when attracting top-notch employees and lenders.

What Potential Suppliers of Capital Look at First

There are four critical areas of the business plan that are important for business success, and investors will weigh them very heavily before deciding whether to participate with you. Make sure that you build a strong case for each of the following areas:

1. Management Team
2. Current and Projected Financials
3. Products and Services
4. Marketing Plan

Management Team

Your management team can make or break your business. This team will sell your business concept better than the best financial projections, the greatest marketing plan, and even the most innovative product or service. Potential investment sources place a tremendous amount of importance on the team of the managers who will be making crucial day-to-day decisions. The success or failure of your enterprise will depend on the skill set, experience, maturity, and common sense of you, your partners, your board of directors, and your management staff.

In your plan, you will want to cover in as much detail as possible why your management team is qualified to drive your business to success. Discuss their experience and their areas of expertise as they relate to the business, and explain their functions within the company.

Any management team needs balance. This balance will give you the ability to provide the organization with four essential elements:

1. Planning
2. Organizational Skills
3. Control
4. Leadership

Balance within the management team as a whole is vital. This includes their behavioral, technical, and conceptual skills and how they apply them to the production and delivery of a product or service, and the overall running of a business enterprise. At a minimum, the management team must have, or develop, skills in the production and marketing of their product or service, in producing and understanding financial data, in running general business operations, and managing others.

The strength of your management team must be well articulated in your business plan.

Honestly judging yourself and each member of the management team is key. If your management team is weak in any of these areas, you should consider bringing in top-notch, experienced individuals to your board of directors for direction as well as inspiration. Outside professionals can offer your enterprise tremendous leverage, without you having to carry them on your payroll.

Develop a formal organizational chart. A company with a formal structure will greatly enhance its ability to raise capital, and achieve its goals in less time and with far less expense. Identify the different managers and departments within your enterprise.

If there are any responsibilities that cannot be fully covered by your management team or if you are the owner and only manager of your small business, make sure that you identify your weak areas. Look at the possibility of hiring someone or contracting with consultants and professionals who specialize in these areas to assist you in your growth and development.

Current and Projected Financials

It will be almost impossible to raise monies from any investment source without having accurate and up-to-date financial statements, including financial statements from previous years and projected financial statements. The financial projections that you document in your business plan should be well thought-out. Plan to devote a fair amount of time to their development and to ensuring that you thoroughly understand them. If you have to refer an investor to your accountant for questions they have about your financial data, what you are essentially telling them is that you have no idea what is going on in your business.

Your set of financial statements should include the following:

• Profit and Loss Statement
• Balance Sheet
• Cash Flow Statement

When calculating your projections for the future, we suggest illustrating monthly figures for the first two years and annually thereafter. The monthly figures will be helpful to the investment source in determining how you are projecting your sales, cost of goods sold, and expenses, as well as seeing how, when, and where your cash will be used. Most investors and lenders are very skilled at reviewing business plans. Do not provide them with unachievable pie-in-the-sky projections. In other words, think about how they will react when they see your projections. Lean more toward the conservative side of projections and you will be far ahead of the game.

Products and Services

Whether or not your products and services are viable in the marketplace is of great concern to an investment source, particularly in the wake of the dot-com bust. During the 1990s, investment sources poured money into businesses that consisted of little more than a concept. They would then sell the companies or take them public through an initial public offering, making huge amounts of money. That is, of course, until the floor caved in.

Most new business start-ups will not mimic the amazing highs and lows of the high-tech dot-coms, but will probably deal with ordinary products and services that most of us use on a daily basis. Either way, the products and services must have quality and substance that is pleasing and acceptable to the marketplace in order for the business to succeed.

It may be important to explain the life cycle of certain products and services to the investment source—what stage the product or service is in and how much money and time must be invested before it will be ready for the marketplace. You may even want to create a simple chart covering the life cycles, time factors, and economic cycles influencing your ability to make money. The basic stages of a typical product or service life cycle are as follows:

1. Introduction Phase—Intense marketing campaign that introduces a new or unique product or service. The cost to purchase the product or service is generally very high, but sales take off and growth occurs.

2. Maturation Phase—The market becomes saturated with the unique product or service. Competition increases as awareness of the product grows, thus causing your sales growth to slow. Customers can now buy the product or service at a competitive rate. The combination of slower sales growth and reduced pricing decreases the sales revenue for that product.

3. Leveling-Off Phase—Newer, more unique products enter the market. Loyal customers continue to buy your product or service. Not-so-loyal customers begin to look at alternative products and services and eventually may shift their business to the newer items. Your product or service is still viable in the marketplace, but there has been a significant impact on sales revenue.

Explain how you will satisfy customer needs and wants. Remember to discuss the characteristics of your products and services and how they differ from similar products and services along with anticipated customer reactions to these characteristics. If applicable, it will be good to discuss your plans for the next generation of products and services that will be introduced in the near future.

Be sure to describe any unique, value-added characteristic your product or service provides to the customers and how this will give your company the competitive edge. Explain how the product works or how the service is used. For example, will your product save your customers time or money? Will your product or service generate more profits for your customers? If so, how? Are there any tests or case studies that have been performed that will help you back up your claims? Obtain that vital information and document it in your plan. If your product or service has evolved over the past few years, explain how and why.

Keep in mind that some investment sources only lend toward certain products and services, and be prepared to contact several different investment sources and groups to discover which capital sources will be most interested in your particular venture. For example, some suppliers of finances will only look at real estate transactions. Others may only consider franchise concepts, while others may wish to invest in a manufacturing enterprise.

Marketing Plan

An investment source will key into your marketing plan because it understands the importance of making your products and services known to the marketplace in a fashion that is cost-effective, timely, targeted at the right audience, and warranted, thus maximizing your sales and profit potential.

This part of the plan requires a fair amount of study and analysis. Although it may seem like a lengthy task at the outset, you can have a lot of fun with it. Here is where you find out who is out there, what the competition offers and what they don't, if your product or service will outsell the competition, what Unique Selling Advantage (USA) you will have over your competitors, etc.

You may even discover that the timing is not right for your enterprise and it would be unwise to go ahead with your plans. Although it may be disappointing to you, this would not be a negative finding because the time and money you will save if you should wait for a better time, or pursue another market, will be invaluable. Your future enterprise may depend on what the market dictates after a carefully designed marketing analysis.

The marketing plan is actually broken into two separate sections, Market Analysis and Marketing Strategies.

Market Analysis describes the existing marketplace in which you plan to operate your business. Some key points in defining the market segment for your products and services are:

- Product features
- Lifestyle of your targeted customers
- Geographical location
- Season or time of the year (if applicable)

It will be important to find answers to these questions as well: How many competitors share your market? How is the share of the market distributed among the major participants? At what rate is the market growing in dollars and percentages? What are the major trends toward the development of the shared marketplace? In writing your plan, summarize your view of the trends and the implied opportunities from your market analysis.

You will also want to list the strengths and weaknesses of your product or service. When covering your strengths, you need to be sure to place at least as much emphasis on marketing as you do on your product, if not more. List several distinct advantages and disadvantages versus your competition in the following areas:

- Actual performance
- Quality and reliability
- Production efficiencies
- Distribution
- Pricing
- Public image or reputation
- Business relationships or references

Marketing Strategies is the science of planning for and executing a promotional campaign that will generate sales for your enterprise. These strategies are meant to enhance, promote, and support the advantages, features, and benefits of your products and services and make the consumer want to buy them. This section should be designed with one word in mind: **strategy.**

When thinking about a strategy, you should be able to specifically define your business activities, strengths, and direction. Think of your competition as the enemy. They absolutely do not want you to succeed. What type of strategy would you put together to get away from an enemy who is bound and determined to see you fail? Your strategy, depending upon how much you want to succeed, should be defined to capture your share of the market in as little time as possible.

An important question you may want to answer in developing your marketing strategy is, how do (or how will) your customers perceive your company and product, relative to the competition? This is critical! Let's say that one more time. How do (or how will) your customers perceive your company and product, relative to the competition? A good way to find out is to ask them. Conduct a market survey. This is an easy and inexpensive way to find out the answer to this important question. What can be said about your competitors' products or services that will change your customers' minds toward your products and services? Determine what your Unique Selling Advantages are over your competitors. (A discussion on this topic follows this section.)

You will need to decide what strategies to use to promote your products and services. Will you use television or radio? Is it better to conduct seminars or participate in trade shows? Will you use telemarketing or outside sales representatives? Do you need to hire a public relations agency? Will you sell your products and services locally, nationally, or internationally? Is using direct mail a consideration? Will you distribute brochures and flyers? What creative ideas and strategies can you come up with that will bring you the sales revenue you desire?

In developing your marketing strategies, here are a few other questions you should give serious consideration:

- Are your strategies consistent with your evaluation of the marketplace and your capabilities?
- Have you defined your targeted market into a narrow window, or does your product appeal to a large market?
- Are your strategies based on facts or assumptions?
- Is your appraisal of the competition open-minded and honest?
- Is the expected return on investment sufficient to justify the risks?
- Have you thoroughly examined other strategies that your competitors are using? Could some of their strategies be adapted to your environment?
- Is your strategy legal?

Hot Marketing Tip

Another tip is to look at the gripes first, then create a marketing strategy around them. Look at everything about your industry that could frustrate or irritate a potential customer. Ask people what irritates them. Try to internalize the same problems and experience your customers' frustrations before creating your marketing strategies. Present your product or service as the solution to their problem.

Create Your Unique Selling Advantage

Your Unique Selling Advantage (USA) is vital to the success of your business. Everyone within an organization from the CEO down through the sales team and on to your clerical staff should have a solid understanding of what sets you apart from the competition.

Your USA is that single unique advantage, benefit, essence,

appeal, or big promise that holds your product or service out to the prospect, one that no other competitor offers or advertises. You should be able to articulate in one or two crisp, clear paragraphs the Unique Selling Advantage of your business product or service, as illustrated in the following example.

> Forward Tech has a wealth of Cisco Certified Internet Experts (CCIE) on staff. Their knowledge is so valuable to Cisco that they have a published Cisco training book on the market. This certification level is recognized worldwide as the highest in the industry. Very few companies can compete on this level.
>
> Low prices with discounts on network equipment make the company even stronger. Forward Tech can provide a total network solution with everything the client is in need of to make sound decisions and have the most state-of-the-art network design available.

Your USA is the backbone of your entire business concept because it will provide the following benefits:
- It is a concept that your entire enterprise should be built around. Your USA is literally the unique advantage that distinguishes and separates your business from any other.
- Based on your USA, you will be able to build a consistent and effective marketing campaign.

Once you have developed your own USA, formulating a winning marketing strategy will become much easier. Therefore, tell it accurately, straightforwardly, and intelligently.

Examples of a USA may be that your product is made entirely of all-natural ingredients or is guaranteed to last twice the amount of time of your competitors' products. Maybe you offer three times more follow-up to your customers after they purchase your product or service. Maybe your product is entirely handmade, the only product in your area, or two years ahead of your competitors' offerings. Maybe your business stays open two hours longer than all of your competitors for added convenience to your customers.

Go ahead! Create an irresistible USA that lets people feel that they cannot live a moment longer without your product or service. You will be surprised how easy this is. Be creative and have fun!

Define Your Business

Write a mission statement in fifty words or less that outlines what you will sell and to whom, and what will make customers want to buy from you and employees want to work for you.

Example: *Our mission is to provide useful, applicable solutions to business owners and managers in the areas of marketing, business planning, finance, accounting, and promotion, and to fully utilize our management team's experience and knowledge to increase revenues of each of our client's enterprises.*

Name Your Business

Our advice is to keep the name straightforward and descriptive. Make it as distinctive as possible and avoid grandiose and overworked adjectives. Your business name should be like the headline of an article. Describe who you are and what you do in your name whenever possible. A dangerous marketing tool is to make customers guess what you do. Your competition may already have a descriptive and straightforward name, so make it easy on yourself and don't be overly creative where it will cost you big dollars to market a name that does not suit the products and services you are providing.

Let's look at some common business names that we are quite familiar with today that have been around for a long time: IBM (International Business Machines), AT&T (American Telephone and Telegraph), and GM (General Motors). There is nothing fancy about any of these names and although their business units have taken on more product and service lines since they were first established, their names match their original products—business machines, telephone equipment, and motor vehicles.

Contents of Your Winning Business Plan

The way you present your data to the reader may vary slightly, but you should consider this general outline of how the business plan should flow:

    I. Cover Sheet
    II. Table of Contents
    III. Executive Summary
    IV. Company Overview
    V. Product and Service Description
    VI. Market Analysis
    VII. Marketing and Sales Strategy
    VIII. Internet Strategy (if applicable)
    IX. Management and Personnel Plan
    X. Financial Projections
    XI. Appendix

The following summary of the ingredients of the business plan is intended to show you the elements needed to compose a winning plan that will attract potential financial resources to your venture and provide your company with a solid road map showing where you are and where you plan to go. (It should be noted that the format of your business plan or the amount of detail it contains or how fancy and image-oriented it is, etc., may vary according to the intended use of your business plan and its readership.)

I. Cover Sheet. If you are appealing to prospective investors, money brokers, bankers, venture capitalists, etc., include a cover sheet, preferably on company stationery. This will help place your winning business plan in a framework of legitimacy.

Keep your cover sheet as simple as possible. Identify yourself, your business, the institution or party to whom you are presenting your winning business plan, and the date the plan is being submitted. Your cover sheet may include the following:

    A. Your business information, including:

        1. Full legal name of business

        2. Location of business including street, city, state, and zip code

        3. Telephone numbers

        4. Main contact person or persons including their titles

    B. A brief business paragraph giving your promotional description of your business goals, potential, and outlook

    C. The amount of capital you are requiring for your current and anticipated future needs

    D. Whenever possible, state the name or names of anyone who has recommended you to the investor source

II. Table of Contents. This will not only help your prospective lender to understand the road map you are placing before him, it will also make a statement about you—that you are organized, thorough, sensitive to the needs of those you are approaching, and able to manage the big picture. How many books have you opened up or read that did not have a table of contents? For most of us, that is where we go first when we want to get a snapshot of what the book is about. We suggest that you type up the table of contents last and include accurate page numbers.

III. Executive Summary. This is the only portion of the business plan that everyone who sees your business plan is sure to read with care. This portion of the business plan must be designed to capture and hold the interest of the party to whom the plan is being presented. Make sure it can be read in a few minutes. Make it exciting so you captivate the reader! A bored reader will simply put your business plan down and go on to the next one.

The executive summary encapsulates the entire business plan in a few paragraphs by giving the most succinct statement possible about the nature and objectives of your business. Take the top concepts that you want to articulate to the investment source in each category of your business plan from your company overview through your appendix. We suggest you keep it short, somewhere between two and five pages of typed copy.

Remember, this summary is a crystallization of the entire business plan in a quick overview format. Don't neglect this section because it will demonstrate that you can focus with clarity on your goals and state in no-nonsense fashion that you know who you are, what you want, and where you are going.

IV. Company Overview. In this section, you will provide information on your company, including who you are, where you have been, where you plan on going, and how your company fits into your industry and marketplace.

Providing a big picture perspective of the industry to which your business belongs will demonstrate how your business fits in, thus giving confidence that your company can be successful in reaching its targeted goals. Identify and discuss the following points in this section:

- The precise nature of your business
- A brief history of the business or how you developed your products and services
- How your facilities will be able to handle your future growth

- Your organizational details, including the legal structure of your business
- Your growth potential
- New products and new developments that have arisen in the recent past that will make your products and services more attractive to the public
- Economic trends that are favorable to your industry
- Any contracts and agreements you have in place guaranteeing future business and revenue

This information and similar details you may include constitute the profile of your business. This section should provide the reader with the concept of how your business works and why it has a unique chance to shine in the marketplace.

V. Product and Service Description. Here, you will tell the investment source exactly what you make or what service you provide, how you make the product or provide the service, and whether you are looking to expand your business by including new and better products and services that will result in increased revenues and a larger bottom line profit.

In writing this section, be sure to carefully explain what your products and services are so they can be easily understood by the investment source. Potential lenders and investment groups will only lend capital if they have confidence that the business plan has been clearly researched, identified, calculated, and thoroughly thought-out.

VI. Market Analysis. As stated earlier in this chapter, you will be describing to the investment source the existing marketplace in which you plan to operate your business. Some key points in defining the market segment for your products and services include product features, lifestyle of your targeted customers, geographical location, and, if applicable, season or time of the year.

When developing a profile of your target market, it is important to remember that your research will determine the strength of your analysis. Your local library and your telephone will be your strongest allies. Use them to their fullest! Take advantage of the information and statistics already available in books, directories, and case studies. Thorough research will impress potential investors more than you can believe. Spend your time wisely here. Be thorough in structuring this market profile. Show that you have done your homework with great care and due diligence.

VII. Marketing and Sales Strategy. Earlier in this chapter, we explained that marketing strategy is the science of planning for and executing a promotional campaign that will generate sales for your enterprise. These strategies should promote and support the advantages, features, and benefits of your products and services and make the consumer want to buy them. This section should be designed with one word in mind: **strategy.**

In reviewing the various strategies available to you, keep in mind that most of them cost money and each of them may target different audiences. It is important to develop a marketing strategy that maximizes your reach to your target audience with the least amount of money spent. Again, it is important that you spend time researching which marketing strategies may be best suited for your company and your products and services because spending money in the wrong areas is like pouring money down the drain. We highly suggest that you track your expenditures in each area along with the results. If an area is showing a strong benefit, you may want to spend more in that area, and if no response is happening in another area, you may want to eliminate spending there. Without proper tracking, you will never know what works and what does not work. We are sure that you would rather have the money stay in your pocket versus going down the drain.

VIII. Internet Strategy. If your business is or will be providing products and services via the Internet, it is important that you carefully develop a cost-effective strategy that will maximize your reach to your target audience. If you are a novice in this area, you may already know the strengths and the pitfalls of doing business over the Internet and you may know the best way to get the results you desire with the least amount of money being spent. If you are unsure how to develop an Internet strategy that will bring optimum results, we highly suggest you research this area thoroughly and discuss it with Internet-savvy consultants.

Your strategy may include doing business on eBay, creating your own domain name, developing your own website with an array of products being sold, using PayPal, or having your own credit card gateway established. Whatever it is, make sure you thoroughly research and clearly articulate your game plan so the investment source does not have to guess at what you are trying to accomplish.

IX. Management and Personnel Plan. Potential investment sources place a tremendous amount of importance on the team of managers that will be making crucial day-to-day decisions. The success or failure of your enterprise will depend on the experience, maturity, and common sense of you, your partners, your board of directors, and your management staff.

It is of the utmost importance that you and your management team fully understand every word, every line, and every component of your winning business plan before you bring it to an investment source. Being fully able to articulate your road map to success will greatly enhance your chances of obtaining the financing or investment capital you are looking for. In addition, you will be assured that your management team is riding on the same bus with you and going on the same journey. This in itself will help you accomplish the goals that you have established in your business plan.

X. Financial Projections. These are the heart of your business plan—the point at which your vision is quantified in terms of dollars and cents and units of time: days, weeks, months, and years. All investment sources reading your plan will go through your financial projections with great care. Your financials should be broken down into monthly projections for years one and two and annually thereafter. You may also present annual summary pages for all the years so the reader can get a quick snapshot of what you are projecting. Minimally, you should have three years of financial projections, although the total amount of years will vary based on the type of business you have or will be starting.

Additionally in this section, you will present your statement of resource needs. If you are using your business plan for generating needed resources from lenders or investors, this item will summarize your precise needs—amount, terms, and date needed—and it will also identify how the resources will be used. In the case of financing, your cash flow projections will reflect how these funds will be repaid.

In the case of capitalization involving equity partners, your projections will give an indication of the growth of equity and the anticipated timetable for the sharing of profits.

XI. Appendix. This section of the business plan might include some or all of the following items in order to support disclosures made throughout your business plan, as well as to provide additional valuable information to the investment source:

• Support of footnotes from the text (for example, added support for economic data presented in your

marketing plan and assumptions used in your financial projections)
- Supporting documents
- Magazine, newspaper articles, and special reports
- Biographies and résumés
- Bibliographies
- Graphs and charts
- Copies of contracts and agreements
- Glossary of terms
- References: lenders, investors, or other bankers, suppliers, trade creditors, etc., who can give positive feedback on your past performance

Be careful not to overload your appendix with too much information. Make sure what you present is pertinent, clearly presented, and logically sequenced.

Anticipated Challenges and Planned Responses

In running your business, you will continually run into obstacles and challenges that could have a major impact on how your business operates. Obviously, if you are able to respond quickly and efficiently, the impact on your enterprise may be minimal; however, if you are slow to respond or unsure how to respond, these situations can have a large negative impact on you.

It is important to know as you are writing your business plan that investment sources will be looking for or identifying potential obstacles to your business plan as they are reading it. That is why it is so important for you to have already identified them and to include how you will respond to them if they do occur. The following are some questions and issues to keep in mind as you are writing your winning business plan.

A. How will you deal with your competition?

1. Identify the similarities and differences between your business and your competitors', including their strengths and weaknesses. What opportunities exist to exploit your competitors' weaknesses? How will you handle your own weak points?

2. Create your competitive edge, your Unique Selling Advantage, which will enable you to prevail and stay on course

3. Determine what roadblocks your competition will try to use to stop you in obtaining market share and develop a plan of action to respond if they occur.

B. What are your weak areas where you believe you may be vulnerable and how do you intend to compensate for them? Areas of weakness may include:

1. Product obsolescence factors
2. Cheaper products on the horizon
3. Cyclical trends in the marketplace
4. Possible economic downturn in the future
5. Turnover of key employees
6. Seasonality of your products and services

  7. Offering a competitive benefits package to your employees

C. How do you anticipate legal factors, issues, and new and revised laws and regulations? Such as:

  1. License requirements that you must satisfy or maintain

  2. Restrictions and regulations under which you must operate given the nature of your business

  3. Future changes in legal or governmental policies that may affect your business, and how you will respond

  4. Any governmental agencies that you need to apply to or be regulated by. (a franchise must comply with the FTC [Federal Trade Commission] regulations; a radio station must comply with FCC [Federal Communications Commission] regulations; etc.)

D. What are your plans to protect your business? They may include:

  1. Patents, copyrights, trademarks, and other protection procedures you have in place

  2. Establishing procedures to assure that business secrets are preserved

E. What key man contingencies (e.g., the absence of key team members) have you prepared for? For example:

  1. Identifying the depth of your management team

  2. Setting management procedures in place to assure continuity of leadership

  3. Planning for responding to the loss of important personnel

F. How will you respond to staffing issues? Such as:

  1. Policies on personnel needs, including overtime, skill requirements, training, and benefits

  2. Policies on minority issues and other equal opportunity issues

  3. Policies on temporary versus permanent staff

  4. Policies on discrimination and harassment

Remember, throughout writing your winning plan, it will be important to demonstrate that you have covered the problem bases and have carefully crafted contingency plans in place. This information will provide your winning business plan with more credibility than you think. Be practical and reasonable. Show that you have really done your homework.

Practical Tips

Be realistic. Build your business plan with a sense of realism and practicality. Make sure that you do your homework carefully and think through every detail that could have a bearing on the success of your project. Your business plan should be a carefully crafted action document, not a speculative piece of fortune telling.

Document your claims. Where you are basing projections on specific assumptions (e.g., projections about market response to your goods or services), give evidence that these assumptions are based as closely as possible on fact. Assemble and apply expert opinion to substantiate your projections. Use newspaper and magazine articles, university studies, interviews with prominent people who are familiar with your market, etc., to back up your claims.

Create a Unique Selling Advantage. If you have an edge that will raise your chances of successes and persuasively identify you as separate from your competitors, emphasize this advantage boldly.

Be flexible. Your business plan is a road map that allows you to check your position, speed, and direction on a constant basis. As you monitor your progress, you will need to implement midcourse corrections periodically. You will certainly need to adjust your business plan from time to time as your assumptions are updated according to real-life feedback from the "trenches" and as market conditions shift.

Use technology to good advantage. Modern computers and computer software can be a tremendous help to you in developing portions of your business plan, especially the financial sections. With the help of computers, you can play "what if" scenarios and gain valuable insight into future outcomes, based on the strategic adjustment of variables (e.g., pricing services in relation to costs). If you need help in this area, contact local accounting experts to assist you.

You may wish to invest in the equipment and software to service your own needs in these regards. Computer hardware and effective software programs are very much within the reach of most budgets these days.

Attend to packaging. The business plan should be clean, conservative, simple, well-prepared, clearly written, error free, and appropriately bound. Your plan should look impressive, but not slick. You don't want to make a statement about being a big spender on superficial items. If you are presenting the business plan to prospective financial sources, you should bind the materials in such a way that they will open flat on a desktop. For internal use, the business plan should be organized in a three-ring binder where updates can be easily incorporated.

Present the plan skillfully and graphically. Consider using projection technology and similar support equipment when presenting your plan to prospective lenders. Presenting economic data, charts, graphs, and financial data in attractive visual ways will help to solidify your position.

CHAPTER 3

100-Plus Questions to Personal and Business Success

Over the many years that we have been working with entrepreneurs and business managers, we have found that one of the best tools for anyone writing a business plan, whether for the first time or the tenth time, is the process of going through a sequence of questions over and over again at various stages in the writing process. We have also discovered the best time to start going through this sequence of questions is right at the beginning of the process. Questions challenge the mind to think beyond the obvious. As you move forward through the business plan process, your mind will actually refer back to a question previously asked, and many times new answers and ideas will be generated, resulting in a more comprehensive and more complete business plan.

The creation of a business plan process is not an overnight occurrence, but rather a process that takes time. During this process, new ideas are created and original ideas are revised or eliminated. What may seem like the perfect answer to a question today may not be the same answer you will have tomorrow or six months from now. Make the time to go through the sequence of questions that follow and answer each of them to the best of your ability. If you are not sure how to answer a particular question at this time, just continue on to the next question. As you write your business plan, remember to continually reread these questions and your answers, and update and revise them if needed.

The following questions have been categorized by key topics and will be helpful to you when you begin writing and organizing your business plan. The key topics include general personal, general business, customers and competition, marketing, sales, advertising, internet strategy, products and services, production and facilities, management, and finance.

So, pick up your pencil and get started. Remember, the business plan process takes time; don't be in a hurry to rush through all the questions. If you need to break the process into a few different sessions, that's fine.

General Personal Questions

1. How do your business skills rate on a scale of 1–5, with 5 being exceptional, in the following areas?
   A. Knowledge of your products and services _____
   B. Ability to produce and provide your products and services _____

C. Knowledge of sales and marketing _____

D. Ability to create and implement marketing and sales programs _____

E. Knowledge of human resource management _____

F. Ability to effectively manage people _____

G. Knowledge of accounting and finance _____

H. Ability to prepare and understand financial statements _____

2. Are you more of a thinker (visionary) or a doer (technical person)? _____

3. Are you an effective leader? _____

4. What can you do to overcome your shortcomings? _____

5. Do you devote time to self-improvement through reading books, taking college classes, or attending seminars? _____

6. How much money do you have to invest in your business? _____

7. Are you willing to risk all of your money? _____

8. Do you feel additional funding may be needed (in addition to your own money)? _____

9. Do you have any experience in the business you plan to start? _____

10. Have you been successful working in this business? _____

11. Do you enjoy working in this business? _____

12. Do you have money saved that will cover your personal expenses while you are starting your new enterprise? _____

13. Are you self-motivated? _____

14. Are you committed to working harder and longer hours? _____

15. Have you explained to your family the risks involved with starting a new business and the extra amount of effort and time it will take? _____

General Business Questions

1. What phase is your business in?
   A. New start-up
   B. Expansion
   C. Cash flow needs
   D. Other _____

2. Why do you want to start or expand your business? _____

   _____

3. What are your goals and objectives for the business? _____

   _____

   _____

4. Have you developed your mission statement? Explain it in fifty words or less. _____

   _____

   _____

_____

_____

_____

5. What corporate structure will your company operate under?

    A. Sole proprietorship

    B. Partnership

    C. C Corporation or S Corporation

    D. Limited liability corporation

    E. Minority or woman-owned

    F. Nonprofit

    G. Other _____

6. What is the nature of your business or the business you are planning to start up (retail, manufacturing, service, etc.)? _____

7. Provide a brief history of the business and tell how you develop your products or services. _____

_____

_____

_____

8. Is your business seasonal? _____

9. If yes, how will you maintain cash flow for the slower times of the year? _____

10. What are the economic forecasts that indicate spending trends are favorable or unfavorable to your business and specific industry? _____

11. Are there any licenses that are required for you to run your business (occupational license, sales tax license, state corporation filings, etc.)? _____

12. What do you want for yourself, both personally and financially, by having your own business?

_____

_____

Customer and Competition Questions

1. What are the profiles of your customers? (Give details on the typical customer that you are targeting.)

    A. Business Customer:

    • Type of business _____

    • Size of business (approximate annual revenues) _____

    • Geographical area _____

    • Number of employees _____

    • Years in business _____

    B. Individual Consumer:

- Age _____
- Income _____
- Sex _____
- Occupation _____
- Family size _____
- Culture _____
- Education _____

2. How would you rank the following in the order of importance to your customers?

   A. Price _____

   B. Convenience _____

   C. Quality _____

   D. Service _____

3. How many competitors share your market? _____

4. Who are they and where are they located?

   A. _____

   B. _____

   C. _____

   D. _____

   E. _____

   F. _____

   G. _____

   H. _____

5. How is your competition currently promoting its product or service? _____

_____

6. What advantages or disadvantages do you have over your competition in the following areas?

   A. Performance _____

   B. Quality and reliability _____

   C. Production efficiencies _____

   D. Distribution _____

   E. Pricing _____

   F. Public image _____

   G. Business relationships _____

7. What strategies may be adapted to your environment that your competition is using?

_____

_____

Marketing Questions

1. Does your marketing strategy incorporate any of the following? If so, please give details.

   A. Executive Selling (owners or managers selling in the field) _____

B. Direct Sales Force _____

C. Manufacturer's Reps _____

D. Distributors _____

2. How do you establish your prices? _____

3. What are your profit margins and how do they relate to industry averages?_____

4. How do you market and advertise your products and services? _____

_____

5. Are there any other markets that you would like to try to establish? _____

6. What are the *strengths* of your marketing plan? _____

_____

_____

7. What are the *weaknesses* of your marketing plan? _____

_____

_____

Sales Questions

1. What is your Unique Selling Advantage? (What makes your product or service unique?)

_____

_____

_____

_____

_____

2. For existing businesses, what were the past three years' prior results?

	Yr. 1	Yr. 2	Yr.3
• Sales	_____	_____	_____
• Cost of sales	_____	_____	_____
• (Variable costs)	_____	_____	_____
• Gross profit	_____	_____	_____
• Operating expenses	_____	_____	_____
• (Fixed costs)	_____	_____	_____
• Profit (or Loss)	_____	_____	_____

3. What would you like to achieve in annual sales volume?

A. Year one $ _____

B. Year two $ _____

C. Year three $_____

D. Year four $ _____

E. Year five $ _____

4. What sales strategies will be implemented in order to achieve your annual sales volume goals?

_____

_____

_____

5. What is your anticipated market share over the next five years? _____

6. Who are your top ten most faithful customers who buy from you on a regular basis?

   A. _____

   B. _____

   C. _____

   D. _____

   E. _____

   F. _____

   G. _____

   H. _____

   I. _____

   J. _____

7. How do you or how will you satisfy your customers' needs and wants? _____

_____

8. Do you or will you have salespeople? If yes, indicate if they will have sales territories, and what their commission and salary structures will be. _____

9. How many salespeople will you have on staff during the next twenty-four months in order to meet your sales goals?

   A. Outside Sales _____

   B. Inside Sales _____

10. How will your company fit into the industry? _____

_____

Advertising Questions

1. How will you promote your products and services (television, radio, seminars, brochures, salespeople, direct mail, etc.)? _____

2. How much will you spend on advertising in a typical year? (List in dollars and as a percentage of gross revenues.) _____

3. What are the associated costs for each area of promotion? _____

_____

_____

4. Have you established a tracking system for charting sales income versus advertising dollars spent for each form of advertisement? _____

Internet Strategy Questions

1. What are the specific products and services you will promote on your site? _____ _____ _____

2. Who will design and build your site? _____

3. What is the flow chart of your site? _____ _____ _____

4. Approximately how many pages are there on your site? _____

5. Will you have a chat room?_____

6. Will you have a shopping cart? _____

7. Will you have an auction site? _____

8. Are your orders placed in batch or real time?_____

9. How does the customer pay you?_____

10. How will you track your site statistics? _____

11. How will you keep a profile of each customer?_____

12. What if they don't purchase, will you be able to send them information in the future?_____

13. Will you promote contests on your site? _____

14. What are the prizes? _____

15. Who will supply your prizes? _____

16. Will suppliers donate the prizes? _____

17. What technology will you use? Why? _____

18. What technical support will you offer? _____

19. Will you have 24x7 support for the uptime of your site? _____

20. Will your site be mirrored? Where? _____

21. Who makes changes to your site? _____

22. How will you drive customers to your site? _____

23. What search engines will your site be listed on? _____

24. What is your Internet marketing budget? _____

25. What will your budget be spent on? _____

26. What are your plans for testing different ideas against others? _____ _____

27. Does your budget allow for testing? _____

28. Will you offer auto-responders to provide real-time information? _____

29. Will you have new members sign in to set up an account? _____

30. What will this look like, and how will you capture important data? _____

31. What technology, front end and back end, will you use? Why? _____ _____

32. How will you accommodate high volume traffic to your site? _____

33. How many technical people will you need internally?_____

34. Will you outsource hosting of your site? With whom? _____

35. Will you be offering free software upgrades or downloads for patches? _____

36. Who are your suppliers of products? _____

37. Do they have an extranet for you to push and pull information from? _____

38. Will your products be drop shipped?_____

39. What are the costs for each piece of drop shipping? _____

40. How will the orders get to your suppliers? _____

41. Who pays for damaged shipments? _____

42. Does the customer call you or the supplier? Why? _____

_____

43. How soon will your orders be shipped? _____

44. How will you provide customer support? _____

45. Will this be staffed 24x7 for customers to talk to live agents? _____

46. Will you allow customers to search your site for information?_____

47. What is your customer profile? _____

48. How do you receive customer information to obtain a profile? _____

49. What are their "hot" buttons? _____

50. Is yours a portal site? _____

51. If so, will customers be able to leave your site and surf your competitors sites? _____

52. Will you offer an online catalog? _____

53. What is your anticipated call volume? _____

54. Will you have Frequently Asked Questions (FAQ's) listed on your site? _____

Products and Services Questions

1. What products or services will you provide to your customers?

2. How do your products or services differ from similar products or services already on the market?

_____

_____

_____

3. What benefits will your products or services provide your customers versus similar products or services sold by competitors?_____

_____

_____

4. What is the life cycle of your product or service? _____

5. Do you have third-party affirmations endorsing, supporting, or promoting your products or services?
   A. Letters of recommendation? _____

B. Endorsements?_____

C. References? _____

6. Is there a benefit to having your product patented? _____

7. If so, have you applied for a patent? _____

8. What is your primary means of distribution (dealers, salespeople, mail order, etc.)? _____

9. What are your coverage areas for distribution? _____

10. Who makes your buying decisions (purchasing agent)? _____

11. Do you get multiple quotes from at least three vendors for all the materials and goods that you buy, including packaging and shipping materials? _____

12. Who are your suppliers?_____

_____

_____

_____

_____

13. Have you established lead times and quantity reorder points for the ordering of inventory?_____

Production and Facility Questions

1. How do you produce your product or service (internally/in-house, externally/subcontract, etc.)?

_____

_____

2. What is your current production capacity in units of output and in dollars on a monthly basis?

_____

_____

3. Will your current production philosophy change in future years? If so, how? _____

_____

4. Does your current facility allow for flexibility with regard to growth? _____

5. Do you plan to lease office/warehouse space or purchase a building? Give details. _____

_____

6. If a new building is being considered, indicate whether you have planned for:

A. Adequate warehouse/office space for future expansion _____

B. Efficient loading docks and ground-level door entrances _____

C. Ease of transportation to roadways, railroads, and airports _____

D. Convenience of location to customers and suppliers _____

7. Have you spoken to an attorney about negotiating and reviewing your lease (lease rates, free rent, term of lease, responsibility for roof repairs and maintenance, etc.)?_____

8. Is your facility accessible to the handicapped? _____

Management Questions

1. Who is your management team?
   A. President: _____
   B. Vice President: _____
   C. Secretary: _____
   D. Treasurer: _____
   E. Controller: _____
   F. Marketing manager: _____
   G. Sales manager: _____
   H. Operation manager: _____
   I. Human resource manager: _____

2. Who is on your outside consultant team?
   A. Legal: _____
   B. Management consultant: _____
   C. Marketing: _____
   D. Accounting: _____
   E. Computer software: _____
   F. Computer hardware: _____

3. What is the background of each member of the management team (education, industry, employment experience, and professional accomplishments)? _____

   _____
   _____
   _____
   _____
   _____
   _____
   _____
   _____

4. What are the *strengths* of your management team? _____

   _____
   _____
   _____

5. What are the *weaknesses* of your management team? _____

   _____
   _____
   _____

Finance Questions

1. Does your business have a current profit and loss statement, balance sheet, cash flow statement, and at least two years' financial projections? _____

2. How often are your business's financial statements prepared (monthly, quarterly, annually)? _____

3. Are your accounting records maintained on a computer? _____

4. When will your fiscal year end? _____

5. What is your break-even point according to your financial statements or projections? _____

6. What are your current asset values?
   Cash $ _____
   Accounts Receivables $ _____
   Inventory $ _____

7. What is your current ratio (the total of current assets divided by the total of current liabilities)? _____

8. How much in accounts receivables do you carry on average?
   A. 0–30 days $ _____
   B. 30–60 days $ _____
   C. 61–90 days $ _____
   D. 91–120 days $ _____
   E. Over 120 days $ _____
   F. Total Accounts Receivables $ _____

9. What type of inventory valuation method do you or will you have?
   A. FIFO (first in, first out)
   B. LIFO (last in, first out)
   C. Other _____

10. What equipment is needed and what do you anticipate the equipment will cost? (Please list the equipment and retail costs, e.g., machinery and equipment, furniture and fixtures, vehicles, office machines and equipment, and telephone systems.)

   _____ $ _____
   _____ $ _____
   _____ $ _____
   _____ $ _____
   _____ $ _____
   _____ $ _____
   _____ $ _____
   _____ $ _____
   _____ $ _____
   _____ $ _____
   _____ $ _____

11. What inventory do you need and what do you anticipate your beginning inventory to cost? (List type of inventory you need.)

_____ $ _____
_____ $ _____
_____ $ _____
_____ $ _____
_____ $ _____
_____ $ _____
_____ $ _____
_____ $ _____
_____ $ _____
_____ $ _____

12. Do you have any existing loans? If so, what are your plans to pay off these loans?

_____

_____

13. Have you contacted state, city, and local governments to see what your obligations are regarding the collection and payment of sales taxes? _____

14. What is the sales tax rate for each state, city, or county in which you plan to transact business? _____

15. If you are looking to raise capital, how will your investors receive their return on investment? (Will you repay the debt? Go public in five years? Be acquired in four years?)_____

16. What type of borrowing structure are you looking for?

   A. Debt only

   B. Debt/Equity

   C. Limited partnership

   D. Stock purchase

   E. Venture capital

   F. Other _____

17. How much capital do you need to accomplish your goals? _____

18. What will the capital be used for?_____

19. What do you have to pledge as collateral (inventory, accounts receivable, fixed assets, stocks, other marketable securities, contracts, etc.)? _____

20. If you are preparing a business plan to obtain financing, do you plan to pay off any existing debt with your new proceeds? _____

21. If so, what and how much? _____

22. Do you have any controlling interests in other businesses? _____

23. Are there any supporting documents you can use that will help you solidify your claims to the investor or lender (newspaper articles, quotes by industry experts, magazine articles, brochures, graphs, charts, copies of contracts, etc.)? _____

_____

_____

Forward Tech, Inc.

Business Plan

2838 S. Main Street
Suite G
Las Vegas, Nevada 84200
Phone: 801-555-0051
Fax: 801-555-1349
Email: gsmith@ForwardTech1.biz
Web Site: www.ForwardTech1.biz

Contact: Gary Smith

March 2005

PROPRIETARY AND CONFIDENTIAL

This is a business concept and not an offering of securities

This document is confidential and has been made available to the individual to whom it is addressed strictly on the understanding that its contents will not be disclosed or discussed with any third parties except for the company's own professional advisers. Investment in new and small businesses carries high risks as well as the possibility of high rewards. It is highly speculative and potential investors should be aware that no established market exists for the trading of shares in private companies. Prospective investors are advised to verify all material facts and to take advice from a professional adviser before entering into any commitments. This plan is strictly for information only and constitutes neither a prospectus nor an invitation to subscribe for shares. Projections in the plan have been compiled by the promoters for illustrative purposes and do not constitute profit forecasts. The eventual outcome may be more.

Published by
Forward Tech, Inc.
Statement of Confidentiality

The information in this business plan is confidential and proprietary. It has been made available solely for consideration and evaluation of this information. In no event shall all or any portion of this executive summary be disclosed or disseminated without the express written permission of Forward Tech.

1.0 Executive Summary

Forward Tech, Inc. (Forward Tech) is a high-end provider of computing hardware, IT consulting, and software solutions. By implementing the Forward Tech solution, organizations are able to incorporate cost-saving features, an enhancement of a customer-centric focus, and integration of the highest security measures available. The purposes of this business plan are to illustrate the tremendous market potential of the rapidly expanding information technology sector and show how Forward Tech is positioned to take full advantage of the opportunities in the market, and to provide a compelling reason to invest in this exciting company.

Forward Tech has expanded from an IT consulting firm into a leader in high-end hardware and IT security solutions. The Company has grown from three employees to twenty-two, and now has offices in Las Vegas, NV; Portland, OR; San Francisco, CA; and Anchorage, AK. It has also recently acquired the assets and sales personnel of a Portland-based computer hardware reseller. The expansion into the Portland area is a key component in the overall corporate strategy. In addition, Forward Tech has secured 51 percent ownership in a new company that caters specifically to the health care market. This wholly owned subsidiary is called XYZ Health Systems and it focuses on software and hardware sales to physicians' clinics and small hospitals.

Forward Tech provides an end-to-end solution from design to implementation to security audits of the network, through project management of the entire solution. The company is able to accomplish this through its employee base of highly experienced sales personnel, engineers with the coveted CCIE designation, and the achievement of high levels of Value Added Reseller (VAR) status with many key IT infrastructure companies.

The core values of the Forward Tech product and service offerings are providing the very best design and implementation strategy possible, and implementing the solution that is custom-tailored to the client's needs. This plan is also written for the purpose of securing additional funding to:

> • Allow the company to free up its lines of credit for hardware purchases that usually exceed $250,000
> • Finance further operations of the company

Forward Tech targets medium to Fortune 1000 companies and government municipalities for its customer base. The primary revenue streams are hardware and consulting sales. The most profitable areas of the business are consulting and software sales. The primary focus of Forward Tech is to promote the fact that the company is well-rounded in all areas of IT, from designing to implementing a solution that is completely catered to the client's needs. Forward Tech provides cost-saving capabilities in the following areas:

> ➢ Hardware and Software Solutions
> ➢ IP Telephony
> ➢ Professional IT Services
> ➢ Wireless Solutions
> ➢ Security

Management Team: The management team consists of highly talented engineering, sales, and administrative managers with over eighty years of combined experience in start-ups, technology, and marketing.

Financial Data: This plan projects rapid growth over the next five years. The Company restructured an earlier partnership in June 2004 and renamed the enterprise Forward Tech, Inc. It has achieved the following revenue over the past three years—2002: $35,000; 2003: $85,000; 2004: $1,200,000; 2005: $1,645,000. By securing the additional funding or line of credit, Forward Tech can execute a rapid and effective campaign that is intended to lead to high rates of return for both Forward Tech and its stakeholders. The Company intends to achieve a revenue stream in excess of $72 million by year five of this plan, with an overall gross profit margin of 18 percent in the same year.

The Company is in need of additional funding in the amount of $250,000 to achieve its immediate goals.

The Market: The information technology (IT) industry was affected by the economic downturn of 2001; however, the U.S. is the world leader in information and communications technology representing almost 35 percent of global spending. According to the Information Technology Association of America (ITAA), "society's next frontier makes information technology the most exciting and creative industry of the 21st Century." Currently 85 percent of Forward Tech's revenue comes from Cisco sales. Forward Tech is a Silver Partner with Cisco, and is very close to achieving Gold status. This is the highest level a VAR can achieve with Cisco. In addition to Cisco, the Company is partnered with HP, Compaq, Computer Associates, Proxim, Motorola, and Best Practices to provide the best equipment and services in the market to its clients. Purchasing in the IT market is continuing to expand and is anticipated to continue its outlook on acquiring new equipment and implementing professional services.

Source: Information Technology Association of America (ITAA) January 2005

1.1 Objectives

The objectives of Forward Tech are to:

1. Expand rapidly into the Oregon and Northern California markets
2. Maintain a Gross Profit Margin of 15–18%
3. Maintain positive growth in sales each month
4. Reach $2 million per month in revenue by June 2005
5. Reach $4 million in monthly revenue by the end of 2005
6. Hire talented personnel that will allow the Company to achieve its goals
7. Be in a position to conduct an acquisition of the Company by year three of this plan
8. Become a Gold Partner of Cisco by June 2005

9. Raise an additional $250,000 in this round of funding to fund further growth and expansion

10. Have commitments or possible other finance options to raise additional capital down the road

11. Provide a remuneration event for all stakeholders in the business through an IPO or acquisition

12. With the proper funding in place, Forward Tech intends to achieve $72 million in revenue in year five of this plan

1.2 Mission

Forward Tech's mission is to offer its clients the highest level of professional IT services, hardware, and software solutions. We will accomplish this by employing the very best people who are passionate about providing stellar customer service. Our guiding principles are to provide superior products and services with the latest in technology, support our clients with superior service, and grow the business by maintaining happy customers.

1.3 Keys to Success

The keys to success in this business are:

- High-quality design and implementation of the solutions
- Speed to market, and rapid penetration into key areas that we have defined
- Consistently striving to obtain the highest margins possible
- Ability to refine and enhance the solutions provided to clients
- Impeccable customer service
- Reliability of the solution

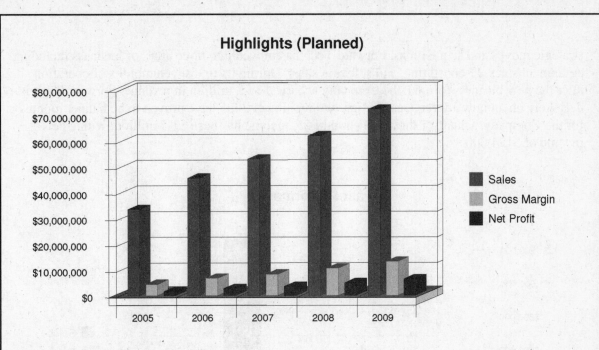

2.0 Company Summary

Forward Tech is headquartered in Las Vegas, NV. It is currently functioning as an S Corporation, operated by its founding members. Expansion costs are estimated to be $250,000, which are offset somewhat by cash flow and current investment as explained in section 2.2. The following section is a more in-depth explanation of ownership and start-up financials.

2.1 Company Ownership

Forward Tech, Inc. is organized as a Nevada S Corporation. Currently the primary owners are the following:

Bill Nish, CEO
Gary Smith, President
Michael Call, VP Operations
Tom Cavin, CTO

Additional ownership is reserved for investors and recruiting industry talent. A plan will be developed for employee options to be exercised.

2.2 Company History

Forward Tech was formed as a result of a prior partnership that was plagued with too many partners that did not catch the vision of running the business for growth. The Company was reformed in June 2004 to focus primarily on IT consulting in the Nevada market. Through strategic moves and acquisitions, Forward Tech has moved into three areas of business including equipment sales, IT consulting, and software sales. During its first seven months of operation after the new business formed, the Company achieved $1.1 million in revenue. Forward Tech is definitely on an upward trend, as the first two months of 2005 have proven to be banner months for the Company. January 1 through February 25, income has been $1.5 million, with a net income of $124,000.

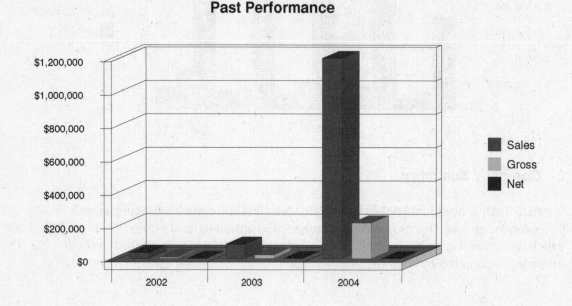

Past Performance

2.3 Company Locations and Facilities

The corporate headquarters are at 2838 S. Main Street, Las Vegas, Nevada. The Company also operates offices in Portland, Oregon (Lake Oswego, OR); San Francisco, CA; and Anchorage, AK. One additional office will be opened in the latter half of 2005 in Phoenix, AZ.

3.0 Products and Services

The products and services offered by Forward Tech are standard offerings in the world of information technology. Yet, two things stand clear of the solutions the Company provides: relationships at high levels and impeccable customer service.

Through the experience of the sales and executive team of Forward Tech, doors are more easily opened due to prior relationships that have been established over the past decade. People buy from those they trust. Forward Tech is able to offer the discounts companies need in order to stay competitive.

The relationships that have been established with the manufacturers allow the Company to get the products at highly competitive discounts. These, along with industry professionals who have a high degree of competency, make Forward Tech an up-and-coming leader in information technology solutions.

3.1 Product and Service Description

Forward Tech solutions are completely tailored to the needs of the client. Whether it is a network security audit, IT infrastructure consulting, specific hardware or software requirements, IP telephony solutions, or wireless network solutions, Forward Tech has developed the team to design and implement the proper solutions for its clients. Designs and implementations range from a simple network security audit all the way up to a complete network design for 4,000 seats.

Network Hardware
Hardware purchases through Forward Tech are painless. We typically have a quote ready for you within an hour of your request—depending on your order, and can have 99 percent of orders to your doorstep by the next day (should you request it). We have partnered with the nation's largest distributors, allowing us to maintain a virtual inventory in over ten warehouses nationwide! Give us a shot.

IP Telephony/VoIP
Convergence is inevitable; you can put it off, but you won't be able to elude it. It is a simple fact; your voice and data networks will become one. Let Forward Tech assist you during this process, and note that it is a process, not a one-time implementation. We will help you with network readiness, hardware/software selection, and help you develop a migration strategy. Do it right the first time.

Network Design/Assessment
The saying is: "If it can be measured, it can be improved." That is our guiding principle while assessing a network's infrastructure. Once a network is measured, methods can be put in place, and strategies can be designed with the end result in mind—efficiency. Our industry-best practices, combined with powerful analyzing tools, will provide a clear path of action for the optimization of your network. Our complete assessment includes a thorough audit of every layer of the OSI model, or we can assess specific issues or problem areas.

Network Security
Obviously, with a name like Forward Tech, we take security very seriously. We view security as a continual process, probably one that will never be complete.

We offer the following security services:

- Security hardware (Firewall, VPN Concentrator, ACS, IDS)

- Security software (Firewall, VPN, IDS, AV)

- Security consulting

- Penetration testing

- Complete security audit

- Written security policies

Telecommunications Services
Forward Tech has chosen to partner with best-in-class telecommunication providers in order to alleviate the hassles of dealing with service providers from our partners.

Roam-enabled Municipal Area Network
The goal of the Roam-enabled Municipal Area Network is to offer a high-speed, wireless municipal solution for public safety and public works systems. We accomplish this by reducing infrastructure costs to the city, enhancing public safety, and providing residents with high-speed Internet connections.

Target Markets
This solution is designed for small to medium municipalities, but can be tailored very easily to hospitality, medical, campus environments, agricultural facilities, and sports arenas.

Wireless WAN/LAN
In addition to vertical market wireless solutions, Forward Tech also offers wireless WAN and LAN products and services. We can assist you with your existing wireless network, help you with proof-of-concept projects, or create your entire wireless infrastructure. As with any other network solution, security is given the utmost consideration throughout the project life cycle.

<h3 style="text-align:center">Equipment Partners</h3>

Cisco Systems continues to dominate the market for equipment used to link networks and power the Internet. The company's bread-and-butter products are routers and switches; Cisco's switch line includes equipment based on Ethernet, Gigabit Ethernet, Token Ring, and ATM technologies. Other products include remote access servers, IP telephony equipment used to transmit data and voice communications over the same network, optical networking components, and network service and security systems. It sells its products primarily to large enterprises and telecommunications service providers, but it also has products designed for small businesses and consumers.

Proxim's products bring broadband nearer. The company is the leader in wireless networking, offering the broadcast range of high performance Wi-fi and fixed wireless products for enterprises, telecom carriers, service providers, venue owners, and small businesses. Proxim makes wireless high-performance multipoint networks more affordable for WISPs and enterprises. The company, formerly Western Multiplex, makes wireless LAN systems that consist of wireless modems and Ethernet bridges and are used to expand private Internet-based networks in homes (Symphony) and businesses (RangeLAN2). Telecom service providers use Proxim's wireless Lynx spread spectrum radios to bridge gaps in their wire line networks. The company sells through distributors including Somera and Tessco; end users include such wireless carriers as Cingular and Nextel. About 75 percent of sales are made in the U.S. The company changed its name to Proxim Corporation after acquiring rival Proxim Inc. in 2004.

3Com is still a major player in the world of network computing. The company sells networking hardware and software through two companies. Its Business Networks Company (BNC) makes LAN-level infrastructure gear (hubs, switches, and servers), networked telephony systems, and wireless networking equipment for enterprises.

Hewlett-Packard (HP) has gotten a whole lot bigger. Now rivaling longtime market ruler IBM in size, HP provides enterprise and consumer customers a full range of high-tech products, including personal computers, servers, storage products, printers, software, and computer-related services. The company has seen extensive restructuring spearheading the largest deal in tech sector history: the acquisition of Compaq Computer in a stock transaction valued at approximately $19 billion.

3.2 Competitive Comparison

The competitive landscape in our target markets is relatively strong. There exists a good mix of equipment VARs and IT consulting firms. Taking a closer look at the competition for Forward Tech's services, a SWOT analysis gives a clearer picture of how Forward Tech compares to current competition. The analysis shows the following:

Strengths
Forward Tech's key strength lies in its engineers. The complexity and scope of the design and implementation of computer networking requires network engineers with a high level of experience, education, training, and certifications. By having a core set of these engineers, Forward Tech can easily design and implement nearly any network solution and resolve nearly any IT issue.

An additional strength of Forward Tech lies in the strategic partnerships it has developed. Due to the negotiations of the agreements with these partners, Forward Tech is capable of competing with even the largest equipment resellers. This allows the company to be competitive on equipment bids and to win contracts much more easily. Prior to these discounts, Forward Tech was not able to win these contracts, let alone even be in the position to bid. Although the equipment is not manufactured by Forward Tech, the actual design of the infrastructure and implementation used is just as proprietary and important as the technology itself.

Weaknesses
Forward Tech's greatest weakness is its current lack of cash for operations. The company's resources are tied up in the day-to-day operations. By getting funds to reallocate those resources to the marketing, sales, and development of the IT solutions, Forward Tech can eliminate this weakness.

Opportunities
The opportunities in IT solutions are abundant. The U.S. is the world leader in information and

communication technology. U.S. spending on IT has increased almost 72 percent since 1992, to almost $813 billion in 2001. Almost 19,500 IT companies in the U.S. employ fifty or more employees each.

During the economic downturn of 2001, productivity growth remained robust at about 2 percent, jumping 5.2 percent in the fourth quarter of 2001 and continuing at 5.1 percent in the third quarter of 2004, in large part due to the contribution of IT.
Across all industries, companies now spend about 3.6 percent of revenue on information technology. Indeed, computer power will transition from the data center and desktop to thousands of points of interaction—whenever and wherever people use information. This "manifest destiny," society's next frontier, makes information technology the most exciting and creative industry of the 21st century.

Source: Meta Group, New Technology Economics, 2004

Forward Tech achieved Gold Alliance Partner status with Cisco Inc. in June 2005. Forward Tech is very close to fulfilling all the requirements outlined by Cisco to receive Gold status. Currently the makeup of certifications of the Forward Tech team is as follows:

Minimum Certified Engineers: 8

Forward Tech has on staff the following certified individuals:

2 – CCIEs

>   Gary Smith

>   Tom Cavin

2 – CCNPs

>   Bill Nish

>   Kurt Norman

2 – CCNAs

>   Brandon Smith

>   Valerie Myers

2 – CSEs

Michael Call

Cade Call

3.3 Sales Literature

Forward Tech is currently developing sales literature to be used in marketing on several fronts. They are:

- Trade shows
- Direct mail
- In-person presentation material
- Web-based presentation material

This material will be available as the sales plan is implemented.

3.4 Technology

Forward Tech provides the highest level of network engineering available. From the high-quality products that the company sells to its engineering capabilities, Forward Tech is in a unique position to win larger, more lucrative contracts. The company utilizes the latest technology for all of its solutions.

3.5 Future Products and Services

Customer service is extremely important to Forward Tech. The company is considering implementing a 24/7 monitoring system to proactively monitor commercial and municipal networks. As equipment experiences any event that should be addressed, Forward Tech will know and be able to take action before it becomes an issue that may lead to network downtime. Although downtime is rare, such a monitoring service would nearly eliminate such an event.

Another possible service is expanding the network to service small business and home use. Although this is discussed throughout this plan, the municipal public safety use is Forward Tech's primary focus.

4.0 Market Analysis Summary

Generally, companies are beginning to loosen up spending on IT solutions, as the need still exists to remain competitive. Since September 2001, many enterprises have decided to curb spending on IT solutions. In its latest report on the IT workforce, the Information Technology Association of America (ITAA) found continued stabilization in the workforce as both hiring and dismissing of IT professionals slowed considerably. The most in-demand tech skills have also held steady since January of 2004. The data shows that although there was a net gain of 147,000 jobs in the third quarter, the number of IT workers hired in 2001 declined to 1,183,000. At the same time, companies cut their spending on IT projects considerably.

The positive news is that IT dismissals have dropped 68 percent since last year, and projects are picking up rapidly. During 2001–2004, the IT industry saw a decline in contractor expenses to approximately 6.5 percent. A recent study conducted by ITAA shows that contractor expense has increased as a percentage of IT payroll—roughly 8 percent on average. This upward trend is expected to continue at a fairly decent pace through 2006.

Source: Information Technology Association of America (ITAA) January 2005

4.1 Market Segmentation

Forward Tech has identified four natural market segments for their product offering. This does not mean that Forward Tech will not consider additional markets, but they believe that focus on more vertical markets yields a greater potential for market penetration and success. The four markets are:
1. Small and medium municipalities
2. Medium enterprises to Fortune 1000
3. Small businesses
4. Physicians' clinics and hospitals

Table 4.1 illustrates the growth potential for each market segment. Small business is by far the largest segment; this fact is recognized by the multitude of IT solution providers in the industry. Forward Tech is in a unique position to capture a significant portion of each of these markets.

Table: Market Analysis

Market Analysis Potential Customers	Growth	2005	2006	2007	2008	2009	CAGR
Fortune 1000	1%	1,000	1,005	1,010	1,015	1,020	0.50%
Medium Enterprises	2%	17,000	17,340	17,687	18,041	18,402	2.00%
Small Business	3%	23,0000	23,6900	24,4000	25,1321	25,8863	3.00%
Hospitals and Physicians' Clinics	2%	900,000	918,000	936,360	955,087	974,189	2.00%
Municipalities	1%	90,000	90,900	91,809	92,727	93,654	1.00%
Total	2.95%	24,008.00	24,717.24	25,447.56	26,199.59	26,973.96	2.95%

Market Analysis (Pie)

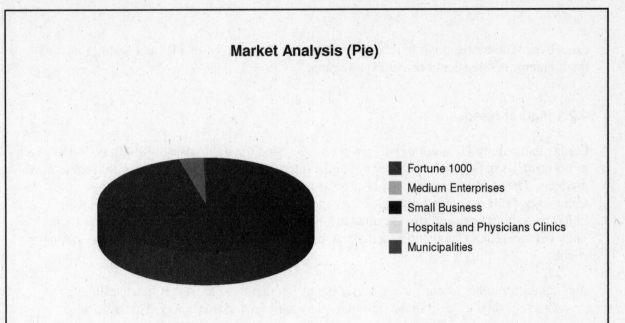

- Fortune 1000
- Medium Enterprises
- Small Business
- Hospitals and Physicians Clinics
- Municipalities

4.2 Target Market Segment Strategy

The most lucrative market for Forward Tech to focus on is the medium to Fortune 1000 enterprises. These companies have large IT budgets to acquire solutions. For Forward Tech to attain market share in this market, it must continue to develop a solid marketing campaign and approach the decision-makers with compelling proposals. These positions within the cities will be motivated by the enhanced public safety, education, and the perceived image of the city itself.

Through its natural arrangement with Primitus Health Systems, Forward Tech is being brought into many opportunities in the health care market. Forward Tech is the vendor of choice to Primitus and to Best Practices, the OEM of V-Chart that is Electronic Medical Record (EMR) software for physicians and small hospitals. Best Practices is building out its nationwide VAR channel, and they make hardware resources available through Forward Tech.

With funding in place, Forward Tech will initiate a national marketing and sales campaign in which seminars will be utilized to gain an audience with these decision-makers. By holding strategic seminars in cities where the new IT solutions are required, Forward Tech intends to capture an audience, explain the technology and solution, and demonstrate the full solution to the audience. The goal for the seminars is to have twenty representatives from different organizations at a single seminar.

Forward Tech will also use the Emergency Medical Services Convention and other such forums to market and sell the remote and wireless solutions. This will give visibility and capture a larger audience than the smaller seminars that Forward Tech will sponsor.

Along with the seminars and forums, Forward Tech will hire two to four additional sales executives. These executives will be a traveling sales force across the United States, touching those enterprises that could not attend a seminar.

4.2.1 Market Needs

Clients that require IT solutions will always have a need for Value Added Resellers (VARs) such as Forward Tech. Original Equipment Manufacturers (OEMs) rely on the VAR channel to move products. The need for experienced IT professionals has never been greater. With new technology being developed, a solid design and implementation of IT solutions is critical. Enterprises, both large and small, cannot afford to do it the wrong way and then try to fix it. They will not remain competitive and the competition will gain too much ground on existing clients.

According to another recent survey, ITAA points out that there are more than a million good reasons to consider a career in the information technology industry today. That's because employers will create a demand in this country for roughly 1.6 million IT workers this year. With demand for appropriately skilled people far exceeding supply, half of these positions—843,328—will likely go unfilled. In a total U.S. IT workforce of 10 million, that shortfall means one job in every dozen will be vacant. This is good for Forward Tech, because these companies will be looking to outside advisors to assist them in the development and rollout of their solutions.

Size of the IT workforce, the demand for qualified workers, and the gap between supply and demand:

- The 10 million strong workforce of IT workers is far larger than one might expect based on previous studies. This number does not include jobs in government, not-for-profit organizations, or small entrepreneurial firms. It provides evidence of a sea change in the nature of work and emphasizes that the Internet and IT have become the twin pistons of the national economy.

- The demand for IT workers is large and growing. Employers will attempt to fill 1.6 million new IT jobs.

- The demand for IT workers is widespread with interesting variations by geographic region. The South has the largest number of IT workers overall. The Midwest has the largest demand for IT jobs—35 percent of the total. The western region is second largest with 28 percent of the total demand.

- The greatest need for IT workers is in the largest segment of the economy—smaller non-IT firms. Companies with 50–99 employees need 1 million IT workers next year or 70 percent of the total demand for all new IT employees. This group also has the highest skills gap; managers from these firms reported the highest rate of unqualified applicants and the greatest difficulty in filling positions.

- While non-IT companies have more aggregate demand, the average IT company has far more jobs to fill—five times as many jobs for tech support representatives, six times as many for Web developers, and twelve times as many for database developers.

The hottest, most in-demand jobs:

- Technical support jobs are in demand by both IT and non-IT companies alike (one-third of all new positions over the next twelve months fall into this category). Required skills ranked highest for technical support jobs by managers were: 1) Troubleshooting (97 percent); 2) Facilitation/customer service (91 percent); 3) Hardware/software installation, configuration upgrades (82 percent); and 4) Systems operations, monitoring, maintenance (67 percent).

- E-business and interactive media are not only stealing headlines and dominating the business press. Demand for workers with Web-related talents is now almost 13 percent of all IT jobs.

- Fifty percent of all jobs are in the two positions that exist in almost every organization: technical support and network administration. While database development and software engineering positions occur in only a portion of firms, they represent 20 percent of new IT positions.

The skills workers need to grab one of these hot jobs:

- The single most important skill is a good knowledge base in the relevant area, according to most (62 percent) of the managers surveyed.

- The second most desirable skill is hands-on experience. However, slightly less than half of responders (47 percent) selected hands-on as a key qualification. This suggests that it is desirable but not required.

- More than one-third of the skills identified by managers as important are non-technical skills such as good communication, problem-solving, and analytical skills, along with flexibility and the ability to learn quickly.

- As one would expect, key skills vary by job. A systematic assessment of the most important skills in each job category is included in the body of this study.

- The largest skills gaps are for enterprise systems integration and Web development positions. These positions have high complexity and a scarcity of qualified applicants.

4.2.2 Market Trends

CIO magazine's January 2005 IT staffing survey shows that layoffs and hiring freezes are making it difficult for CIOs to meet demands on IT. While a small percent of existing IT staff are being retrained for new roles within the department, the majority of CIOs surveyed are using external sourcing options like contractors or outsourcing to fill in gaps and complete projects.

The good news is that turnover rates in IT have dropped 20 percent over the past six months from 5 percent in July 2004, down to 4 percent in January this year, according to the 290 IT executives surveyed. But many IT departments are running lean, with close to half of companies included in our survey saying they reduced IT staff in the past six months, close to one third of those positions being eliminated permanently.

According to the 290 IT executives surveyed, managing workloads and preventing burnout were their top staffing concerns. In terms of the IT skills most in demand, application development topped the list followed by project management, networking, and database expertise.

Key Findings

Retraining IT executives included in the survey will allocate an average of 7 percent of their 2005 IT budget on IT training for their staff, including travel and lodging. On average, CIOs are training 14 percent of their staff for a new, primary function or job within the IT department, down slightly from 17 percent reported in July of last year.

Outside sourcing options have gained favor during the past twelve months. The majority (73 percent) of IT executives surveyed have increased their use of outside sourcing options. CIOs are most frequently relying on contractors/contingent staff (68 percent), onshore outsourcing (23 percent), and part-time staff (21 percent) to supplement their internal, permanent IT staff. Roughly one quarter (27 percent) of those surveyed said they are not using outside sourcing options currently.

Close to half (42 percent) of the survey respondents reported that their organization will increase its use of outside sourcing options in the next twelve months. The sourcing options that will be used most frequently included contractors/contingent staff (47 percent), offshore outsourcing (18 percent), and onshore outsourcing (16 percent).

IT Skills in Demand

When asked to indicate which IT skills were most in demand, IT executives surveyed listed application development (65 percent), project management (59 percent), networking (54 percent), database management (53 percent), and security (51 percent).

Turnover Rate Slowing

Close to half (44 percent) of the IT executives surveyed said their IT organization had layoffs in the past six months. Six months ago, only one third of companies surveyed reported layoffs. On average, IT departments were reduced by 13 percent in the second half of 2004, and one third of the "laid-off" positions were eliminated permanently.

Skills Most in Demand

When asked to indicate which IT skills were most in demand, IT executives surveyed listed application development (65 percent), project management (59 percent), networking (54 percent), database management (53 percent), and security (45 percent) most frequently.

Compared to our mid-2004 staffing survey, the list of top skills in demand is the same. However, a higher percentage of CIOs indicated that these skills were needed in their organizations. The good news is that 41 percent of companies surveyed are currently hiring these skills or will hire within three months. Twenty-one percent of survey respondents will hire later this year, while close to one-third (32 percent) will not hire until 2006.

Twenty-nine percent of the survey base worked at companies with fewer than 500 employees. Twenty-six percent were from companies with 500 to 2,500 employees. Thirty-six percent worked in companies with more than 2,500 employees. (Nine percent did not answer the question.)

When asked about company revenue, 33 percent reported annual company revenue of less than $100 million, and 29 percent reported revenue between $100 million and $999.9 million. The remaining 27 percent reported company revenue greater than $1 billion. (Eleven percent did not answer the question.)

Source: *CIO* magazine January 2005 issue and March 2005 issue

4.2.3 Market Growth

Methodology
CIO magazine's survey on IT staffing was administered online from January 1, 2005, through January 28, 2005. Visitors to CIO.com and readers of the CIO Insider electronic newsletter were invited to take a survey. Results were based on 290 IT professionals. (Not all respondents answered all questions.)

Survey respondents represented a range of industries including computer-related (15 percent), manufacturing (11 percent), medical/dental/healthcare (11 percent), finance/banking/accounting (10 percent), insurance/real estate/legal (9 percent), and government (5 percent).

In terms of title, 45 percent of the survey respondents were CIOs, CTOs, or vice presidents in charge of IT. Others were directors or managers of IT (45 percent), and IT staff or consultants (10 percent).

4.3 Service Business Analysis

Wireless network manufacturers and providers range from major international name-brand companies to thousands of small companies. One of Forward Tech's challenges will be establishing itself as a "real" wireless solution, positioned as a relatively risk-free municipal purchase.

4.3.1 Main Competitors

The main competitors to Forward Tech come in different forms.
In the equipment reseller space, local resellers, or VARs have a client relationship that is sometimes difficult to break into.

Equipment VARs
Mountain States—The other Cisco Silver dealer (Forward Tech and Mountain States are the only two Cisco Silver dealers in Nevada.)

Connecting Point—Recognizable name in the market; mostly government sales; sells hardware mainly with some IT networking services; does not typically employ high-end networking IT personnel

Source One—Voice and data technology solutions; database and e-Business solutions; data storage

UBS—Twenty-five years in the Wasatch Valley market as a large volume dealer of HP, Compaq, Microsoft, Novell, and Oracle products

Totally Awesome Computers—Sells mostly to small businesses based on low-priced, in-house computers

Office Depot—Sells mostly to small businesses based on low-priced computers and printers

Office Max—Sells mostly to small businesses based on low-priced computers and printers

Staples—Sells mostly to small businesses based on low-priced computers and printers

Computer networking companies that compete with Forward Tech in the Clark County Region:

Competitors in Computer Networking
Network Solutions—HP Authorized; services Linux, Microsoft, and Novell

Consonus—High-end server and storage co-location facility; CCIEs on staff; LAN/WAN design and engineering; security experts

MicroWorks—Microsoft, Novell, Citrix, and Cisco experts on staff; equipment sales; network engineering and day-to-day administration of networks

Wasatch Communication Technologies—Guarantees one-hour response time; data hosting; telephony and voice networks; security experts

UBS—Network support; project management; part-time outsourcing of help desk; e-Business experts

NetWize—Network Specialists; design, backup, and storage; wiring and cabling services

5.0 Strategy and Implementation Summary

The primary strategy in positioning Forward Tech in the minds of the decision-makers is to clearly illustrate Forward Tech as a leader in computer network technology. Forward Tech is the only partner they will need to provide the custom solution that will work for their network enterprise. Design, implementation, project management, low equipment prices, voiceover IP, telecom solutions, etc. This is accomplished through one professional organization with all ranges of networking expertise. From CCIEs to help desk support, Forward Tech can provide everything for their networking needs.

5.1 Value Proposition

Forward Tech is in business to provide the highest level of networking equipment and expertise to make the investment in technology a sound decision for its customer base. As a trusted advisor, Forward Tech personnel work directly with C-level executives as well as frontline network support people to design the proper solution for the client. It's their network, their way—with a little advice on the best solution.

5.2 Competitive Edge

Forward Tech has a wealth of Cisco Certified Internet Experts (CCIE) on staff. Their knowledge is so valuable to Cisco that they have a published Cisco training book on the market. This certification level is recognized worldwide as the highest in the industry. Very few companies can compete on this level.

Low prices with discounts on network equipment make the story even stronger. Forward Tech can provide a total network solution with everything the client is in need of to make sound decisions and have the most state-of-the-art network design available.
In addition, its health care division, Primitus, is one more compelling reason for hospitals and physicians' clinics to choose Forward Tech over the competition.

5.3 Marketing Strategy

The primary strategy for Forward Tech is to engage its sales personnel to contact its clients and prospects directly and ask what their needs are. This has been the primary strategy in the past, and it has worked quite well. With the additional funding in place, the company will launch a marketing campaign that consists of new sales literature, direct mail campaigns, seminars, and trade show exhibits.

The company also plans to develop a corporate newsletter that is sent out once a month to clients and prospective clients. This is to establish further credibility by providing valuable information and timely offers, in hopes that it keeps the Forward Tech name in front of the decision-makers.

5.3.1 Positioning Statements

Forward Tech intends to position itself as a market niche provider to organizations, specifically to decision-makers in its chosen market segments previously outlined. Then, as Forward Tech is entrenched in several cities across the western United States, Forward Tech will begin to offer additional services that are targeted to the government entities in certain cities and counties. By this point, Forward Tech will hold such a significant market share of municipal markets that larger competitors will be caught off guard. Such an advantage will make it difficult for the competition to catch up.

5.3.2 Pricing Strategy

Pricing will be based on the following:
- Size of the order
- Type of equipment
- Volume discounts

One of the greatest advantages that Forward Tech has to offer is the quality of service and technology for a price that small and mid-sized companies can actually afford. Competition is stiff and IT managers expect the discounts that Forward Tech is able to offer to them.

5.3.3 Promotion Strategy

Since Forward Tech intends to take its market share in a stealth manner instead of blasting the market, the promotion will be kept very targeted. Promotion will continue to be done with direct communication via telephone, email, and direct mail. As the client base continues to grow, word of mouth will spread quickly. Once a stable base is established, a mass attempt to reach additional market segments may make sense. Releasing mass information any sooner runs the risk of cash-enabled competitors moving in and attempting to copy Forward Tech's solution and make it an offering of their own.

5.3.4 Marketing Programs

Marketing will continue to be accomplished through the following:
- Direct solicitation
- Trade shows
- Word of mouth
- Partners
- Primitus Health Systems

After additional funding is in place, the additional marketing efforts will be added:
- Advertisements in magazines targeted toward IT decision-makers
- Possibly radio ads
- Web broadcasts
- Seminars

5.4 Sales Strategy

The strategy for acquiring sales is a three-fold mission of the company:

1. Work with existing clients to continue to order equipment and provide IT consulting services

2. Work closely with strategic alliances to develop new opportunities that we may not be aware of

3. Develop new channels within the health care and emergency services markets through Primitus

5.4.1 Sales Forecast

The sales forecast is shown in Table 5.4.1.

Table: Sales Forecast (Planned)

Sales Forecast

Sales	2005	2006	2007	2008	2009
Hardware	$31,608,954	$42,250,297	$48,587,841	$55,876,018	$64,257,420
Software	$866,153	$996,076	$1,145,488	$1,317,311	$1,514,908
Consulting	$798,974	$1,718,820	$2,157,119	$2,696,399	$3,370,498
Primitus Dividends	$274,125	$612,000	$1,122,000	$2,116,500	$3,187,500
Total Sales	$33,548,206	$45,577,193	$53,012,448	$62,006,227	$72,330,326
Direct Cost of Sales					
Hardware	$28,448,058	$38,025,267	$43,729,057	$50,288,416	$57,831,678
Software	$649,615	$747,057	$859,116	$987,983	$1,136,181
Consulting	$39,949	$85,941	$107,856	$134,820	$168,525
Primitus Dividends	$2,741	$6,120	$11,220	$21,165	$31,875
Subtotal Direct Cost of Sales	$29,140,363	$38,864,385	$44,707,249	$51,432,384	$59,168,259

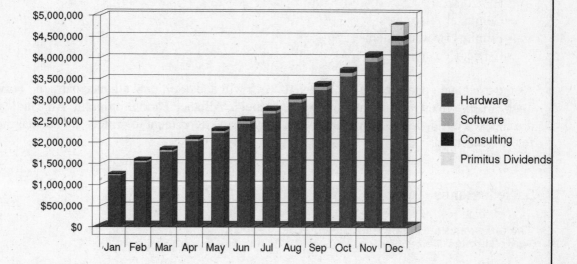

Sales Monthly (Planned)

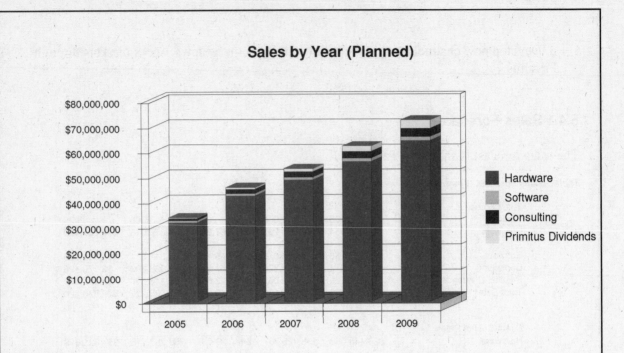

5.5 Strategic Alliances

Forward Tech understands and believes in forming Strategic Alliance Partnerships (SAP) to strengthen its position in the market. Forward Tech currently has strategic alliances with:
- Cisco
- Proxim
- HP/Compaq
- Computer Associates
- Primitus Health Systems
- C-Lect Consulting

As the need and opportunity arise, Forward Tech will add additional alliance partners. Forward Tech is very selective whom it lets into the Strategic Alliance Partner program. All candidates are checked out in detail and put under a nondisclosure agreement to protect intellectual property for all concerned.

5.6 Milestones

The milestones are detailed in Table 5.6.

Table: Milestones (Planned)

Milestone	Start Date	End Date	Budget	Manager	Department
Complete Funding	5/1/2005	5/25/2005	$1,000	Gary	Finance
5 Sales Personnel in Portland Office	1/15/2005	3/1/2005	$4,000	Bill	Sales
Marketing Collateral Complete	2/15/2005	3/15/2005	$7,500	Exec Team	Marketing

Primitus Paperwork Complete	1/20/2005	3/1/2005	$500	Bill	Operations
$100K/mo. in Consulting Revenue	2/1/2005	8/1/2005	$24,000	Michael	Sales

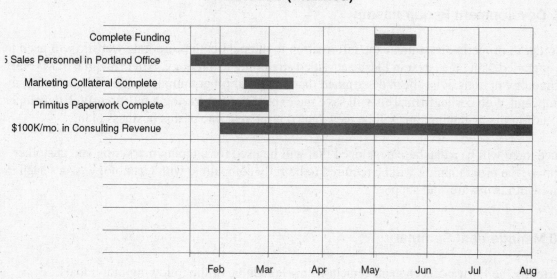

Milestones (Planned)

6.0 Web Plan Summary

The Corporate website is currently an information site that provides general information about our products and services. The site will eventually be upgraded with new options and menus for our clients to receive real-time information and have the capabilities of viewing an online presentation.

The strategy is to develop a dynamic, robust site that has real streaming video capabilities to show how our solution works. This will be a six- to seven-minute overview of the products and services with a call to action. The call to action will provide the prospect or client with the opportunity to choose three options:

• Register and send their information via the Internet to receive a response call
• Sign up for our newsletter
• Take a brief assessment of where they are and where they would like their technology to be

One additional key area of the website will be a training and development section that will allow the technical personnel of our clients to become educated on the company's capabilities in technology. This area will consist of general technical information as well as practice tests that are meant to assist the local technical analyst on troubleshooting and resolution information.

As strategic alliances are further developed with well-known industry names, a link from the

Forward Tech website to the strategic partner's site is in place, thus creating a portal of technical and municipal general information for our clients and prospects. Management will work closely with vendor marketing personnel to place the most strategic link to their site and to develop a seamless alliance between Forward Tech and the vendor.

6.1 Development Requirements

In order to properly disseminate the information to the public, the corporate website will need to be upgraded using the latest in Flash and video streaming technology. After research of several technology options, it has been determined that the initial programming will be outsourced to a competent Web design firm. This will save the expense of not having a full-time Web developer on staff in the beginning, but will be reevaluated after year one of this business plan.

Since there will be a database developed that will be used for ongoing marketing and customer support, the programming will be required to be fully compatible with technology issues such as bandwidth, software, and support.

7.0 Management Summary

Currently the Forward Tech management team is made up of the following individuals:
Bill Nish, President, CEO
Gary Smith, Executive Vice President, CIO
Michael Call, Vice President Operations
Tom Cavin, Partner, Board Member

The management team is experienced in technology, sales, operations, and project management, and has over forty years combined experience. As with any organization, the management team drives the business to success. The products and services are solid within the company, yet it has been the management team and its board of advisors that has been responsible for the strategic moves to this point.

7.1 Organizational Structure

The following shows Forward Tech's organizational structure:

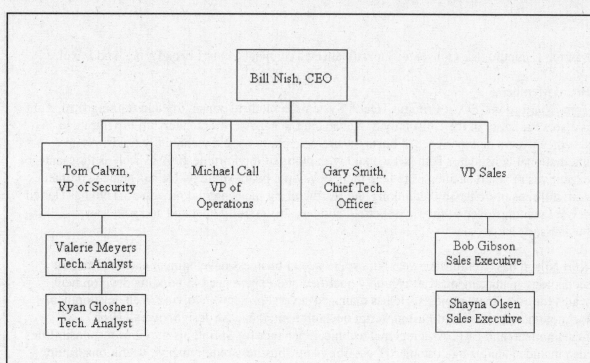

7.1.1 Management Team

Forward Tech's management team is comprised of four partners. Listed below are the management team and a brief description of each member.

<u>Bill Nish, CEO</u> Bill has fourteen years of experience in the world of technology. He has been involved in the sales process all the way through operations and implementation. He has been salesman of the year four times as a sales executive for IBM, and he has received other important awards and recognitions as a manager in several previous jobs.

<u>Gary Smith, Chief Technology Officer</u> Gary has extensive technical and management experience with companies such as Sprint, INS, Lucent, Apple, AAA Auto, and functioned as the chief network engineer for the District Courts of the United States of America. Gary obtained his CCIE in 2001, has a Bachelor of Arts from Nevada State University in business information systems, and is co-author of "CCNA Practical Studies" by Cisco Press.

<u>Michael Call, Vice President of Operations</u> Michael brings an extensive corporate technical training background from Hewlett Packard, where he trained engineers for companies such as Ingram Micro, Gates Arrow, Tech Data, Synnex, UBID, Insight.com, as well as others. As manager of training programs for the VAR channel, Michael managed twenty-seven regional VAR trainers in a mentoring environment. Michael has also obtained industry certifications for WAN technologies, and network peripherals management. He also brings an extensive background in technical sales, support, and personnel management.

<u>Tom Cavin, VP of Security</u> Tom is currently the technical lead on the Forward Tech engineering team. He has obtained his CCIE, MCSE, and CCSI. Tom has worked for companies such as

Mentor Technologies, Consonus, Inc, Advanced Technical Center, BroadWing, and Level3.

Board Members:

Tom Bradford is CEO of Primitus Health Systems, a medical consulting and training firm. Tom is also a Professor at the University of Nevada in the MBA Entrepreneurship Program. He has seventeen years of experience in business/strategic planning and technology fields. As an international consultant, Tom has worked with many of the Fortune 1000 as well as thousands of executives of small businesses to help them develop a better strategy. He has helped companies save millions of dollars by rethinking and restructuring their internal processes. Tom has started several ventures over a thirty-year period, and has successfully operated and sold four businesses.

Kurt Nilson has over thirteen years of experience in business development and information technology management. Kurt is highly qualified and experienced in building development teams for e-Business projects. He has managed several projects involving Web development technologies such as Cold Fusion, script development, database design, overall Web development, and ERP. As a regional technical manager for Sprint, his previous responsibilities also included analyzing customer IT environments, business requirements, operations, future growth, and determining maturity of operations. His experience aligning IT goals and objectives with business goals has been instrumental in helping Fortune 1000 companies gain an understanding and control over their environments.

Larry Instead has over seventeen years of experience in information technology engineering and management. Larry spent nine of those years as the project manager for Intermountain Health Care (IHC). Larry has also been involved in several successful start-up companies that have been acquired.

7.2 Management Team Gaps

Forward Tech's current management team has performed well in developing the company and surviving recent challenges in the wake of a global slowdown in corporate and government purchasing. However, the current management team has done an excellent job in bringing the company to its present stage of business. They have learned some of the valuable lessons of the pitfalls of a start-up and have made contingency plans to weather the storms they have encountered.

To assist with HR issues, management has decided to outsource all HR functions to a competent HR and benefits company. This will free up the management team from highly important yet very time-consuming operations such as payroll, HR issues, dealing with taxes, quarterly filings, etc.

The biggest area of neglect currently is the director of marketing position. This position will eventually need to be filled by a competent individual with solid experience marketing to IT decision-makers.

7.3 Personnel Plan

The personnel plan takes into consideration the growth in the customer base and the personnel required to support the intended growth. The number of personnel and the costs associated with the development of the staff are outlined in Table 7.3.

Table: Personnel (Planned)

Personnel Plan

	2005	2006	2007	2008	2009
Technical	$176,667	$203,167	$233,642	$268,688	$308,991
Sales	$1,174,187	$1,595,202	$1,855,436	$2,170,218	$2,531,561
Sr. Executives and Administrative	$436,667	$480,333	$528,367	$581,203	$639,324
Marketing	$24,000	$25,000	$30,000	$35,000	$40,000
Finance	$30,000	$42,500	$45,000	$48,000	$60,000
Bonuses	$12,058	$46,924	$53,849	$62,062	$71,598
Total Payroll	$1,853,578	$2,393,126	$2,746,293	$3,165,171	$3,651,474
Total People	26	46	57	66	76
Payroll Burden	$370,716	$478,625	$549,259	$633,034	$730,295
Total Payroll Expenditures	$2,224,294	$2,871,751	$3,295,551	$3,798,206	$4,381,768

8.0 Financial Plan

The most important element in the financial plan is the critical need for improving several of the key factors that affect cash flow.

1. The Company must at any cost emphasize its plans to sell both equipment and services to clients, and develop better customer service policies than the competition. This should also be a function of the shift in focus toward service revenues to add to the product revenues.
2. Management hopes to bring the gross margin to 20 percent and the net profit margin to 10 percent by the end of fiscal year 2007. This, too, is related to improving the mix between product and service revenues, because the consulting and software revenues offer much better margins.

The Company plans to borrow $250,000 to $500,000 in equity financing and have commitments to fund acquisitions. These amounts seem in line with the balance sheet capabilities.

8.1 Important Assumptions

The financial plan depends on important assumptions, most of which are shown in Table 8. The key underlying assumptions are:
1. The Company assumes a moderate-growth economy, without a major recession.
2. The Company assumes that there are no unforeseen changes in business and technology to make its products immediately obsolete.
3. The Company assumes access to equity capital and financing sufficient to maintain the financial plan as shown in the accompanying tables.
4. In the Sales Forecast, the term "Equipment" refers to computer network equipment.
5. In the Sales Forecast, the term "Consulting" refers to IT services and outsourcing projects.
6. In the Sales Forecast, the term "Software" refers to selling software solutions with Computer

Associates software.

7. In the Sales Forecast, the term "Primitus Dividends" refers to the annual dividends associated with ownership in Primitus Health Systems. These dividends will be paid to Forward Tech as long as the financial commitments from Forward Tech to Primitus are met.

8. The gross margin on equipment is calculated at 10 percent.

9. Also listed in the Sales Forecast are the associated costs for the products and services in the following manner:

- Equipment—90%
- Software—75%
- Consulting—5%
- Primitus Dividends—1%

10. The breakdown of specific lines of business and the percentage of total revenue in year 2005 and then again in 2009 for each area of business looks like this:

2005	2009
Equipment—94%	Equipment—89%
Software—3%	Software—2%
Consulting—2%	Consulting—5%
Primitus Dividends—1%	Primitus Dividends—4%

Table: General Assumptions

General Assumptions	2005	2006	2007	2008	2009
Short-term Interest Rate %	10.00%	10.00%	10.00%	10.00%	10.00%
Long-term Interest Rate %	10.00%	10.00%	10.00%	10.00%	10.00%
Tax Rate %	25.00%	25.00%	25.00%	25.00%	25.00%
Expenses in Cash %	10.00%	10.00%	10.00%	10.00%	10.00%
Sales on Credit %	90.00%	90.00%	90.00%	90.00%	90.00%
Personnel Burden %	20.00%	20.00%	20.00%	20.00%	20.00%

8.2 Key Financial Indicators

The plan shows an assumption of a 20 percent personnel burden for additional items such as vacation, insurance, and sick leave. As far as long-term and/or short-term debt, the plan has figured in an interest rate of 10 percent. This plan outlines a 25 percent tax burden.

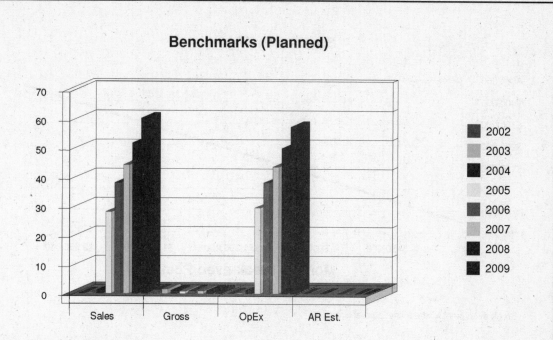

8.3 Break-even Analysis

For the break-even analysis, the plan assumes monthly running costs of approximately $149,000 in month seven of 2005, which includes our full payroll, rent, utilities, interest, telephone, and an estimation of marketing costs.

Margins are harder to assume. The overall average of $225,000 per unit sold is based only on the revenue generated from an average sale to a municipality. However, there are three primary products and services that Forward Tech sells. Calculated in this plan is an average variable cost of 75 percent for each unit sold. The Company hopes to attain a margin that will remain high in the future.

The breakeven per month is three units per month sold, which means that the company will need to generate in excess of $599,000 per month to break even.

Table: Break-even Analysis

Break-even Analysis:	
Break-even Monthly Units	3
Break-even Monthly Sales	$599,867
Assumptions:	
Average Per-unit Revenue	$225,000.00
Average Per-unit Variable Cost	$168,750.00
Estimated Monthly Fixed Cost	$149,966.67

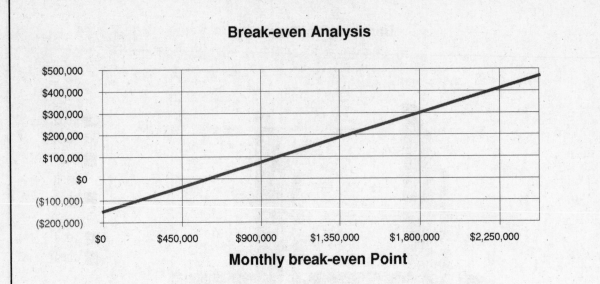

Break-even Analysis

Break-even point = where line intersects with 0

8.4 Projected Profit and Loss

The most important assumption in the projected profit and loss statement is the gross margin, which is estimated to be 13.4 percent through 2005, and 18.2 percent at the conclusion of 2009 of this plan. Month-by-month assumptions for net profit margin are intended to achieve 5 percent through April 2005 and 10 percent at the conclusion of 2007.

Table: Profit and Loss (Planned)

Pro Forma Profit and Loss

	2005	2006	2007	2008	2009
Sales	$33,548,206	$45,577,193	$53,012,448	$62,006,227	$72,330,326
Direct Cost of Sales	$29,140,363	$38,864,385	$44,707,249	$51,432,384	$59,168,259
Other	$0	$0	$0	$0	$0
Total Cost of Sales	$29,140,363	$38,864,385	$44,707,249	$51,432,384	$59,168,259
Gross Margin	$4,407,843	$6,712,808	$8,305,199	$10,573,843	$13,162,067
Gross Margin %	13.14%	14.73%	15.67%	17.05%	18.20%
Operating Expenses:					
Marketing and Advertising	$23,000	$30,000	$33,000	$36,300	$39,930
Travel	$34,000	$45,000	$55,000	$65,000	$75,000
Miscellaneous	$6,000	$9,000	$12,000	$15,000	$18,000
Payroll Expense	$1,853,578	$2,393,126	$2,746,293	$3,165,171	$3,651,474
Payroll Burden	$370,716	$478,625	$549,259	$633,034	$730,295
Depreciation	$14,000	$14,700	$15,435	$16,207	$17,017
Professional Fees	$12,000	$13,200	$14,520	$15,972	$17,569
Phones	$23,100	$25,410	$27,951	$30,746	$33,821
Insurance	$2,400	$2,640	$2,904	$3,194	$3,514
Rent	$63,000	$96,000	$96,000	$96,000	$96,000

Other	$9,000	$9,900	$10,890	$11,979	$13,177
	------------	------------	------------	------------	------------
Total Operating Expenses	$2,410,794	$3,117,601	$3,563,251	$4,088,604	$4,695,796
Profit before Interest and Taxes	$1,997,049	$3,595,207	$4,741,948	$6,485,239	$8,466,271
Short-term Interest Expense	$0	$0	$0	$0	$0
Long-term Interest Expense	$0	$0	$0	$0	$0
Taxes Incurred	$499,262	$898,802	$1,185,487	$1,621,310	$2,116,568
Extraordinary Items	$0	$0	$0	$0	$0
Net Profit	$1,497,786	$2,696,405	$3,556,461	$4,863,930	$6,349,703
Net Profit/Sales	4.46%	5.92%	6.71%	7.84%	8.78%

Profit Monthly (Planned)

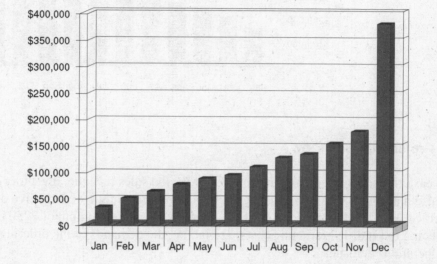

Profit Yearly (Planned)

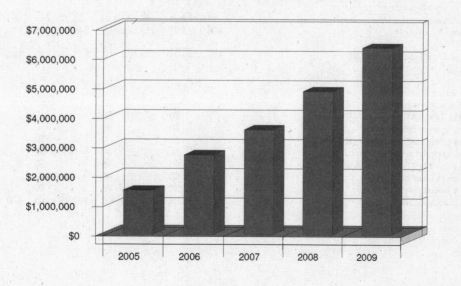

Gross Margin Monthly (Planned)

8.5 Projected Cash Flow

The cash flow depends on assumptions for projected sales revenue, inventory turnover, payment days, and accounts receivable management. The projected time of forty-five days for collection is critical, and it is also reasonable. The Company needs a minimum of $250,000 in new financing to fund: 1) Marketing costs, 2) Meeting the demands of the ordering of products, and 3) Operations demands.

Table: Cash Flow (Planned)

Pro Forma Cash Flow	2005	2006	2007	2008	2009
Cash Received					
Cash from Operations:					
Cash Sales	$3,354,821	$4,557,719	$5,301,245	$6,200,623	$7,233,033
From Receivables	$26,030,083	$39,526,687	$46,788,495	$54,689,485	$63,816,082
Subtotal Cash from Operations	$29,384,904	$44,084,407	$52,089,740	$60,890,107	$71,049,115
Additional Cash Received					
Extraordinary Items	$0	$0	$0	$0	$0
Sales Tax, VAT, HST/GST Received	$0	$0	$0	$0	$0
New Current Borrowing	$0	$0	$0	$0	$0
New Other Liabilities (Interest Free)	$0	$0	$0	$0	$0
New Long-term Liabilities	$0	$0	$0	$0	$0
Sales of other Short-term Assets	$0	$0	$0	$0	$0
Sales of Long-term Assets	$0	$0	$0	$0	$0
New Investment Received	$0	$0	$0	$0	$0
Subtotal Cash Received	$29,384,904	$44,084,407	$52,089,740	$60,890,107	$71,049,115

Expenditures					
Expenditures from Operations:					
Cash Spent on Costs and Expenses	$2,982,613	$4,000,904	$4,616,044	$5,334,409	$6,159,885
Wages, Salaries, Payroll Taxes, etc.	$2,224,294	$2,871,751	$3,295,551	$3,798,206	$4,381,768
Payment of Accounts Payable	$23,276,381	$34,790,282	$40,808,700	$47,150,535	$54,451,720
Subtotal Spent on Operations	$28,483,288	$41,662,937	$48,720,295	$56,283,150	$64,993,373
Additional Cash Spent					
Sales Tax, VAT, HST/GST Paid Out	$0	$0	$0	$0	$0
Principal Repayment of Current Borrowing	$0	$0	$0	$0	$0
Other Liabilities Principal Repayment	$0	$0	$0	$0	$0
Long-term Liabilities Principal Repayment	$0	$0	$0	$0	$0
Purchase Other Short-term Assets	$0	$0	$0	$0	$0
Purchase Long-term Assets	$0	$0	$0	$0	$0
Dividends	$0	$0	$0	$0	$0
Adjustment for Assets Purchased on Credit	$0	$0	$0	$0	$0
Subtotal Cash Spent	$28,483,288	$41,662,937	$48,720,295	$56,283,150	$64,993,373
Net Cash Flow	$901,616	$2,421,470	$3,369,444	$4,606,957	$6,055,741
Cash Balance	$901,616	$3,323,086	$6,692,530	$11,299,487	$17,355,229

Cash (Planned)

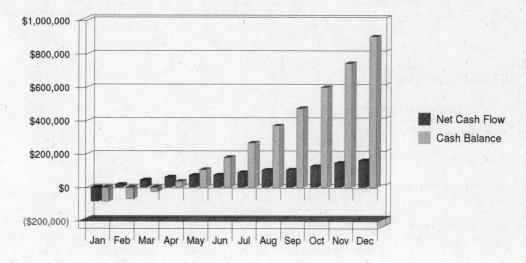

8.6 Projected Balance Sheet

The projected balance sheet is quite solid. The Company does not project any real trouble meeting its debt obligations, as long as it can achieve the funding requirements and meet specific objectives.

Table: Balance Sheet (Planned)

Pro Forma Balance Sheet

Assets

Short-term Assets	2005	2006	2007	2008	2009
Cash	$901,616	$3,323,086	$6,692,530	$11,299,487	$17,355,229
Accounts Receivable	$4,163,302	$5,656,089	$6,578,798	$7,694,917	$8,976,129
Other Short-term Assets	$0	$0	$0	$0	$0
Total Short-term Assets	$5,064,918	$8,979,175	$13,271,328	$18,994,405	$26,331,358
Long-term Assets					
Long-term Assets	$0	$0	$0	$0	$0
Accumulated Depreciation	$0	$0	$0	$0	$0
Total Long-term Assets	$0	$0	$0	$0	$0
Total Assets	$5,064,918	$8,979,175	$13,271,328	$18,994,405	$26,331,358

Liabilities and Capital

Accounts Payable	$3,567,132	$4,784,983	$5,520,675	$6,379,823	$7,367,073
Current Borrowing	$0	$0	$0	$0	$0
Other Short-term Liabilities	$0	$0	$0	$0	$0
Subtotal Short-term Liabilities	$3,567,132	$4,784,983	$5,520,675	$6,379,823	$7,367,073
Long-term Liabilities	$0	$0	$0	$0	$0
Total Liabilities	$3,567,132	$4,784,983	$5,520,675	$6,379,823	$7,367,073
Paid-in Capital	$0	$0	$0	$0	$0
Retained Earnings	$0	$1,497,786	$4,194,192	$7,750,652	$12,614,582
Earnings	$1,497,786	$2,696,405	$3,556,461	$4,863,930	$6,349,703
Total Capital	$1,497,786	$4,194,192	$7,750,652	$12,614,582	$18,964,285
Total Liabilities and Capital	$5,064,918	$8,979,175	$13,271,328	$18,994,405	$26,331,358
Net Worth	$1,497,786	$4,194,192	$7,750,652	$12,614,582	$18,964,285

8.7 Business Ratios

Table: Ratios (Planned)

Ratio Analysis

	2005	2006	2007	2008	2009	Industry
Sales Growth	2695.68%	35.86%	16.31%	16.97%	16.65%	0.00%
Percent of Total Assets						
Accounts Receivable	82.20%	62.99%	49.57%	40.51%	34.09%	0.00%
Inventory	0.00%	0.00%	0.00%	0.00%	0.00%	0.00%
Other Short-term Assets	0.00%	0.00%	0.00%	0.00%	0.00%	100.00%
Total Short-term Assets	100.00%	100.00%	100.00%	100.00%	100.00%	100.00%
Long-term Assets	0.00%	0.00%	0.00%	0.00%	0.00%	0.00%
Total Assets	100.00%	100.00%	100.00%	100.00%	100.00%	100.00%
Short-term Liabilities	70.43%	53.29%	41.60%	33.59%	27.98%	0.00%
Long-term Liabilities	0.00%	0.00%	0.00%	0.00%	0.00%	0.00%
Total Liabilities	70.43%	53.29%	41.60%	33.59%	27.98%	0.00%
Net Worth	29.57%	46.71%	58.40%	66.41%	72.02%	100.00%
Percent of Sales						
Sales	100.00%	100.00%	100.00%	100.00%	100.00%	100.00%
Gross Margin	13.14%	14.73%	15.67%	17.05%	18.20%	0.00%
Selling, General, and Administrative Expenses	8.67%	8.81%	8.96%	9.21%	9.42%	0.00%
Advertising Expenses	0.07%	0.07%	0.06%	0.06%	0.06%	0.00%
Profit before Interest and Taxes	5.95%	7.89%	8.94%	10.46%	11.71%	0.00%

Main Ratios

Current	1.42	1.88	2.40	2.98	3.57	0.00
Quick	1.42	1.88	2.40	2.98	3.57	0.00
Total Debt to Total Assets	70.43%	53.29%	41.60%	33.59%	27.98%	0.00%
Pre-tax Return on Assets	39.43%	40.04%	35.73%	34.14%	32.15%	0.00%
Pre-tax Return on Net Worth	133.33%	85.72%	61.18%	51.41%	44.64%	0.00%

Business Vitality Profile

Sales Per Employee	$1,290,316	$984,705	$926,557	$940,328	$950,809	$0
Survival Rate						0.00%

Additional Ratios

Net Profit Margin	4.46%	5.92%	6.71%	7.84%	8.78%	n.a
Return on Equity	100.00%	64.29%	45.89%	38.56%	33.48%	n.a

Activity Ratios

Accounts Receivable Turnover	7.25	7.25	7.25	7.25	7.25	n.a
Collection Days	25	44	47	47	47	n.a
Inventory Turnover	0.00	0.00	0.00	0.00	0.00	n.a
Accounts Payable Turnover	7.53	7.53	7.53	7.53	7.53	n.a
Total Asset Turnover	6.62	5.08	3.99	3.26	2.75	n.a

Debt Ratios

Debt to Net Worth	2.38	1.14	0.71	0.51	0.39	n.a

Liquidity Ratios

Net Working Capital	$1,497,786	$4,194,192	$7,750,652	$12,614,582	$18,964,285	n.a
Interest Coverage	0.00	0.00	0.00	0.00	0.00	n.a

Additional Ratios

Assets to Sales	0.15	0.20	0.25	0.31	0.36	n.a
Current Debt/Total Assets	70%	53%	42%	34%	28%	n.a
Acid Test	0.25	0.69	1.21	1.77	2.36	n.a
Sales/Net Worth	22.40	10.87	6.84	4.92	3.81	n.a
Dividend Payout	$0	0.00	0.00	0.00	0.00	n.a

8.8 Long-term Plan

The long-term plan is to dominate the public safety market quickly and move into other markets such as the hospitality, residential, and commercial alarm monitoring markets as quickly as feasible. This is intended to build the Company into a profitable and desirable enterprise that can lead to a profitable exit strategy for all stakeholders in the Company.

Confidentiality Agreement

The undersigned reader acknowledges that the information provided by _____ in this business plan is confidential; therefore, reader agrees not to disclose it without the express written permission of _____.

It is acknowledged by reader that information to be furnished in this business plan is in all respects confidential in nature, other than information which is in the public domain through other means and that any disclosure or use of same by reader, may cause serious harm or damage to _____.

Upon request, this document is to be immediately returned to _____.

_____
Signature

_____
Name (typed or printed)

_____
Date

This is a business plan. It does not imply an offering of securities.

SECTION 2

Writing Your Winning Business Plan

CHAPTER 5
Company Overview

Knowing Who You Are

How important is it to know where you are now, where you have been, and where you plan to go? Extremely important! Whether your company is a start-up or an established company, potential lenders and investment groups will want to know with confidence that you have a clear understanding of the business you're in, as well as your strengths, weaknesses, and goals.

If you are an existing business with years of history behind you, it may be easier for you to know the path you are on, but are you certain you're going in the right direction? If you are a recent business start-up looking to take your business to the next level, do you truly know where you are going? Have you really done the research to assure that your assumptions are correct? If you are looking to start a new business, have you examined where you have personally been in your business career and are you certain that your experience will take you and your business where you want to go?

In all the time that we have worked with business owners and managers, we have never met a business owner who did not think differently about their business after doing a thorough written winning business plan. Even longtime business owners and managers would find invaluable information that would help their business to be so much more, and at the end of the process, could tell anyone in two minutes the who, why, what, where, and how of their business.

How many times have you asked people what business they are in only to find that they cannot clearly communicate what they do? "I'm a lawyer," they say. Great, that tells me a lot! Then you have to ask twenty questions to get a sense of what they really do: Do you have your own firm? What areas of law do you specialize in? How long have you been practicing? Wouldn't it have been nice if the person gave you what is known in business networking as a two-minute elevator speech? Well, the key in writing your business plan is to know your business inside and out so that when you speak with anyone about it, especially lenders and investment sources, they are convinced that you do.

Your Company Overview

Items to include when preparing this section of your business plan include the name of the company, when and by whom it was started, its legal structure, its mission statement, its vision statement, its present situation, its goals and objectives, and any other issues or items that you feel may be important to communicate.

Your mission statement should articulate the essence of what the company is about including its values, purpose, and direction and should be concise but impactful so it will inspire and motivate everyone in your organization. Your vision statement should clearly and concisely identify where you believe your company will be at a future date. It should be clearly communicated to everyone in your organization so they can be encouraged to work together to achieve a common purpose.

Use the following questions to help guide you as you write your mission statement.

- *Purpose Statement*—Why does your organization exist and what is the ultimate result of your work?
- *Business Statement*—What activities or programs has your organization chosen to pursue?
- *Values*—What beliefs do your organization's members hold in common and endeavor to put into practice?

In the company overview section, you should highlight existing key areas briefly; for example, your market environment, products and services, customers, management team, manufacturing and distribution facilities, and financial position, along with listing your goals and objectives.

We have put the following statements and questions together to help stimulate your thought process in writing about your present situation.

- Explain the current market environment. Is it undergoing changes in technology, demographics, competition, customers, or financial conditions?
- What is the present stage of your industry, for example, infancy, growth, or mature stage?
- Are there any factors that could contribute to the growth or decline of your product? Indicate both the weak and strong points here. It will look like you really have done your homework (and you should).
- Where are your products assembled or manufactured?
- What is your product's average life cycle?
- With regard to pricing and profitability, are current prices from suppliers increasing, decreasing, or remaining constant? Indicate how you plan to make whatever adjustments are necessary to manage these possible changes in prices.
- How will your customers use your products and services?
- Where will your main office and distribution center be? Do you have any plans to open other offices and distribution centers? If so, indicate when and where.
- Give some additional information about your management team. Have all members been selected? Will you need to hire additional managers or seek advice from outside consultants?
- Provide information about your current financial resources. How much cash is available? How much inventory do you have on hand and is any of it obsolete?

For both your short-term and long-term goals and objectives, you must formulate a vision of where you want to be in a few years. It is important to make sure that you balance your enthusiasm with realism when you visualize your company's progress. In order to achieve your goals, set a few simple objectives as well as aggressive but reachable objectives for each of the next five years.

Let's Start Writing!

Now that you know who you are, let's begin telling the "Company Story." Remember to refer back to your answers to the questions in chapter 3 when writing this section of your winning business plan because most of your answers that are already developed will be used in writing your business plan.

Start this section of your winning business plan by providing a main heading of either "Company Overview" or "Company Description" and then begin telling why and by whom the corporation was started along with any other relevant information that you feel may be important. Then, explain what your company mission statement is and what your company vision statement is. Please note that the font size of headings throughout each section should be smaller than the main heading that begins each section of your winning business plan. Use the boxed examples as a starting point.

Company Overview

Michael X. Swann formed Home Improvements Inc. as a C Corporation in the state of Arizona in 2005 to provide high-quality exterior aluminum siding and superior customer service to residential customers throughout the Southwest region.

Mission Statement

To provide customers with high-quality exterior aluminum siding and double pane windows, to take pride in the integrity and craftsmanship of each product sold to the end user, and to offer superior customer service throughout the warranty phases of the product, always remembering that each customer may be a tremendous source of referral business to our company.

Vision Statement

To become a nationally recognized company and a leader in our industry, develop a training, education, and advancement program for all employees to participate in, and to give back to our communities through volunteer outreach and charitable donations.

Start Writing:

_____

_____

_____

_____

_____

_____

_____

_____

_____

_____

_____

_____

_____

Next, explain the present situation of the company by briefly providing information on the company's key areas as defined earlier in this chapter. If you are a business start-up, let the reader of your business plan know what phase you are in regarding your start-up and let them know the present situation of the marketplace that you plan to enter along with the products and services you will be providing. In addition, let them know the business and transferable skill set of everyone on your management team, including yourself, along with how much capital you have available for your business start-up. Begin with the heading "Present Situation."

Present Situation

Home Improvements Inc. has had an exciting and promising year. We have recently completed a move to a larger and more efficient facility, which has enabled the company to streamline its method of operation and increase its bottom line.

The marketplace is undergoing tremendous technological change. New aluminum siding technology is making our product increasingly attractive, stronger, and less costly. We are now poised to take advantage of these changes and expect to become a major supplier of exterior aluminum siding and double-pane windows nationally.

Our core products are in the mature stage since our products have been in the marketplace for over thirty years; however, annual revenues in the industry continue to increase because of the high demand for new construction as well as an increase in the number of homeowners upgrading the exterior of their current homes. Although current prices are increasing for materials and labor, we have been able to pass these costs on to the customer without having a negative effect on sales volume.

Our current customers are using our exterior aluminum siding and double-pane windows for added home value, energy savings, storm protection, and noise reduction; and they frequently request that we continue to promote our products in their area so the value of their neighborhoods will continue to increase, especially when the real estate market tightens.

We currently have one distribution center in Phoenix, Arizona, with plans to open additional offices in Indianapolis, Indiana, and Knoxville, Tennessee. Once in place, these centers will reduce freight costs and damage that occurs during shipment and will reduce lead times to our customers.

The management team is the strength of our company with over twenty-five years of combined experience directly related to the industry. They are poised to handle the challenges that will occur once the company begins its campaign to open new markets nationally.

The financial status of the company is strong under current conditions with cash assets of $22,500 and total assets totaling $170,000. By establishing a new line of credit of $150,000, our company will be able to begin its national expansion.

Start Writing:

_____

_____

_____

_____

_____

_____

_____

_____

_____

_____

_____

_____

_____

_____

_____

_____

_____

Next, give a brief yet comprehensive statement on the various goals and objectives you wish to reach over the next five years, or longer if needed. As discussed in chapter 1, it is important to quantify both your short- and long-term goals by being specific, realistic, aggressive, and consistent. Goals are important because they will affect just about everything you do as you plan and operate your business. Goals are not just the destination you're driving toward, but they're also the painted white lines that keep you on the road. Your goals may include when you will be opening the doors to your new business, when you will be hiring your employees, and when you anticipate your business will become profitable. Remember to keep goals realistic and reachable because most lenders and investors are smart enough to recognize pie-in-the-sky rhetoric and will call you on it; after that, your chances to obtain capital will be slim. Begin with the heading "Objectives" or "Goals and Objectives."

Objectives

The long-term goal of Home Improvements Inc. is to become a nationally recognized company to our target market of middle- to upper-income households. With the working capital provided, management intends to expand into rural America by purchasing the inventory and equipment required to meet the demand for our products and by advertising and promoting our business to the marketplace.

Our short-term goals are to solidify our existing location and bring the company to a more profitable position while we are pursuing financing. Once financing is achieved, the primary objectives of our organization are to:

- Open new sales and distribution offices
- Increase our advertising spectrum through television and radio
- Purchase additional inventory direct from OEMs
- Attend national and international trade shows
- Hire new personnel and increase sales training
- Purchase new equipment

For the company to reach these goals, the line of credit must be structured to long-term debt because it will better match the terms of the loan with the use of the proceeds. In addition, the following will be needed to position us for growth:

- Study and understand customers, competition, and industry
- Provide top-grade products, services, distribution, and customer service
- Improve product and service life cycles
- Balance team members, management, and business goals
- Operate at fifty employees
- Develop morals, values, and culture
- Hire the best people

Start Writing:

_____

_____

_____

_____

_____

_____

_____

_____

_____

_____

_____

_____

_____

_____

_____

_____

_____

_____

_____

_____

_____

Let's Do a Quick Review!

Those who have been in business for a number of years may feel that they know their business inside and out. Most probably do know it very well, but there is always something to learn, maybe a way to do things better, or in certain cases you find things that you should stop doing. Those who have been in business for a shorter period of time and those looking to start a new business may feel overwhelmed with all that there is to learn. Regardless of where you are, it is important to remember that a potential investor or lender will hone in on you and will ask you tough questions about where your business was, how you got to where it is now, and how you plan on taking it to the next level. Go back to chapter 3, "100-Plus Questions to Personal and Business Success," and review your answers to all the questions. Make sure all your answers have been thoroughly thought out, researched, and answered fully and completely and that you have incorporated all pertinent information into your winning business plan. We must reiterate just how important this process is. Writing a business plan involves revisiting information already written because as you go through the process, thoughts, ideas, and perceptions change. Is it overwhelming? It can be. Will it take time to do? Yes, of course. The key question is, will it produce better results? The answer is a definite yes. It is important to challenge the mind and stimulate thought so you will think beyond the obvious. When you do, you will increase your chances of reaching your established goals and objectives.

When we sit with new business start-ups and existing-business owners, we go over these questions with them many times. As we get deeper into writing the plan, they begin to see a new light and a clearer path resulting in new ideas, concepts, and directions that are beneficial to the company. You may find it helpful to share your business idea with someone you know who is business-savvy and have him review these questions with you. Ask him to challenge you to dig deeper so you may formulate a deeper understanding of where you are, where you want to be, and how you plan to get there.

Not only is it important to know your business inside and out, it is just as important to make sure that you can tell others what your business is all about in a short, concise, and clear manner. You do not want to get in front of an investor or lender and be like a deer in headlights. For example, we were referred to one successful client who contacted us to help him with a business plan because he was looking to get a $50,000 credit line to expand his business. Upon our initial meeting, he informed us that he had been to his bank, and they were uncertain about the direction he wanted to take his business. Although he was in good credit standing with them, this was not enough to convince them to provide the line of credit he was asking for. They suggested that he put together a business plan and come back to them. After working with our client on preparing a winning business plan, we were able to fine-tune several areas and create a road map that was clear and concise. In addition, our client who felt that he knew his business inside and out had a whole lot more to learn—and he did. Once he honed his presentation skills, our client went back to his bank and was approved for a $50,000 credit line. We are proud to say that this client was able to grow his business and sell it for a substantial amount several years later.

CHAPTER 6
Product and Service Description

Making It Count

Your capacity to produce and provide marketable products and services to your customers is extremely important. Whether your company is a start-up or an established company, potential lenders and investment groups will only lend capital if they are satisfied with the company's ability to efficiently procure, produce, and provide marketable products and services to their customers in a timely and profitable manner.

Many entrepreneurs starting their own business go into an industry that they already know. Our experiences with our clients show that the majority of them have a good handle on how to produce their products and provide their services because that is what they have been doing for a number of years. If you are looking to start a business, this may be the same situation you are in. A word of caution, though: knowing how to produce products and provide services is just the beginning. Keep in mind as you are writing your winning business plan that there is so much more to know in this area that will make your business more effective and more profitable. Choosing the right business location and leasing the proper amount of space, effectively negotiating your building and equipment leases, establishing purchasing polices and procedures that allow you to maximize your cash flow by ordering inventory on a just-in-time basis, creating a process flow that allows you to move your products and services in the most efficient manner, and implementing a delivery system that is cost-effective and timely will all affect your ability to produce and provide your product or service.

For your product and service description, cover the main points, including what the products and services are and how they work, what technology is needed in order to make it feasible, what your manufacturing costs are, how you intend to distribute and deliver them, what your packaging looks like (point out any specific designs or colors you use and why), how you derived your pricing, whether or not your products are handmade or even customized, etc. Also describe what customer need your products and services fill. What are their important features and benefits?

When including features and benefits of your product(s), remember that benefits are generally much more important than features. Many entrepreneurs tend to describe features more than benefits.

Manufacturers tend to think in features first, but benefits are what make the products sell. Become a marketer and describe products that are rich in features, technologies, handling, superior materials, etc. With a high-tech automobile, for example, you may be tempted to talk about the technology and the features—aerodynamic design and a 400hp engine. But what the customer wants to hear is that he will look cool driving a metallic red fireball that hugs the corners going 65 mph and attracts babes like there is no tomorrow!

Finally, describe your product offerings in terms of customer types and customer needs, and you'll often discover new needs and new kinds of customers to cover. This is the way ideas are generated.

For anyone looking to start a business in an industry in which they have no experience, be aware that there are many training options available to you to help you get started. To start or purchase any of these businesses may require an intensive amount of capital or only require a little amount of capital. So, what are your options if you fall into this category? First, you can buy an existing business where the owner will agree to stay with the company for a certain amount of time in order to train you on all aspects of the business. Second, you can get a franchise business, where part of your franchise payment is to cover your training and setting up your business; plus they should always be there for you if you have any questions or concerns. Third, you can start a home-based business, usually with a small investment, where training and initial study books and materials are provided, and if it is a direct marketing company, you will have the support of the individuals throughout your organization. Whichever way you go, make sure you fully understand what products and services you are selling and make sure you can fully articulate your knowledge of your products and services to whomever you speak with.

Before choosing to get into any business, we highly suggest you do a thorough investigation into the business and industry, including making sure the products and services being offered are viable, before making a commitment. In addition, in order to protect yourself financially (and even physically and mentally because yes, big mistakes will make you sick and drive you crazy!), make sure you hire a top-rated law firm to review and advise you on any contracts before you obligate yourself to any situation. We have had a number of clients, friends, and family members sign contracts and put up their personal cash without doing due diligence or consulting with a law firm, and in the end they have all asked themselves the same question, "What did I do?"

Let's Start Writing!

This section of the business plan is where you will begin telling the "Product and Service" story. Remember to refer back to your answers to the "Products and Services Questions" and the "Production and Facility Questions" in chapter 3 when writing this section of your plan.

Start this section of your winning business plan by providing information on what products and services you offer featuring any highlights that you feel are important. For companies that have an immense product line with commonly known items, listing the various categories should be adequate; however, if you have any dynamic hot-selling items within these categories, you will want to mention them specifically. It will be important that your products and services are easily recognizable and understood by lending organizations, so you must clearly identify and explain them, as well as the purchasing, manufacturing, packaging, and distribution aspects of your products and services.

Product and Service Description

Our exterior aluminum siding and double-pane windows are manufactured in Korea, Florida, and South Carolina in bulk and are shipped into Phoenix, Arizona, where they are cut and assembled into finished goods. Utilizing state-of-the-art tooling and strict quality control procedures throughout the process, we can continually produce high-quality finished products out of custom hardened aluminum alloy that are dependable and long lasting.

The products are specially designed to withstand all weather conditions in all parts of the United States from the dry desert conditions of Arizona to the wet, bitter-cold conditions of New England. Each siding panel is technologically slotted and overlaid on high-density fiberglass insulation that provides extra insulation value to every home on which it is installed. Decorative trim pieces and eave under panels made of extruded aluminum give the final touches to an attractive product and when installed with our double-pane windows, homeowners are assured of additional energy efficiency to the home.

The siding products are immediately available in eight colors: white, cream, dark brown, dark wood grain, beige, sky blue, aqua green, and sunflower yellow. Forty additional custom colors are available; however, they must be specially ordered from one of our manufacturers and it increases our delivery time from thirty to sixty days over our normal delivery time of two weeks. Our double-pane windows are available in black or white. An analysis of our sales history shows that less then 5 percent of our orders are custom colors.

Start Writing:

_____

_____

_____

_____

_____

_____

_____

_____

_____

_____

_____

_____

_____

_____

_____

_____

_____

Next, expand upon the benefits that customers will receive by purchasing your products and services. For example, "our patented 16 SEER heating and air conditioning unit has been proven to reduce utility bills in excess of 20 percent, which for the average homeowner of a 2,000 square foot home is $960.00 annually." Remember to keep this information factual, based on historical data tracked and provided by an independent party responsible for the testing. If something sounds too good to be true, it probably is and most investors and lenders will recognize it and will call you on it—and that is not a good thing! When appropriate, footnote the source of the data and if you choose, you can include supporting documentation in the appendix section of your business plan. Begin with a heading that is appropriate to the benefit you are emphasizing. Please note that the font size of headings throughout each section should be smaller than the main heading that begins each section of your winning business plan.

Payback Period

For most customers, our aluminum siding and double-pane windows will pay for themselves in terms of energy savings within twelve years. Independent research has shown that each homeowner may realize energy savings of 10 to 15 percent. During the hotter months, our products intercept solar radiation, thus providing an insulation value that allows air conditioners to work about 30 percent less. In the winter, our products provide a pleasant insulating blanket that keeps the cold air from entering and keeps heat inside the home.

In addition to utility savings, savings from never having to paint their home again will shorten the payback period further for homeowners, particularly in especially hot, cold, or wet climates where frequent repainting costs can be extremely high.

Start Writing:

_____

_____

_____

_____

_____

_____

_____

_____

_____

Next, in brief and concise paragraphs, provide additional information that you feel will be of benefit in promoting and supporting the viability of your products and services, including added value or unique features, third-party tests, approvals, and validations such as test ratings and approvals by government regulators, product and service life cycles, warranties, and guarantees. Again, begin with a heading that is appropriate to the benefit you are emphasizing.

Tests and Product Life Cycle

Tests subjecting our aluminum siding to impact by hard and soft objects, performed in accordance with the common rules of the Product Durability Testing Requirements set forth by U.S. regulations, have demonstrated a performance that is highly superior to that required by the regulations.

It has been determined that the product life cycle of our aluminum siding and double-pane windows is sixty years based on historical climate and weather conditions that have occurred throughout the United States. The manufacturer's warranty covers all exterior parts for five years for any manufacturing defect that occurs.

Start Writing:

_____

_____

_____

_____

_____

_____

_____

Let's Do a Quick Review!

You may feel that investors and lenders are not really that interested in your products or services, especially if they are everyday items, but investors and lenders are concerned with more than just a basic description. Give details about the whole process, starting with where you are located, where the products and services are procured, how you obtain them and for how much, where and how you manufacture and inventory them, how much you sell them for, how you distribute and deliver them, and how you manage your workforce and cash flow during this process. We have seen many an entrepreneur start a business because they thought no one could produce a widget as well as they could. Well, in some cases they were probably right. The only problem was that there is a whole lot more to do when owning a business besides manufacturing a widget. If this is you, we say, "Entrepreneur, beware." Go back to chapter 3 and review your answers to the "Products and Services Questions" and "Production and Facility Questions." Make sure all your answers have been thoroughly thought out, researched, and answered fully and completely and that you have incorporated all pertinent information into your winning business plan.

It is truly important that you understand the processes required from beginning to end that will maximize your bottom line regarding your products and services. You must be able to speak with investors and lenders without hesitation; otherwise, they will pass on providing you financing. For example, we had one successful client who was growing at a good pace and was looking for additional capital for inventory. Upon reviewing his inventory and purchasing methods, we discovered that he was losing production time waiting for raw materials to arrive and he was paying more than others in the same industry for the same materials. We put together a program with one of his key vendors that guaranteed just-in-time shipment of products and we negotiated a price point for each of the items purchased below what others were paying in the same industry. Upon going to the bank, our client was well versed in all his business matters, and when he informed the banker of the arrangement with his vendor and how he was able to increase production while putting more money to the bottom line, the banker was pleased to extend him the credit line increase he had requested. We are proud to say that this client has continued to grow over the years and he runs a very successful company.

CHAPTER 7
Market Analysis

Doing Your Homework

How important is your determination to research, study, and investigate your market and do a thorough analysis of it? Extremely important! Whether your company is a start-up or an established company, potential lenders and investment groups will focus on the potential of your market and make a determination of whether you can successfully run a profitable business in it. They will know if you have done your homework in this area so you had better make sure you do; there is no cramming allowed when writing this section of your winning business plan.

Many of you already in business may feel that you have a good handle on your marketplace, and that may be true, but have you done a full-blown market analysis? If you have not, dig in and start the process because you may be surprised at what you will find out about who your target market really is and what your competitors are all about. For those who have recently started or plan to start a business, now is the time to do your detailed market analysis. It is what you find in researching, studying, and investigating your market that will enable you to create the marketing and sales strategies that will bring the greatest amount of return on your investment dollar. Give investors and lenders what they are looking for.

Again, when developing a profile of your target market, it is important to remember that the quality of your research will determine the strength of your analysis. The time you spend on this section should be spent wisely. Your local library, chamber of commerce, the Internet and telephone, and marketing consultants may be your strongest allies. Use them to their fullest! Take advantage of the information and statistics already available in books, directories, case studies, and on the Internet. Thorough research will impress potential investors more than you can believe, so be thorough in structuring this market profile. Show that you have done your homework with great care and due diligence. Spend your time wisely.

Determine Who You Are Targeting

It is imperative for you to know who your target market is and where they are. You must precisely state whom the consumers of your products and services are and where they are located—and we do mean precisely.

For the individual consumer, your data findings must include the demographic scope of your market, including total population size, population by gender, age, occupation, culture, education, marital status, family size, number of homeowners, number of renters, income per individual and per household, and income by gender. You must also determine their buying and spending habits as they relate to personal items like clothes and household goods, social time like restaurants and movies, work expenses like business outfits and business supplies, vacation time like weekend trips and cruises, relaxation time like reading books and magazines or watching television while enjoying a beverage, and luxury items like boats and fancy cars. You need to know what makes your target market tick and what gets them to spend money! You must also include the geographic scope of your market, identifying your target area or areas and how the demographics of the target area will be sufficient for you to meet your goals and objectives.

For the business customer, often referred to as business-to-business sales or B2B sales, your analysis must include the geographic scope of your market as defined above, and your demographic scope must include the type and size of business you are selling to, the number of employees they have, and the number of years they have been in business, along with what their buying and spending habits are. You will need to determine if they are currently buying or plan to buy what you are selling, and most important, you must determine how much they currently buy and how much they plan to spend.

A word of warning: if at the conclusion of researching, studying, and investigating your market, you determine that the market is not sufficient to support your business, give a lot of thought to not opening your business, at least not in that target market. If you are already in business and realize that the target market is not enough to support your business, you may want to look at alternative products that you can sell that will be supported by your market. See if it is feasible to increase the size and/or location of your market, or you may want to consider developing an exit strategy to get out of the business.

Determine Who Your Competition Is

It is imperative for you to know who and where your competitors are and what they are doing to obtain business. You must precisely determine whom the competitors are for your specific target market, where they are located, how they are promoting their products and services, how much market share each has, and if additional new competitors can be anticipated or expected.

This must be done whether you are selling to individual consumers or business customers. You need to know everything about your competitors that you can possibly find and you can do this in a number of ways. Determining who and where your competitors are can be done in several ways based upon the size of your target market. You can use resources such as industry trade publications, directories, and magazines, Yellow Pages, online business directories, and walking or driving through your target market area. Make sure you clearly define all your competitors—any businesses that are competing for the same purchasing dollar as you are.

Let's say you are looking to open a sandwich shop. Your first thought might be to look only at competing sandwich shops, but you shouldn't stop there. You must also look at all other eateries where an individual can buy a meal for around the same price you are offering and get it in the same amount of time. You may have to look at businesses that sell hamburgers, chicken sandwiches, all-you-can-eat salad, and pizza, because you and these other businesses are all competing for the same purchasing dollar. A perfect example of this is the food court at a large mall. Here you usually have six to ten companies trying to entice you to get in their line and buy from them, so what do you do? You go around to each one of them and take a look at the food they are presenting and usually, unless you have a craving for something in particular, you get in line of the business that has the best food presentation, which normally has the longest line. (Unless, of course, you are in a huge rush and then you get in the shortest line and after you are done eating you wish you hadn't.)

After you determine who your competitors are, you need to find out what your competitors are doing to obtain business. You can do this in few ways including shopping them yourselves or having someone you know shop them for you along with sitting outside their place of business and watching their traffic flow. You must do whatever it takes to discover what they are doing to be successful. This will help you create your marketing and sales strategies to effectively compete with them and help you toward obtaining your desired market share.

Let's Start Writing!

Now that you know whom you are targeting, let's begin telling the "Market Analysis" story. Remember to refer back to your answers to the "Customer and Competition Questions" in chapter 3 when writing this section.

Start this section of your business plan by providing a main heading of "Market Analysis" and then begin providing a market analysis overview along with any other relevant information that you feel may be important. In other words, in this section of your plan you will want to provide specific information about the size of the market in dollar volume and by number of competitors. Include industry statistics on growth for the past five to ten years and where experts feel the industry is headed. Add in information about buying trends and certain buying patterns that have been prevalent during the past five years. And provide the reader with information about your target market and why it will be inclined to purchase your products and services.

Please note that the font size of headings throughout each section should be smaller than the main heading that begins each section of your business plan.

Market Analysis

Currently, nine businesses share the Phoenix, Arizona, market and our company enjoys approximately 30 percent of this market share. It is estimated that four major competitors share 60 percent of the market while the remaining competitors share the remaining 10 percent. The stability of the market segment is expected to increase as the exterior aluminum siding market has been growing at a fast pace and the overall United States market is virtually untapped.

Over the past three years, companies have developed additional features and have focused on the use of technological advances to steadily improve the quality of aluminum in exterior siding, thereby creating larger demand for the products. New Consumer Product Reports also states that firms selling home value added products will prosper greatly in the coming decade.

Strengths

Our most powerful assets are the uses of television and radio for advertising and promotion. The public awareness for our products and services has been greatly enhanced due to our intense advertising campaigns. Because of our successful marketing strategies and superior customer service, Home Improvements Inc. has garnered 30 percent market share, the largest share of the market in this industry.

Weaknesses

The only notable marketplace disadvantage is the inaccurate perception homeowners have regarding the prices they will have to pay for our products. Once consumers realize how affordable our products are, closing the sale becomes much easier. Typically, an average job will cost around $13,000 if the entire home is covered with siding and double-pane windows.

Corporate weaknesses at this time consist only of not enough sales personnel; however, we are taking steps to interview competent sales professionals, which we feel will alleviate this problem.

Start Writing:

_____

_____

_____

_____

_____

_____

_____

_____

_____

_____

_____

_____

_____

_____

_____

_____

Customers

The average household earnings of our customers range from $50,000 to $80,000 per year for married couples still in the workforce and retired persons living in the middle- to upper-income class with a larger amount of disposable income. The person who influences the decision to buy is typically the housewife or woman of the household, and she will be the one to permit the purchase to be made. Generally, she will also be the one who will choose the color and the areas where the siding and double-pane windows will be added to the home.

It is likely that potential customers are going to be familiar with aluminum siding and double-pane windows and that they will readily accept our advertising approach, provided that we educate them in the proper manner. It is also important to point out that our marketing and advertising efforts have been targeted to people concerned about energy efficiency and adding value to their homes and to retired homeowners. It is easy to understand why the principal buying motives are geared toward our products because retired persons and housewives are looking for added comfort and beauty in and around their homes in addition to adding value and energy efficiency.

Historical data and research indicates that these groups of customers are not sensitive to pricing differences among competitors and it indicates that these consumers are willing to spend their money on ways that will improve their way of life. It is our constant task to educate the customer on the superior quality of our products and services.

The demographics of our target market are as follows:

Housewife:		Married Couple:	
Age:	35–65	Age:	35–55
Income:	Fixed	Income:	Medium to high
Sex:	Female	Sex:	Male or Female
Family:	Children living at home	Family:	0 to 2 children
Geographic:	Suburban	Geographic:	Suburban
Occupation:	Housewife	Occupation:	Varies
Attitude:	Security minded	Attitude:	Security minded, energy conscious

Older Couple:		Elderly:	
Age:	55–75	Age:	70+
Income:	High or fixed	Income:	Fixed
Sex:	Male or Female	Sex:	Male or Female
Family:	Empty nest	Family:	Empty nest
Geographic:	Suburban	Geographic:	Suburban
Occupation:	White-collar or retired	Occupation:	Retired
Attitude:	Security minded, energy conscious	Attitude:	Security minded, energy conscious

Next, explain who you are targeting and where they are located. Begin with the heading "Customers." Start Writing:

_____
_____
_____
_____
_____
_____
_____
_____
_____
_____
_____
_____
_____
_____
_____
_____
_____
_____
_____
_____
_____
_____
_____
_____
_____

Next, explain who your competitors are, where they are located, and how you match up against them. Begin with the heading "Competition."

Competition

Our competitive threats come from three primary competitors and three secondary competitors in Phoenix, Arizona. Our research indicates that in comparison our products provide more features and have superior performance over our competitor products. In most cases, the number of differences is substantial. A complete technical comparison has been made and is available for review.

Companies that compete in the U.S. market are Home Siding 4 You (HSY), U.S. Aluminum (USA), North East Siding (NES), and Quality Home Products (QHP). All of these companies charge competitive prices and supply similar products with similar features. Our products are made of superior aluminum (a higher grade of material than our competitors use) and we are able to compete with them although our pricing is higher, because our customers receive a greater value for the money they are spending.

To support our claim of a superior product, our aluminum siding has been subjected to many trials of impact with hard and soft objects in accordance with the common rules of the Product Durability Testing Requirements set by U.S. regulations. The results showed our products to be high above what the regulations require.

Competitive Roundup

Based on our research of the competition, the following chart illustrates how we feel our company compares with the competition, HSY, USA, NES, and QHP, in several different key areas with 1 being weak and 5 being strong:

	Competition	Home Improvements Inc.
Estimated Market Share	60%	30%
Product Line	4	5
Quality	4	5
Technology	4	5
Advertising	2	5
Sales Force	3	5
Distribution	3	4
Price	4	4
Installation	4	5
Ease of Use	4	5
Appearance	3	5
Design	4	5
Useful Life	4	4
Responsiveness	3	5
Availability	1	5
Technical Expertise	4	5
Repair Service	3	5
Efficiency	3	5
Guarantee/Warranty	5	5
On Time Capability	4	5
Industry Reputation	3	5

It appears from the above information that some of our competition is faring well; however, it is apparent that our company is offering superior products and services at a competitive price.

Start Writing:

_____
_____
_____
_____
_____
_____
_____
_____
_____
_____
_____
_____
_____

Let's Do a Quick Review!

You may have asked yourself, do I really have to do all this researching, studying, and investigating? Can't I just make quick assumptions based on what I already know? The answer is an absolute no. This information is so critical to your business that you must not take it lightly and brush it off. Investors and lenders will be placing a lot of focus in this area and they will know whether or not you have done your homework. If you are not able to convince them that you have a viable market and you know how to successfully compete in it, you can anticipate that you will be waving good-bye to any potential financing. Don't sell yourself short; make sure you go and do a thorough job on your market analysis.

Putting forth the time and effort required to get to know your market inside and out is a part of creating marketing and sales strategies that will increase your bottom line. For example, we had one successful client who after years of being in business decided to go back and shop his competitors, and retained us to do so. For years his marketing strategy was to be the low price leader because he felt that low prices were what propelled customers into his retail stores to buy from him. When shopping the competitors, we asked how they felt about the products he sold and from each of them we got the same answer: "You get what you pay for." So, in effect, by setting his prices so low, the business owner was telling potential customers that his quality wasn't as good as the competition's. We wondered how many of these customers never made it to his store and even worse, told others that his products weren't very good. After several discussions with our client, we were able to convince him to raise his prices (although he was reluctant and scared to do so) closer to the prices his competitors were charging for similar products. The year after raising his prices, he sold over 30 percent more product at larger margins that increased his overall profit by over $120,000. We're certain we earned our consulting fee on that one, and we are proud to say that the client has continued to successfully grow his business year after year.

CHAPTER 8
Marketing and Sales Strategy

Planning for Gold

How important is your ability to take the information you gathered from your market analysis and create effective revenue-producing marketing and sales strategies? Extremely important! Whether your company is a start-up or an established company, potential lenders and investment groups will want to know your plans for promoting market recognition of your company and your products and services and they will make a determination on whether or not you have a clear and concise focus in doing so in a cost-effective manner.

We have seen great businesses with a super location and a unique product go broke and close their doors. In most cases, this tragic ending can be traced to poor marketing and promotion because the owner of the business did not do a thorough market analysis to determine how to properly market his products and services and as a result spent time and money unwisely. Many business owners make the mistake of thinking they don't have to advertise or promote their "superior products or services." Well, in many cases they are flat-out wrong! Many business owners ignore or forget four key marketing areas and this usually has a negative impact on their business. These four critical areas are:

1. Publicity
2. Promotion
3. Merchandising
4. Market research

How do you reach your customers to let them know who you are and what services you provide? First you must define your market. Who or what is your targeted audience? Who will listen to your story and who will buy from you once they have heard your case?

Before completing your marketing and sales strategy, it is advantageous to have done a thorough market analysis as described in chapter 7. *Entrepreneur* magazine gives us a super idea in this area: "All you have to do is forget that you are selling your product or service and put yourself in your customer's place." The article suggests asking yourself questions such as these:

• Where do I go to buy it?

- What makes me buy it?
- What media do I watch, read, and listen to that makes me decide to buy?

Simply put, you must know what media your market is drawn to. Once you do, you must develop a rock-solid marketing plan. Your profits will literally rise or fall on the basis of how well you develop and implement your marketing plan. Carefully consider the following ideas and strategies and include a discussion of each one of them in your plan if applicable.

- Marketing strategies that you will be focusing on.
- Pricing your products and services. Remember to "charge what the market will bear." Don't over or under price what you are selling.
- Your timetable to market your products and services.
- Your marketing budget.
- Guarantee policies.
- Presentation and packaging.
- Professional resources you will need to implement your plan.
- Your method for monitoring the response of the market to your campaign.
- Your method for testing one approach against another.
- Advertising and promotional intentions.
- Media you will use to promote your enterprise and related costs.

Establish Marketing Objectives

When establishing your marketing objectives for your next campaign, you will want to consider four critical goals and objectives:

1. Increasing brand awareness by a specific percentage
2. Generating high-quality leads for your sales force (even if your sales force is just you)
3. Improving the morale of your direct sales force
4. Increasing sales by a specific percentage within a certain time frame

Once the campaign is underway, begin tracking results. Conduct a few preliminary studies a few weeks into the campaign to measure the results, but don't expect these results to be final. In most cases, you should give your campaign a significant amount of time to realize final results. Your target expectations may be realized sooner, which would be the result of a well-planned and well-executed marketing strategy. However, if you are not getting the results that you were anticipating, you must review your plan to try to determine why it is not working and then alter or stop your plan based on the results of your review.

Advertising and Promotion Ideas

Begin by developing a realistic budget for advertising. You may follow a general rule of thumb by allocating about 5 to 10 percent of expected annual revenues. Obviously the percentage can dramatically change from industry to industry, so in your market analysis, look to see if there is a percentage indicator in your specific industry. Include in your advertising campaign a good mixture of promotional items. If your budget is relatively small—for example, about $100 to $200 per month—you should definitely include business cards, letterheads, envelopes, a brochure, and stamps at a minimum. These items will give your business plenty of exposure if you carefully follow up on literature that is sent out.

There are so many different ways to promote your business without spending a lot of money. Make sure you do research on the costs associated in each of the following areas.

- A company newsletter is another inexpensive way to keep your name in front of your customers. You could possibly charge for a subscription or send it out free each month or every quarter to existing, new, and prospective customers.

- T-shirts, pens, coffee mugs, paperweights, hats, etc., are a relatively inexpensive way to advertise your business. Check the costs by interviewing several advertising specialties companies and include this in your business plan. These promotional items are a subtle reminder to your clients every time they see your name.

    Send out promotional products with your corporate name, logo, and phone number imprinted on the item to your best customers and prospects. This can be a great way to keep your name in front of them for a long time. Focus on items such as pens, notepads, hats, calendars, shirts, and other items that will remain on their desktop or be used regularly.

- Advertise on one radio station during morning drive time hours (6:00–9:00 a.m.) where your target audience is listening and the price of advertising is cost-effective.

- Give a free or low-cost seminar at a convention hall, hotel, auditorium, gymnasium, classroom, library, etc., that holds thirty to fifty people at one time were the cost is minimal. Make sure you clearly define the costs of promoting and holding seminars, including costs for the room, beverages, overhead projectors, writing boards, tables, chairs, microphones, pens and paper, and your printed material.

- Broadcast a live-remote radio campaign from your location where your customers can come to your store to meet the radio talent and receive promotional giveaways. For certain industries, this type of promotion is a tremendous investment.

- Write a powerful and exciting press release and send it to various media sources like the editor of a newspaper or a producer of a radio or television show, which can often give you free press or airtime, especially when they like your idea or concept. Sometimes they will conduct an interview about you, your company, and your products and services. Your only costs may be the price of a few letters and stamps. Look in the Yellow Pages under television stations, radio stations, newspapers, and magazines for the telephone numbers. Call and ask for the name of the business editor or producer and send them a personalized, double-spaced press release that is one or two pages in length. Then, follow up in a week or so to see if they received your material. Don't ask them if they are going to do a story on you. Simply remind them about your unique product, service, or idea. Don't be surprised if you do not hear from them for many months; it often takes quite a while for an opening to become available. In some instances you may not hear from them at all, but don't let that aggravate or concern you; sometimes things just fall through the cracks.

- Offer to give public speeches to several different organizations. You will be pleasantly surprised at the enormous number of organizations you probably never knew existed as you scan the Yellow Pages or various reference sources available in the library. The speaking and seminar business will enable you to promote your products and services at a relatively low out-of-pocket cost. Some organizations to choose from are:

A. Business and trade organizations
B. Civic groups
C. Convention planners
D. Service organizers
E. Business firms and organizations
F. Political affiliations
G. Fraternal organizations
H. Athletic clubs
I. Professional associations

Selling Tactics

This is where you will determine how you will take your products and services to market and where you will create your unique selling advantages. First, you will need to identify the ways you can effectively sell your products. Will you sell them yourself, hire an inside sales staff that tries to find and sell customers over the telephone, hire an outside sales force that goes directly to the customers, enlist manufacturing representatives, or sign on independent contractors? The direction that you take will vary depending on your particular industry or business. The key is to establish a process to get in front of a customer so you can present your products and services and give yourself the chance to close a sale and generate revenue.

Defining the Unique Selling Advantages of your products and services is paramount in helping you get in front of customers and close the sale. Customers are always looking for the sizzle of a good deal because they want to feel good about the buying decision they are making; therefore, it is your job to add the sizzle and make a mouth-watering sales presentation so they will buy what you are selling. Anything less may result in a lost opportunity, and in the games of sales and business, that is a direct negative hit on your bottom line. So start up the grill and begin cooking up what makes your products and services unique from your competitors.

Let's Start Writing!

Now that you have determined how you are going to market and sell your products and services, let's begin telling the "Marketing and Sales Strategy" story. Remember to refer back to your answers to the "Marketing Questions," "Sales Questions," and "Advertising Questions" in chapter 3 when writing this section of your winning business plan.

Start this section of your winning business plan by providing a main heading of "Marketing and Sales Strategy" and then begin providing your overall marketing strategy along with any other relevant information that you feel may be important.

Please note that the font size of headings throughout each section should be smaller than the main heading that begins each section of your winning business plan.

Marketing and Sales Strategy
Marketing Strategy

Our marketing strategy is to enhance, promote, and support the fact that our products and services are superior to others in the market. The overall marketing plan is based on the following fundamentals:

1) The segment of the markets we plan to reach
2) The distribution channels we intend to use to reach the market segment, including television, radio, mail order, and direct sales
3) The share of the market that we expect to capture over a fixed period of time

To prove the value of our exterior aluminum siding and double-pane windows we will demonstrate two features that sell our product because they are of great concern to our customers—added home value and energy efficiency. Because our product is constructed with a high-grade aluminum and installed over superior insulation, an extra value is added to the home year-round. According to a study release by County Gas & Electric, based on actual comparisons, our product saves our customers 10 to 15 percent in energy costs.

Product Strategy and Positioning

Our exterior aluminum siding and double-pane windows should be treated as a long-term product as our customer can recoup their investment within the term of a thirty-year mortgage, if one only considers energy savings. However, if one factors cost saving from painting and maintenance on the home as well as the increase in equity in the home, the return on investment is more than worth the price. Our siding and windows are seen as products that protect customers' homes as well as their pocketbooks.

In terms of market segmentation advantages, we can use these factors to arrive at a winning market position. By repositioning our product from a cost to an investment in one's home and as an overall attractively appealing package, exterior aluminum siding and double-pane windows become a smart investment for any customer.

Outside Media

We are presently using the firm Superior Media Marketing for all of our television and radio marketing, and we have had a good relationship that has lasted since the inception of the company. Superior Media Marketing has the buying power and technical and marketing expertise necessary for a successful campaign.

Start Writing:

_____

_____

_____

_____

_____

_____

_____

_____

_____

_____

_____

_____

_____

_____

_____

Next, explain your main plans to advertise and promote your products and services along with your objectives for reaching your target audience. To do this you must determine what the best ways to promote your business are. Of course, there are the basics that we have previously discussed, but you will need to decide what is best for your business and your target market(s). For example, Yellow Pages advertising may be the best advertising medium for local attorneys, doctors, and CPAs. However, the best form of advertising a website or e-business may be through search engines. You will need to decide what your budget can handle, and remember to test one medium or ad against others and come up with the best point that creates sales. Begin with a heading that is appropriate to the benefit you are emphasizing.

Advertising and Promotion Objectives

Home Improvements Inc. recognizes that the key to success at this time requires an extensive and aggressive promotion campaign on a wide scale. This will position our company as the leading supplier of exterior aluminum siding and double-pane windows in the U.S. market.

Additionally, our plan will generate sales leads for field sales representatives who will be able to take quick action in presenting and closing sales. This will be accomplished by using the campaign to generate greater awareness among potential customers, thus eliminating 80 percent of the time spent prospecting. Our experience has shown that sales representatives can optimize their time by using this type of promotional campaign.

Our primary objective is to start a television and radio campaign that will give us greater public awareness and recognition and will establish us as a solid company that is very professional, completely reliable, highly visible, and a leader in the market. Our secondary objectives are to send press releases to major radio stations, newspapers, and magazines, to run radio advertising on secondary stations, to attend major industry tradeshows throughout the United States, and to write product-related articles and stories for industry trade journals and technical conferences.

Media Strategy

It is the aim of senior management to position the company in select primary publications, radio stations, and television stations with high specific market penetration; therefore, it is important to schedule adequate frequency to impact the market with a positive corporate image and superior products and services. Plans are to work with a reputable advertising agency to maximize ad life with monthly and weekly exposure of the advertisements. *cont...*

---

cont...

To obtain optimum results with our promotional budget for media coverage, we will focus on two target audiences:

1) Households who are concerned about home value and energy efficiency

2) Retired individuals in high-income areas

An advertising campaign will be built around the added value and energy efficiency of our products beginning with a "who we are" position and supported by ads that reinforce the added value and energy efficiency message. It is important that a consistent message and frequency be maintained throughout the advertising campaign.

Advertising Campaign

The best way to reach our potential customers is to develop an intense advertising campaign promoting the company's basic premise, "Value you can count on!" To maintain our stable image, the delivery and tone of promotional statements will be based on hard driving reality that creates a sense of urgency to protect one's largest asset and energy savings. Ads will convey the look and feel of a home that is attractive, comfortable, and energy efficient. Research indicates that television and radio advertising is not heavily used by any of our competitors, which gives us a distinct advantage.

Ideally, after becoming familiar with our company and our products and services, customers will be able to take action by calling a toll-free number to place their order, request that additional information be sent to them, or set up an appointment with a sales representative. To eliminate objections to immediate action, the advertisements must address known and anticipated objections, for example, how much their property is worth.

Our company has created a system of research and response to ensure the maximum benefit of its advertising dollars. One way to measure the effectiveness of its advertising is to count the number of responses and purchases per one hundred customers given a particular advertisement. Research shows that television commercials will bring in an average of forty-eight leads per day and further research shows that for every one hundred phone-in leads, the following results are typical:

- 29 percent are not really interested at the time of the call.
- 18 percent do not own their home or are not interested in a future purchase.
- 3 percent give incorrect information, for example, wrong phone numbers.
- 10 percent request that we call at a later date.
- 40 percent turn into actual appointments.

From the actual appointments, our research indicates that approximately 20 percent of appointments—one in five—turn into an actual sale.

Start Writing:

_____

_____

_____

_____

Next, explain any other plans you have to advertise and promote your products and services that you feel will be of benefit, including advertising specialty and promotional items, direct mail, company brochures, and sales materials. Begin with a heading that is appropriate to the benefit you are emphasizing.

Incentives

As an extra incentive for customers to remember Home Improvements Inc.'s name and the services that we provide, we plan to distribute coffee mugs, hats, and T-shirts with the company name, logo, and slogan. This will be a gratis service that will keep our company name and image in front of the customers.

Sales Support Materials

An additional form of advertising in the home will be used, as each sales representative will play a company introduction DVD as part of their home sales presentation. The DVD will be designed to give an accurate description of all the benefits of having exterior aluminum siding and double-pane windows, and it will enable the representatives to close more sales.

Also, our sales representatives will carry a presentation binder that is in a flip chart format to keep their thoughts in a unified and easy-to-understand style. The following is a list of items that will assist the communication process during their sales presentations:

- Ads
- Brochures
- Business cards
- Catalogs
- Charts
- Data sheets
- Direct mailers
- DVDs
- Résumés
- Handouts
- Newsletters
- Postcards
- Price lists
- Promotions
- Proposals
- Questionnaires
- Reports
- Stationery
- Telephone scripts
- Letters of recommendation

Advertising and Promotion Budget

For the first twelve months of the project, advertising and promotion will require $48,000. On an ongoing basis, we feel that we can budget 15 percent of total anticipated sales. This figure is necessary because of the specific goals we plan to reach. Industry averages for dollars spent on advertising and promotion are considerably less because competitors are not using television and radio as a marketing tool.

Start Writing:

_____
_____
_____
_____
_____
_____
_____
_____
_____
_____
_____
_____
_____
_____
_____
_____
_____
_____
_____
_____
_____
_____
_____
_____
_____
_____
_____
_____

Next, explain your sales strategies, including how you plan to sell your products and services to the customer, how you will provide customer support throughout the sales process, and what your Unique Selling Advantage is along with any other relevant information that you feel may be important. Begin with a heading of "Sales Strategies" or "Selling Tactics" or with a heading that is appropriate to the benefit you are emphasizing.

Sales Strategies

Our sales strategies are to sell our products through several sales channels, including executive selling, a direct sales force, distributors, mail order and direct response cards, telemarketing, and joint marketing relationships.

Because our customers tend to be highly conscientious about spending large amounts of money, it is important that our company president and senior managers present our products and services to our customers on occasion. The majority of sales will be generated through direct sales by our outside sales staff. We anticipate hiring ten additional sales representatives to cover additional territories and markets to sell specific products.

We have chosen to use a direct sales force because our products and services require considerable customer education and post-sales support directly from our company. Our sales price point, cost structure, and profits are such that our system allows sales to be handled on an individual basis in this manner.

One of the key elements designed into the marketing plan is the targeting of distributors who will buy our products and then sell them to homeowners. It will be important to select existing distribution channels with the right customer base and staffed with professionals possessing appropriate backgrounds. This strategic marketing approach takes full advantage of the tremendous momentum inherent in the fact that these professionals are involved with parallel products and services. They already have expertise in the industry and have been practicing in their field for a long time.

By operating within these distribution channels in this manner, we feel that we can maintain control of our market and we can generate growth at a reasonable pace and obtain excellent sales results.

Customer Service

Historical data shows that our customers emphasize superior customer service as a major concern for them. They are consistently impressed with the support we provide, especially our hotline service, currently available to all customers who are enrolled in a maintenance support program. Also, we provide free post-sale consultations for customers to ensure customer satisfaction and loyalty. In addition, these consultations allow us to increase sales by gaining customer referrals and repeat business.

Returns and Cancellation Policy

Currently, general trade policy for handling cancellations is to provide a full refund of any down payment if a cancellation occurs within three business days of the signing of the contract. For product already shipped, refunds are made only on the price of the product and applicable taxes, and the refund does not include shipping costs. Credit card refunds are credited to the customer's account and cash or check payments are refunded within thirty days of receipt of returned merchandise in good condition.

Start Writing:

_____

_____

_____

_____

_____

_____

_____

_____

_____

_____

_____

_____

_____

_____

_____

_____

_____

Let's Do a Quick Review!

Many entrepreneurs writing their business plans may think all they want to do is open the doors of their business and start selling without really laying out a master marketing and sales strategy beforehand. Don't go in front of investors and lenders with this mindset because they will turn you around and have you walk right back out the door. They know, as you should by now, how every component of your business plan is extremely important. Doing what is right versus what you want to do or currently know how to do is the difference between making money and losing money. If you want to lose yours, go right ahead, but investors and lenders are keen on protecting their assets.

One of the points that we want to drive home here is that you must consider all of the aspects of your marketing and sales strategies that we have covered in this chapter. Some things will work wonderfully well for your business, while others may not work at all. You must weigh the odds of developing a solid marketing mix, and incorporate the best mediums and strategies that will accomplish better brand recognition, plus drive sales. Those are in fact, the two primary goals when you create your marketing and sales campaigns.

When trying something new, even with well thought-out strategies, you will experience trial and error. That is why it is important to track where you are spending money and what kind of return you are getting on it. For example, we have one successful client who was spending $8,000 per month on four different advertising mailers produced by four different companies and was very happy with the results. We asked him how he was tracking his advertising dollars and which mailer brought the best results. He had no answer because he had no tracking system in place. We explained to him the importance of tracking his advertising dollars to make sure he was getting a return on them. Six months after creating a tracking system and putting it into place, he discovered one of the mailers, the most expensive one at $4,000 per month, was not even paying for itself, as it was returning under $3,000 per month in revenue. At this point, our client discontinued use of this mailer and began trying a new one at a much lower price which began to pay for itself in the first three months. This is a good lesson on how not to waste your money. We are proud to say that this client has continued to grow immensely over the last two years and the future looks very promising.

CHAPTER 9
Internet Strategy

Selling Your Website

The design, layout, and flow of your website cannot be overstated. It is very important to pay critical attention to these crucial aspects. Whether your company is a start-up or an established company, potential lenders and investment groups will want to be certain that your website is user-friendly, so browsers can easily navigate through it and purchase products and services on it. They will also want to know that there is a bona fide online market for the products and services you are offering, that they can be easily purchased and delivered in a timely fashion, and that your company can support the entire process.

For many business owners today, it is important to have a website for others to learn more about what they do, what products they offer, and how the customer can purchase their products online. In most cases, your Internet strategy should include a two-pronged approach, first to educate others about your business, including your products and your services, and second to sell your products online to an ever-increasing online consumer base.

You should explain what role your corporate website plays in your overall marketing mix and what general information it provides about the company's products and services. For example, you will want to illustrate how your strategy may be to develop a dynamic, robust site with video streaming capabilities and a five-minute overview of the products and services with a call to action. The call to action may provide the prospect or client with the opportunity to choose three options:

- Register to receive future information via the Internet
- Sign up for a newsletter
- Purchase a product online

Consumer behavior and your particular business or industry should be the principal determining factors of your corporate Internet or e-commerce strategy; consumer loyalty may likely differ significantly between online booksellers and providers of financial services. Two factors seem critical in predicting behavior and determining an appropriate e-commerce strategy. Your task is to figure out what your customers want from your website and how they would like it delivered.

First, review your company's sales history reports to determine what the duration of the relationship between your company and the buyer is. In other words, does the buyer have a relationship with you as a favorite seller, in which they return again and again to purchase from you, or does the buyer search for a different electronic vendor for each interaction? The first scenario suggests a stable relationship between you and the consumer, and the second scenario is an opportunity for fine-tuning your offerings.

Second, what is the scope of goods and services linking you and the buyer? Does the consumer purchase a single good or service from you or a bundle of related goods and services? The first scenario suggests the consumer searches for the provider of the best individual goods and services, while the latter suggests a search for the best provider of a collection of goods and services. Combining these would indicate that you might find yourself in one or more of four competitive landscapes.

Bear in mind, consumers buying products that buy on price alone will exhibit no loyalty. Each purchase may be from you or from a different vendor—and there is no one-stop shopping. For example, they may buy a ticket from Delta Airlines one day and United Airlines the next and book their hotels separately. Your goal is to provide as many products or service offerings in a user-friendly environment that are competitively priced to keep your customers on your site. Yours should be a site that provides general information about your company and a convenient shopping setting which makes it easy to navigate and ultimately purchase something.

Consumers buying in categories that may be described as "loyal customers" will still have preferred providers. Basically, they will count on these providers for a range of offerings. For example, they may work with a financial consultant at Merrill Lynch who helps pick stocks, draft a will, arrange guardians for their children, find a lawyer, and review their insurance. These integrated services are so effective that the consumer may seldom consider switching providers.

Each of these environments has a different competitive feel and requires a different strategy and use of different assets. This is as true in the physical world, where companies understand it pretty well, as it is in the dot-com world, where companies often struggle to develop profitable strategies.

There are loyal customers and you should pursue these with loyal link strategies. But in reality, some customers may use a website for spot purchases and others may show great loyalty. The challenge for you is to guide the consumer to the behavior matching your strategy. When this is not possible, you should match your strategy to the customer's behavior. The approach given here may help you discover the forces that determine your best strategy.

In order to properly disseminate the information to the general public, your corporate website may need to be upgraded using the latest in Flash and video streaming technology. Use video and Flash when you want to tell them a story, or explain in detail what your product does and why it is superior to the competition. You will also want to use Flash or video when you have technical information to share about your products and services. This would be the time to provide a short overview of the products when you feel the consumer can receive all of the important data relating to the products they will purchase. In a brief, two- to five-minute overview, you can accomplish a great deal of marketing and/or data sharing that will provide the consumer with the necessary details to either make a decision or save a phone call to your office.

The initial programming can be outsourced to a competent Web design firm. This will save the expense of not having a full-time Web developer on staff in the beginning. Since there may eventually be a database developed that will be used for ongoing marketing and customer support, the programming will be required to be fully compatible with technology issues such as bandwidth, software, and support. Just be aware that this may cost a few thousand dollars to accomplish the e-commerce site you are planning.

You may be tempted to try to soften the consumer's perception of the competition by creating quality differences and ensuring that your buyers are aware of them. However, this type of branding must be based on real differences, since even with nearly perfect information it is difficult to deceive consumers. But in most instances, consumers will buy from you if your business is a trusted products and service provider.

The Internet can also be used for supply-chain management and logistics to ensure the lowest cost structure and prices. It also supports access to information about your company and allows for a more accurate setting of prices based on cutting out elements of the sales process that include human intervention for sales and marketing expenses. Part of your Internet strategy will be to provide general information that is compelling and accurate, but also sells the sizzle of who you are and why you are different. You should spend some time asking yourself what your true Internet strategy is based on, and what you would like to accomplish. Remember to refer back to your answers to the "Internet Strategy Questions" in chapter 3 to see if you have incorporated important answers into this section of your winning business plan.

How to Calculate ROI for Your Website

Measuring Return on Investment (ROI) for a traditional e-commerce site, a company that exists only on the Web, is rather simple. Calculate the investment by asking, "How much does it cost to run the company?" Calculate the return by asking, "How much did I sell?" The difficulty in measuring ROI takes place when a company sells on the Web and through other channels. Customers may browse on the Web but buy retail. A website may contribute to an off-site sale when the user looks at what's available, the price, and customer reviews, but decides to buy the product elsewhere. Trying to determine how much the Web contributed to a purchase is a nebulous situation.

A company with strong on-site customer support offers good potential for ROI. In practice, customers prefer to find answers on their own rather than contact customer service, but most sites are designed so poorly that answers are difficult to find. While a website can't solve every problem, if you can minimize the number of support calls you're receiving, the customer is happy and you save money.

Remember the magic formula: *A company that is always there for its customers generates repeat business.*

Tracking Your ROI

Tracking where your customers are coming from and why and how much they are buying from you is integral in maximizing your return on investment. Just as with marketing and sales strategy, it is important to track where your advertising dollars are being spent and what amount of income is being generated from it, the same rules apply here. The following are four ways to track Internet leads.

- **Track leads.** Ask clients why they bought and how they heard of you, either in person or through surveys. Track where leads come from as well as how many leads are converted to sales.
- **Track advertising.** Advertising on the Web is measured by click-through rates. However, a good rate does not always mean an increase in business. It's easy to get a high click-through rate if, for example, you offer a freebie, but keep in mind that those who take you up on such offers are not necessarily people you will do or will want to do business with in the future. A good way to measure ROI through advertising is to install *cookies* to determine which ads bring customers in and should get credited for conversion.
- **Track Web traffic.** Track Web traffic to determine the number of unique visitors coming to your site and how many of them turn into loyal, repeat users. Is the information on your site so good that users are getting to the product page? Determine how many users navigate through your site and actually read about your product and you'll know if your site is working. Do an online survey of a few users once they get to the product page. Ask, "Did you find what you are looking for?" and "Is the information we provide helpful?"
- **Track sales.** If you offer products for sale on your site, you will want to track how many times you convert prospects into paying customers. This is where the "rubber meets the road," and you will be able to get a clear picture of how your website is generating sales for you. Your Internet Service Provider, or ISP, will be able to provide you with statistics of the number of visits to your site, where visitors came from, how long they remained on your site, and when a purchase was made. In addition, your ISP will be able to show you how many times your site was visited hourly, weekly, monthly, or annually. You will want to build a spreadsheet that allows you to view this information each month. Ultimately, you will want to test your Internet strategy to make certain that you are maximizing sales. The primary objective here is like any other sales strategy: to track how many prospects you turn into paying customers.

Let's Start Writing!

Now that you have determined how you are going to market and deliver your products and services through your company website, let's begin telling the Internet story. Remember to refer back to your answers to the "Internet Strategy Questions" in chapter 3 when writing this section of your winning business plan.

Start this section of your winning business plan by providing a main heading of "Internet Strategy" and then begin providing information on what your strategy will be to advertise your products and services so they are appealing, easy to see and understand, and easy to purchase along with your anticipated return.

Internet Strategy

The Corporate website currently provides general information about our products and services. The site will eventually be upgraded with new options and menus for our clients to receive real-time information and view an online presentation.

The strategy is to develop a dynamic, robust site that has real streaming video capabilities to show how our exterior aluminum siding and double-pane windows operate. This will be a six- to seven-minute overview of the products and services with a call to action. The call to action will provide the prospect or client with the opportunity to choose three options:

1) Register and send their information via the Internet to receive a response call

2) Request our product information brochures

3) Take a brief assessment of where they are and what they would like their homes to look like

As strategic alliances are further developed with our new distribution customers, a link from our website to the strategic partner's site will be put in place, thus creating a portal of technical and general information for our clients and prospects to view. Management will work closely with vendor marketing personnel to place the most strategic link to their site and to develop a seamless alliance between Home Improvements Inc. and the vendor.

Development Requirements

In order to properly disseminate information to the general public, the corporate website will need to be upgraded using the latest in Flash and video streaming technology. The initial programming will be outsourced to a competent Web design firm once the various options have been researched. This will save the expense of not having a full-time Web developer on staff in the beginning, but will be reevaluated after year one of this business plan.

Since there will be a database developed that will be used for ongoing marketing and customer support, the programming will have to be fully compatible with technology issues such as bandwidth, software, and support.

Start Writing:

_____

_____

_____

_____

_____

_____

_____

_____

_____

_____

_____

_____

Let's Do a Quick Review!

Many business owners writing their winning business plan may feel an Internet strategy is not needed; however, there are many businesses that can benefit in some way by having a website. To put it simply, with an Internet presence, you are able to accomplish two things: 1) You can provide your prospects and customers with information about your company and its products and services, and 2) You will be able to sell products online without the direct intervention of salespeople. Many consumers just want information in order to assist them in making a decision—without the pressure of someone trying to sell them something. Give proper attention to your Internet strategy because investors and lenders are very savvy in this area, and will expect your business to have an Internet presence.

It is important that a website is developed in such a way that a user can easily move around and navigate through it. Complicated and confusing websites are frustrating and unless someone is looking for something they can only purchase on that particular site, they will probably leave the site aggravated and without having even come close to buying anything. We had one successful client who was struggling with the growth of his Internet sales. He felt the growth rate should have been double what it was the previous year. In reviewing his website and asking him what had occurred over the last twelve months, we found out that on numerous occasions his system crashed, sometimes for days at a time, and at times there were issues with orders not flowing through the system correctly and getting lost. He mentioned that this really frustrated his customers. He resolved to find a reputable company to host his website where zero downtime was guaranteed and his program would be corrected to make sure orders were correctly sent through the system. Within several months of these changes, his customers were in better spirits and began placing orders on a more regular basis, increasing his sales accordingly. We are proud to say that this client has continued his growth and has moved into a larger and more efficient facility.

CHAPTER 10
Management and Personnel Plan

Leading the Way

How important is your business management team? Extremely important! Whether your company is a start-up or an established company, potential lenders and investment groups will only finance a company with a management team that has balance and the ability to provide four essential elements:

1. Planning
2. Organization
3. Control
4. Leadership

What is meant by balance? The management team as a whole must have the people skills (the ability to relate to others), technical skills (the ability to perform the tasks assigned to them), and conceptual skills (the ability to see beyond today)—skills applicable to both the production and delivery of your products and services today and tomorrow. At a minimum, it is a must for your management team to have experience managing the marketing, sales, finance, and operation departments of your company.

The strength of your management team must be clearly communicated in your business plan. An organization with a formal structure (figure MT.1, page 128) will enhance its ability to raise capital and will be that much closer to achieving its goals. This will be done in less time and with less expense.

After reviewing figure MT.1, take some time to mentally review your proposed or existing management team. Remember to use honesty in the judgment of yourself and each member of the team. Do not let thoughts like "he's a nice guy" or "he never misses a day's work" influence your assessment.

Refer to data chart MT.1 (page 129) and complete for each key management team member.

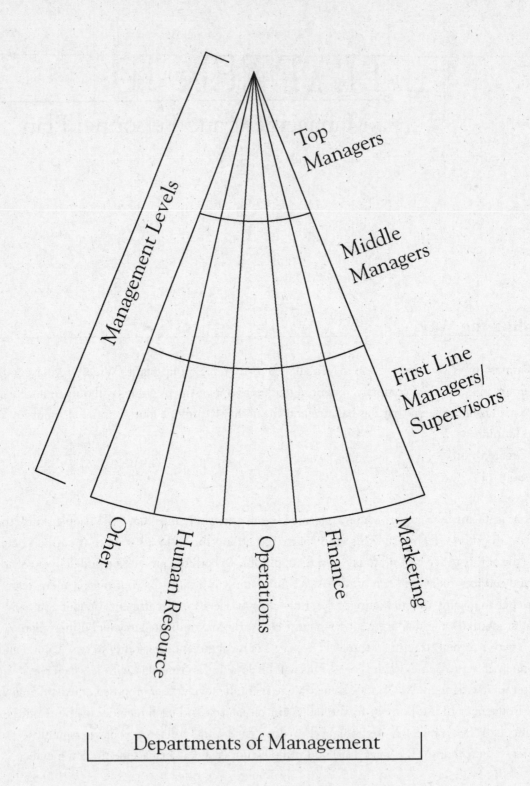

Figure MT.1
Depending on the structure and size of your organization, the number of management levels and departments will vary.

Department Manager _____

Name of Manager _____

Skills	Grade	Grading Key
Conceptual		1 = Exceptional
Technical		2 = Good
		3 = Average
Human		4 = Should not be manager

Describe Strengths of Manager:

Describe Weaknesses of Manager

Overall Grade (see key above)

Data Chart MT.1

Your Formal Organization

After fully completing data chart MT.1, begin to develop a formal organizational flow chart. One important item to remember is the structure and size of your organization. It is reasonable for small to medium-sized businesses to have a management team consisting of only one or possibly two key management personnel. If this is the case, it is highly suggested that outside consultants and professionals be hired to fill in the gaps, if applicable, to provide expertise that is necessary to strengthen your management team. Example MT.1 (page 131) provides a useful example of an overall organizational structure, while example MT.2 (page 132) shows a further breakdown by department.

Incorporate Your Management Team into Your Formal Organization

At this point, you have identified the abilities of your key management team and the formal organizational structure of your company. Now, in the final step, we must blend the two together to see if each key function within your organization can be met by at least one team member. Examples of functions include:

- Marketing
- Advertising
- Sales
- Accounting
- Finance
- Inventory control
- Purchasing
- Operations
- Production
- Distribution
- Receiving
- Human resources
- Legal

Use data chart MT.2 (page 133) to incorporate key management personnel with key functions. For any responsibilities that cannot be covered by current management, check the column for outside services required. You may want to consider contacting outside consultants and professionals who specialize in these areas to assist you.

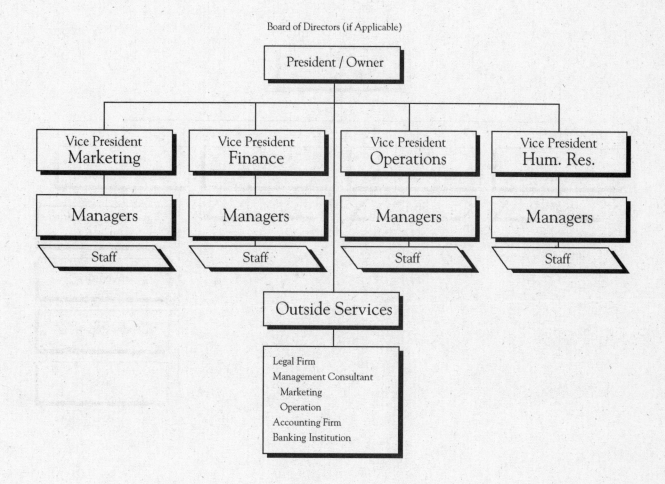

Example MT.1

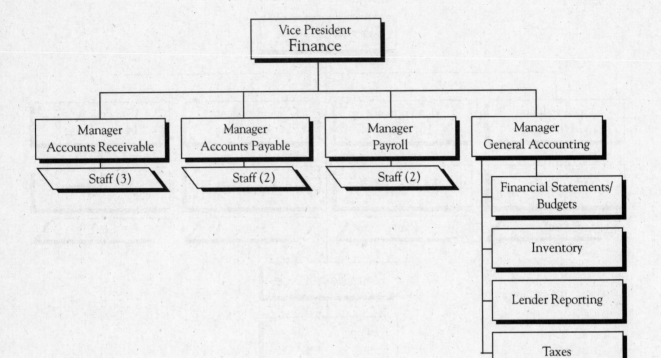

Example MT.2

Managers / Key Functions					Outside Services Needed

Data Chart MT.2

Let's Start Writing!

Now that you have determined your management structure and who should be a part of your management team, let's begin telling the management story. Remember to refer back to your answers to the "Management Questions" in chapter 3 when writing this section.

Start this section of your winning business plan by providing a main heading of either "Management and Personnel Plan" or "Management." Then begin telling why and by whom the corporation was started along with any other relevant information that you feel may be important. You can have the best financial projections, the greatest marketing plan, and even the most innovative product or service to sell to the world; but if your management team is not solid, and does not have the necessary experience to drive the business to success, none of this will matter. Your management team can literally make or break your business. This team should sell your business concept better than anyone else.

Cover the basic information about your team up front. This would include how much relevant experience your team possesses, how many years of experience selling your product(s) or service(s) the team has, the type of key employees the company has, who the founders of the business are and what they own, etc.

Is your team complete, or are there gaps that still need to be filled? Is your organizational structure sound, with job descriptions and logical responsibilities for all the key members? Particularly with start-up companies, you may not have the complete team as you write the plan. If this is the case with your business, be sure to point out the gaps and weaknesses and how you intend to fill them. One way to help with this problem (especially if you are a one-person show in the beginning) is to include outside resources that are not on your payroll as part of your team. Include professionals such as your attorney, your accountant, your outside consultants, your insurance agent, and even an advisory board.

Creating an advisory board, or better yet, a board of directors that are willing to assist you in being a sounding board or help you make decisions as you grow your business, will be invaluable as you try to raise capital.

You will also want to cover in as much detail as possible why your management team is qualified to drive your business to success. Discuss your team's experience and their areas of expertise as they relate to the business.

Finally, explain their functions within the company, and why they are best suited to direct the affairs of their particular assignment.

Management and Personnel Plan

Michael X. Swann, who after a careful study of the exterior aluminum siding industry, found a tremendous void of quality products and superior service, founded Home Improvements Inc. in 2005. This lack of quality products and services was the principal reason that Mr. Swann decided to start his own company in the industry, and the opportunity to create an entity that offered high-quality products and superior service became the driving force behind his enthusiasm to establish and start-up Home Improvements Inc.

There are several key executives making up the management team. They are:

Michael X. Swann, President

Mary V. Jonstone, Vice President, Finance

Roger Armstrong, Director of Sales

John Herber, Warehouse Manager

The founder and key executives have over twenty-five years combined experience in the exterior aluminum siding industry in the areas of manufacturing, distribution, service, and installation. The strength of the management team stems from hands-on management skills and techniques, the ability to identify profitable target markets and create effective marketing and sales strategies, and expertise required to produce and provide high-quality products and superior service.

The leadership and alignment characteristics of the management team have resulted in broad and flexible goal setting to meet the ever-changing demands of the marketplace requiring our products. This is evident when the team responds to situations requiring innovation and is reflected in the company's outstanding results over the past year.

Start Writing:

_____

_____

_____

_____

_____

_____

_____

_____

_____

_____

_____

_____

_____

Next, list each manager separately and explain his or her various responsibilities. Begin with the heading "Responsibilities." Please note that the font size of headings throughout each section should be smaller than the main heading that begins each section of your winning business plan.

Responsibilities

Michael X. Swann, President

Manage market planning, advertising, public relations, sales promotion, merchandising, and facilitating staff services. Identify new markets, maintain corporate scope, and perform market research.

Mary V. Jonstone, Vice President, Finance

Protect the assets of the company, including cash, accounts receivables, inventory, and marketable securities. Prepare and analyze financial statements, manage the day-to-day activities of the accounting department, administer employee records and employee company benefits, and maintain strong banking relationships.

Roger Armstrong, Director of Sales

Manage the sales organization, including inside and outside sales personnel, sales territories, sales quotas, and customer service and sales support staff.

John Herber, Warehouse Manager

Supervise all warehouse functions, including receipt and organization of product from vendors and timely and accurate shipments to customers. Maintenance and safeguarding of warehouse equipment and building facilities.

Start Writing:

_____

_____

_____

_____

_____

_____

_____

_____

_____

_____

_____

_____

_____

Next, if applicable, list all outside professional consultants, industry experts, and members of your board of directors or advisory committee who give support to your management team. They may include your law firm, accounting firm, management consultant, marketing consultant, and computer consultant. The heading for this section can be "Outside Support" where you identify everyone under this heading or it can be specific for each outside support category you are presenting, for example, "Board of Directors" or "Management Consultant."

Outside Support

Knight, Smith, and Cordova, Attorneys at Law, with over forty years of combined experience, provide the company with legal expertise in the areas of employee hiring and related issues, contract formation and document reviews, legal correspondence, equipment and building leases, debt collection, and general business advisement.

A1 Computer Corporation, with over ten years of experience in servicing distribution companies, has been a key ingredient in the success of our company. A1 implemented a state-of-the-art computer system along with a top-rated accounting and management program that allows our company to maintain maximum efficiency with minimal labor hours. Their company is on call 24/7 with a one-hour guaranteed response time that is a unique advantage to assuring our systems will always function when needed.

Start Writing:

_____

_____

_____

_____

_____

_____

_____

Next, give a brief yet comprehensive résumé of the qualifications of each manager. Remember to highlight qualities that would give the reader of your business plan confidence that the management team has the ability to successfully lead the company, make it profitable, and return the investment required by the lender or investor. Begin with the heading "Management Team."

Management Team
Michael X. Swann, President

Mr. Swann's professional experience extends to many different areas in the sales and distribution arena. He has been involved in sales, marketing, and distribution for large corporations, including Big Shoe Stores, Fresh Pine Inc., and Home Siding 4 You Corporation. He has received several awards as the top salesperson for his efforts.

After learning the basic techniques of the siding industry, Mr. Swann, as sales manager, worked

cont...

cont...

with the development of sales and distribution for Home Siding 4 You Corporation. He was then responsible for the implementation of marketing and sales programs that increased the company's revenue by 45 percent in the first year with consistent double-digit growth thereafter for the next five years he was with the company.

During his time at Home Siding 4 You, he was promoted to national sales manager and he enjoyed considerable success. He became interested in developing a more efficient way to operate a company within the same industry. With that idea in mind, he conducted a feasibility study to determine the viability of a product capable of competing in the siding industry that was of higher quality yet priced competitively. The results of the study indicated that such a product could be developed and could compete in the marketplace, which became Mr. Swann's impetus at which time he formed Home Improvements Inc.

Mary V. Jonstone, Vice President, Finance

Ms. Jonstone's diverse employment background includes work in accounting, finance, human resources, and management. She served as controller for a combined twelve years at Value Department Stores Incorporated and House and Yard Company.

She has been overseeing the accounting and personnel departments for Home Improvements Inc. since the company's inception and has done an outstanding job in preparing accurate and timely financial statements, budgets, and reconciliations; maintaining strong relationships with banks, customers, and vendors; and managing employee records and benefits.

Roger Armstrong, Director of Sales

Mr. Armstrong's background in sales and marketing has been a big asset to the company. After earning his degree in marketing, he went to work as a sales representative for Steel Boxes, Inc. He enjoyed much success during his five-year career there, including the successful launch of a new product line of silver-coated boxes that increased the company's sales by 4 percent.

Upon earning his MBA from the University of Gainesville, he was offered a regional district management position with the multinational corporation Better Products Incorporated. As Regional District Manager, he was responsible for managing the day-to-day operations of his designated region, including sales, marketing, hiring and training personnel, and developing departmental policies and procedures. During his tenure, his region was ranked number one out of all regions in the company across the nation for two consecutive years.

As sales director with Home Improvements Inc. he has enjoyed a high degree of success, including the development of the present sales and marketing structure of the company, training and assisting the sales staff, and employing market research programs that have opened new revenue opportunities.

John Herbert, Warehouse Manager

With a solid ten years of experience in warehouse procedures and management specifically in the siding industry, Mr. Herbert brings a wealth of knowledge to the company. His proven ability to streamline the process of receiving, storing, and shipping product has been paramount in improving the company's bottom line since he joined the company last year.

Start Writing:

Next, list the current and future needs of anticipated company staff. Estimate the number of employees as well as the positions needed to effectively operate the business and its forecasted growth. Please note, this information will also be needed when you are preparing your financial statements as you decide what people will be hired to support the expansion of your business along with how much you plan to pay them. Begin with the heading "People and Talent Required."

People and Talent Required

In preparing for our future growth, it has been determined that additional team members will be required to properly support the increase in business in all areas of the company including management, marketing, sales, customer service, engineering, administration, accounting, human resources, distribution, skilled assembly labor, and field service technicians. Currently the company has a staff of eight, but we forecast that in order to meet the demands of the projected market over the next five years, our employee headcount will reach fifty team members.

Start Writing:

_____

_____

_____

_____

_____

Let's Do a Quick Review!

You may be a one-person company or you may only plan to hire a few people. You may not anticipate your company growing rapidly, but you may see it growing at a steady pace where the expectations of adding employees are low. Whether you are an experienced manager or a new manager-to-be, it will be important for you to understand what qualities potential investors or lenders look for in leaders. Go back to chapter 3, "100-Plus Questions to Personal and Business Success," and review your answers to the "General Personal Questions," "General Business Questions," and "Management Questions."

You must truly take a good look at yourself and identify all your strengths and weaknesses as they relate to your business knowledge and experience and as they relate to your personal knowledge and experience. When starting your own business, it is usually impossible to separate the two. If your weaknesses are in critical areas, you must find ways to cure them, whether it is through self-learning and self-improvement or bringing on outside assistance.

An investor or a lender puts much weight on the business owner or management team when determining whether or not to provide financing to a company. We had one successful client who needed expansion capital. He had been dealing with the same bank and banker for a number of years, and they had an excellent relationship; however, the banker was unwilling to increase his line of credit by $200,000 because he was not confident that the client would be able to handle the growth with his current management team. The banker did, however, state that if our client would hire a business consultant firm or a qualified staff member to oversee and help with his expansion, it would be possible to get the credit line increase. We worked with our client to prepare a business plan for the expansion and went in with our client to meet the banker. After several meetings, the banker was confident that with our help, our client would be successful in growing his business, and he approved the credit line increase. We are proud to say that this client has continued to grow over the years, is very successful, and is a leader in his industry.

CHAPTER 11
Financial Projections

Counting the Money

The financial projections form the heart of your business plan, the point at which your vision is quantified in terms of dollars and cents, and units of time: days, weeks, months, and years. All persons reading your plan will go through your financial projections with great care. For most entrepreneurs, the development of an idea or concept is the easy part. Turning it into a profitable reality takes thorough research, especially as it relates to determining the following:

1. Potential markets
2. A realistic selling price for your products and services
3. Assets needed to produce and deliver your products and services
4. Costs associated to produce and deliver your products and services
5. Advertising and promotion dollars needed to obtain market share
6. Fixed general and administration costs necessary to support the above, including what employee head count is needed to support and operate your enterprise

In this section, you will develop a set of financials that will include profit and loss statements, balance sheets, and cash flow statements. You will also develop an assumptions page, a break-even analysis, and statement of resource needs (use of proceeds table). A thorough understanding of how your financial statements and forecasts are conceived and developed must be a top priority, whether they were prepared by you or someone else. Presenting potential lenders or investors with a set of financials is meaningless if they are a foreign language to you. Therefore, before you dive in and begin crunching numbers, become familiar with the financial statements presented in the "Sample Business Plans," included with our book along with chapter 17, "Financial Ratios, Glossary, and Chart of Accounts."

The chapter on financial ratios (page 213) will explain to you how to calculate key ratios that investors and lenders look for such as your current ratio, return on sales percentage, inventory turns, and debt to net worth. Including every ratio in the financial section of your business plan is not always necessary, although you may want to make them a part of your appendix, but it is important to calculate them and understand what they mean because they are key indicators to help you run your business more efficiently.

Investors and lenders will also key into them when reviewing your financial statements and projections and will make judgments and determinations on them. The glossary (page 215) will explain many accounting terms including the accrual basis of accounting and the cash basis of accounting. The "Chart of Accounts" (page 221) will show you what accounts are included in the profit and loss statement, for example, sales, cost of goods sold, selling expenses, and general and administration expenses and what accounts are included in the balance sheet, for example, cash, accounts receivable, inventory, accounts payable, and owners equity.

If you need to brush up on your overall knowledge and understanding of financial statements, it is suggested you do one or more of the following:

- Pick up accounting reference books and workbooks from a local bookstore or library
- Take an accounting class at an accredited college or university
- Obtain help from an outside accounting firm familiar with your line of business

Your Financial Management Tool

We feel it is important for every business to prepare financial statements on a monthly basis, regardless of its size or structure. Many business owners and managers feel that monthly financial statements are just not needed in their business. This is a big mistake! Financial statements are key management tools. Taking the time to learn and interpret what the financial statements are telling you could mean the difference between success and failure for your business.

Determining Your Numbers

By this stage of the game, whether you are a start-up or an existing business, you must fully understand how to project, forecast, estimate, and calculate all items included in your financial statements. If assistance is needed, we suggest you contact a competent accounting firm that will be able to assist you in the completion of this portion of the business plan and will fully explain the statements to you so you can fully articulate them to potential investors and lenders.

Pro forma schedules that will aid you in the preparation of your financial statements can be found later in this chapter. Please note that one copy is provided for the profit and loss statement, balance sheet, and cash flow statement. We suggest you use these as a master set and make copies of each blank form to use for each forecasted year. If you are computer savvy and have a good working understanding of Microsoft Excel, we highly suggest you format your financial statements in Excel, including the use of headers to identify and title your pages.

Your financials should be broken down into monthly projections for years one and two and annually thereafter, especially for your profit and loss statement. For smaller companies, it is possible to present your balance sheet and cash flow statement quarterly for years one and two. You may also present annual summary pages for all the years so the reader can get a quick snapshot of what you are projecting. The total number of years to be used will vary based on the type of business you have or will be starting. Minimally, you should have three years of financial projections; a good rule of thumb is five years. If your plan is a long-term one where lenders and investors will not see their full return on investment for several years, then it is a good idea to include all years until they can see when they will receive their ROI.

Remember, it is important that you use realistic numbers and assumptions when preparing your financial statements, and you must be totally capable of backing them up. Investors and lenders know what is real and what is pie in the sky; if your numbers are not based on realistic assumptions, you should not expect them to support your business plan.

Profit and Loss Statement

As the title indicates, the profit and loss statement shows you how much money you are making or losing. It does this by indicating the amount of sales being made along with the costs being incurred to make what you are selling, usually referred to as variable costs, as well as expenses incurred in order to run and operate your business, usually referred to as fixed costs.

The marketing and sales plan you have developed will be used in determining projected sales and revenues in your financial forecasts. Typically, projections eventually become outdated given the impact of all the variables at work in a given enterprise and its market environment; therefore, adjustments will need to be made constantly as you implement mid-course corrections over time. For the purpose of projecting sales numbers for your winning business plan, remember to use historical data if applicable, to be realistic in your projections, and to be able to substantiate your projections, especially if you are a start-up business with no historical data to rely on.

Based on the mix of your projected sales, your cost of goods and/or services sold (COGS) must be calculated. For businesses with many products and services, you may use historical data to determine an overall product mix, and for business start-ups, you will have to best project what your product mix may be.

The difference between your total sales and your total COGS is your gross profit or gross margin. This is the amount of profit that is available to cover all of your other company expenses, including selling expenses and general and administrative expenses.

Expected selling expenses and general and administration expenses, like wages, commissions, travel, rent, office expenses, and postage, needed to support the sales function as well as the overall running of the company are then recorded. Most of these costs are usually fixed, meaning they will exist on a continued monthly basis regardless of your monthly sales volume. Some variable costs (which fluctuate with revenue volume) include sales commissions and freight costs if not included in COGS.

The net difference of gross profit or gross margin less total selling and general and administration expenses will determine the profit or loss of your enterprise.

Balance Sheet

The balance sheet gives a profile of your company's worth at a given moment in time. This statement lists all of the company's assets (cash, accounts receivable, inventory, machinery and equipment, real estate, etc.) and all of the company's liabilities (accounts payable, notes payable, taxes and interest payable, salaries and wages currently owned, etc.).

The difference between the assets and the liabilities constitutes the net worth of the company, also called owner's equity, at any particular moment in time. If, for instance, you are expanding your business as you write your business plan, then the balance sheet may show considerable equity. If you are starting out with a new venture, the balance sheet may be very simple and show little equity. Work with your accounting team to develop the details of the balance sheet if you feel that assistance is needed.

Cash Flow Statement

In simple terms, your cash flow statement tracks where cash is coming from, known as the source of funds, and where cash is going to, known as the use of funds. Cash flow totals are a critical index of how successful your business will be as cash is key to the efficient functioning of any business. Be sure to identify all cash flow changes by account type in detail.

Statement of Resource Needs (Use of Proceeds Table)

Do you have a pretty good idea of what areas in your business need capital and what amount of capital will be needed in each of these areas to launch or expand your venture? Where will you find the funding? Let's first take a close look at the financial requirements of your venture. For this we will need to turn our attention to a simple but highly effective table called the Use of Proceeds Table (page 147).

This table will help you see where and how much capital you will need in order meet your goals and objectives. And it is meant to give you a clear picture of the total amount of capital needed, broken down by individual areas of the business. Completing this breakdown is a critical exercise that helps potential investors and lenders gain a crystal-clear understanding of what your overall capital needs are.

Begin by developing a list of individual costs that require capital, such as marketing and advertising expenses, raw materials, rent and utilities, legal costs, and machinery and office equipment.

Next you will want to concentrate on how much capital each individual area of business will require before the business can begin generating enough cash flow to support itself. In other words, how much will your business need for marketing and advertising costs, to cover legal expenses, to hire employees and rent and utilities, etc.? Take the necessary time to think through your answers carefully and thoroughly. You will be questioned about your knowledge of the use of proceeds and you will need to give clear, concise, and justifiable answers about the amounts you list in your table. You will also want to note how much you have invested or plan to invest in to your venture.

The Use of Proceeds Table is a simple illustration of your thought process and your budget for all aspects of launching or expanding your business. The following Use of Proceeds Table is a good example of what you may consider when you begin looking for the amount of capital that will be required to not only launch or expand, but also to sustain growth, and for lack of a better term, "keep the wolves away until you can afford to run the business on your own."

Use of Proceeds Table

Legal	$ 2,500			
Marketing & Advertising*	$230,500	*** Marketing & Advertising Mix**		
Travel	$ 48,000	Radio	$ 98,500	
Raw Goods	$ 75,000	Literature	$ 4,500	
Insurance	$ 10,400	Print Ads	$ 75,000	
Free Up Line of Credit	$ 40,000	Direct Mail	$ 45,000	
Total Expenses	**$406,400**	Email	$ 5,500	
		Web Design	$ 2,000	
Assets Needed		**Total**	**$230,500**	
Additional inventory	$ 70,000			
Other Short-term Assets	$ 20,000			
Total Short-term Assets	**$ 90,000**			
Long-term Assets	$ 0			
Total Assets	**$ 90,000**			
Total Requirements	**$496,400**			

Now that you have a better understanding of what you should include in your Use of Proceeds Table, you are ready to fill in the blanks and come up with your capital needs. Spend some time assessing your business needs and enter the appropriate amounts in the sample template.

There are a couple of extra rows to enter "Other" data that may be pertinent to your business such as the purchase of a new building, leasehold improvements to your new or existing building, and the purchase of new vehicles for your business. As you prepare your financial statements, you will incorporate these areas and amounts into them accordingly. If any of your capital needs change while you are preparing and analyzing your financial statements, such as realizing that two additional vehicles may be needed to accomplish your goal, then make sure you add them to your Use of Proceeds Table as well as your financial statements.

Legal	$ _____
Marketing & Advertising	$ _____
Travel	$ _____
Sales Commissionss	$ _____
Insurance	$ _____
Free Up Line of Credit	$ _____
Rent	$ _____
Other	$ _____
_____	$ _____
_____	$ _____
_____	$ _____
Total Expenses _____	$ _____

Assets Needed

Additional inventory	$ _____
_____	$ _____
_____	$ _____
_____	$ _____
Other Short-term Assets	$ _____
Total Short-term Assets	$ _____
Long-term Assets	$ _____
_____	$ _____
_____	$ _____
_____	$ _____
Total Assets	$ _____
Total Requirements _____	$ _____

Assumptions Page

When developing your financial projections, you will need to create a set of assumptions that must be clearly articulated to the potential investor or lender. It is understood that since these are forecasts and no one can perfectly predict the future, qualified assumptions based on historical data, current economic information, and realistic foreseeable economic projections must be made. Some of the assumptions may include annual sales growth, product costs, number of employees by department, payroll benefit costs, annual pay increases, legal and accounting fees, rent increases, income tax rates, average time anticipated to collect accounts receivable and pay accounts payable, inventory kept on hand, and new equipment purchases.

Remember to keep your assumptions realistic and be able to substantiate them; otherwise, potential investors and lenders may send you back to the drawing board.

Break-even Analysis

As defined in the glossary section of chapter 17, a break-even analysis is the method of determining the exact point at which the business makes neither a loss nor a profit. In general terms, it is the point where sales exactly balance out expenses so that sales minus all costs, including cost of goods sold, selling expenses, general and administration expenses, and any other expenses, whether fixed or variable, equals zero. This is very important to know as it relates to either generating or losing cash flow. If you are below the break-even point, you can be assured that you will be losing cash. If you are above it and have been managing your money wisely, you will probably generate cash. The key in developing your financial statements is to see how much capital will be needed to sustain your business operations until it can generate its own cash. There is no set time frame for when a business should reach the break-even point or when it can expect to be profitable, as there are many variables, including type of business, timing of the business' start or expansion, location of the business, etc. Of course, the sooner you can reach the break-even point and become profitable, the better.

In order to properly calculate your break-even point, you must first know what your fixed costs are, those business costs that essentially do not vary when sales volume changes, and what your anticipated variable costs are, costs that vary directly with sales, including raw material costs, certain utility costs, labor, and sales commissions.

For example, if in a given month, fixed costs for your business equaled $10,000, cost of goods sold (COGS) was 50 percent of every sales dollar made, and your sales commission was 10 percent of every sales dollar made, how many sales dollars would be needed to break even? The answer would be $25,000 and it is supported as follows:

Monthly sales	$25,000	
Less: COGS	12,500	(50% of $25,000)
Sales commission	2,500	(10% of $25,000)
Fixed cost	10,000	(per above)
Profit (Loss)	$0	

To calculate your monthly break-even point, first calculate your total monthly gross profit margin (100% minus your total monthly variable cost percentage). Then take your total monthly fixed costs and divide it by the monthly gross profit margin. Using the above example, it would be as follows:

monthly gross profit margin = 100% - total monthly variable cost percentage

monthly break-even point = monthly fixed costs/monthly gross profit margin

$10,000 (fixed costs) divided by .4 (100% minus 60%, the total of COGS and sales commission percentages) = $25,000.

Fixed costs divided by the gross profit margin percentage equals total monthly sales needed to break even.

Let's Start Writing!

Now that you know what is needed in your financial projections, let's begin presenting the financial story. Remember to refer back to your answers to the "Finance Questions" in chapter 3 when writing this section of your winning business plan.

Start this section of your business plan by providing a main heading of "Financial Projections" and then explain why you are looking to raise capital and the assumptions you are using in your financial projections along with any other relevant information that you feel may be important. Please note that the font size of headings throughout each section should be smaller than the main heading that begins each section of your business plan.

Financial Projections

Financial Plan

To accomplish our goal of propelling our company into a prominent market position, we have developed a comprehensive plan to intensify and accelerate our marketing activities; product development, services expansion, engineering, distribution, and customer service. To implement our plans we require a line of credit of $150,000 for the following purposes:

1. Purchase one container of aluminum materials for inventory: $50,000
2. Expand current operations into the rural areas of the United States: $30,000
3. Add new production and computer equipment: $60,000
4. Allow for additional working capital: $10,000

Important Assumptions

Current Assets:

1. Cash reflects limited amount of cash on hand at any balance sheet date. Positive generation of cash is to be applied against outstanding loan.
2. Accounts receivable are minimal as the company policy dictates payment before installation or approved financing from reputable finance companies on the majority of projects.
3. Inventory is to be purchased on a container-load basis at a precalculated reorder point determined by lead times provided by the manufacturers. Product on hand will be items already categorized as "work in process." Stock available for sale is scheduled to turn over in a six- to eight-week period.

Fixed Assets:

1. Production and assembly of the aluminum siding requires light machinery. The major piece of equipment required is a twenty-inch radial arm saw for cutting. This equipment will be purchased on an as-needed basis with available cash funds.
2. Thirty thousand dollars has been scheduled for the first quarter of 2007 for the purchase of new commercials, equipment, and office furniture.
3. Depreciation: All equipment and furniture has been considered either seven- or five-year property. Whole year depreciation has been estimated on all equipment.

Liabilities:

1. Accounts payable includes amounts due on inventory purchases as well as noninventory items

cont...

cont…

such as supplies, tools, telephones, travel, and entertainment.

2. Taxes payable for unpaid federal, state, FICA, FUTA, SUI, and medical withholding based on current and expected headcount.

Selling, General, and Administration Expenses:

1. Officer wages have been reflected at market value for all years.

2. Employee wages includes all employees including sales, general administration, and warehouse staff. Wage increases for nonofficer employees are calculated at 5 percent per annum.

3. General administrative expenses have been increased annually by approximately 6 percent to reflect inflationary increases.

Start Writing:

_____

_____

_____

_____

_____

_____

_____

_____

_____

_____

_____

_____

_____

_____

_____

_____

_____

_____

_____

_____

_____

_____

_____

_____

_____

_____

_____

_____

_____

_____

Next, present your break-even analysis. Remember, you will be showing the investor or lender the exact point at which the business makes neither a loss nor a profit. It is imperative to know at what point you will be covering your monthly expenses, that is, how much in sales will be needed to cover your monthly expenses.

Break-even Analysis

For the break-even analysis, the financial projections assume monthly selling expenses of $7,000 and general and administrated fixed costs of approximately $16,000 for the first three months of 2006, thus the business will need to generate $34,000 per month to break even. Cost of goods sold for materials and labor is anticipated to be near 33 percent, thus resulting in a gross margin percentage of approximately 67 percent.

Sales	$34,000	
COGS: Materials	$ 6,800	
Labor	4,200	
Total COGS		11,000
Gross Profit		$23,000
Selling Expenses: Commissions	$3,400	
Advertising	3,600	
Total Selling Expenses		7,000
Profit before G&A Expenses		$16,000
Total G&A Expenses		16,000
Break-even		0
		======

Start Writing:

_____
_____
_____
_____
_____
_____
_____
_____
_____
_____
_____
_____
_____
_____
_____
_____
_____
_____
_____
_____
_____
_____
_____
_____
_____
_____
_____
_____
_____
_____

Next, present your profit and loss statements, your balance sheets, and your cash flow statements for each year you are forecasting as well as any other financial information that you feel will be relevant, such as financial ratios.

	HOME IMPROVEMENTS INC.				
	PROFIT & LOSS STATEMENT				
	YEAR ONE: 2006				
	Jan	**Feb**	**Mar**	**Apr**	**May**
SALES	**30,000**	**30,000**	**30,000**	**40,000**	**40,000**
COGS-Materials	6,000	6,000	6,000	8,000	8,000
COGS-Labor	3,600	3,600	3,600	4,800	4,800
TOTAL COGS	**9,600**	**9,600**	**9,600**	**12,800**	**12,800**
GROSS PROFIT	**20,400**	**20,400**	**20,400**	**27,200**	**27,200**
Selling Expenses:					
Commissions	3,000	3,000	3,000	4,000	4,000
Advertising	3,600	3,600	3,600	4,800	4,800
TOTAL SELLING	**6,600**	**6,600**	**6,600**	**8,800**	**8,800**
General & Administration Expenses:					
Salaries—Employees	8,800	8,800	8,800	8,800	8,800
Salaries—Officers	2,000	2,000	2,000	2,000	2,000
Payroll Taxes	1,000	1,000	1,000	1,000	1,000
Vehicle Expense	300	300	300	300	300
Insurance	200	200	200	200	200
Legal & Accounting	200	200	200	200	200
General Office Expense	100	100	100	100	100
Postage	100	100	100	100	100
Office Supplies	200	200	200	200	200
Telephone	500	500	500	600	600
Rent	800	800	800	800	800
Utilities	200	200	200	200	200
Depreciation	900	900	900	900	900
Travel	200	200	200	200	200
Entertainment	100	100	100	100	100
Miscellaneous	100	100	100	100	100
TOTAL G&A	**15,700**	**15,700**	**15,700**	**15,800**	**15,800**
PROFIT (LOSS) BEFORE TAX	**(1,900)**	**(1,900)**	**(1,900)**	**2,600**	**2,600**
Estimated Income Taxes	-	-	-	-	-
PROFIT AFTER TAX	**(1,900)**	**(1,900)**	**(1,900)**	**2,600**	**2,600**

cont…

June	July	Aug	Sep	Oct	Nov	Dec	Total
40,000	40,000	40,000	40,000	50,000	50,000	50,000	480,000
8,000	8,000	8,000	8,000	10,000	10,000	10,000	96,000
4,800	4,800	4,800	4,800	6,000	6,000	6,000	57,600
12,800	12,800	12,800	12,800	16,000	16,000	16,000	153,600
27,200	27,200	27,200	27,200	34,000	34,000	34,000	326,400
4,000	4,000	4,000	4,000	5,000	5,000	5,000	48,000
4,800	4,800	4,800	4,800	6,000	6,000	6,000	57,600
8,800	8,800	8,800	8,800	11,000	11,000	11,000	105,600
8,800	8,800	8,800	8,800	8,800	8,800	8,800	105,600
2,000	2,000	2,000	2,000	2,000	2,000	2,000	24,000
1,000	1,000	1,000	1,000	1,000	1,000	1,000	12,000
300	300	300	300	300	300	300	3,600
200	200	200	200	200	200	200	2,400
200	200	200	200	200	200	200	2,400
100	200	200	200	200	200	200	1,800
100	200	200	200	200	200	200	1,800
200	300	300	300	300	300	300	3,000
600	600	600	600	700	700	700	7,200
800	800	800	800	800	800	800	9,600
200	200	200	200	200	200	200	2,400
900	900	900	900	900	900	900	10,800
200	200	200	200	200	200	200	2,400
100	100	100	100	100	100	100	1,200
100	100	100	100	100	100	100	1,200
15,800	16,100	16,100	16,100	16,200	16,200	16,200	191,400
2,600	2,300	2,300	2,300	6,800	6,800	6,800	29,400
-	-	-	-	-	-	-	7,400
2,600	2,300	2,300	2,300	6,800	6,800	6,800	22,000

HOME IMPROVEMENTS INC. QUARTERLY BALANCE SHEET YEAR ONE: 2006	March	June	Sept	Dec
ASSETS:				
Current Assets:				
Cash		45,000	38,600	36,300
Accounts Receivable	6,000	8,000	8,000	10,000
Inventory	120,000	120,000	120,000	120,000
TOTAL CURRENT ASSETS	**178,500**	**173,000**	**166,600**	**166,300**
Fixed Assets:				
Machinery & Equipment	30,000	30,000	30,000	30,000
Furniture & Fixtures	10,000	10,000	10,000	10,000
TOTAL FIXED ASSETS	**40,000**	**40,000**	**40,000**	**40,000**
Accumulated Depreciation	8,200	10,900	13,600	16,300
NET FIXED ASSETS	**31,800**	**29,100**	**26,400**	**23,700**
TOTAL ASSETS	**210,300**	**202,100**	**193,000**	**190,000**
LIABILITIES & STOCKHOLDERS' EQUITY:				
Current Liabilities:				
Accounts Payable	30,000	30,000	30,000	30,000
Payroll Taxes Payable	1,000	1,000	1,000	1,000
TOTAL CURRENT LIABILITIES	**31,000**	**31,000**	**31,000**	**31,000**
Long-term Liabilities:				
Leases Payable	20,000	19,000	18,000	17,000
Bank Loan Payable	150,000	135,000	120,000	105,000
TOTAL LIABILITIES	**201,000**	**185,000**	**169,000**	**153,000**
STOCKHOLDERS' EQUITY				
Common Stock	10,000	10,000	10,000	10,000
Prior Year Profit (Loss)	5,000	5,000	5,000	5,000
Current Year Profit (Loss)	(5,700)	2,100	9,000	22,000
TOTAL EQUITY	**9,300**	**17,100**	**24,000**	**37,000**
TOTAL LIABILITIES & STOCKHOLDERS' EQUITY	**210,300**	**202,100**	**193,000**	**190,000**

		March	June	Sept	Dec	Total
HOME IMPROVEMENTS INC.						
QUARTERLY CASH FLOW STATEMENT						
YEAR ONE: 2006						
		March	**June**	**Sept**	**Dec**	**Total**
NET INCOME		**(5,700)**	**7,800**	**6,900**	**13,000**	**22,000**
SOURCE:						
Depreciation		2,700	2,700	2,700	2,700	10,800
USE:						
Purchase—Property& Equipment		-	-	-	-	-
SOURCE (USE) From Operations:		**(3,000)**	**10,500**	**9,600**	**15,700**	**32,800**
(Increase) Decrease:						
Accounts Receivable		(20,000)	(2,000)	-	(2,000)	(24,000)
Inventory		(95,000)	-	-	-	(95,000)
Increase (Decrease):						
Accounts Payable		(2,000)	-	-	-	(2,000)
Payroll Taxes Payable		-	-	-	-	-
Leases Payable		-	(1,000)	(1,000)	(1,000)	(3,000)
(Increase) Decrease:						
Cash		(30,000)	7,500	6,400	2,300	(13,800)
Distribution to Stockholders		-	-	-	-	-
CHANGE IN LOAN BALANCE		**(150,000)**	**15,000**	**15,000**	**15,000**	**(105,000)**
Balance Beginning of Quarter		-	150,000	135,000	120,000	-
LOAN BALANCE END OF QUARTER		**150,000**	**135,000**	**120,000**	**105,000**	**105,000**

	HOME IMPROVEMENTS INC.				
	PROFIT & LOSS STATEMENT				
	YEAR TWO: 2007				
	Jan	**Feb**	**Mar**	**Apr**	**May**
SALES	**70,000**	**70,000**	**70,000**	**80,000**	**80,000**
COGS-Materials	14,000	14,000	14,000	16,000	16,000
COGS-Labor	9,100	9,100	9,100	10,400	10,400
TOTAL COGS	**23,100**	**23,100**	**23,100**	**26,400**	**26,400**
GROSS PROFIT	**46,900**	**46,900**	**46,900**	**53,600**	**53,600**
Selling Expenses:					
Commissions	7,000	7,000	7,000	8,000	8,000
Advertising	10,500	10,500	10,500	12,000	12,000
TOTAL SELLING	**17,500**	**17,500**	**17,500**	**20,000**	**20,000**
General & Administration Expenses:					
Salaries—Employees	14,400	14,400	14,400	14,400	14,400
Salaries—Officers	5,000	5,000	5,000	5,000	5,000
Payroll Taxes	1,600	1,600	1,600	1,600	1,600
Vehicle Expense	400	400	400	400	400
Insurance	300	300	300	300	300
Legal & Accounting	300	300	300	300	300
General Office Expense	200	200	200	200	200
Postage	200	200	200	200	200
Office Supplies	300	300	300	300	300
Telephone	800	800	800	800	800
Rent	800	800	800	800	800
Utilities	300	300	300	300	300
Depreciation	1,200	1,200	1,200	1,200	1,200
Travel	300	300	300	300	300
Entertainment	200	200	200	200	200
Miscellaneous	200	200	200	200	200
TOTAL G&A	**26,500**	**26,500**	**26,500**	**26,500**	**26,500**
PROFIT (LOSS) BEFORE TAX	**2,900**	**2,900**	**2,900**	**7,100**	**7,100**
Estimated Income Taxes	-	-	-	-	-
PROFIT AFTER TAX	**2,900**	**2,900**	**2,900**	**7,100**	**7,100**

cont…

June	July	Aug	Sep	Oct	Nov	Dec	Total
80,000	100,000	100,000	100,000	110,000	110,000	110,000	1,080,000
16,000	20,000	20,000	20,000	22,000	22,000	22,000	216,000
10,400	13,000	13,000	13,000	14,300	14,300	14,300	140,400
26,400	33,000	33,000	33,000	36,300	36,300	36,300	356,400
53,600	67,000	67,000	67,000	73,700	73,700	73,700	723,600
8,000	10,000	10,000	10,000	11,000	11,000	11,000	108,000
12,000	15,000	15,000	15,000	16,500	16,500	16,500	162,000
20,000	25,000	25,000	25,000	27,500	27,500	27,500	270,000
14,400	16,000	16,000	16,000	16,000	16,000	16,000	182,400
5,000	5,000	5,000	5,000	5,000	5,000	5,000	60,000
1,600	1,700	1,700	1,700	1,700	1,700	1,700	19,800
400	400	400	400	400	400	400	4,800
300	300	300	300	300	300	300	3,600
300	300	300	300	300	300	300	3,600
200	300	300	300	300	300	300	3,000
200	300	300	300	300	300	300	3,000
300	400	400	400	400	400	400	4,200
800	1,000	1,000	1,000	1,000	1,000	1,000	10,800
800	800	800	800	800	800	800	9,600
300	300	300	300	300	300	300	3,600
1,200	1,200	1,200	1,200	1,200	1,200	1,200	14,400
300	300	300	300	300	300	300	3,600
200	200	200	200	200	200	200	2,400
200	200	200	200	200	200	200	2,400
26,500	28,700	28,700	28,700	28,700	28,700	28,700	331,200
7,100	13,300	13,300	13,300	17,500	17,500	17,500	122,400
-	-	-	-	-	-	-	43,400
7,100	13,300	13,300	13,300	17,500	17,500	17,500	79,000

HOME IMPROVEMENTS INC.				
QUARTERLY BALANCE SHEET				
YEAR TWO: 2007				
	March	June	Sept	Dec
ASSETS:				
Current Assets:				
Cash	6,200	13,100	16,700	11,400
Accounts Receivable	14,000	16,000	20,000	22,000
Inventory	130,000	130,000	150,000	150,000
TOTAL CURRENT ASSETS	**150,200**	**159,100**	**186,700**	**183,400**
Fixed Assets:				
Machinery & Equipment	50,000	50,000	50,000	50,000
Furniture & Fixtures	20,000	20,000	20,000	20,000
TOTAL FIXED ASSETS	**70,000**	**70,000**	**70,000**	**70,000**
Accumulated Depreciation	19,900	23,500	27,100	30,700
NET FIXED ASSETS	**50,100**	**46,500**	**42,900**	**39,300**
TOTAL ASSETS	**200,300**	**205,600**	**229,600**	**222,700**
LIABILITIES & STOCKHOLDERS EQUITY:				
Current Liabilities:				
Accounts Payable	37,000	37,000	37,000	37,000
Payroll Taxes Payable	1,600	1,600	1,700	1,700
TOTAL CURRENT LIABILITIES	**38,600**	**38,600**	**38,700**	**38,700**
Long-term Liabilities:				
Leases Payable	26,000	25,000	24,000	23,000
Bank Loan Payable	90,000	75,000	60,000	45,000
TOTAL LIABILITIES	**154,600**	**138,600**	**122,700**	**106,700**
STOCKHOLDERS EQUITY				
Common Stock	10,000	10,000	10,000	10,000
Prior Year Profit (Loss)	27,000	27,000	27,000	27,000
Current Year Profit (Loss)	8,700	30,000	69,900	79,000
TOTAL EQUITY	**45,700**	**67,000**	**106,900**	**116,000**
TOTAL LIABILITIES & STOCKHOLDERS EQUITY	**200,300**	**205,600**	**229,600**	**222,700**

	March	June	Sept	Dec	Total
HOME IMPROVEMENTS INC.					
QUARTERLY CASH FLOW STATEMENT					
YEAR TWO: 2007					
NET INCOME	**8,700**	**21,300**	**39,900**	**9,100**	**79,000**
SOURCE:					
Depreciation	3,600	3,600	3,600	3,600	14,400
USE:					
Purchase—Property& Equipment	30,000	-	-	-	30,000
SOURCE (USE) From Operations:	**(17,700)**	**24,900**	**43,500**	**12,700**	**63,400**
(Increase) Decrease:					
Accounts Receivable	(4,000)	(2,000)	(4,000)	(2,000)	(12,000)
Inventory	(10,000)	-	(20,000)	-	(30,000)
Increase (Decrease):					
Accounts Payable	7,000	-	-	-	7,000
Payroll Taxes Payable	600	-	100	-	700
Leases Payable	9,000	(1,000)	(1,000)	(1,000)	6,000
(Increase) Decrease:					
Cash	30,100	(6,900)	(3,600)	5,300	24,900
Distribution to Stockholders	-	-	-	-	-
CHANGE IN LOAN BALANCE	**15,000**	**15,000**	**15,000**	**15,000**	**60,000**
Balance Beginning of Quarter	105,000	90,000	75,000	60,000	105,000
LOAN BALANCE END OF QUARTER	**90,000**	**75,000**	**60,000**	**45,000**	**45,000**

	HOME IMPROVEMENTS INC.		
	PROFIT & LOSS STATEMENT		
	YEARS THREE TO FIVE		
	2008	**2009**	**2010**
SALES	**1,240,000**	**1,430,000**	**1,640,000**
COGS—Materials	260,000	300,000	350,000
COGS—Labor	160,000	190,000	220,000
TOTAL COGS	**420,000**	**490,000**	**570,000**
GROSS PROFIT	**820,000**	**940,000**	**1,070,000**
Selling Expenses:			
Commissions	124,000	143,000	164,000
Advertising	186,000	215,000	246,000
TOTAL SELLING	**310,000**	**358,000**	**410,000**
General & Administration Expenses:			
Salaries—Employees	288,000	294,000	300,000
Salaries—Officers	72,000	78,000	84,000
Payroll Taxes	28,000	30,000	31,000
Vehicle Expense	6,000	7,000	7,000
Insurance	4,000	5,000	5,000
Legal & Accounting	6,000	7,000	7,000
General Office Expense	4,000	5,000	5,000
Postage	4,000	5,000	5,000
Office Supplies	5,000	6,000	6,000
Telephone	12,000	13,000	13,000
Rent	14,000	14,000	14,000
Utilities	6,000	7,000	7,000
Depreciation	17,000	20,000	23,000
Travel	5,000	6,000	6,000
Entertainment	3,000	4,000	4,000
Miscellaneous	3,000	4,000	4,000
TOTAL G&A	**477,000**	**505,000**	**521,000**
PROFIT (LOSS) BEFORE TAX	**33,000**	**77,000**	**139,000**
Estimated Income Taxes	8,000	20,000	47,000
PROFIT AFTER TAX	**25,000**	**57,000**	**92,000**

HOME IMPROVEMENTS INC.			
BALANCE SHEET			
YEARS THREE TO FIVE			
	2008	**2009**	**2010**
ASSETS:			
Current Assets:			
Cash	24,000	71,000	126,000
Accounts Receivable	25,000	25,000	30,000
Inventory	150,000	170,000	200,000
TOTAL CURRENT ASSETS	**199,000**	**266,000**	**356,000**
Fixed Assets:			
Machinery & Equipment	70,000	90,000	110,000
Furniture & Fixtures	30,000	40,000	50,000
TOTAL FIXED ASSETS	**100,000**	**130,000**	**160,000**
Accumulated Depreciation	48,000	68,000	91,000
NET FIXED ASSETS	**52,000**	**62,000**	**69,000**
TOTAL ASSETS	**251,000**	**328,000**	**425,000**
LIABILITIES & STOCKHOLDERS' EQUITY:			
Current Liabilities:			
Accounts Payable	65,000	65,000	75,000
Payroll Taxes Payable	5,000	5,000	5,000
TOTAL CURRENT LIABILITIES	**70,000**	**70,000**	**80,000**
Long-term Liabilities:			
Leases Payable	40,000	60,000	55,000
Bank Loan Payable	-	-	-
TOTAL LIABILITIES	**110,000**	**130,000**	**135,000**
STOCKHOLDERS' EQUITY			
Common Stock	10,000	10,000	10,000
Prior Year Profit (Loss)	106,000	131,000	188,000
Current Year Profit (Loss)	25,000	57,000	92,000
TOTAL EQUITY	**141,000**	**198,000**	**290,000**
TOTAL LIABILITIES & STOCKHOLDERS' EQUITY	**251,000**	**328,000**	**425,000**

HOME IMPROVEMENTS INC.			
CASH FLOW STATEMENT			
YEARS THREE TO FIVE			
	2008	**2009**	**2010**
NET INCOME	**25,000**	**57,000**	**92,000**
SOURCE:			
Depreciation	17,000	20,000	23,000
USE:			
Purchase—Property& Equipment	30,000	30,000	30,000
SOURCE (USE) From Operations:	**12,000**	**47,000**	**85,000**
(Increase) Decrease:			
Accounts Receivable	(3,000)	-	(5,000)
Inventory	-	(20,000)	(30,000)
Increase (Decrease):			
Accounts Payable	28,000	-	10,000
Payroll Taxes Payable	4,000	-	-
Leases Payable	17,000	20,000	(5,000)
(Increase) Decrease:			
Cash	(13,000)	(47,000)	(55,000)
Distribution to Stockholders	-	-	-
CHANGE IN LOAN BALANCE	**45,000**	-	-
Balance Beginning of Quarter	45,000	-	-
LOAN BALANCE END OF QUARTER	**-**	**-**	**-**

NOTES:

Start Writing:

HOME IMPROVEMENTS INC.
PROFIT & LOSS STATEMENT

	Jan	Feb	Mar	Apr	May
SALES					
COGS—Materials					
COGS—Labor					
TOTAL COGS					
GROSS PROFIT					
Selling Expenses:					
Commissions					
Advertising					
TOTAL SELLING					
General & Administration Expenses:					
Salaries—Employees					
Salaries—Officers					
Payroll Taxes					
Vehicle Expense					
Insurance					
Legal & Accounting					
General Office Expense					
Postage					
Office Supplies					
Telephone					
Rent					
Utilities					
Depreciation					
Travel					
Entertainment					
Miscellaneous					
TOTAL G&A					
PROFIT (LOSS) BEFORE TAX					
Estimated Income Taxes					
PROFIT AFTER TAX					

June	July	Aug	Sep	Oct	Nov	Dec	Total

HOME IMPROVEMENTS INC.
QUARTERLY BALANCE SHEET

	March	June	Sept	Dec
ASSETS:				
Current Assets:				
Cash				
Accounts Receivable				
Inventory				
TOTAL CURRENT ASSETS				
Fixed Assets:				
Machinery & Equipment				
Furniture & Fixtures				
TOTAL FIXED ASSETS				
Accumulated Depreciation				
NET FIXED ASSETS				
Other Assets:				
TOTAL ASSETS				
LIABILITIES & STOCKHOLDERS' EQUITY:				
Current Liabilities:				
Accounts Payable				
Payroll Taxes Payable				
TOTAL CURRENT LIABILITIES				
Long-term Liabilities:				
Leases Payable				
Bank Loan Payable				
TOTAL LIABILITIES				
STOCKHOLDERS' EQUITY				
Common Stock				
Prior Year Profit (Loss)				
Current Year Profit (Loss)				
TOTAL EQUITY				
TOTAL LIABILITIES & STOCKHOLDERS' EQUITY				

HOME IMPROVEMENTS INC.
QUARTERLY CASH FLOW STATEMENT

	March	June	Sept	Dec	Total
NET INCOME					
SOURCE:					
Depreciation					
USE:					
Purchase—Property & Equipment					
SOURCE (USE) From Operations:					
(Increase) Decrease:					
Accounts Receivable					
Inventory					
Increase (Decrease):					
Accounts Payable					
Payroll Taxes Payable					
Leases Payable					
(Increase) Decrease:					
Cash					
Distribution to Stockholders					
CHANGE IN LOAN BALANCE					
Balance Beginning of Quarter					
LOAN BALANCE END OF QUARTER					

Let's Do a Quick Review!

If you have never looked at a financial statement before and you are concerned and confused as to how and go about it, seek help from qualified accountants. Remember, it is important that you fully understand all information in your financial statements and projections including a profit and loss statement, balance sheet, and cash flow statement, use of proceeds table or written statement, and your assumptions used, regardless of whether someone else did them. Make sure they carefully and slowly walk you through each line item, over and over again, until you have a full understanding on the how and whys of them. To go in front of investors or lenders without this knowledge would not be advisable. It will be a waste of their time and yours.

Preparing and reviewing financial statements and supporting documentation is a lot of work, but these documents are also key management tools. We were referred to one successful client who was struggling with cash flow. His company was always months behind in producing their financial statements and analyzing key balance sheet items and the owner couldn't care less because he thought that it didn't make a difference. After several months of working with his company's accounting department, we were able to implement a system by which they were able to create and produce timely and accurate financial statements, including support analysis of all balance sheet and profit and loss items. As this process developed, they began seeing how cash was being tied up in accounts receivable and inventory as well as where money was being spent foolishly on things that were not really needed. Once they tightened their belts in these areas, cash started flowing right into their bank account. We are proud to say that this client has continued his growth over the last three years and continues to add new employees and new products.

CHAPTER 12
Executive Summary

Preparing Your Sizzle

The executive summary is one of the most critical pieces of your business plan as it is the section that everyone will read first. Before they dig into the detail portions of your business plan, investors and lenders must first be enticed to do so, and it is up to the executive summary to do the enticing. In some cases, investors and lenders will ask for just your executive summary along with your financial projections. It is imperative that you get their attention! If they like what they see, they will request your entire business plan for further review and consideration, otherwise they will let you know they are no longer interested.

In essence, the executive summary capsulizes your entire business plan in summary, usually in two to three pages. By preparing the executive summary last, you will be able to write it more easily and with far greater impact because you will have already compiled all of your data in the other sections of your business plan. Writing the executive summary involves transferring the "sizzle" of the plan into several concise, informative, and intriguing paragraphs in the same order that the material is presented throughout your winning business plan. Remember, even though you are writing it last, it will be presented first when packaging your business plan as described in chapter 2. (See page 29.)

Based upon the business you are in, it is possible that you may have to write different executive summaries for each of the audiences you are presenting to. When searching for a job, you adapt your résumé to the position that is being offered. The same goes for when you are trying to raise capital. It will be beneficial to you if you are able to get a feel for what excites and intrigues the investor or lender. Whether it is high technology products or steady growth products, you must tailor your executive summary to their tastes.

Let's Start Writing!

Now that you understand the purpose of the executive summary, let's begin telling the executive summary story. Remember to refer back to the detail portion of your winning business plan, take the sizzle from each section, and include it in the executive summary.

Start this section by providing general highlights about your company and your mission statement along with a summary of each section of your business plan. The summaries should be brief and to the point. You only have a few seconds to capture and keep the reader's attention. As you will see in the following example, Home Improvements Inc. provides a succinct overview of the company and then leads into their mission statement.

Executive Summary

Home Improvements Inc. (HII) was formed in 2005, and during the past year, the company has positioned itself as a leader in the sales and distribution of durable and energy-efficient aluminum siding and double-pane windows. The purpose of the operation of the company is to provide customers with exterior aluminum siding that is attractive, yet provides a high degree of durability and energy efficiency to homeowners and business owners.

The company is now entering two separate phases that are projected to cut operating cost by 15 percent and increase sales by 30 percent. First, by buying direct from the manufacturer, HII will realize better purchasing power and gain hands-on control of the manufacturing and assembly process. This will also cut down on delivery time to the customer resulting in a faster cash flow to the company. Second, with an intense television and radio campaign we will continue to be recognized as the leader in our market and as the company with a well-deserved positive and stable reputation.

Mission Statement

To provide customers with high-quality exterior aluminum siding and double-pane windows where we can be proud of the integrity and craftsmanship of each product sold to the end user and offer superior customer service throughout the warranty phases of the product, always remembering that each customer may be a tremendous source of referral business to our company.

Start Writing:

_____

_____

_____

_____

_____

_____

_____

_____

_____

_____

_____

_____

_____

_____

_____

Next, write a clear and concise statement on each of the detailed sections of your winning business plan starting with the "Company Overview."

Company Overview

For many years, people have had one of two choices when considering purchasing exterior siding for their home or office:

1. Purchase high-quality aluminum siding at a premium price
2. Settle for a low quality exterior siding made of wood composite, steel, or low-grade aluminum offered at a lower price.

Potential customers need to be educated on the important fact that all exterior siding is not the same. When they settle for a lower-quality product, the results are frustrating and costly.

At HII, we only sell the most highly rated siding on the market today; however, to maintain this standard, we are currently forced to purchase materials from a single distributor. This presents a problem because our company does not have an alternate source for the product at a lower price, thus it must pass the additional cost on to the customer and as a result, potentially lose revenue due to higher prices.

Senior management has decided to buy raw materials in container load quantities direct from other manufacturers in the United States and in Asia. These companies have mastered the art of designing and manufacturing aluminum siding through advanced technology and the product they provide is superior to any other on the market. Buying direct from the manufacturer will enable our company to save tens of thousands of dollars in the upcoming years, whereby the company can become highly price competitive while adding additional profit to the bottom line.

Objectives

Our objective at this time is to propel the company into a prominent market position within the next five years that will put HII in a suitable position for an initial public offering or profitable acquisition. We have developed a comprehensive plan to intensify and accelerate our marketing activities, product development, services expansion, engineering, distribution, and customer service. To implement our plans, we require a line of credit of $150,000 for the following purposes:

1. Purchase one container of aluminum materials for inventory: $50,000
2. Expand current operations in the rural areas of the United States: $30,000
3. Procurement of production and computer equipment: $60,000
4. Use for general working capital: $10,000

These items will enable HII to maximize sales with an extensive campaign to promote our products and services, and it will reinforce customer support services to handle the increased demands created by the influx of new orders and deepened penetration into new markets.

Start Writing:

_____

_____

_____

_____

_____

_____

_____

_____

_____

_____

_____

_____

_____

_____

_____

_____

_____

_____

_____

_____

Next, write a clear and concise statement on your "Products and Services."

Products and Services

The condition of the industry today is such that people are rapidly becoming aware of the need to protect their real estate assets more than ever before. It has been shown that aluminum siding not only protects your home, but the beauty and attractiveness also adds to its value.

Compared to many competitive products, ours is superior because it is made of the highest quality aluminum, whereas many competitive products use lower-grade aluminum or steel and wood composites that do not have the durability of our product.

The ability to educate our customers on the superior quality of our product is a capability unique to our trained salespeople. Each of the company's sales personnel is required to complete a four-week course before selling to the general public. This is absolutely essential to the success of our business since our higher price requires our salespeople to be able to convince customers of our product's added value in order to make the sale. Upon procuring container-load inventory direct from the manufacturer, we will be able to pass along some of the cost savings to the customer, which will result in our sales team closing more sales, thus generating more company revenue.

Start Writing:

_____

_____

_____

_____

_____

_____

_____

_____

_____

_____

_____

_____

Next, write a clear and concise statement on your "Market Analysis" and "Market and Sales Strategy."

Market Analysis

The typical customer profile falls into two separate categories:

1. Households with an annual income of $50,000 to $80,000

2. Retired persons in medium- to upper-income neighborhoods

HII is rapidly moving into its third marketing phase, namely expansion of its market base into rural geographical areas. Responses from customers indicate that our current product is enjoying an excellent reputation, and inquiries from prospective customers suggest that there is considerable demand for exterior aluminum siding and double-pane windows throughout our target market. Conservative estimates suggest that our market share with our intensified and accelerated marketing plan is about 30 percent in the Arizona market.

Marketing and Sales Strategy

The fundamental thrust of our marketing strategy consists of television, radio, printed advertising, and one-on-one selling in the home. Television and radio advertising have been the most successful marketing methods for HII, compared with flyers, direct mail, and display ads in magazines and newspapers.

We intend to reach prospective clients through continued advertising via television and radio. The marketing promotion tactics will consist of a new leads flow system; the customer calls the 1-800 number and the leads are forwarded to HII, whereby we will send out product information. A subcontracted telemarketing firm will then call the original leads and set appointments for the sales personnel to go on.

None of our competitors is advertising as intensely as we are. Our company can be characterized through our marketing efforts as the business that creates a positive and stable image for customers to see. HII enjoys an established track record of excellent support to our customers. Their expressions of satisfaction and encouragement are numerous, and we intend to continue our advances in the marketplace with more unique and instrumental offers.

Start Writing:

_____

_____

_____

_____

_____

_____

_____

_____

_____

_____

_____

_____

_____

_____

_____

_____

_____

_____

Next, write a clear and concise statement on your "Management and Personnel Plan."

Management

Our management team is comprised of individuals whose backgrounds consist of thirty years of corporate development experience with major organizations, as well as over twenty-five years of sales and design experience within the home improvement industry.

Personnel

The HII development team recognizes that additional staff is required to properly support marketing, sales, accounting, and production. Currently our company is composed of eight individuals with plans to expand our employee headcount to fifty team members over the next five years.

Start Writing:

_____

_____

_____

_____

Next, write a clear and concise statement on your "Financial Projections."

Financial Projections

Our operation was producing $200,000 in sales by the end of 2004, which represents eight months of operation. These results exceed industry standards for a start-up enterprise of our size. Projected revenue for the current year ending December 31, 2005, is $320,000.

Revenue projected for calendar year 2006 is expected to be $480,000, with annual growth thereafter to be projected at 15 percent per year through 2010.

In thirty months, we will have reached our stated goals and objectives and our lending institution will be able to collect its return on investment. The original loan will be paid down to a balance of zero as projected by the end of the third quarter of year three, 2008.

Start Writing:

_____
_____
_____
_____
_____
_____
_____
_____

Let's Do a Quick Review!

The primary purpose of the executive summary is to provide the reader with an exciting and intriguing snapshot of your venture. This is accomplished by giving them a summary of each section of your plan, the body of which should contain the most interesting points that you make.

Remember, the executive summary must contain the "sizzle" of your business plan. If you do not get the attention of the investor or lender here, you probably will not get it ever. Take your time in preparing and writing your executive summary, and if you feel parts of your business plan need to be rewritten to add more fire to it, then go back and do it. We suggest having business associates, family, and friends read your executive summary to see if it catches their attention and if it is easily understood. If not, go back and add some spice to it and clarify any confusing and unclear areas.

CHAPTER 13

Appendix Section of Your Business Plan

Supporting Your Claims

Your appendix section should include all of the backup documents that include or support the data you have already shared. You will want to provide any supporting documents that are significant to back up your winning business plan and all data, statements, and claims presented in it. There are several sources to find most of your important information, including the Internet, the library, industry magazines and publications, and your customers and competitors.

Through the Internet, you can go to various search engines and begin your search for whatever information you are seeking. In chapter 18, "Helpful Internet Links," we have provided some links that we feel may be useful to you when researching the different sections of your winning business plan.

Your public library should carry previously written articles, publications, newsletters, reports, statistics, etc., that will help you identify and verify your claims. Also, look for market survey data that has been performed by an independent surveying company. A lot of this information, including industry magazines and publications, is usually in the reference section of the library.

Your best customers may be your strongest ally to validate the quality of your products and services as well as the overall character of your company. If you can persuade loyal, satisfied customers and respected people in the community to write you a letter of recommendation, you will be miles ahead of your competition. If possible, get them to write their letter of recommendation on their letterhead.

In order to support any claims about your competitors, you may need to personally shop your competitors or get someone to do it for you. Gather as much written information from them as possible, including product brochures, pricing, and information on lead times; how long they have been in business; and what they feel separates them from their competition. Remember, in order to compete, you need to know who and what you are competing against.

As stated previously, in chapter 2, the appendix section of your winning business plan might include some or all of the following items in order to support disclosures made throughout your plan as well as providing additional valuable information to the investment source or lender.

- Support of footnotes from the text, for example, added support for economic data presented in your marketing plan and assumptions used in your financial projections

- Supporting documents
- Magazine and newspaper articles and special reports
- Biographies and résumés
- Bibliographies
- Graphs and charts
- Copies of contracts and agreements
- Glossary of terms
- References and supporting statements from lenders, investors, or other bankers, customers, suppliers, trade creditors, magazine and newspaper articles, etc., who can give positive feedback on your past performance as well as the products and services you provide
- Brochures and product information sheets
- Mechanical designs of your product
- Customer contracts
- Media information
- Surveys

Be careful not to overload your appendix with too much information. You don't want to overwhelm or confuse your reader. An appendix is not mandatory for a winning business plan, so make sure you include only what is pertinent, clearly presented, and logically sequenced. Everything in your appendix should add value to your winning business plan.

SECTION 3

Implementing Your Winning Business Plan

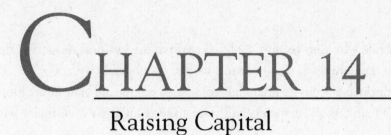

CHAPTER 14
Raising Capital

A Winning Business Plan Is a Must

Although the writing, researching, compiling, editing, and rewriting can at times be tedious and unpleasant, the process of writing a winning business plan can be highly rewarding if you follow a simple system and the proper outline. Beyond that—and this is big—*the written business plan is the means to get the capital that you need in order to launch or expand your enterprise.*

You may have been told by an investor or a banker: "I'm sorry, but before I make a decision, I will need to see your business plan." If you are looking at outside funding for your business or idea, a business plan today is as essential as a business card and an email address. Convince yourself that you must absolutely concentrate on crafting a superior winning business plan to create excitement in your venture and ultimately get the investors or bankers to believe in your business or idea and to back that belief up with funding.

Basic Principles of Getting Funded

Let's look at a few key principles that are basic steps in getting funding. Follow them carefully as you plan your business, and you will be far ahead of your competition. We've seen millions of investment dollars raised by entrepreneurs who followed these principles. As you review this list, think about where you are in your thought process and if you have implemented some of these key principles thus far.

- Investors will want to know the market potential and how your products or services will fit in and how they will take a healthy piece of the market.
- Your plan must communicate how well you have researched the opportunity and you must lay out a road map from beginning to end showing the investors how and when you will achieve your goals and objectives.
- Investors will want you to prove you can capitalize on your market strategy and generate the amount of sales revenues you are projecting.

- Your plan must describe why your team is qualified to drive the business to success. Surround yourself with a solid management team that investors will be comfortable with.
- You must create realistic and accurate financial projections supporting your future growth potential. This is a key area of focus, as all financiers will want to see how their investment will be returned to them.

"Those who fail to plan, plan to fail." This adage is not only profound and true; it is a simple process to follow. When you leave for a trip to a location you have not been before, you wouldn't just hop in the car, drive to the airport, book the first flight, show up at a destination with no lodging plans, no car, no money, and no sense of what you would like to do while you are there, without a sense of how long you would like to stay, people you would like to meet, and places you would like to visit.

The same is true with planning your business. Have a winning business plan, and commit your winning business plan to writing. Put some serious thought behind it. Do your research. Come up with a compelling strategy that will make others want to participate with you, whether they are potential investors or key employees. Explain how you will compete in the market and what your critical path to customer acquisition is or when you will start selling your products and services.

If you don't have a plan, don't plan on getting any funding. It's that simple. Don't kid yourself into thinking that you can show up with an idea and wow the investors into submission. Those days are over. Today you must clearly illustrate and articulate that there truly is an opportunity out there and that you are the one to seize it and turn it into a viable, profitable business.

As you develop your winning business plan, it will be to your advantage to go through the process of researching, writing, crafting, strategizing, packaging, and persuading with a written winning business plan. Two important things will occur in the process:

1. You will better understand your business and will probably appreciate it more.

2. You will know if there really is an opportunity out there for you to snatch up your own piece of the American Dream.

Answer the #1 Question on Their Minds

Every investor or banker wants to know one thing: "When will I get a return on my investment?" This is the silent question they will ask after every section of your plan. They are risking their capital in a venture that may succeed or fail. Therefore, when you are researching and eventually writing your winning business plan, keep this question in your mind because it will definitely be on the minds of your funding sources.

Sounds almost too simple but make no mistake, if you can put a business plan together that illustrates how you have thought the business through completely, you can raise the capital you need. As you write your winning business plan, it is important for you to keep these things in mind as you research and compile your data:

- When you describe your goals and objectives, show how you are going to provide a good return on investment.

- When you present your management team, illustrate how this team is highly qualified to look out for the bottom line.
- When you craft your marketing plan, explain by example how sales will occur as a result of your market analysis and marketing strategies.
- When you develop your financial projections, show that you have clearly thought through the numbers presented and that they are achievable.
- When you make promises, make sure that you can keep them.
- When you provide supporting documentation, identify as many sources as you can to validate your idea or business concept.
- When you write your winning business plan, don't allow yourself to provide too much fluff. Make sure you can validate every claim you make in your winning business plan. Excitement for your idea is one thing, but deception is never a good strategy.

In order to fully answer the #1 question, there are a few funding questions that you should be aware of as you develop your plan. We have come up with fifteen key questions (qualifying investment questions) that probably will be asked by venture capital firms and angel investors. The best place to reach these investors is to start at the local level. Almost every state has some type of angel investor group that will be interested in hearing pitches by entrepreneurs. Most investors will look to their home state first for deals to fund. Do a search of angel investors on the Internet and you will find several listings to help you get started in finding the right source. For example, www.gatheringofangels.com, www.ventureworthy.com, www.gobignetwork.com, and www.fundingpost.com.

The fifteen questions listed below are an excellent primer to help you understand the mindset of investors, and the types of questions they will ask you. If you can answer these questions, you will be well on your way to receiving financing. There is no guarantee that you will get funded, but your responses to these questions will help you figure out how much work you still need to do, and what types of deals the investment community is looking for.

The primary sources of capital that you will want to consider are:
- Your savings
- Family members
- Loans from a bank or other financial institution
- Credit cards
- Angel investors
- Venture capital firms
- Receivable factoring companies

Qualifying Investment Questions
1. Can you explain your product or service in forty-five seconds or less?
2. What are the top three value-added applications of your product or service to the consumer?
3. Who is your management team and what are their credentials?
4. Who is your target market?

5. Why does the market need your product or service?

6. How much capital do you have in the venture?

7. Do any other investors own part of the company?

8. Who owns the company and what is their percentage?

9. How much capital do you need?

10. What is your intention for use of proceeds?

11. What are you doing in the business currently?

12. What is your exit strategy?

13. If you were to advertise your product or service, what would you say in thirty seconds to persuade your target market to buy?

14. What is your projected sales revenue for each of the next three years?

15. What are your projected profits for the next three years?

The key is to be able to answer every one of these questions. As you answer each question, it will be like moving to the next level in succession. If you don't or can't answer one of these questions, you will not advance. Yours may be a nice idea, but you'll have a hard time convincing an investment group that it's worthy of their attention.

Investment groups can wade through many business ideas fairly quickly (usually in about ten to fifteen minutes) to determine whether it's a project they want to spend their time and money on. Make sure that you are able to answer each one of these questions in order to move to the next round of being seriously considered for funding.

Hone Your Presentation Skills

The following list of items is also a helpful source of information compiled from several different sources of angel investors. An angel investor is an entrepreneur who has money and is willing to take smaller risks with their capital by investing a few hundred thousand or sometimes a few million dollars into other ventures. They will usually take a stake in the business and spend time on your management team or board of directors assisting in the operations of the business.

Take a few minutes to become familiar with the presentation outlined below. In our experience, this has proved to be highly successful in helping entrepreneurs to clearly present their ventures in a logical order. Angel investors usually meet on a set day and time each month, for example, the second Wednesday of each month, and they generally hear from three presenters:

9:00–10:00 a.m. with Company A

10:00–11:00 a.m. with Company B

11:00–12:00 p.m. with Company C

You will want to check with the group leader to find out what they feel is appropriate attire, but business casual is usually appropriate.

Depending on the number of investors in the audience, you will want to bring as many copies of your business plan as they tell you to. You will also want to bring the same number of your handouts and whatever audio and visual equipment you need. Also, check with the group leader and ask them if they would like a ten-, fifteen-, or twenty-minute presentation presented to the group.

Each of these points are important to the investors in the audience, and they will certainly want to know about each of these as they relate to your venture. Try to provide an overview of each of these elements in your presentation, and be prepared to answer questions about each. Keep your presentation to ten minutes using PowerPoint and your business plan, and leave at least ten minutes of your allotted time for the investors to ask you questions. If they like your deal, they will take more time to ask you questions.

Presentation Outline

Presentation (ten minutes)
- Management introductions
- Investment terms and exit strategy
- Company overview
- Product and service
- Industry overview
- Competitor analysis
- Marketing plan
- Historical performance
- Financial projections
- Requested capital and expected usage

Questions (ten minutes)

Your presentation will obviously follow the information provided in your business plan, but you will also need to deliver a professional presentation of some sort. The most common is a PowerPoint slide presentation that you should be able to deliver in ten to twenty minutes. This presentation is very important. Your winning business plan is what got you to the meeting, but your presentation is your sales pitch that will make or break your chances of getting funding.

Brian puts it this way: "As a judge for the Utah Entrepreneur Challenge, I have seen many good business plans get torn apart in the presentation phase of the competition. This is a statewide business plan writing competition with a lot of young, bright, and energetic college students all competing for the chance to win $40,000. For the past five years, we have received over 250 entries each year. We narrow these down to twenty-five final business plans and then down to ten finalists.

"It never ceases to amaze me how the top ten business plans seem to transform from great written plans to abysmal presentations. We have the ten finalists give a ten-minute, live presentation, just as they would if they were presenting to a group of investors. Winners of the competition are judged on their business plans, their overall idea, the true opportunity, the resources they have gathered, and the management team. The final piece of the puzzle is the one that is crucial for the competition, 'Can you present to a group of individuals that will ask you tough questions, and how do you handle yourself under pressure?' Being able to present a professional presentation that builds on the overall venture from slide to slide is key in winning the competition."

The presentation is a summary of your business plan, and each slide or concept presented should build on the previous concept/slide. As you build on the idea, you keep the investors' attention and answer their unspoken questions as you move from slide to slide. Investors love the "the build." As you follow the presentation outline provided above, you will be building on concepts in a logical fashion that is easy to follow and clearly outlines your strategy.

Your presentation may not be given in a formal setting in front of a panel of judges or investors, but you will eventually need to give your pitch. When it comes to raising capital, the presentation will need to be honed to a fine-tuned offering. Don't let the fact that you are simply taking the key points out of your winning business plan and presenting them fool you; the presentation is often not as simple as it sounds, so keep practicing until you've got it nailed.

Backyard Funding

Can't find money anywhere? Maybe you're searching too far from home. Try raising that capital in your own backyard.

One entrepreneur, an office furniture manufacturer based in northern California, felt looking for funding was like looking for a needle in a haystack. He had grown his company to $6 million in revenues and fifty employees over twenty-seven years. Now the company was ready to launch its own branded product line, but the CEO wasn't sure where to turn for the necessary funding to get the project going.

He was reluctant to take on any more bank debt, but was completely realistic about his chances of finding equity financing. "It's extremely difficult for a company like ours to go to the VC market," he says. "We might as well say it's virtually impossible. We're a small low-tech company that is never going to go from $6 million to $60 million in two years. It's just not going to happen."

Five months after the search for capital began, this small manufacturing company hooked up with a venture capital firm in Silicon Valley that saw potential. This particular venture firm targets businesses in low-income communities in the Bay Area. At the conclusion of their due diligence, the venture firm invested $250,000 in the company in exchange for a 6 percent stake.

What aspect of the business caught the venture firm's eye? There were two very surprising elements. First was the company's commitment to training and advancing its blue-collar workforce, and second, its socially responsible business practices, especially its commitment to sustainable forestry.

Those qualities may not seem as if they would be particularly attractive to a typical venture capital firm. But this VC firm was hardly typical. As one of some fifty funds involved in community-development projects throughout the country, the venture firm seeks both practical and altruistic compensation, referred to by those within the community development arena as a "double bottom line." The dual goal is to see a financial return on an investment and a return to the local community in the form of such things as jobs for low-income workers, inner-city property revitalization, and opportunities for women and minorities.

This particular CEO's secret weapon in making his pitch to the venture firm was his company's business plan. He drew up a traditional document, including an overview of the marketplace, a list of his company's competitive strengths and weaknesses, and what he saw as the market opportunities for his new product line. He also included information about his company's diverse workforce and made forecasts about job-growth potential. He saw those elements as a critical part of his company's identity and thought the venture firm would be particularly interested in his community development commitment.

He was right, says a senior portfolio manager at the Bay Area venture firm. "The thing that really caught our attention about the company from a social-return point of view was the willingness of the CEO to implement training programs for low-income workers within the company," he recalls.

After sixty days of due diligence, during which the venture firm challenged the owner on his financial projections and his expectations for the new product line, the CEO walked away with $250,000. He also gained access to the venture firm's advisory program, a free service through which it links its portfolio companies with Bay Area executives who volunteer their time and expertise in such business-critical areas as finance, marketing, and strategic planning to companies that could otherwise never dream of being able to hire them.

An Investor-Ready Business Plan

Put simply, an investor-ready business plan is crafted with the reader and potential investor in mind. As discussed earlier, the business plan is a fantastic tool for the business owners and managers, but when it comes to securing capital, there are certain key points the plan's writer must keep in mind. What do investors really want to see in your business plan? What data is important to them in order to make a decision for funding? How should you present your information to make it persuasive? What silent questions do you need to answer?

We have covered at least fifteen questions that you will need to provide persuasive answers to, but let's take it one step further. To keep it simple, just remember five easy points in presenting your ideas in writing. In fact, if you can learn to think like an investor, you're 80 percent there! Think about it this way: when you have an interest in purchasing something and you can get all of your questions answered in a satisfactory way, you make the purchase. The same goes for potential investors.

Point #1

What is the problem you are solving? OR Why is your company's product or service *needed*?

Point #2

What is your sustainable competitive advantage? OR How will you stop other *competitors* from taking your customers?

Point #3

What are your barriers to entry? OR Why will you *succeed* where others have failed?

Point #4

What is the true market opportunity? OR How many *customers* can you reach?

Point #5

What is your critical path to customer acquisition? OR When will you start selling?

In chapter 2, we discussed the four most important things investors will look for in your business plan. And we introduced the reasons why investors placed so much emphasis on these four areas. Just to review, they are:

1. Solid management team

2. Realistic financials and projections

3. Marketable products and services

4. Achievable marketing plan (analysis and strategy)

Now that you have learned some of the more important aspects of crafting a winning business plan, let's add one more thing for you to consider as you research and compile your plan:

5. Rewards outweigh the risks

In other words, to make this a true investor-ready business plan, you must provide enough documentation and data to clearly illustrate that the rewards do, in fact, outweigh the risks.

The reward or the "exit strategy" is the cherry on top of the sundae. Your crowning moment of signing new clients, selling a big deal, or even just keeping your growth on a steady pace will lead you to an event that will be a good thing for both you and your investors.

Of course, many small businesses will not require an investor. However, consider yourself, the inside investor, or the bank that you are taking your business plan to. The "exit strategy" for a bank will be when you pay off your loan or line of credit. The exit strategy for you personally may be a merger, an acquisition, or even your annual bonus for a job well done.

In order to help you fully understand the concept of rewards outweighing risks, crafting a winning business plan is an essential and important exercise that will provide you with the initial steps of raising the capital you need for your venture. Since you and the investors are risking capital, time, and reputation, it is important for you to implement these principals outlined and craft your winning business plan in a manner that will help you achieve success quickly. Good luck!

CHAPTER 15

The Future and Building Your Business

The Good and the Bad

When it comes to growing your business, there is both good news and bad news. Before we get into a discussion on *strategy* and how you can continue to grow your business, let's discuss some numbers that can help you as you formulate a winning strategy.

First, let's get the bad news out of the way. And, by the way, don't shoot the messenger here, but according to a report by Dun and Bradstreet in 2004, there are a few statistics that you should be aware of.

- Businesses with fewer than twenty employees have only a 37 percent chance of surviving four years and only a 9 percent chance of surviving ten years.
- Restaurants only have a 20 percent chance of surviving two years.
- The failure rate for new businesses seems to be around 70 percent to 80 percent in the first year, and only 50 percent of those who survive the first year will remain in business the next five years.
- In the SME business sector, nine out of ten business failures in the U.S. are caused by a *lack of general business management skills and planning*.
- 88.7 percent of all business downturns and failures are due to management mistakes.

(Source: Dun & Bradstreet Report 2004)

A report released by the U.S. Chamber of Commerce in the same year offers some good news. The chamber report agrees with some of the previous bleaker statistics for small to medium enterprises; however, they also point out a few areas of business that shed light on the other side of the equation, the successful side of things:

- Between 2000 and 2004, U.S. employer firms grew 18 percent from 5.5 million to 6.7 million.
- In 2004, small enterprises, fewer than 500 employees, made up the bulk of the total number of companies, yet within the total number of employer firms, medium-sized firms had also grown at a steady pace.
- In 2001, there were just over 100,000 medium enterprises. In 2004, there were over 116,000 medium-sized companies in the U.S. (Source: the U.S. Chamber of Commerce 2004)

As of this writing in 2006, some 591,000 jobs were created in the world's largest economy in the first three months of this year. America's March unemployment rate of 4.7 percent matches January's four-and-a-half-year low. (Source: U.S. Federal Reserve) The good news is that small businesses are popping up all over, especially in newly created industries. Millions of entrepreneurs are starting or expanding an existing business and creating jobs. Bankruptcy rates are now declining after hitting an all-time high for the past several years.

Business ventures involve much risk, but as Ewing Mario Kauffman, founder of Marion Laboratories and owner of the Kansas City Royals, has said, "You take a risk, sometimes you lose…but sometimes it pays off big!"

Sharpening Your Tools

Starting a business or growing an existing business can be a fun and rewarding experience as long as you have the proper tools at your disposal. We plan to give you a few more tools to help you along the way. To begin, we want to focus a little attention on creating a powerful marketing plan.

First, focus on the CUSTOMER. Since they are the ones that will be paying you for your products and services, it makes sense to break this down in three simple steps.

Step One: Define your market

Step Two: Describe your target customer

Step Three: Create a communication strategy

Defining your market is a convoluted way of saying "who will you sell to?" Will it be twenty- to twenty-six-year-old males who are athletic, enjoy the outdoors, and eat pizza twice a week? Or is your market baby boomers age forty-two to sixty who own a second home in the mountains, have a retirement fund, and who enjoy eating out four times a week?

To keep on top of your game and continue to compete and grow your business, you will need to keep asking yourself questions like these. The answers you provide may change along the way. We defined some of those marketing questions earlier, so refer back and take a look at your answers. Don't rest on your laurels and think that you have figured it out. IBM used to think that way, and today they don't even make systems any longer—their PC group was sold to Lenovo in 2004. During the 1990s, IBM was the eight-hundred-pound gorilla to compete against. The same holds true for any small business that does not keep focused on growth and retention.

If someone were to ask you to *describe your typical customer*, could you do it in thirty seconds or less? If you can, then you are among the elite business owners who really do know their business and who bring in the money. If you can't, take time to figure out who buys from you and practice this over and over.

In order to grow, you will need to *communicate to your customers* and clients who you are, what you are offering, and how much they will be expected to pay for it. Think of the many inserts and circulars in the Sunday paper. These companies are communicating with their customers. They are reaching out to stay competitive and to provide members of their target market with compelling reasons to buy from them.

Likewise, the way the entrance of your business looks, the way your people dress, the signage that you have, the marketing materials you present, and the website you create are all ways to communicate with your customers.

Your communication strategy should consist of several key components, but remember this one very important principle: **Communicate with your customers at least three times every month.**

You can accomplish this through an email, a mailer, a letter, a phone call, a news article, a story written about your business, a speech that you give, or even attending a networking meeting at your local chamber of commerce. Just keep your name visible at least three times per month.

Always make time for marketing and be sure to maintain a budget to keep marketing your business. As an owner of a small business, expect marketing to take up 60 percent of your time. You should be relentless about telling people about your business and helping your customers understand that your products and services are the best in the market.

One more tip: remember the four P's of marketing: **P**roduct, **P**rice, **P**lacement, and **P**romotion. As you do so, you will be organizing your thoughts about knowing what motivates people to buy. In some cases, you will become an amateur psychologist as you analyze what hot buttons you can push to get them to open up their wallet and purchase from you.

Remember, people buy on DESIRES, not just on needs alone, especially the generation of young people coming up in the world. Sometimes it seems no matter what the cost is, luxury, beauty, relaxation, time, and ease seem to dominate the buying patterns for members of several different age groups. We have become a society that has grown impatient, and we want things now.

The following list of faster, smaller, more convenient things that we just can't live without was conceived in less than six minutes:

- Blackberry phones with email
- Camera phones
- Digital cameras
- Digital camcorders
- Fast-food restaurants with dual drive-through windows
- ESPN scores and game updates 24/7
- Speed dial
- Faster Internet speeds
- Faster computers
- Faster cars
- Microwave dinners
- Better graphics
- MP3 players
- Books on tape/CD
- Remote controls
- Pay at the pump
- ATMs on every corner
- All-in-one printers/fax/copiers
- Online ordering
- Overnight deliveries
- More freeways and bi-ways
- Smaller and more compact phones

- Rapid charge battery chargers
- Internet search engines

You get the picture. So, where are *your* products headed? What services will become obsolete? What products will be obsolete, and how soon?

If you are an engineer or in manufacturing and you want to market a product, take some advice from someone in sales and marketing. When it comes to features and benefits, the features are certainly important, but the benefits will sell your products faster. Here is a simple example:

- Features and benefits—sell the benefits
- Manufacturing talks about *features*
- Good marketing discusses *benefits*

Aerodynamic design with lightweight alloy wheels...	versus	**Style, exhilaration, and performance. Hugs the corners tightly going 95 mph...**

In 2005, Jaguar came out with a clever ad that sold the idea about their cars performing better than any other luxury car. The ad read: "R Performance is a mindset, born of the belief that racing does indeed improve the breed. By demanding innovation in the way a car is engineered to accelerate, steer, and stop, and by rewarding drivers with supercharged power, computer-aided stability, and precisely executed design, Jaguar R Performance models are truly born to perform." Then a picture of the car was shown. Once again, the point is to sell the benefits more than the features. The ad makes you feel like R Performance is a very cool thing to have. "Born to perform" is a benefit that is stated in a way indicating that demanding drivers will be rewarded when they experience R Performance.

As you write your plan and you define your marketing strategy, keep in mind that investors may ask, "What is your critical path to customer acquisition?" This is just a fancy way of asking, "When will you start selling?" By defining this in your plan, you should be able to point out how you are selling the benefits of your products, and not just the features.

You can answer this question by defining whom your customers are, how you will get them to buy from you, and telling them *why* they should buy from you.

Practicing "Nichecraft"

Many companies today have carved out a certain niche of customers that they sell to on a regular basis. From the local dry cleaners to the national retail chain, they have created a need for their products and services by catering directly to the needs of a smaller, much more conscientious consumer. Here are just a few examples:

- Dell: Eliminate the middleman and sell for less. Dell's built-to-order boxes allow for lower inventories, lower costs, and higher profit margins.
- Wal-Mart: Always low prices.

- Wendy's: Old-fashioned hamburgers with fast, friendly service.
- The Home Depot: You have home projects, we stock the things you need to do it yourself.
- Hunter Ceiling Fans: Distinctive designs with exceptional performance.
- Lexus Automobiles: For the driver who craves luxury, with a premium level of craftsmanship.

Niche marketing today means targeting, communicating with, selling to, and obtaining feedback from the heaviest users of your business's products or services.

Picking the right segment of the market is important to achieving sufficiently large sales volume and profitability to survive and prosper as a company. Picking the right market segment means that it is:

- Made up of consumers who will buy from you
- Measurable in quantitative terms
- Substantial enough to generate planned sales volume
- Accessible to your company's distribution methods
- Sensitive to planned and affordable marketing spending events

In identifying your niche and the segment of the market you will target, it is also important to examine other factors that could affect your company's success. You will want to consider:

- Strength of competitors to attract your niche buyers away from your products
- Similarity of competitive products in the buyers' minds
- Rate of new product introductions by competitors
- Ease of entry/protectability in the market for your niche

Perhaps the driving force behind "niche" marketing or "segmentation" is the need to satisfy and keep those consumers who really love your products or services. Consumers become increasingly more sophisticated and demanding. Product choices continue to expand with prosperity and global competition.

Even large companies have embraced niche marketing, continuing to refine and target their product offerings to different buyer groups. As an example, Nike restaged a multi-billion dollar company that had plateaued by pursuing a segmentation strategy. Nike designed and marketed athletic shoes for each different sport, often further segmenting with specialized models within each sport. For example, "Air Jordan" represented by Michael Jordan, and "Flight" basketball shoes represented by Vince Carter; "Vick III D" football cleats represented by Michael Vick, the Warrior Pro iD series represented by Troy Napalotano, and "Mercurial Vapor" represented by Damarcus Beasley for Team USA soccer.

It also is important to be able to identify and estimate the size of your target market, particularly if you're thinking about a new venture so that you can tell if the customer base is large enough to support your business or new product idea. Remember that it is not enough that people like your business concept. There must be enough target buyers on a frequent enough basis to sustain your company sales, spending, and profits from year to year.

For example, selling a product or service that people may need only once in a lifetime, such as an indestructible pair of shoes, may not be a sustainable business, unless a large number of people need it at any given time or unless everyone needs it eventually (as with funeral services) or your profit margins generate a substantial income.

What niche does your product or service fill? What needs are out there that are not being filled by you or anyone else? Brainstorm for just a minute. Think about what you would like to see improved upon that your business can directly affect. In other words, if the world were perfect, what would your product do and what services would you provide?

How to Segment Your Market

If the universe of all potential buyers is your market, then the market can be divided up into sections or segments based on any number of factors. For example, you might divide your customers by age group and find that you sell most of your products to people aged eighteen to thirty-four. You might divide that segment up by family size and find that you sell most of your products to married couples with young children. You could divide that segment up by economic status and find that you sell most products to families with an annual income of about $60,000 to $100,000. You may even sort again, this time by geographic location, and find that you sell most of your products to people living within two specific zip codes.

Many small businesses stop there, thinking that they have enough information to be able to identify and communicate with their most likely customers. However, larger companies will attempt to push on further and find out even more information about their customers' lifestyles, values, life stage, and so forth. Let's define some terms:

Demographic data refers to age, sex, income, education, race, martial status, size of household, geographic location, size of city, and profession.

Psychographic data refers to personality- and emotion-based behavior linked to purchase choices; for example, whether customers are risk-takers or risk-avoiders, impulsive buyers, etc.

Lifestyle refers to the collective choice of hobbies, recreational pursuits, entertainment, vacations, and other non-work time pursuits.

Belief and value system refers to religious, political, nationalistic, and cultural beliefs and values.

Life stage refers to the chronological benchmarking of people's lives at different ages, for example, preteens, teenagers, and empty nesters.

How can you find out more about your customers? By doing thorough market research.

Larger companies segment their markets by conducting extensive market research projects, consisting of several rounds of exploratory research as follows.

Customer and product data collection: Researchers gather data from users of similar products regarding:

- Consumable products purchased and how often they are consumed
- Number and timing of brand purchases
- Reasons for purchases
- Consumers' attitudes about various product attributes
- Importance of the product to the lifestyle of the consumer
- Category user information (demographics, psychographics, media habits, etc.)
- Seasonal uses and seasonal colors

Factor and cluster analysis: Researchers analyze the data collected in ways to find correlations between product purchases and other factors as a basis for identifying actionable consumer target clusters. Clusters are defined as niche markets where there are identifiable numbers of buyers or users who share the same characteristics and who thus can be reached by adept advertising and promotion.

Cluster identification and importance ranking: Researchers then determine whether clusters are large and viable enough to spend marketing funds on them and whether potential marketing niche clusters fit strategic company objectives, for example, does marketing to this group fit your existing image and long-term goals?

What can your company do to segment its markets?

Smaller companies also can conduct informal factor and cluster analysis by:

- Watching key competitors' marketing efforts and copying them
- Talking to key trade buyers about new product introductions
- Conducting needs analyses from qualitative research with individuals and groups

You can segment markets by geography, distribution, price, packaging, sizes, product life, and other tangible factors in addition to clustering by demographic, lifestyle, and psychographic data. Service businesses will want to go as far as developing a cluster of clients based on a radius within a certain geographical area. For example, an interior designer may want to focus on a fifty-mile radius, and a math tutor may look at a twenty-mile radius for servicing customer needs. Some service businesses, such as dry cleaners, will even tighten down the radius to about three to five miles. You decide how large the radius around your business should be, but put some type of limits to where you are physically capable of servicing your customers' needs.

Can a radius define your market? If so, how big?

What are some of the other segments that can be defined for your business/customers?

Age range: _____

Income: _____

Education background: _____

Male or female: _____

Neighborhood: _____

Buying patterns: _____

Life stage: _____

Use of product/service: _____

So how do you develop a niche for your business? Ask yourself these questions and give an honest attempt of real answers:

- Are you going in too many directions at once?
- Have you asked colleagues, friends, clients, or customers to tell you what business they would say you are in? After the feedback, make adjustments and ask again.
- Is your business compatible with what's most important to you in life? Review your life's goals and priorities.
- What opportunities are in the market that you can fill?
- Which things do you do best?
- What are you already best known for?
- What are you most eager to promote?
- What comes most naturally for you?

Next, take the action steps listed in the seven-step niche process that follows. This brief list can help you concentrate on some key elements of moving closer to your niche marketing ideas.

1. Make a wish list of what you want to market.

2. Focus: Don't target every Tom, Dick, Harry, Jane, and Jill.

3. Describe the customers' view on what is needed. The customers must want the product or service in order for your business to succeed.

4. Carefully plan your strategy.

5. Become one of a kind, "the only game in town."

6. Your products and services must evolve with the market needs and you must test, test, test, one strategy against another.

7. Go get it done!

Finding Your Hidden Resources

Have you taken some time lately to think about and write down some of the hidden resources in your business? This section of the book will help you think about these hidden resources and begin to define a plan of action for using those resources to your benefit.

First, we need to define what "Resources" we are referring to. Refer back to the free enterprise model and remember the five basic elements, or resources that we referred to, namely, people, tools, technologies, capital, and industry best practices. Now, look at the following list of items that are resources for you to consider. Are they hidden? Maybe not, but you may not be fully utilizing them.

- Inventory
- Customer list
- Intellectual property
- Employees
- Physical assets
- Strategic partnerships
- Internal knowledge base
- The Internet
- Experience
- Skills
- Contacts/network
- Software
- Hardware
- Family
- Friends
- Passion to succeed
- Technology
- Databases
- Marketing ideas
- The media

- Free press (press releases)
- Internal assessment of resources to free up assets

For example, do you have inventory that is costing you money? You may have a few items that you can sell to free up capital and space.

What about your employees? They may have some hidden talents that you are unaware of. Try sitting down with them and asking a few key questions about their skills and talents, and what they feel they could do to help you grow your business. Some employees will surprise you with their ideas.

Take the concept of sitting down with key people a little further and contact a few of your strategic alliance partners. Take them to lunch and let them know that you value their expertise, then share a new marketing idea with them. Ask them for feedback on how to improve.

The media can also be a tremendous resource for you. A simple press release can catch the attention of a reporter or editor that needs to fill space in their newspaper. One press release can generate multiple stories about your company, and it can even begin with a small hometown paper.

Have some fun with this and let your mind run wild with new ideas. Come up with at least three new ideas of how to better utilize your hidden resources. Write them down, follow up in one week, and readjust your course if necessary. Don't stop at three...keep going. Come up with as many as your brain can handle, then take these to associates, friends, and family and get their input. Refine your original ideas and come up with more. This is a perpetual process that has no boundaries or limits. The next steps are to figure out where you should look first in your business for potential resources.

Where should you look first?

There are five basic elements to help you gauge how well you are utilizing your resources. You, as well as your team, should measure these five elements periodically. Spend some time exploring alternatives and asking hard questions. This may not always be easy, especially if you have family members or close friends involved in your business, but you must remember that this is your business and your livelihood, and move past the emotions. Come up with the best possible resources to drive your business to success.

The five elements are as follows:

1. People: Are we really tapping into everyone's talents and skills?
2. Capital (costs): Are we getting the best rate possible for the money we've borrowed?
3. Tools: Is our equipment working for us or against us?
4. Technology: Is our technology up-to-date or obsolete?
5. Industry best practices: What have we learned and what have other companies learned that we can study?

What are you looking for?

- Process improvement
- Cost-cutting opportunities
- Morale improvement

- Revenue growth
- More networking opportunities
- Free press
- New strategic alliance partners
- Fresh, new ideas
- Sales growth
- Better budgeting practices
- Hidden talents
- Leaders
- Experts
- New technology

Funding Future Growth

How will you fund the future growth of your business? Will it come from sales or should you start considering outside financing? If you land a sizeable contract, how will you finance the parts, equipment, additional personnel, travel, professional fees, etc.? If this happens, would it be possible to finance the actual contract, for example, guaranteed income that the bank will take a close look at? Have you looked into receivable financing or factoring?

In the previous chapter, we discussed at length many of the financing options available to small businesses. This topic deserves a brief review as you turn your thoughts to building your business.

Asset-based Financing

Asset-based lending is a type of business financing or alternative financing where your business assets are used as collateral to secure capital or to develop cash flow. Asset-based lending is a straightforward concept matching a company's assets to its borrowing needs. Unlike traditional bank debt that relies heavily on balance sheet ratios and cash flow projections as loan criteria, asset-based lending uses a client's business assets as its primary focus for lending. The result is usually far greater borrowing power than what can be achieved from a traditional cash flow banking approach.

Other examples of collateral are inventory, including marketable raw materials, machinery and equipment, owner-occupied real estate, and personal assets.

Asset-based lending is advantageous if you are looking for quick financing decisions, less red tape, and fewer borrowing restrictions.

Asset-based lending improves your cash flow and funds business growth. It is a proven cash flow solution and an alternative business financing technique. Asset-based lending can be used when a company has negative cash flow or is over-leveraged, and asset-based lending is flexible and cost-competitive.

Asset-based lending is beneficial to manufacturers, wholesalers, distributors, and service companies. It is increasingly used in the agricultural industry and in health care financing.

An important aspect of asset-based lending is that prospective borrowers do not always have to be profitable or have a minimum net worth. A business with tangible assets and a qualified management team can use its assets to create additional working capital to help carry out its business plans.

Accounts Receivable Factoring

Factoring, also known as accounts receivable factoring and factoring accounts receivable, is the sale of invoices for immediate cash. Factoring frees up your money locked up in accounts receivable, unpaid customer invoices, for long periods of time. With accounts receivable factoring you can turn unpaid invoices into immediate cash to pay bills, improve cash flow, expand your business, pay off debt, and take advantage of new opportunities.

Factoring provides a business with debt-free cash if it has invoices for delivered services or products to commercial businesses or federal, state, and local government. Factoring accounts receivable is already earned income (you have performed a service or delivered a product), so there is no debt associated with it. Accounts receivable factoring is a cash flow solution that does not require borrowing or giving up ownership in your business.

Typically, an accounts receivable factoring company makes cash available to you from 65 to 90 percent of the face value of your invoices. The factoring company pays the balance, less a service fee, to you when your customer, the one who receives the invoice, pays the invoice in full. In the meantime, you have a large portion of your money to use as you see fit. The factoring company then waits to be paid instead of you. Although accounts receivable factoring is a respected financing tool that has been around for decades and is used by small and large businesses, *it is not for every business*. It may not be suited for a business that is not growing or for a business with timely and prompt invoice payments. If you commonly experience lag time between rendering services and receiving invoice payments, factoring may be a worthwhile option to consider.

Factoring is beneficial to growing companies, enabling them to continue to grow and expand. It is a ready source for cash for businesses too new to have, or growing too fast for adequate traditional financing, such as bank loans.

Government Factoring

A factoring company can assist your business with the unique challenges that typically arise when factoring U.S. government receivables and negotiating the Federal Government Assignment of Claims Act. Seek out a factoring company that has experience dealing with the special assignment provisions that pertain to government factoring. They should understand your government contract cash flow problems. Large contracts can use up all your operating capital and are not collected for thirty to ninety days, if not longer. This can cause cash flow shortages that affect weekly payroll and fixed overhead expenses. Government factoring allows you to leverage government receivables and turn them into immediate cash to pursue additional contracts.

Advantages of Factoring

- Quick cash: Usually within twenty-four to forty-eight hours
- Frees up cash tied up in accounts receivable and eliminates waiting thirty to ninety days or more for invoice payments
- Your credit history is not important for factoring, no financial statements are required, and there are no long-term contracts to sign
- Can provide a continuous source of cash as your business grows
- No debt creation as factoring is a sale of invoices, not a loan
- Improves cash flow to meet payroll, pay taxes, pay vendors, and fund business growth
- Convenient and flexible: Start, stop, or continue factoring as needed and you are always in control

If you are a government contractor or subcontractor seeking government factoring or a company seeking factoring/debt factoring, contact several competent factoring companies and let them show you how to maximize the value of your company's unpaid invoices/accounts receivables by turning them into cash today. Remember, they do charge you a fee. It can vary greatly between companies so make sure you take the time to research and interview several factoring companies before making the decision to factor your receivables. This is to assure that it is in the best interest of you and your company.

CHAPTER 16

Other Considerations and Helpful Hints

Developing a Center of Influence

In order to jump-start your business, try to focus on whom you know. Next, focus on whom others may know and how they may be helpful in raising capital, creating sales, and introducing you to key suppliers and vendors. These people will be your Centers of Influence; they can provide referrals for you, give you some advice on your products or service offerings, introduce you to key players in your market, and even purchase from you.

Selling is a key element of running a business. Although there are many aspects of running a successful enterprise, nothing else happens if you don't sell something. The argument could be made that if you go out and raise capital for your venture, you have money in the bank to build the rest of the enterprise and selling is then only necessary to build the business down the road. True, but how did you get the money from the investor, bank, or your rich uncle Bill? You had to *sell* them on the idea that there really is an opportunity out there and you are just the one to make a business venture work. You must sell the concept of your venture to your Centers of Influence, and they in turn can assist you, the entrepreneur, in building your business.

Let's take a few minutes and discuss the Centers of Influence in your life. Keep in mind that your Centers of Influence can be family members; business colleagues; former students and professors; local politicians; members of your church, synagogue, mosque, or other place of worship; neighbors; etc. Your job is to identify who they are and how they can help you obtain business. After all, word-of-mouth advertising is the most powerful—not to mention the cheapest—form of getting the word out and also establishing credibility.

Example of What a Center of Influence Can Do for You

When setting out to build an IT consulting enterprise, Brian realized fairly quickly that his target market, information technology (IT) managers in large corporations, wanted to deal with name brand companies. They felt comfortable buying products and services from well-established, well-known companies for one primary reason—a bad decision that ends up costing the company a lot of money could cost the IT manager his job. These IT managers needed assurance that the solutions they were acquiring from a third-party vendor would really work and work as well or better than what they could get elsewhere.

In the beginning, Brian's business was not a well-known name in the industry and he had a very difficult time getting folks to sit down with him and listen to what he had to offer. He developed a plan to begin working with the vendors that were already calling on these same IT Managers. These vendors would become strategic alliance partners (SAPs) to help open a few more doors that had previously been closed to anyone outside of the *good ole boy network*.

Presentations were made to the managers and salespeople of several well-known companies in the IT industry. The word started getting out among IT analysts that there was a real player in town who could assist on IT projects. The key was to call on well-known hardware and software vendors that had nothing to do with IT consulting. Brian did not want to appear as a threat to these SAPs, rather as a solid choice to enhance their current relationship with their customers and make them look good. By bringing someone from the outside that did well on the projects assigned, the vendors would be perceived as companies looking out for their customers.

The plan worked and soon a small Center of Influence developed. This center of influence opened up a few key doors in the beginning. As time went on, the first year in business developed a few key relationships that turned into over $600,000 in sales. The next year turned into over $5 million in sales, and the business kept growing.

Who are your Centers of Influence?
Let's list a few of the Centers of Influence that you can think of:

Business associates

_____

_____

Angel investors

_____

_____

Venture capital firms

_____

_____

Bankers

_____

_____

Chamber of commerce executives

_____

_____

Church members

_____

_____

Family members

_____

_____

Uncles, aunts, cousins, second cousins

_____

_____

Parents of your kids' friends

_____

_____

Local business owners

_____

_____

College professors

_____

_____

Your doctors

_____

_____

Other doctors

_____

_____

Local radio talk show hosts

_____

_____

Local newspaper reporters

_____

_____

Local television reporters

_____

_____

Your CPA

_____

_____

Other CPAs

_____

_____

Your attorney

_____

_____

Other attorneys

_____

_____

Associations catering to your market

_____

Your printer

_____

Your local PTA president

_____

Your local principal

_____

Local politicians

_____

Your barber, hairdresser, or beautician

_____

_____

Once you have gone through this exercise, it should spark a few ideas of people you can contact to assist you with launching or growing your business. This list is not a complete list unless you add additional names from areas in your life that are not listed here. Remember, the best way to get business is to work with people who know and trust you, or someone who can recommend you and your services.

Brainstorming for New Ideas

Brainstorming is an incredible tool that all executives should engage in with their team on a regular basis. In just a few short minutes, you can literally create new ideas that will move your company to the next level of success or even start a new industry.

Brainstorming is the name given to a process where individuals meet as a group to generate new ideas around a specific area of interest. Using rules that remove inhibitions, people are able to think more freely and move into new areas of thought, thereby creating numerous new ideas and solutions.

In traditional brainstorming, the participants call out ideas as they occur to them and then build on the ideas raised by others. All the ideas are noted down and none are criticized. Only when the brainstorming session is over are the ideas evaluated.

The aim is to provide you with the methods of traditional brainstorming and then to move on to the next level and introduce a series of advanced techniques.

- Brainstorming is a tried-and-tested process for generating new ideas.

- Brainstorming is a technique by which a group attempts to find a solution for a specific problem by amassing all the ideas offered spontaneously by its members.
- Brainstorming sparks and encourages new ideas that might never have surfaced under normal circumstances.
- Brainstorming is a fun way to unlock all those exciting ideas that a group may have buried in their minds but are too busy to think about.
- Brainstorming requires surprisingly little effort to generate some great ideas.

Exactly what you apply brainstorming techniques to depends on what you want to achieve. You can brainstorm to develop new products and services or to rethink how you approach certain processes within the company. Naturally, there are techniques and environments that suit certain people better than others, but brainstorming is flexible enough to be able to suit everyone.

Whether you brainstorm with a group of excited colleagues or by yourself will be up to your personal preference and circumstance. Both will be successful if you read and follow the process described below.

The history and use of brainstorming started in 1941. Alex Osborn, an advertising executive, found that conventional business meetings were inhibiting the creation of new ideas and proposed some rules designed to help stimulate creative thinking. He was looking for rules that would give people the freedom of mind and action to generate and reveal new ideas. To "think up" was the original term he used to describe the process he developed and that, in turn, came to be known as "brainstorming." The four rules he came up with are:

1. No criticism of ideas
2. Go for large quantities of ideas
3. Build on each other's ideas
4. Encourage wild and exaggerated ideas

Osborn found that when these rules were followed, a lot more ideas were created and that a greater quantity of original ideas gave rise to a greater quantity of useful ideas. Quantity produced quality.

These new rules reduced people's natural inhibitions that previously had prevented them from putting forward ideas that they felt might be considered "wrong" or "stupid." Osborn also found that generating "silly" ideas could spark very useful ideas because they changed the way people thought.

Rules of Brainstorming

Rule 1: Postpone and withhold your judgment of ideas.

Do not pass judgment on ideas until the completion of the brainstorming session. Do not suggest that an idea won't work or that it has negative side effects. All ideas are potentially good, so don't judge them until afterward. At this stage, avoid discussing the ideas at all, as this will inevitably involve either criticizing or complimenting them.

Rule 2: Encourage wild and exaggerated ideas.

It is much easier to tame a wild idea than it is to think of an immediately valid one in the first place. During a brainstorming session, the wilder the idea the better. Shout out bizarre and unworkable ideas to see what other ideas they spark. No idea is too ridiculous. State any outlandish ideas. Exaggerate ideas to the extreme. Use creative thinking techniques and tools to start your thinking from a fresh direction.

Rule 3: Quantity counts at this stage, not quality.

Go for quantity of ideas at this point and narrow down the list later. All activities should be geared toward extracting as many ideas as possible in a given period. The more creative ideas a person or a group has to choose from the better. If the number of ideas at the end of the session is very large, there is a greater chance of finding a really good idea.

Keep each idea short and do not describe it in detail. The key is to capture its essence. Brief clarifications can be requested. Remember to think fast and reflect later.

Rule 4: Build on the ideas put forward by others.

Build and expand on the ideas of others. Try to add extra thoughts to each idea. Use other people's ideas as inspiration for your own. Combine several of the suggested ideas to explore new possibilities.

It's just as valuable to be able to adapt and improve other people's ideas as it is to generate the initial idea that sets off new trains of thought.

Rule 5: Every person and every idea has equal worth.

Every person has a valid viewpoint and a unique perspective on the situation and solution. In a brainstorming session, you can always put forward ideas purely to get other people thinking. Encourage everyone to participate, even if they feel they need to write their ideas on a piece of paper and pass them around.

You will know that you have created a healthy brainstorming environment if everyone feels comfortable contributing. Don't hold back! Give it a go, and see how surprisingly effective a good brainstorming session can become in producing effective, even profitable results. Good luck!

Patents, Copyrights, Trademarks, and Secret Formulas

There are countless stories about multimillion dollar companies whose origination was based on a Ralph Waldo Emerson notion: "Build a better mousetrap and the world will come knocking at your door." Emerson's quotation was never more true than it is today in the world of high technology and expanding markets. Companies from far and wide are being developed on a worldwide basis to produce and distribute products that were never even dreamed of just ten years ago.

If you are a start-up business or even an established business that has new products, ideas, or technology that will improve someone's standard of living, and want to place your product on the market, your products should be patented or trademarked and all your written material should be copyrighted.

There are various types of patents—utility, design, and plant. There are also two types of utility and plant patent applications—provisional and nonprovisional. Each year the United States Patent and Trademark Office (USPTO) receives approximately 350,000 patent applications. Most of these are for nonprovisional utility patents.

Provisional Patents—Since June 8, 1995, the USPTO has offered inventors the option of filing a provisional application for patent, which was designed to provide a lower-cost first patent filing in the United States. Applicants are entitled to claim the benefit of a provisional application in a corresponding nonprovisional application filed not later than twelve months after the provisional application filing date. Under the provisions of 35U.S.C. § 119(e).

Nonprovisional or Utility Patents—A nonprovisional utility patent application must be in the English language, or be accompanied by a translation in the English language, a statement that the translation is accurate, and a fee as set forth in 37 CFR §1.17(i).

Utility Patents—In general terms, a "utility patent" protects the way an article is used and works (35 U.S.C. 101), while a "design patent" protects the way an article looks (35 U.S.C. 171).

Design Patents—A design consists of the visual ornate characteristics embodied in, or applied to, an article of manufacture. The USPTO further states that "since a design is manifested in appearance, the subject matter of a design patent application may relate to the configuration or shape of an article, to the surface ornamentation applied to an article, or to the combination of configuration and surface ornamentation. A design for surface ornamentation is inseparable from the article to which it is applied and cannot exist alone. It must be a definite pattern of surface ornamentation, applied to an article of manufacture."

The United States Patent and Trademark Office examines applications and grants patents on inventions when applicants are entitled to them. The patent law provides for the granting of design patents to any person who has invented any new, original, and ornamental design for an article of manufacture. A design patent protects only the appearance of the article and not structural or utilitarian features.

Plant Patents—A plant patent is granted by the government to an inventor (or the inventor's heirs or assigns) who has invented or discovered and asexually reproduced a distinct and new variety of plant, other than a tuber propagated plant or a plant found in an uncultivated state. The grant, which lasts for twenty years from the date of filing the application, protects the inventor's right to exclude others from asexually reproducing, selling, or using the plant to reproduce. This protection is limited to a plant in its ordinary meaning:

- A living plant organism that expresses a set of characteristics determined by its single, genetic makeup or genotype, which can be duplicated through asexual reproduction, but which can not otherwise be "made" or "manufactured."

- Sports, mutants, hybrids, and transformed plants are comprehended; sports or mutants may be spontaneous or induced. Hybrids may be natural, from a planned breeding program, or somatic in source. While natural plant mutants might have naturally occurred, they must have been discovered in a cultivated area.

- Algae and macro fungi are regarded as plants, but bacteria are not.

For more information regarding different patent types, please visit the United States Patent and Trademark Office website at www.uspto.gov/web/patents/types.htm

Government Contracts

Many new businesses have been established just to handle government contracts. If you are establishing a new business to handle government contracts or if you are already established and handling government contracts, this should be totally revealed in your business plan.

There are many advantages and disadvantages to this. You must use your own knowledge and expertise to determine these factors. Obtaining a contract is not easy. Yet the government spends hundreds of billions of dollars annually on just about everything you can think of. Government contracts are a very lucrative source of business.

The specifics of your business and your experience will determine whether you are capable of handling a government contract. You must bid for a government contract, and if you are successful, this business could mean your ultimate success.

On the other hand, many government contracts are subject to cancellation or withdrawal, in which case you may have spent many thousands of dollars that cannot be recovered. All contracts carry a "save or hold harmless" clause. So beware!

SECTION 4

Knowledge Building for Preparing Your Winning Business Plan

CHAPTER 17

Financial Ratios, Glossary, and Chart of Accounts

This chapter has been created to help you in the writing and preparing of your winning business plan. Our years of experiences has shown us that for many business owners and first time entrepreneurs, their knowledge and understanding of accounting, accounting terms, and financial ratios is usually limited. We felt that this information would be helpful to you even though it will not make you an accounting wizard.

As it takes four years to earn an accounting or finance degree, we would not be able to teach you these skills in a few pages, nor should you expect to learn them in such a short period of time. Rather, this information will provide you with some of the basics so when you are discussing business issues with consultants, business leaders, investors, lenders, etc., you will have a basic knowledge foundation to assist you.

Remember, outside consultants, especially experienced degreed accountants, will be able to assist you in preparing the financial section of your business plan as well as explaining it to you so you will fully understand what has been incorporated into it. Also, you may want to look at taking accounting classes at a local college, attending accounting seminars and workshops, and buying self-study books on accounting. As previously discussed, it is imperative to know your financial situation and financial information inside and out before presenting your business plan to potential investors and lenders.

Financial Ratios

Financial ratios are used to show what condition the business is in. They assist in determining the actual meaning of financial statements and are especially accurate for comparing similar businesses. Financial ratios are a combination of dividing, adding, and multiplying one entry of the financial statement by another.

There are four major categories of financial ratios:

1. Solvency Ratios, which describe your ability to pay debts.
2. Profitability Ratios, which measure relative profitability.
3. Efficiency Ratios, which measure how efficiently funds are used.
4. Leverage Ratios, which measure the indebtedness of the business (i.e., how much debt the business is carrying).

Whenever you are looking to raise capital, borrow money, lease equipment, or establish a line of credit, potential financial sources will use a variety of financial ratios to judge the condition of your business. Here are a few of the possible ratios they may use in their judgment.

Solvency Ratios

Quick Ratio. Cash plus accounts receivable divided by current liabilities. The larger the number, the better the protection to short-term creditors. A ratio of 1.0 or better is taken as a statement that the business is in a "liquid" condition.

Current Ratio. Current assets divided by current liabilities. The larger the number, the better the margin of safety for covering current liabilities. A ratio of 2.0 or better is considered good.

Current Liabilities to Net Worth (%). Current liabilities divided by net worth times 100. The lower the %, the better the protection to investors and creditors. As a rough guide, anything less than 66% is considered reasonable.

Total Liabilities to Net Worth (%). Total liabilities divided by net worth times 100. The lower the %, the better the protection to creditors. As a rough guide, anything over 100% is a red flag to creditors and investors.

Fixed Assets to Net Worth (%). Fixed assets divided by net worth times 100. This ratio varies significantly from industry to industry. The lower the %, the better the use of capital.

Profitability Ratios

Return on Sales (profit margin) (%). Net profit (after taxes) divided by net sales times 100. The higher the %, the better.

Return on Total Assets (%). Net profit (after taxes) divided by total assets times 100. The higher the better. Indicates the efficiency of the use of assets employed.

Return on Equity (net worth) (%). Net profit (after taxes) divided by net worth times 100. This is one of the most quoted ratios. It measures the management's ability to make a good return for the net worth of the business.

Return on Investment (%). Net profit (after taxes) divided by the invested capital times 100. This is another popular ratio, indicating management's ability to make satisfactory profit on invested capital.

Efficiency Ratios

Collection Period (days). Accounts receivable divided by annual sales and multiplied by 365. Extremely low or high numbers are problematic. In theory the lower the number of days the better, but too low a number may lead to lost sales due to credit problems.

Net Sales to Inventory (inventory turns). Annual sales divided by inventory. In theory the higher the better. A low number may indicate too much inventory on hand. An excessively high number may indicate sales are being lost due to too little inventory on hand.

Net Sales to Working Capital. Annual net sales divided by working capital. This measures the efficiency of management's use of working capital. The higher the number the better.

Cost of Sales to Inventory. Annual cost of sales divided by inventory. This is very similar in concept to inventory turns. The only difference is that it uses the more accurate cost-of-sales figure.

Accounts Payable to Sales (%). Accounts payable divided by annual sales times 100. A low % may mean the business is not getting good terms from its suppliers. An excessively high % may indicate a problem in paying suppliers.

Cost of Sales to Accounts Payable. Annual cost of sales divided by accounts payable. An excessively low ratio may indicate a problem in paying suppliers. An excessively high ratio may mean that management is not getting good terms from its suppliers.

Leverage Ratios

Fixed Assets to Net Worth. Fixed assets divided by net worth. The lower the number, the better for creditors; however, a low number may also indicate an inefficient or obsolete facility.

Debt to Net Worth. Total liabilities divided by net worth. The higher the number, the greater the risk to creditors.

Glossary

Accounts Payable. The monies owed to suppliers of goods and services to the business.

Accounts Receivable. The monies that are owed the business from the sales of goods and services.

Accrual Basis Accounting. The accounting method that is used by larger businesses. It records the sale, expense, or other event when it actually occurs, rather than when the cash changes hands. It is not the actual receipt of payment that is important but the "right" to receive it. The sales or costs are said to be "accrued."

Administrative Expense. Such expenses as salaries, stationery, printing, office supplies, telephone, depreciation of office equipment, and rent.

Amortization. The gradual payment of a debt through a schedule of payments or the process of writing off an intangible asset against expenses over the period of its economic useful life.

Back-End Selling. Selling additional products and services to existing customers that have previously purchased from you at an earlier date.

Backward Integration. Where a company owns or controls the suppliers of goods or services to its primary operation.

Bad Debt. Debts to the business that are either uncollectible or likely to be uncollectible.

Balance Sheet. Describes the assets, liabilities, and net worth of the company on some fixed day.

Board of Directors. A group of individuals elected by stockholders, who, as a body, manage the corporation.

Bookkeeping. See *Single-Entry Bookkeeping, Double-Entry Bookkeeping.*

Break-Even Analysis. The method of determining the exact point at which the business makes neither a loss nor a profit. It is usually calculated as a point where sales have grown at a greater rate than costs and the two lines cross.

Budgeting. The planning and coordination of the various operations and functions of a business to attain, over a specific period of time, and the control of variations from the approved plan to achieve the desired results.

Business Plan. A written document that describes the business, its objectives, strategies, operating plans, business environment, and marketing strategies, together with a financial forecast. It is the road map for managing the business.

Business Receipts. Sales and/or receipts from the operations of the business.

Capital. The general term for monies invested in the business.

Capital Plan or Capital Budget. A plan that describes the purchase of capital items such as equipment, buildings, and plant.

Cash Basis Accounting. An accounting system where the sale or expense is recorded only when the transfer of cash occurs. It is primarily used by small businesses that operate with cash.

Cash Flow, Cash Projection. The systematic charting of the sources and uses of cash in a business.

Collateral. Personal or business assets that a borrower assigns to the lender to help ensure debt payment. If the loan is in default, then the lender may assume possession of the asset.

Company Thrust. Describes the overall direction of the company.

Convertible Loan. A loan to the business whereby the lender has the option of either repayment of the loan or taking part ownership of the business at some future date.

Corporation. An organization formed under a state statute for the purpose of carrying on an enterprise in such a way as to make the enterprise distinct and separate from the persons who are interested in it.

Cost of Goods and Services. Also known as variable cost. Cost directly associated with making or providing the goods or services. These usually include raw material costs, certain utility costs, labor, and variable overhead.

Critical Issues. Issues that are currently unresolved or unpredictable or outside your control that could affect the performance of business.

Current Assets. Cash and property in your possession that can be liquidated quickly in a short period of time.

Current Liabilities. Debts that must be met within a relatively short time, such as short-term loans, accounts payable, and accrued taxes.

Customer Profile. Is the description of the customer, including type, characteristics, and habits (see also *Demographics*).

Cyclical. Is the rise and fall of the business in some relationship to the economic ups and downs.

Debt Financing. The use of borrowed money to finance a business. The loan is repaid and the lender does not receive part ownership of the business.

Demographics. Profiling the customers by age, sex, family size, income, occupation, education, religion, culture, social class, etc.

Depreciation. Is the process of expensing the decrease in value of a fixed asset over its' useful life.

Direct Labor. Labor costs directly associated with production or contract work.

Double-Entry Bookkeeping. A bookkeeping method where transactions are first entered in a journal or log, then posted to ledger accounts to show income, expenses, assets, liabilities, and net worth. In the double-entry system, each account has a left side for debits and a right side for credits.

Equity. The value of the assets minus the liabilities for the business. Also known as net worth.

Equity Financing. A method of securing monies from an investor in which the investor becomes part owner of the business for the investment.

Exit. The ability of an investor to exit a venture by turning his investment and profit into cash or other easily traded instrument.

Expenses. See *Operating Expenses.*

Exporting. Selling products and services outside a company's general geographical area. Usually associated with the conduct of overseas trade through several types of well-established channels for foreign distribution.

Fiscal Year. The definition of the year for a company for financial, accounting, planning, and tax purposes. Usually twelve calendar months.

Financial Reports. Reports that show the financial status of a company at a given time.

Financial Statement A written presentation of financial data prepared from the accounting records. The usual financial statements include a balance sheet, income statement (or profit and loss statement), and cash flow statement.

First In, First Out (FIFO). A method of valuing an inventory of merchandise. This method assumes that the goods first acquired are the goods first sold, in typical grocery store style. It is the method in most common use, largely because it conforms most nearly to the physical flow of the inventory.

Fixed Asset. Equipment, plant, buildings, machinery that are not sold in the normal course of business.

Fixed Expenses, Fixed Costs. Those business costs that essentially do not vary when sales volume changes.

Forecasting. The calculation of all reasonable probabilities about the business future.

Forward Integration. Where a company owns or controls the marketing or distribution of its products or services.

Franchise. A business that is contractually bound to operate on another company's concept and operating principles.

General and Administrative Expenses. Expenses that are directly associated with the management of the business and not with either making or selling the product or service.

Geographic Market Factors. Geographic service area of the business and the different natural clusters of population.

Goals. See *Objectives.*

Goodwill. An intangible asset related to the customers' positive attitude or perception of the business. It often includes a complete listing of customers.

Horizontal Integration. Where a company owns or controls many like businesses in the same industry.

Importing. Buying products and services from individuals or companies outside the general geographical area of a business. Usually associated with buying from overseas.

Income Statement. A standard accounting method for determining the profit and loss of a business over some time period. Usually yearly, quarterly, or monthly.

Incorporation. The act of forming a corporation.

Industry Life Cycle. The almost universal cycle of events that virtually every industry undergoes from embryonic, through growth, maturity, and finally slow retrenchment.

Inside Sales Force. Those personnel who are in direct contact with customers but who do not leave their place of work in the performance of their duties.

Intangible Asset Assets that are associated with goodwill, trademarks, patents, copyrights, formulas, franchises, brands, customer lists, and mailing lists.

Interest. The amount paid on borrowed money.

Interim Financing. Acquisition of funds for a short term when it is planned that by the end of that period, necessary financing for a longer term will be provided.

Inventory. Items that have been produced or purchased and will ultimately be sold. May include raw material inventory, work in progress inventory, and finished goods inventory.

Inventory Financing. (1) The process of obtaining needed capital for a business by borrowing money with inventory used as collateral or (2) as in the case of a trade acceptance, a method used for financing the purchase of inventories.

Joint Venture. Partnership (often short term) between two or more businesses to accomplish some task or business.

Last In, First Out (LIFO). A method of valuing an inventory of merchandise. This method is the inverse of the first-in-first-out method and assumes that the units sold are those most recently acquired and that the units on hand are those first acquired.

Leverage. The use of credit/borrowing to increase the ability to buy a business or conduct business. Highly leveraged means a business that has a high debt level.

Line of Credit. An advance commitment by a bank to lend up to the amount indicated. Business people who anticipate the financing of current operations by bank loans usually ask their banks for a line of credit in order that they may know in advance how much they can borrow at a particular bank, without collateral, should the need arise.

Liquidity. The degree of cash that can be generated in a short time from the sale of assets.

Management Consultant. A specialist outside a business who advises the business on management matters. Professional consultants have three basic advantages over company officers and employees:

1. They bring in a point of view attained by experience with many enterprises; they can see things in proper perspective.

2. Their approach to problems is generally impartial, but it is advisable for management, when retaining a consultant, to emphasize that a predetermined result is not being sought.

3. Since such investigations are the consultants' operations, efforts are more concentrated on your investigation.

Market. A clearly defined group of people, area, or group of things that can be classified together as having some common need or other common trait.

Market Analysis. Process of determining the characteristics of the market and the measurement of its capacity to buy a commodity. It investigates the potential market for an industry.

Marketing. The act of identifying, satisfying the needs of, selling to, and servicing customers.

Marketing Mix. The array of marketing methods used to sell customers.

Marketing Plan. The combination of market analysis and marketing strategies that defines who your competitors and customers are and how you will promote your business to successfully get customers to buy from you.

Market Research. The act of discovering information about a particular market. The information typically relates to the type of customers in that market, their buying habits, unfilled needs, product or service information, plus many other factors.

Market Segments. The logical breakdown and grouping of customers or customer needs or products.

Market Share. The sales of your business divided by the total sales of your industry for either your local market or the national or international market. Usually expressed as a percentage.

Net Income. See *Net Profit.*

Net Profit After Taxes. Net profit before taxes less federal, state, or local income, or franchise taxes.

Net Profit Before Taxes. Net sales or total receipts less all cost and expense items and before federal, state, or local income, or franchise taxes.

Net Sales. Total sales less discounts, returned goods, and freight costs.

Net Worth. The value of the assets minus the liabilities for the business.

Net Worth of a Customer. A calculated formula used to indicate the dollar value of a customer's patronage every time he or she buys from you. (Total number of purchases divided by twelve.) This formula is used to calculate monthly advertising and marketing expenditures.

Notes Payable. An account in the general ledger showing the liability for promissory notes incurred by the business.

Notes Receivable. An account in the ledger showing the amount of negotiable promissory notes received (1) from customers in payment for goods sold and delivered, and (2) from other debtors.

Operating Expenses. Those expenses of the business that are not directly associated with the making or providing of the goods or services. They usually include administrative, technical, and selling expenses.

Operating Statement See *Income Statement.*

Operational Plan. The detailed action plan you will take to implement the strategies and to reach desired goals. It usually covers the near-term action items, up to one, two, or three years in the future.

Outside Sales Force. Personnel who perform their selling function and meet with customers either at the customer's location or outside the salesperson's business office.

Partnership. The Uniform Partnership Act defines the arrangement as an "association of two or more persons to carry on as co-owners of a business for profit."

Patent. An exclusive right granted by the federal government to make, use, and sell an invention for a fixed period of time.

Preferred Stock. Stock that is given a preference over other forms of stock within the same corporation primarily with respect to dividend payments.

Product Mix. The grouping of products into categories so that the change in their relative amounts can be compared.

Profit. See *Net Profit.*

Profit and Loss Statement. See *Income Statement.*

Pro Forma. A projection of future (often financial) activity.

Projected Financials. An estimation of future financial earnings and expenses.

Proprietorship, Sole. An individual owner of a business who has not incorporated or does not have a recognized partner. The owner is liable for all the debts of the business to the full extent of his or her property.

Public Offering. When a business goes into the financial market to secure capital financing by offering shares or stock in the company to the public.

Quick Ratio. Cash plus accounts receivable divided by current liabilities.

Receivable. See *Accounts Receivable*.

Reorganization. A process involving a recasting of corporate capital structure, which the corporation may be compelled to undergo because of either imminent or immediate insolvency.

Retained Earnings. Net profit after taxes that is retained in the business as working capital and not paid out as dividends to stockholders.

Return on Equity. Profit on the total equity in the company.

Return on Gross Operating Assets (RGOA). Profit on the total assets used in the business.

Return on Investment (ROI). Profit on the invested capital.

Return on Sales. Profit on net sales.

Revenues. Used interchangeably with sales. Often used for businesses that do not physically sell something, such as rental companies, contracting businesses.

Seasonality. Annual rise and fall of the business according to seasonal demand variances.

Securities and Exchange Commission (SEC). Government body that is chartered to maintain order and rules of the stock and securities exchanges.

Selling Expenses. Expenses incurred in selling or distributing a product or service.

Single-Entry Bookkeeping. A simple system of recording business transactions where single entries are made into a daily, weekly, or monthly journal.

Small Business Administration (SBA). An independent agency of the Federal Government, under the general direction and supervision of the president. The SBA is authorized to furnish credit either as a maker of a direct loan or as a guarantor in part of a loan made by a bank to a business.

Strategic Role. A term used by larger, more mature businesses that identifies the type of business, its charter, and operating boundaries.

Strategic Opportunity. An opportunity or goal that will change the basic thrust or strategies of the business.

Strategy. The basic method used to reach the goal.

Tactical Plan. See *Operational Plan*.

Taxes. A "four-letter" word that most people hate, others become nauseated when it is spoken, and still others downright detest.

Trade Receivables. See *Accounts Receivable*.

Trade Payables. See *Accounts Payable*.

Unemployment Insurance. A Federal-State system that provides temporary income for workers when they are unemployed due to circumstances beyond their control.

Unique Selling Advantage (USA). The essential appeal a business owner develops to share with staff members and customers. It is all the unique reasons why customers should buy from your company, all stated in one crisp, easy-to-understand paragraph.

Unsecured Loan. A loan made with no actual collateral or security posted to guarantee payment of the loan.

Variable Cost. Costs that vary directly with sales. These include raw material costs, certain utility costs, labor, and sales commissions.

Variances. An accounting term for the difference between what was forecast and what actually happened.

Venture Capital. A pool of investment dollars made by private investors who provide counsel designed to enhance the investment, and who usually will require controlling or a major interest in the company.

Vertical Disintegration. The breakings up of manufacturing and supply operations into discrete smaller units that are completely separate entities, often independently owned.

Working Capital. Current assets less current liabilities.

Sample Chart of Accounts

BALANCE SHEET ACCOUNTS:
Current Assets:
Checking Cash
Savings Cash
Payroll Checking
Petty Cash
Accounts Receivable
Allowance for Bad Debts
Inventory
Prepaid Insurance
Prepaid Taxes
Loans and Exchanges
Other Prepaid Expenses

Property and Equipment:
Land
Building
Accumulated Depreciation—Building
Building Improvements
Accumulated Depreciation—Building Improvements
Leasehold Improvements
Accumulated Depreciation— Leasehold Improvements
Machinery and Equipment
Accumulated Depreciation—Machinery and Equipment
Furniture and Fixtures
Accumulated Depreciation—Furniture and Fixtures

Office Equipment
Accumulated Depreciation—Office Equipment
Vehicles
Accumulated Depreciation—Vehicles
Other Fixed Assets
Accumulated Depreciation—Other Fixed Assets

Other Assets:
Officers' Loan Receivable
Utility Deposits
Goodwill
Accumulated Amortization—Goodwill
Organization Costs
Accumulated Amortization—Organization Costs

Current Liabilities:
Accounts Payable
Employee Health Insurance Payable
Sales Taxes Payable
Federal W/H Tax Payable
FICA W/H Taxes Payable
State W/H Taxes Payable
Local W/H Taxes Payable
Accrued Interest
Accrued Salaries/Bonuses
Other Accrued Expenses
Notes Payable—current portion
Current Portion of Long-Term Debt

Long-Term Liabilities:
Long-Term Debt
Note Payable Officer
Note Payable—Long Term Equity

Equity:
For a Corporation:
  Common Stock
    Additional Paid-in Capital
    Retained Earnings

For a Partnership:
  Partner's Capital #1
  Partner's Capital #2
  Partner's Drawing #1
  Partner's Drawing #2
For a Sole Proprietor:
  Capital
  Drawing Sales

PROFIT AND LOSS ACCOUNTS:

Sales:
Sales
Sales Discounts
Sales Returns and Allowance

Cost of Goods Sold:
Cost of Materials
Cost of Labor
Purchase Discounts
Purchase Returns and Allowance

Selling Expenses:
Salaries
Bonuses
Taxes Payroll—Sales
Auto Expense
Commissions
Advertising + Promotion
Travel
Entertainment
Miscellaneous Expenses—Sales

General and Administrative:
Salaries—Office
Salaries—Officers
Bonuses
Taxes—Payroll
Outside Services
Auto Expense
Bank Service Charges

Contributions
Dues and Subscriptions
Insurance—Property and Casualty
Insurance—Medical
Insurance—Other
Interest Expense
Legal and Accounting
Miscellaneous Expense
Office Expense
Postage Expense
Equipment Rental Rent Expense
Utilities
Repairs and Maintenance
Depreciation Expense
Amortization Expense
Supplies Expense
Taxes—Other
Telephone
Travel
Entertainment
Income Taxes
Federal Income Tax
State Income Tax

CHAPTER 18
Helpful Internet Links

This chapter has been created to help you find links to websites that will be useful to you in a number of ways in writing your winning business plan and running and expanding your business. At the time of the writing and publication of this book, these links were active and provided good information.

We hope that you are computer/Internet savvy and know how to navigate around the World Wide Web and find the information you need. If you have avoided buying, using, or going near a computer, your time has come. It is important to know that going into business goes hand in hand with having a computer and being knowledgeable on how to use it along with basic software programs like Microsoft Word and Excel. In addition, having access to the Internet may be very helpful to some and critical to others.

Remember, outside consultants, especially experienced degreed computer professionals, will be able to assist you in getting the hardware and software you need to get started. Also, you may want to look at taking computer classes at a local college, attending computer seminars and workshops, and buying self-study books on computers and the Internet.

Sites	Links	Notes
adforce.com	www.adforce.com	Pay per click marketing
agoa.gov	www.agoa.gov/	African Growth Opportunity Act
allsmallbiz.com	www.allsmallbiz.com	Search Engine
associatioins.com	www.associations.com	Listing of Associations
bcentral.com	www.bcentral.com	Support and tools for small business
bizbuysell.com	http://www.bizbuysell.com/	Buy or sell a business
bizminer.com	http://www.bizminer.com/business-research.asp	Business Research
bizmove.com	http://www.bizmove.com/go11-grants.shtml	Government Grants
bizoffice.com	http://www.bizoffice.com/	Small business resources
bizplanit.com	www.bizplanit.com	Business plan consulting firm
bizwiz.com	www.bizwiz.com	Internet business network
bluestreak.com	www.bluestreak.com	Web marketing engine

Sites	Links	Notes
bringmebiz.com	www.bringmebiz.com	Optimization
business.gov	http://www.business.gov	Official business link to the U.S. Govt
businessweek.com	http://www.businessweek.com/smallbiz/index.html	Magazine
census.gov	http://www.census.gov/statab/	U.S. Census data
cfda.gov	www.cfda.gov/	Database of all Federal Govt programs
clickz.com	http://www.clickz.com/resources/adres/	Internet advertising and marketing resources
cnet.com	www.cnet.com	Business software, equipment, tools, and resources
corporate.com	www.corporate.com	Online incorporation for small business
entrepreneur.com	www.entrepreneur.com	Magazine
entreworld.org	www.entreworld.org	Kauffman Foundation, grants, capital
export.com	www.export.gov	Online trade resources for international exporting
familybusinessmagazine.com	http://library.familybusinessmagazine.com	Magazine
gecapital.com	http://www.ge.com/capital/smallbiz/contactus.html	Capital resources for business
google.com	www.google.com	Search Engine
hoovers.com	www.hoovers.com	Research engine for publicly traded companies
inc.com	www.inc.com	Magazine
infousa.com	www.infousa.com	List reseller
irs.gov	http://www.irs.gov/businesses/small/	The IRS
jackstreet.com	www.jackstreet.com	Streaming media network for emerging e-businesses
junglegroup.com	www.junglegroup.com	Small business consulting
knowthis.com	www.knowthis.com	Marketing virtual library
lacher.com	http://www.lacher.com/toc.htm	Excel spreadsheet templates for business
legalzoom.com	http://www.legalzoom.com/	Save time and money on simple legal issues
lycos.com	http://hotbot.lycos.com/	Search Engine
mep.nist.com	http://www.mep.nist.gov/	Manufacturers Extension
moodys.com	www.moodys.com	Partnership with the Federal Govt
pharmaceutical-business-review.com	http://www.pharmaceutical-business-review.com/	Research site for Pharmaceutical companies
prweb.com	www.prweb.com	Provider of independent business credit ratings and research data

Sites	Links	Notes
quicken.com	www.quicken.com	Financial and accounting software
salesandmarketing. com	http://www.salesandmarketing.com/	Magazine
sba.gov	www.sba.gov	Small Business Administration site
smallbusiness.com	www.smallbusiness.com	How-to basics for small business
smallbusiness.yahoo. com	http://smallbusiness.yahoo.com/index.php	Search engine and small business tools
smartpages.com	www.smartpages.com	Yellow pages listings for businesses
surveysez.com	www.surveysez.com	Register Internet domains
tacticalentrepreneur .com	tacticalentrepreneur.com	Business consulting
tradeshows.com	www.tradeshows.com	Link to trades shows in the U.S. and international sites
tucows.com	www.tucows.com	Software and shareware download site
utah.gov	http://www.utah.gov	State of Utah site
virtualpromote.com	www.virtualpromote.com	Search engine optimization and marketing
wave.net	http://www.wave.net/upg/immigration/sic _index.html	Standard Industrial Classification (SIC) Code site
wsj.com	www.wsj.com	*The Wall Street Journal* online
zdnet.com	www.zdnet.com	Technology site for business software and hardware

SECTION 5

Samples of Winning Business Plans

ABC Consulting & Training

Business Plan

ABC Consulting, LLC
12450 So. 4000 Street
Suite K
Downtown, AZ 84020
Telephone: (602) 555-3333
Fax: (602) 555-4444

Prepared by:
Bill Moss and Bob Jones

August 2005

PROPRIETARY AND CONFIDENTIAL

This is a business plan for evaluation purposes and is not an offering of securities.

Published by
ABC Consulting, LLC
Statement of Confidentiality

The information in this business plan is confidential and proprietary. It has been made available
to you solely for consideration and evaluation of this information. In no event shall all or any
portion of this Business Plan be disclosed or disseminated without the express written permission
of ABC Consulting.

© 2005 ABC Consulting, LLC. All Rights Reserved

Table of Contents

1.0 Executive Summary

ABC Consulting is a strategic planning tools, training, and consulting company specializing in strategic planning training, business plans, online Web-based training, small business productivity kits, and business consulting.

The company is in its second round of funding to fund growth and to roll out new products that have been developed. The products that have been developed are in high demand, and the company is currently marketing and selling strategic planning workshops, seminars, consulting services, and business assessment products. The additional funding will allow **ABC Consulting** to fund the growth of the company as well as new product development for online training, small business products for an infomercial, and expansion of our consulting practices.

Success in today's business environment requires that business leaders have the ability to create a vision of the organization's future *direction* as well as the *course* it needs to take to get there. **ABC Consulting** provides client companies with the tools and leadership required to obtain *superior strategic results*.

This focus allows us to intimately understand the special needs, resources, and capabilities of our client's business. We have positioned our organization to understand the unique challenges typically faced by our clients by installing the systems and practices necessary to support growth, while maintaining the entrepreneurial spirit that is typically the foundation of their success.

The foundation of our product and service offerings is built upon the Excellence in Planning™ Model and Process developed by company founder Bill Moss. It is a streamlined, hands-on methodology designed to ensure the proper course and direction a business should take utilizing limited resources.

Products and Services: ABC Consulting provides high-end strategic planning and business planning products and services to all types of Small to Medium Enterprises (SMEs), and Fortune 1000 enterprises. The Company sells products and services including Web-based training packages, business planning and strategic planning consulting, Excellence in Planning™ Workshops and seminars, and business assessment and improvement products.

By capitalizing on the experience of the management team, **ABC Consulting** provides high-level management consulting and strategic planning to meet enterprise solutions. With the Excellence in Planning™ Model and the Excellence in Planning™ Workshops, the company has become a trusted ally to its clients. Implementation tools, including Mr. Moss's new book: *Excellence in Planning: The New Era in Strategic Thinking* guidebook and a wide offering of audio and video tapes, books, and computer software programs that enable clients to retain and effectively utilize concepts and skills. With the funding in place, **ABC Consulting** will facilitate online training by presenting users with a host of applications and other information they are authorized to access.

Management: The management team brings with them many industry best practices and combined experience of over sixty-five years in strategic planning, management, sales, general business management, and information technology-based applications. This solid team of professionals continues to drive revenue and profit goals to meet investor expectations. Our founder, Bill Moss, is a best-selling author and has written fifteen books. One of his titles was named the number one book on business planning and one of the best books ever written on marketing.* Bill has seventeen years experience in corporate management and strategic planning.

Financial Status: ABC Consulting has been funded to date by Mr. Moss and bank loans. Although this has been a necessary step to get the business off the ground for the first fourteen months of operation, capital resources have been depleted, and an injection of additional funding is needed. The company anticipates reaching $800,000 in revenue for fiscal year 2005, and $3.1 million in revenue for fiscal year 2006. With the additional funding, **ABC Consulting** intends to achieve $18 million in revenue with an intended net profit margin of $6.6 million in fiscal year 2008. By focusing on its strengths, its key customers, and the underlying values they need, **ABC Consulting** intends to increase annual sales, while also improving the gross margin on sales, cash management, and working capital.

Use of Funds: The Company plans to raise $5 million to fund growth, further develop its corporate training and licensing programs, fund further software- and Web-based training development, expand its employee and consultant base, purchase additional equipment, and provide marketing capital for the new products and services.

Financial Data and Exit Strategy: The Company intends to be acquired or conduct an initial public offering (IPO) after year five of this business plan. **ABC Consulting** may even opt to purchase back the shares of outside investors.

Any one of these options is intended to provide a remuneration event for the investors and personnel who built the company. In addition, the Company intends to be actively involved in mergers and acquisitions in year three of this business plan. This will require additional capital in the amount of $10 million.

Name and Company Logo: The corporate name was chosen to illustrate a Good Thinking™ organization that focuses on strategic planning products and services. The logo was designed to show the confusion that often exists in corporations and departments with their individual strategic plans. **ABC Consulting** encircles the confusion and assists the organization to move in a clear, forward direction.

(*Note, Sources: *Small Business Press*, 2004; SmallBizPlanit.com, 2005)

1.1 Objectives

1. Begin breaking ground by January 2006 for Corporate Retreat

2. Bring in executives from around the world to experience the Corporate Retreat

3. Average twenty-five executives per week after six months of operations

4. Operate a highly successful enterprise that provides professional solutions for small to medium enterprises (SMEs)

5. Develop business packages that provide the very best strategic planning solutions in the market

6. Raise an additional $5 million for the expansion of the enterprise consulting services and new products and services, as well as have commitments for an additional $10 million for acquisitions

7. Provide an exit strategy after 2009

8. Continue to develop new products and services that enhance efficiencies and reduce costs for our clients

9. Achieve $3.1 million in revenue in 2006, $8.3 million in 2007, and $18 million in 2008

10. Develop a solid team of business consulting professionals to work with all types of business enterprises

11. Create a program for high school and college students to help them acquire business planning skills and strategic planning knowledge

12. Become a highly recognized name to the SME market, venture capital firms, and eventually Fortune 1000 companies

13. Develop a coaching methodology for SMEs that is of high value to our customers

14. Develop strategic alliances with well-known companies that service the same companies **ABC Consulting** does

15. Develop an international presence with our Web-based training and workshops

1.2 Mission

ABC Consulting's mission is to assist business leaders in thought leadership, which helps to create a successful enterprise. We assist companies in the efficient allocation of their resources through products and professional services that no other consulting firm offers. Our guiding principles are: promote client independence, expand strategic thinking, collaborate with others, ensure our own competence, and act as one organization.

To impact profoundly:

- The way in which a company is managed and operated

- The manner in which an enterprise generates revenue and turns a profit

- The overall manner in which an enterprise conducts business

We envision an ever-increasing global movement to restore and revitalize the strategic planning efforts in companies worldwide. **ABC Consulting** will be a recognized contributor and leader in that movement.

1.3 Keys to Success

The keys to success in this business are:

- Marketing: providing value to our customers as a strategic partner to help them achieve their goals and objectives by solving problems through strategic planning

- Provide a unique and life-changing experience in the beautiful scenery of Wisconsin as the executives spend time at our picturesque and charming facility

- High degree of training, consulting, and product quality

- Management: products and services delivered on time, costs controlled, marketing budgets managed; remove the temptation to fixate on growth at the expense of profits

- Technology: provide the most up-to-date online training solutions for organizations and development of the enterprise through our strategic planning and assessment tools

- Investor relations: provide a solid return on investment

In today's market, companies and individuals do not have the expertise and time to put together a successful business plan or provide proper strategic planning training. Rather, they must shop around for separate products and programs that all too often leave them hanging with not enough direction. More often than not, those looking to craft the proper plan do not know where to start. Given this daunting task, individuals and companies alike need an intermediary who can coach and mentor, conduct research, provide planning, establish relationships, provide strategic planning training, and provide outside assistance with a "third party point of view." **ABC Consulting** is that company.

With over forty products and services specifically geared to three different levels of products and services, **ABC Consulting** can offer a wide variety of consulting services and software products to organizations. The purpose of **ABC Consulting** is to be a resource company to other enterprises that are looking to reduce costs, increase productivity, raise funding, and/or gain a better focus.

Risks

Every business faces risks in today's economy and the products and services **ABC Consulting** offers are no exception. Three areas are especially risky. The first is putting too much trust into one area of the business that is intended to drive revenue. If we do not have a solid mix of products and services, we may be vulnerable to market downturns and budget cuts.

The second area that represents a risk is allocating the right amount of capital to the development of all three lines of business: consulting, assessment services, and training and education. We must continue to provide the necessary capital to attract the top talent in the industry.

Training Young Entrepreneurs

One additional highly important initiative to **ABC Consulting** is the development of entrepreneurial and managerial skills for high school and college students. Mr. Moss is currently an adjunct professor at the University of Wisconsin and has developed a system for young people to learn cutting-edge processes in strategic planning and business

planning. This system includes Mr. Moss's books, which have been named the number one business planning books on the market, and allows students to raise their business acumen for operating a highly successful enterprise. It is **ABC Consulting's** belief that a strong foundation of business acumen in the early stages of business will give the advantage to young people who will be competing in a highly diverse business climate.

Contingency Plans

Management has developed contingency plans to mitigate the risks that were described in the last section. By providing a balanced mix of services and products, these risks should be reduced. Seminars, workshops, one-on-one consulting, software, and retail product sales are intended to make up a solid mixture of products and services. Additionally, **ABC Consulting** will expand its sales efforts to increase the number of corporate accounts in its core business to offset the time required to enter this market and generate revenue.

2.0 Company Summary

ABC Consulting is a limited liability company registered in the state of Wisconsin. The Federal Employer Identification Number (EIN) for **ABC Consulting** is 87-06608129523.

History of the Company

ABC Consulting was a concept that was first developed in 1999. The first products and services of the company have been worked on for the past eighteen months and have been drastically improved upon. Several products and services have been refined, marketed, and tested since September of 1999 with our customer base. These include a professionally designed website, the Excellence in Planning Model™, the Excellence in Planning Workshops™, Bill Moss's book *Excellence in Planning: The New Era in Strategic Thinking*, the Excellence in Planning™ CD, *The Small Business System* CD, thirty different seminars, strategic alliances and partnerships, professionally designed literature, business methodologies, and more. Thus, the learning curve has been dramatically shortened as we have developed many new products and services in the past eighteen months.

Bill Moss, CEO founded the company with a part-time focus, and worked hard to develop the concept into a reality. Bob Jones and Sally Thomas have been highly instrumental in getting projects, development of software solutions, and developing a solid brand identity.

Founders of the Company

Bill Moss is the founder of **ABC Consulting.** Bill has been involved in business planning, strategic planning, and running successful enterprises for seventeen years. Bill has written five books on business planning and strategic planning and has produced two CDs. Two of his books are college textbooks, and another book was named the best book ever written on business planning in 2001. His latest work, *Excellence in Planning: The New Era in Strategic Thinking,* is the manual used in the **ABC Consulting** strategic planning training courses. Bill is currently an adjunct professor at the University of Wisconsin, teaching courses in the newly developed entrepreneurship program, and he is also a frequent guest on radio talk shows throughout the country.

Bill sits on the board of advisors for the Phoenix Chamber of Commerce and the Las Vegas Chamber of Commerce, and is a co-chairman of the National Small Business Advisory Council. During the early phases of the Internet, Bill started a Phoenix, Arizona-based ISP that was soon voted the number three ISP in the state of Arizona. He sold his interests in this business. Bill was a member of the legislature for the state of Wisconsin and is the father of six children, with two sets of twins. He and his lovely wife of sixteen years, Judy Moss, live in Mesa, Arizona.

Bob Jones is Chief Operations Officer and co-founder of the Company. Bob holds a Bachelors Degree in business information systems and is completing an MBA at the University of Phoenix. He has over thirteen years experience in business development and information technology management. Bob is highly qualified and experienced in building development teams for e-Business projects. He has managed several projects involving Web development technologies such as Cold Fusion, script development, database design, overall Web development, and ERP.

Prior to **ABC Consulting,** Bob held the position of regional technical manager for Sprint. This management experience lead to a regional professional consulting management position with Sprint Enterprise Network Services. Bob managed the Next Town, Wisconsin; Denver, Colorado; and Las Vegas, Nevada regions. His previous responsibilities also included analyzing customer IT environments, business requirements, operations, future growth, and determining maturity of operations. His experience aligning IT goals and objectives with business goals has been instrumental in helping Fortune 500 companies gain understanding and control over their environments.

Bob is currently responsible for building customer relationships, partnerships, and business opportunities for **ABC Consulting.** He has worked successfully in a variety of industries including manufacturing, healthcare, city emergency services, consulting, information technology, telecommunications, and government. This wide spectrum of experience has given Bob the background necessary to be highly effective in the business and strategic planning arenas.

2.1 Company Ownership

ABC Consulting has four shareholders with the majority of the shares being owned by Bill Moss, 75 percent; Bob Jones, 15 percent; and Randy Hills and Jeff Nielsen own a combined 10 percent. Plans are to bring on the most talented personnel in the areas of business strategies, marketing, administration, and sales as quickly as possible to round out the team, and drive new business.

2.2 Company History

ABC Consulting was officially formed as a limited liability company in June 2000. Since September 1999, the products and services have been in the marketplace and further refined since that time. The startup/learning phase of the business is winding down. The products and services are already being marketed and sold to many companies. The Company has recently formed several key strategic alliance partnerships with well-known names in the market including IBM, NIST/MEP, Paradigm Ventures, Pinnacle Technology Partners, Cerebral Sales, Mountain West Business Brokers, and Wells Fargo Financial Services.

Past Performance			
	FY2002	FY2003	FY2004
Sales	$41,667	$376,333	$798,000
Gross Margin	$31,250	$282,250	$598,500
Gross % (calculated)	75.00%	75.00%	75.00%
Operating Expenses	$37,500	$283,638	$495,087
Collection Period (days)	0	60	60
Inventory Turnover	0	1	1
Balance Sheet			
Short-term Assets	FY2002	FY2003	FY2004
Cash	$52,667	$15,500	$24,800
Accounts Receivable	$5,000	$142,000	$108,000
Inventory	$500	$5,000	$5,000
Other Short-term Assets	$55,000	$275,000	$350,000
Total Short-term Assets	$113,167	$437,500	$487,800
Long-term Assets			
Capital Assets	$15,000	$385,000	$390,000
Accumulated Depreciation	$500	$5,400	$12,080
Total Long-term Assets	$14,500	$379,600	$377,920
Total Assets	$127,667	$817,100	$865,720
Capital and Liabilities			
	FY2002	FY2003	FY2004
Accounts Payable	$4,000	$12,000	$62,000
Short-term Notes	$0	$175,000	$210,000
Other ST Liabilities	$0	$25,000	$25,000
Subtotal Short-term Liabilities	$4,000	$212,000	$297,000
Long-term Liabilities	$0	$275,000	$175,000
Total Liabilities	$4,000	$487,000	$472,000
Paid in Capital	$25,000	$175,000	$200,000
Retained Earnings	$98,667	$155,100	$193,720
Earnings	$0	$0	$0
Total Capital	$123,667	$330,100	$393,720
Total Capital and Liabilities	$127,667	$817,100	$865,720

Other Inputs	FY2002	FY2003	FY2004
Payment Days	30	30	45
Sales on Credit	$0	$282,250	$340,000
Receivables Turnover	0.00	1.99	3.15

2.3 Company Locations and Facilities

ABC Consulting is headquartered at 12450 S. 4000 Street, Suite K, Downtown, AZ. The leased facility has approximately 2000 square feet of space. The cost for the office space is $10.75 per square foot, with the term lease expiring in September 2006, and an annual extension clause. Plans are underway to expand to a new facility at 106 S. 3000 Street in Downtown, AZ. This facility would show a more high-scale consulting model much better than the current facility.

2.4 Company Website

The Company website has been a work in progress and will continue to be updated on a regular basis. The Company has invested considerable time and capital into programming the site to allow for our online training modules.

3.0 Products and Services

ABC Consulting has developed products and services that correspond to three key areas:

- Training and education
- Professional consulting services
- Coaching packages

3.1 Product and Service Description

Training and Education

Online Training

ABC Consulting intends to upgrade and provide better learning processes for its client base through a state-of-the-art online training method. The courses offered by **ABC Consulting** personalize e-Learning by adapting content to the user. Our system teaches the way learners want to be taught. Through a strategic alliance with IB Training, our unique technology personalizes e-Learning content to every learner. Courses are delivered to the learner, based on their PREFERRED learning style, as with a personal tutor.

Learning styles utilized include analogy, abstract, problem solving, demonstration, discovery, example, procedure, and simulation. Text, audio, video, graphics, and Flash are tools used within these learning styles.

As the learner studies online, the intelligent ibtraining.com engine observes and detects their learning style preference, then DYNAMICALLY modifies the presentation of course materials for them.

The market is accepting and adopting online learning. Our proprietary online adaptive e-Learning system (patent pending) allows courseware to be dynamically delivered based on the learner's preferred learning style.

In other words, as the learner is studying an online training course, the engine detects and understands the type of learner they are, then intelligently and dynamically modifies the presentation of the materials for them. As such, they learn faster, comprehend more fully, and retain the material longer. The goal is to spend much less time training, but more important, to have significantly better retention and improved application of knowledge and skills learned. Research shows that traditional instruction yields an average 20 percent retention rate, while instruction catered to individual learning preferences increases retention up to as high as 90 percent.

In addition, the engine tracks the learning progress module by module, allows the leaner to review materials previously completed, assesses their knowledge and comprehension, and allows the learner to "test out" of areas already understood. Any training material can be presented, such as leadership, sales skills, forklift safety, or mathematics.

Training Workshops and Seminars

ABC Consulting has developed workshops for the executive in need of strategic planning mentoring. The Company is also building the back-end capabilities to offer Web-based training on strategic planning, developing a business plan, brainstorming, and several other educational offerings. This capability will be introduced by mid-2006. **ABC Consulting** offers one- and two-day workshops designed to give a company's management team a comprehensive understanding of the Excellence in Planning™ Process. The workshops are similar to what is presented at our popular public workshop.

Both the one- and two-day formats present all of the elements of the Excellence in Planning™ Process. The two-day format allows additional time for questions and more in-depth discussion of concepts.

Topics include:

- Purpose of strategic planning

- Strategic planning process flow

- Information, analysis, decision making, and implementation required to complete a strategic plan

- Instruction on how to complete required worksheets

- Hands-on exercises specific to your company

Getting Started Workshop

This session is designed for companies who are just beginning the strategic planning process.

This workshop features the following topics/exercises:

- Purpose of strategic planning

- Process flow

- Team and leadership issues

- Instructions on how to gather market and competitive information needed for the process

- Overview of the information analysis, decision making, and implementation that flows out of each section of the process

- Hands-on exercises specific to your business and the particular challenges it faces

Interim Assessment Workshop

This session is designed for teams that have begun the Excellence in Planning™ Process, but have encountered difficulties in moving forward or sustaining momentum to see the process to completion.

This workshop will include:

- A review of progress

- Instruction in relevant strategic planning concepts

- Ideas on information gathering

- Hands-on exercises as appropriate

The session will highlight areas of the existing plan that may need rework and will provide a checklist of what is required to bring the planning process to completion.

Implementation Workshop

This workshop is for teams that have completed the "planning" portion of the process and are looking for help with successful implementation.

The workshop will include:

- A review of action plans

- Linking strategic objectives with strategy

- A review of the monitoring process and scheduling

- Effective way of communicating the strategic plan

This workshop guides successful implementation of your team's strategic plan in order to achieve the company's desired goals.

In all cases, the workshops provide an in-depth study of the Excellence in Planning™ Model developed by Mr. Moss.

Professional Consulting Services

SME Consulting

ABC Consulting will continue to provide business planning consulting to SMEs. This lucrative and steady market is in dire need of a professional consulting organization that understands the success of proper planning. Our business analysts provide one-on-one consulting and support to our customer base. In many cases, our business analysts will actually write the plan for the customer. In other cases, an hourly rate will apply for their expertise.

The products and services that fall under this category are business plans, strategic planning, business plan reviews, management consulting agreements, marketing consulting, and e-Business consulting.

Fortune 1000 Consulting

In the past, Bill Moss and **ABC Consulting** have been approached on several occasions to work with many large enterprises in the area of strategic planning. Mr. Moss's knowledge and expertise in planning and marketing have also assisted these large enterprises in creating new products and services. Fortune 1000 companies represent a solid portion of the direct sales for **ABC Consulting**. The reason for this is due to the hands-on consulting and the onsite workshops that **ABC Consulting** conducts on a regular basis.

With a mixture of consulting, strategic planning, and management workshops, **ABC Consulting** plans to become a key partner with several industry leaders who rely on up-to-the-minute strategic focus on their overall direction.

Coaching and Mentoring Services

Upon funding, **ABC Consulting** will increase its coaching program to include a solid team of business coaches. Coaches sell coaching programs to pre-qualified customers through a process that includes giving a presentation over the phone; qualifying the customer for time, motivation, and money; and closing the sale. They will also prepare payments through proper channels, and work with compliance operations to ensure the sale is finalized.

Coaching has been identified as one of the fastest-growing segments of the training industry. Demand for qualified coaches is rapidly expanding, as more and more people are discovering the benefit of an ongoing, supportive relationship with a trained and certified coach.

Coach Certification within an Organization

ABC Consulting will train and certify individuals within organizations to act as change agents, working one-on-one with employees to ensure that training initiatives have impact beyond the event.

Olympic athletes use coaches to win gold medals. These athletes already compete at the highest levels in their given sport, but they understand the measurable value of that "extra something" that comes from having someone work directly with you—someone to point out blind spots, someone to keep encouraging and challenging someone to move beyond their perceived limitations. In other words, someone who will bring out the best within and help you achieve results that surpass your expectations of what was possible!

The goal is to have someone in the clients' corner who always believes in them, is infinitely patient yet has the courage to push when needed, and who can help them tap into the special skills and talents that most of us never have had the good fortune of discovering, much less leveraging.

Having a partner keeps people on track, makes them more accountable, and keeps them continually progressing forward and seeing the results they really want.

Who hires a coach and why?

All types of people hire coaches, but they all share the following characteristics:

- They want more of something in their lives

- They want to grow and improve themselves

- They want their lives to work better and more easily

That's all there is to it really. A coach will help you get all three quickly.

So what's the difference between coaching and therapy?

Coaching is not therapy. More simply put, therapy focuses on the "why?" and coaching focuses on the "why not?!" Coaching is a form of consulting—all of our coaches are consultants, but few consultants are coaches. As an example, if you were interested in learning how to ride a bike, a consultant would show you how to balance yourself, where the brakes are, and perhaps point out flaws in your riding technique.

In contrast, a coach would do all of the things the consultant does and then continue to run alongside you in case you were to fall or need support on the fly. A coach will stay with you to help you implement the skills and changes that are crucial to your long-term success.

How does coaching work and how much does it cost?

Coaches generally work with their clients over the phone three times a month for one half-hour call per week. Of course, there are deviations from this model, but this is the one **ABC Consulting** will use the most. Fees generally range between $200–$1000 a month for this service. Experienced coaches and corporate coaching and programs typically cost more.

Coaching Policies

- Client agrees to make a good-faith, six-month commitment

- Client comes to each session prepared

- Client agrees to make him/herself a priority in her/his life

- Payment is due by check or credit card on the fifth of the month

- 24-hour notice is required for canceled appointments

- Client calls coach at the scheduled time

- Client voices any concerns immediately

- Client thoroughly enjoys the coaching process

3.2 Competitive Comparison

Plans are to continue to differentiate **ABC Consulting** as a business partner with the vision of a company that wishes to be a strategic ally. Company offerings must continue to offer a real alliance.

ABC Consulting benefits include many intangibles such as: vision, confidence, strategic direction, reliability, superior products, high-end knowledge base, and the knowledge that someone will be there to answer questions and help at the important times.

These are complex products and services that require serious knowledge and experience to use. There are a few companies that offer competing products, yet they do not offer the full suite of products and services that **ABC Consulting** offers.

Competitors for the Corporate Retreat are as follows:

The primary competitor in the strategic planning training and consulting area is Center for Modern Strategic Planning (CMSP). CMSP has been doing strategic planning training for eighteen years. Focused mostly on the East Coast, CMSP has developed a solid reputation in training over 12,000 executives in strategic planning. However, CMSP's training manual does not cover even 25 percent of the concepts that Mr. Moss's training manual covers.

3.3 Sales Literature

ABC Consulting has developed sales literature that illustrates a highly professional organization with vision. Our literature also illustrates how our services and products add tremendous value to any type of enterprise. There will always be additional pieces of literature that need to be developed. To accomplish this, **ABC Consulting** is constantly refining its marketing mix through a number of different literature packets. These include:

- Workshop brochures
- Seminar flyers
- Press releases
- New training manuals
- Email marketing campaigns
- Website content
- Television advertisements

(Copies of **ABC Consulting** advertisements and sales literature are attached in the Appendix at the end of this document.)

3.4 Sourcing

ABC Consulting outsources the design and packaging of the CD products, The Business System, online training, email pop-mercials, and eventually the Online Business Plan software to different partners. We are currently working on finding the right packaging and distribution partners to allow us to effectively handle the product orders.

Seminar fulfillment will be outsourced as well. This has been fulfilled in-house in the past; however, management recognizes that others offer this as their core business and they are experts that can drive sales faster. Plans are underway to turn this completely over to a strategic alliance partner by November 2006 to drive this area of the business.

3.5 Technology

ABC Consulting technology management involves processes and activities that will establish standards and monitor the direction in all areas of our distributed computing environment. The further establishment of our standards and direction include our operating systems, network cabling, LAN/WAN topologies, hardware, applications, and networking protocols.

The technology used for online training is planned to be powered by a professional content development firm that develops training curriculum.

3.6 Future Products and Services

Within the next two to six years, **ABC Consulting** intends to open additional offices to support the development of nationwide services. The following cities are targeted for opening a new office to support our growth plans. Each office will have a set of guidelines to follow such as office location, space requirements, personnel requirements, etc. The following cities are targeted for new offices:

-Phoenix, AZ September 2007

-Las Vegas, NV October 2007

-Los Angeles, CA February 2008

-Dallas, TX May 2008

-San Francisco, CA August 2008

-Seattle, WA TBD

-Boise, ID—TBD

-Denver, CO—TBD

-Kansas, MO—TBD

-Raleigh, NC—TBD

-Atlanta, GA—TBD

-Tampa, FL—TBD

Obviously, meeting goals and objectives will drive how soon each office will open. Financial requirements are also a big part of determining when the time is right to go into a new market with an office. These needs will be assessed and evaluated by the management team and board of directors before making any commitments to open other offices.

4.0 Market Analysis Summary

The SME consulting market is worth an estimated $30 billion in end-user value in 2004, and is projected to grow at 10 percent per year, according to professional forecasts published by the Small Business Association.

Source: The Small Business Association 2004

Small Business consulting will continue to be a strong area for expansion. The Small Business Administration (SBA) increases its loan portfolio and financial services each year. During fiscal year 2004, the SBA maintained a guaranteed-loan portfolio of more than $29 billion in loans to 200,000 small businesses, and backed over 49,400 loans totaling a record $10.9 billion to America's small businesses. The SBA made a record 2,700 investments worth $2.37 billion through its venture capital program and provided 50,000 loans totaling $1.1 billion to disaster victims for residential, personal property, and business losses. It also extended management and technical assistance to nearly 900,000 small businesses through its 12,400 Service Corps of Retired Executives volunteers and approximately 1,000 small business development center locations. And, according to the SBA, America's 23 million small businesses:

- Employ more than 50 percent of the private workforce

- Generate more than half of the nation's gross domestic product, and

- Are the principal source of new jobs

Source: The Small Business Administration 2004

Management consulting (SIC code 8742) and general business consulting (SIC code 8748) continue to lead all consulting fields. With an estimated $30 billion in annual revenue, this number is projected to grow at 10 percent per year.

Most small- to medium-sized companies do not have a strategic plan, but those that do are outpacing their peers while displaying a greater-than-average interest in customer and employee satisfaction. During the last twelve months, strategic planners experienced higher increases in sales, profits, and number of employees than nonplanning companies and anticipate above-average growth rates in the future.

More than three-quarters, 77 percent, of those with strategic plans conduct customer surveys of one kind or another, while 57 percent of nonplanners do. Furthermore, 28 percent of companies with strategic plans conduct formal surveys or assessments of customer satisfaction, while about half as many nonplanners do.

The strategic planning companies also invest more in their internal "customers"—employees. On average, they anticipate spending 3.4 percent of revenues on training, while nonplanners anticipate spending only 2.5 percent. Strategic planners also are more likely to offer more employee benefits than the nonplanners.

With regard to financing, 67 percent of companies with strategic plans know the market value of their company, while 46 percent of nonplanners do; and the planners have a more calculated approach. For example, 25 percent of nonplanning companies use credit cards for "instant financing," and 21 percent use private loans. Of companies with strategic plans, 18 percent use credit cards for cash, while 14 percent rely on private loans.

In addition, fraud is a potential threat to every company, and there is plenty to learn from the 17 percent of small companies that were victimized in just the past year alone. Processes and controls can be put in place to help manage the risk of employee fraud. On an ongoing basis, the possibility of employee fraud should be evaluated and monitored as one of the many business risks faced by every small business.

Companies that have strategic plans...

...gain a competitive edge with strategic planning

...have an average size of forty-four employees

...know the market value of their company

...offer performance-based incentives

...export

...are likely to have changed business in the last year

...use computers to do business

...offer more benefits, bonuses, and tuition reimbursement

...are more likely to conduct business abroad

...conduct customer surveys

...spend money on training

...are less likely to use credit cards and bank loans for financing

"Mind your own business," has taken on a new meaning with the increase in employee theft. Small businesses are now forced to divert valuable time from growing their business, to wondering who might steal their business—from within.

Editor's Note:

Study results are based on 966 surveys of owners of small and mid-sized businesses. Results were weighted using U.S. Bureau of the Census business establishment data.

Growth leaders are small and mid-sized companies that experienced increases greater than 10 percent in sales/revenues, profits, employee compensation, and number of employees during the last twelve months.

Source: National Small Business United 2005 (NSBU)

In 2000, the economic census indicated that there were 752,000 medium-sized businesses in the U.S. A medium-sized business has 100 to 4,000 employees. By calculating a 15 percent annual increase in the number of medium-sized companies, the number has grown to over 1 million firms in 2004.

Source: 2004 Economic Census, US Census Bureau

4.1 Market Segmentation

Our market segmentation scheme allows some room for estimates and nonspecific definitions. We primarily focus on the SME market and the Fortune 1000. We have targeted manufacturing, municipalities, and finance (venture capital) vertical markets as viable and profitable options. Our target enterprises are large enough to need the high-quality consulting and information, but too small to have a separate consulting team that solely focuses on strategic planning, e-Business, or general business.

Our target market enterprises have 25 to 1,000 employees for most of the products and services that **ABC Consulting** offers. For strategic planning workshops and training, our target market is enterprises with 500 to 10,000 employees. In general, we assume that there is broadband as well as specific needs for all types of enterprises. In short, **ABC Consulting** can assist many types and sizes of organizations through its consulting services and product offerings.

Start-up and small enterprises have a hard time justifying a $5,000 to $50,000 expenditure for our consulting services. Medium-sized enterprises hire us to assist in the development of their strategic plan, or a business plan to raise funding. These enterprises have a better understanding of the value in hiring a professional consulting firm to point out things that will springboard them ahead of the competition.

The Fortune 1000 have a need for managers to be trained, and have training budgets set aside—sometimes these budgets are in the tens of millions. Each of these enterprises has a need for process improvement and therefore requires the services of professional consulting and the products **ABC Consulting** offers.

The point is this: **ABC Consulting** has a laser focus on promoting products and services to other enterprises.

For example, small and start-up businesses usually can only pay for products that will help them, and they end up doing it on their own. They are more prone to purchase the products first, then realize they may need assistance and end up hiring **ABC Consulting** to consult with them.

Medium-sized enterprises take advantage of the products and services like consulting, business plans, strategic plans and training. These types of enterprises tend not to have a big need for our products.

Fortune 1000 companies are most likely to send their managers through the online training and individual workshops, and then hire us to assist their team in finishing their strategic plan.

The typical customer of **ABC Consulting** varies with the different product and service offerings. Business planning services and products are made available mostly to start-up enterprises. Excellence in Planning™ Workshops and online strategic planning training are mostly held for larger, established organizations. The **ABC Consulting** *Business Game Plan* and assessment services are generally marketed to small and medium enterprises.

The average customer is between 25 and 45 years old, is a C-level or VP-level executive, and is a college graduate.

Typical segments for customers are as follows:

- Age: 25 to 45

- Sex: 74% male, 26% female

- Family life: Mostly married

- Income: over $75,000 annually

- Education: Some college to college graduate

- Ethnic background: Mostly Caucasian

- Social class: Upper

- Personality: Ambitious, self-confident

- Lifestyle: Mostly conservative

Market Analysis

Potential Customers	Growth	2006	2007	2008	2009	2010	CAGR
Small Businesses	4%	23,000,000	23,920,000	24,876,800	25,871,872	26,906,747	4.00%
Large Enterprises	3%	50,000	51,500	53,045	54,636	56,275	3.00%
Medium Enterprises	15%	2,300,000	2,645,000	3,041,750	3,498,013	4,022,715	15.00%
VC Firms	2%	5,000	5,100	5,202	5,306	5,412	2.00%
Start-Ups	5%	1,500,000	1,575,000	1,653,750	1,736,438	1,823,260	5.00%
Total	5.14%	26,855,000	28,196,600	29,630,547	31,166,265	32,814,409	5.14%

Market Analysis (Pie)

- Small Businesses
- Large Enterprises
- Medium Enterprises
- VC Firms
- Startups

4.2 Target Market Segment Strategy

Our choice of target markets is strategic. We assume that it reflects our strengths and weaknesses. We are not only selling to the self-reliant customers, we are also selling to the service-seeking clients whose needs match our strengths.

The SMEs in manufacturing and finance will be looking for specific needs to be filled. They need experts to show them how to assess their business and IT strategies, raise capital, gain a strategic focus on their future direction, develop processes that are tailored directly to their needs, and have a mentor close by. Large enterprises will look to have their managers gain specific knowledge in strategic planning. This can most often be accomplished through the **ABC Consulting** Excellence in Planning™ Workshops.

4.2.1 Market Needs

Since our target markets look to outside advisors to assist them, the most important market needs are process improvement, training, coaching, planning project management, customer service, and follow-up support. One of the key points of our strategy is the focus on target segments that know and understand these needs and are willing to pay to have them filled.

All business owners and managers need outside support and service. However, they won't always admit it. The self-reliant people, however, supply those needs themselves. Among the businesses, these are businesses that have people on staff.

The service seekers may be as knowledgeable as the self-reliant users, but prefer to seek outside advice and assistance. They prefer the consulting firms with professionals and products like those that **ABC Consulting** offers. The underlying needs are related to assurance and dependence. Our customers depend on a plan and products that will help them achieve their goal and objectives. They need the assurance that they can find help when they need it.

4.2.2 Market Trends

The most obvious and important trends in the market are the increasing lack of time and lack of knowledge. The need for outside professionals to provide a second opinion on the overall direction of a company is becoming more and more valuable. This has been true for years, but the trend seems to be accelerating. We see many companies trying to reinvent how they do business and trying to capture Internet business. This new economy is global in nature and most SMEs require outside professionals to help them accelerate in the global economy. We see many new tools and technologies being introduced to companies, and their staff becoming overwhelmed with projects. There are simply not enough hours in the day to keep their staff fully updated on process improvement, business analysis, and technology management. In addition, SMEs are constantly looking for ways to expand their business through capital acquisition.

The Big 4 accounting firms are providing a valuable service to the marketplace, but they are massive and impersonal, and tend to focus more on the Fortune 500. The market needs a major player who can spend the time to work through problems and be more of a strategic partner.

This may be related to a second trend, which is an ongoing auditing system to keep companies on track. Through personal experience, companies are searching for a strategic partner to complete an internal assessment of where they are, and make recommendations of how to get where they want to be. They are looking for a partner to provide ongoing support and audits to help them stay on track. Too many large consulting firms charge huge sums of money for the assessment, then deliver a massive document that no one spends meaningful time digesting. The company is then left to figure things out on its own after "reading the document." This is not a good practice, and there is a huge market for a company that can provide this type of service.

A third trend is the rise of online training. Many companies are realizing a greater return on their education investments by allowing their employees to utilize online training. The Internet is attracting a growing number of distance-learning companies, presenting opportunities for both students and corporations. According to the Learning to Learn Network, Inc., a private company testing the online education waters, there is plenty of money to be made in online adult education. U.S. organizations spend more than $60 billion each year on continuing education and training for employees and managers. This trend is going to continue to grow in the coming years.

4.2.3 Market Growth

Market growth for SME consulting has been on a steady growth pattern for the past decade. With the growth of supply chain management, strategic direction, online training, the need for capital and e-Commerce initiatives, many SMEs are looking for outside assistance from consulting firms that have a wide range of services and products to meet their needs. The demand for knowledgeable consulting firms in the market is expected to continue to grow.

4.3 Industry Analysis

ABC Consulting is part of the business consulting and training industries, which includes several kinds of products and services:

1. Business Consultants: There are many business consultants who focus on specific categories such as business planning, marketing, sales, and finance.

2. Strategic Planning Firms: These include Big 4 accounting firms, IT consulting firms, CSSP, and colleges and universities.

3. IT Consulting Firms: The market is served increasingly by IT strategy and integration businesses that offer aggressive pricing of implementation and operational support services. Yet these firms are usually poor strategic planners, and don't offer strategic planning and auditing services for their clients.

4. Software: There are many other channels through which people buy their business software. **ABC Consulting** will aggressively pursue SMEs to provide assessment tools and consulting.

The entry point into new markets for **ABC Consulting** is based on three principles:

- Leverage current relationships with customers and prospects
- Aggressively market our services
- Aggressively pursue strategic alliances

Many SMEs have turned their efforts to partnering with outside companies like **ABC Consulting** to assist in the development of their ongoing strategies. As an example, IBM tries to sell small businesses on the benefits of e-Commerce. An article in *Sales Tips and Trends* magazine explains how "IBM with $81.7 billion in revenues and nearly 300,000 employees is out to prove that it can also look out for the little guy. In early May 2000, IBM began to offer hardware and software bundles as well as training and consulting for small companies on effective use of technology. All of the offerings are specifically designed for businesses with fewer than one hundred employees. The program focuses on establishing an ongoing relationship with customers.

"After years of struggle and disappointment in trying to sell to small businesses, industry analysts believe IBM is finally on the right track. IBM is headed in the right direction. It has the tools and the wherewithal to provide solutions to small business."

Source: Sales Tips and Trends magazine, *August 2004 issue*

4.3.1 Distribution Patterns

SME buyers are accustomed to buying from vendors who visit their offices. They expect the copy machine vendors, office products vendors, and office furniture vendors, as well as the local graphic artists, freelance writers, or whomever, to visit their office to make their sales. Part of our service offering will be very similar as our sales executives and analysts visit with customers. However, with Web-enabled products and services, we will not solely depend on face-to-face visits.

4.3.2 Competition and Buying Patterns

The SMEs understand the concept of service and support, and are much more likely to pay for it when the offering is clearly stated.

There is no doubt that **ABC Consulting** competes much more against all the consultants than against other service providers. For **ABC Consulting** to effectively compete for business, we will go above and beyond the normal consulting practices by offering quality products that no other consulting firm offers the SME market.

Our focus group sessions indicated that our target SMEs think about price, but would buy based on quality service if the offering were properly presented. We have very good indications that many would rather pay 10 to 20 percent more for a relationship with a long-term vendor providing back-up and quality service and support; they end up with the uncaring, and often unprofessional, consultants because they aren't aware of the alternatives.

Availability is also very important. The SME buyers tend to want immediate, local solutions to problems.

4.3.3 Main Competitors

There are several competitors in the consulting market, yet they do not offer a full-service package for small, medium, and large enterprises. Our strategy works, and we will have differentiated ourselves sufficiently to not have to compete against these firms.

Strategic Planning Training Firms

Strengths: Experience in training thousands of executives; several trainers on staff

Weaknesses: Canned approaches to strategic planning without a whole lot of customization; mostly academics on staff.

Big 4 Accounting Firms

Strengths: National image; high volume; high hourly rates; large staff; experience in the market

Weaknesses: Lack of product variance; poor service and support afterward; lack of personal attention

IT Consulting Companies

Strengths: Can focus on IT integration; up-to-date skills in technology; sometimes national presence

Weaknesses: Do not understand strategic planning; too narrowly focused; do not audit their work

College Professors

Strengths: They have time to study

Weaknesses: Knowledge usually based on theory and not practicality; little time to focus on things outside of academics

Small Consulting Firms

Strengths: Customer attention; focus; lower hourly rates

Weaknesses: Small staff; unable to take on many projects; limited in resources; limited geographical coverage

Software Firms

The primary competitors in the software arena are national companies with large advertising budgets.

Strengths: National image; high volume; aggressive pricing; economies of scale

Weaknesses: Impersonal, high volume sales expected from dealers where customer service lacks. Box pushes that are interested selling software, not providing one-on-one consulting without charging expensive fees.

5.0 Strategy and Implementation Summary

ABC Consulting focuses on a few practices that will maintain healthy growth. These are:

1. Emphasize service and support.

We must continue to differentiate ourselves from the canned presentation and box pushers. We need to establish our business offering as a clear and viable alternative to the price-only kind of buying for our target markets.

2. Build a relationship-oriented business.

Build long-term relationships with clients, not single-transaction deals with customers. Become their partner, not just a vendor. Help them understand the value of the relationship.

3. Focus on target markets.

We need to focus our offerings on small business and medium enterprises as the key market segment we should own. Our values—training, consulting, products, service, support, and knowledge—are more clearly differentiated in this segment.

4. Differentiate and fulfill the promise.

We can't just market and sell service and support; we must actually deliver as well. We need to make sure we have the knowledge-intensive business and service-intensive business we claim to have.

5. Market products that no one else offers.

The product mix for **ABC Consulting** is unique in that each product is written and developed in house. With the use of the founder's books, manuals, models, and assessment tools, we can provide custom designed solutions for the SME. An aggressive marketing and sales campaign for our assessment services and products is at the forefront of our strategy. The assessment tool uncovers strengths and weaknesses in an organization that opens the door for additional consulting and training.

5.1 Strategy Pyramids

For placing emphasis on service and support, our main tactics are strategic planning, business planning, consulting, excellent training, assessment tools, and online training. Our specific programs for developing the consulting practice include direct calls, mailers, and seminars. Specific programs for training include direct mail promotion, "train-the-trainers" programs, and pop-mercials sent via email. For developing our own proprietary systems, our programs are utilizing direct mail marketing and working with VARs.

The second strategy is emphasizing relationships. Through strategic alliance partners, **ABC Consulting** has developed new business opportunities, where doors were initially opened by partners. These have turned into very good engagements for the company. Therefore, the tactics are marketing the company (instead of the products), more regular contacts with the customer, and increasing sales per customer. Programs for marketing the company include new sales literature, revised ad strategy, seminars, workshops, and direct mail. Programs for more regular contacts include callbacks after consultation, direct mail, and sales management. Programs for increasing sales per customer include upgrade mailings and sales training.

5.2 Value Proposition

Unique Selling Advantage

ABC Consulting is a Good Thinking™ Company. We offer the most advanced products and services in business planning, marketing strategies, strategic planning, and training. Our Excellence in Planning™ series of products and services help business owners and managers gain a tighter focus that leads to increased profitability and efficiency—thereby reducing overall costs. We bring in-depth knowledge and experiences to the table, and guarantee the results that we promise, or clients pay nothing for our solutions. We have assembled a team of professionals and partners that enable clients to reach a pinnacle of success faster and with less pain. And, we highly value each of our client's business and hope to provide them with all the tools they need to run their business better.

Value Proposition

ABC Consulting offers uniquely premium goods and services that are easily adaptable to all forms of business enterprises. Every organization needs to prepare for the short term as well as long-term operations. This is done through proper planning. **ABC Consulting** is the company that can be a strategic partner to help other companies achieve their goals. The products and services that we offer meet the needs of many different market segments. Particularly in the areas of strategic planning and business plans, we offer comprehensive, yet simple products and services. In addition to simplicity, our product and service offerings cover several different levels of pricing.

5.3 Competitive Edge

ABC Consulting's competitive edge is our positioning as a strategic ally with our clients when they need a partner to act as a "general contractor" coordinating other vendors. By building a business based on long-standing relationships with satisfied clients, we simultaneously build defenses against competition. The longer the relationship stands, the more we help our clients understand what we offer them and why they need it.

5.4 Marketing Strategy

The marketing strategy is the core of our main business strategy:

1. Emphasize service and support

2. Build a relationship business

3. Focus on SMEs in manufacturing, medical, and financial markets

4. Keep our name in front of customers through a comprehensive marketing mix

5. Strengthen existing relationships and build new relationships with partners

6. Provide a broad mix of products and services that can be spread out to reduce risk

7. Work with many customers to reduce any risk of too much business in one area that may be vulnerable

8. Assist enterprises to improve the quality of internal processes

The strategy moving forward is to emphasize the products that have been, and are being, created. In addition to this, **ABC Consulting** will continue to focus on strategic alliances with outside partners that will increase revenue streams from both the products and services that are offered.

5.4.1 Positioning Statements

For business people who want to be on the cutting edge of strategic direction, **ABC Consulting** is a trusted strategic ally who makes certain that customers' needs are paramount. Our customers' needs are simple: be more efficient and productive while reducing costs. The products and services **ABC Consulting** promotes will bring our customers to the front of their competitive markets as they deploy our products to increase efficiency while employing our services to reduce costs.

5.4.2 Pricing Strategy

ABC Consulting charges appropriately for the high-end, high-quality services and products we offer. Our revenue structure must continue to match our cost structure. The salaries we pay hopefully assure good service and support as they are balanced by the prices we charge.

The hourly fees for consulting range from $95 per hour to $195 per hour.

Products have a wide range of prices. The breakdown of the products is as follows:

- Workshops $1,195
- Online training package $950
- Business plans $12,000 (average)

- Strategic planning engagements $50,000 (average)

- Seminars range from $195 to $395

- *The Business Game Plan* $395

- Enterprise assessment tool $1,500

- Coaching plan $2,500

- Fees for raising capital range from 3 to 10 percent, depending on the amount raised.

- Business broker fees are 10 percent of the sale, and may be shared in the event there is a co-broker.

5.4.3 Promotion Strategy

We depend on our website, email campaigns, email newsletters and direct mail advertising, seminars, and local television as our main marketing avenues to reach new clients. As we change strategies, however, we need to change the way we promote ourselves:

1. Advertising

Our core positioning message is "Strategic planning partners with a vision into the future" to differentiate our products and services from the competition. We intend to continue to use local radio and television advertising, cable television, our website, and email promotions to promote our products and services.

2. Sales Brochure

Our collaterals sell the idea of a strategic partner who has expertise in business strategy, IT strategies, and e-Business.

3. We must radically improve our direct mail and telemarketing efforts, reaching our established customers with training, support services, upgrades, and seminars.

4. We will continue to work closely with the local media. Currently, there is a commercial running on local television and at a mega, seventeen-theater complex in the downtown Wisconsin area. These ads are bringing in an average of three leads per day. These numbers will increase as we add more stations, and as we develop the radio ad campaign.

5. One additional advertising medium presently being considered is to offer the local market a radio talk show on topics about small business. As an example, Mr. Moss was a radio talk show host for the largest AM station in Phoenix, Arizona—KPPM AM 570. His show was called "Learning Small Business" and it covered many different topics such as marketing, sales, business planning, legal, human resources, customer service, and general business practices. This type of format can be easily adopted and successfully implemented in the local market.

5.4.4 Marketing Programs

Our most important marketing program is the various direct email campaigns, which will include information to drive business to our website. These programs are intended to show the world how easy it is to purchase products via the Internet, and that good, quality products are online and are affordable. Achievement is intended to be measured by the number of SMEs we reach with the campaign. Both of these campaigns will drive traffic to the **ABC Consulting** website where the customer will be able to purchase products and sign up for workshops, online training, and additional **ABC Consulting** services.

With over 25 million SMEs in the U.S., and 17 million in Europe, our sales projections are based on only reaching 1/1000th of a percent of the U.S. market. This low percentage is based on these enterprises purchasing our products and services. The success of this campaign will be determined on exceeding this expectation, as well as selling additional products and services.

5.5 Sales Strategy

The Company will continue to sell to its current customer base and broaden its sales territory to the western U.S. and some international business.

1. We sell **ABC Consulting** as a Good Thinking™ Company and not just our products and services.

2. We have to sell our services and support. The products are like the razor, and the support, service, software services, training, and seminars are the razor blades. We need to serve our customers with what they really need.

3. As we segment different vertical markets, the strategy is attacking each market as well. For example, email campaigns will require a robust website, e-Commerce for online purchasing, and proper follow-up. Consulting services require one-on-one selling to high-level executives, proper proposing of solutions, and proper follow-up.

The yearly total sales chart summarizes our ambitious sales forecast. We estimate sales to increase from $800,000 for year 2005 to more than $3 million in 2006, $8.3 million in 2007, and to more than $18 million in year 2008 of this plan.

ABC Consulting will continue to send out press releases to the media. The press release will provide important information on events that focus on the Company and the community.

5.5.1 Sales Forecast

The important elements of the sales forecast are shown in the total sales by month in the following table.

Sales Forecast

Sales	FY2006	FY2007	FY2008
Professional Consulting Services	$850,000	$1,700,000	$2,975,000
Workshops and Seminars	$675,175	$1,728,900	$3,457,800
Online Training	$636,500	$2,850,000	$7,125,000
Coaching	$310,000	$600,000	$1,650,000
Other Products	$711,000	$1,422,000	$2,844,000
Total Sales	$3,182,675	$8,300,900	$18,051,800
Direct Cost of Sales	FY2006	FY2007	FY2008
Professional Consulting Services	$85,000	$170,000	$297,500
Workshops and Seminars	$168,794	$432,225	$864,450
Online Training	$31,825	$142,500	$356,250
Coaching	$15,500	$30,000	$82,500
Other Products	$35,550	$71,100	$142,200
Subtotal Cost of Sales	$336,669	$845,825	$1,742,900

Sales Monthly

5.5.2 Sales Programs

1. Direct mail: We intend to continue to use direct mail to invite business owners and managers to seminars and executive briefings. Direct mail will continue to be used as a medium for special offers.

2. Seminars: We intend to continue to conduct informative seminars on topics like: general business planning, business valuation, corporate IT strategy, developing a powerful e-Business, enterprise resource planning, and corporate strategic planning.

3. Internet: The Internet is a tool that allows us to reach millions of potential clients with minimal costs. It helps us build brand awareness through direct marketing via email. Increasingly, companies are testing the direct marketing model, sending complex emails to highly targeted lists of prospects. This technique works much the same way as off-line direct marketing campaigns: **ABC Consulting** has built a database of email addresses by enticing customers to register on our site in exchange for information or access to a special offer. We also send entertaining emails to customers that contain music and other audio enhancements.

We intend to start an email newsletter. Customers will register to receive the newsletter, which will include tips for business owners and managers, as well as special offers.

The Web is one of the few places where we can combine the two (banner advertising and direct marketing).

4. Face-to-face visits: Of course, we will continue to visit with our customers one-on-one. Our sales executives will call on C-level executives to explain our strategic services and objectives. We want to be their long-term partner, and have the skills and talents on staff to help them reach *their* goals and objectives.

5. Television, radio, and theater: With the current television and theater ad campaign, **ABC Consulting** is generating an average of three new prospects per day. With only one television station, and one large seventeen-theater complex, this campaign can be broadened into other stations and additional markets. We intend to continue our radio ad campaign during the remainder of 2000 on local AM stations as well.

With everything we do, we want to create greater awareness of other products and services that **ABC Consulting** offers. Each one of our promotions from our seminars to our workshops and even our email campaigns must be intertwined with driving traffic to the **ABC Consulting** website. These various sales promotions will accomplish four things:

- They drive the traffic to the ABCConsulting.com and mwbusinessbrokers.com sites
- They create sales revenue

- They invariably create big opportunities for our consulting services
- They build our database for future promotions

5.6 Strategic Alliances

We depend on our alliances with IBM, NIST/MEP, Cisco, AT&T, Sprint, Morgan Stanley, and Schwab to generate continuous leads for our add-on products. In addition, the company is constantly forming alliances with CPA firms, law firms, marketing firms, venture capital companies, SBICs, IT consulting firms, insurance companies, chambers of commerce, the SBA, and other enterprises that support the critical need of strategic planning. We need to make sure that personnel and especially our strategic alliances are aware of our support and reciprocation.

5.7 Milestones

The accompanying table lists important program milestones, with dates and managers in charge, and budgets for each. The milestone schedule indicates our emphasis on planning for implementation.

Milestones

Milestone	Start Date	End Date	Budget	Manager	Department
Complete Funding	7/1/2006	11/1/2006	$10,000	Bill	Finance
Complete Online Training	9/1/2006	12/1/2006	$25,000	Bill	Marketing
Complete Business Game Plan	8/1/2006	1/31/2007	$25,000	Bill	Production
Spanish Translations	7/1/2006	9/1/2007	$2,000	Curtis	Marketing
Chinese Translations	9/1/2006	12/1/2006	$5,000	Curtis	Marketing
Hire Sales Personnel	9/1/2006	11/1/2006	$15,000	Curtis	Operations
Develop Manufacturing Vertical	3/15/2007	Ongoing	$5,000	Bill/Tal	Sales
Develop Municipality Vertical	1/20/2007	Ongoing	$5,000	Bill/Tal	Sales
Develop VC Vertical	5/1/2008	Ongoing	$5,000	Bill/Curtis	Sales
Develop Strategic Alliance Partners	7/1/2009	Ongoing	$2,500	Bill	Marketing
Totals			$99,500		

6.0 Management Summary

Our management philosophy is based on responsibility and mutual respect. People who work at **ABC Consulting** want to work here because of an environment that encourages creativity and achievement. The initial team includes six employees, growing to twelve employees by the end of year 2006, thirty-two personnel by year 2007, forty-eight by the end of year 2009, and seventy-two by the end of fiscal year 2010. The increase is needed to support the effort to move beyond the local region.

Members of our Management Team brings with them many industry best practices and combined experience of over forty-eight years in strategic planning, general business, finance, information technology, and Internet-based applications. This is a solid team of professionals that can drive revenue and profit goals to meet investor expectations.

We will continue to work with outside consultants and our board of directors to assist with corporate strategic direction, as well as part-time people to handle shipping and packaging, errands, phone back-up, etc.

Our corporate law firm is Rain, Sunshine and Martin located in Next Town, AZ. Julie Westin is the Company's personal attorney. Ms. Westin has an office in Next Town, AZ. Our corporate CPA firm is Tomson & Company located in Murray, AZ.

6.1 Organizational Structure

The Company is managed by a highly talented team of professionals. The team consists of Bill Moss, Chairman and Chief Executive Officer; Bob Jones, Chief Operations Officer; Thomas Phill, Chief Technology Consultant; Sally Thomas, Training and Education Director; Jody Topaz, Senior Technical Consultant; Bradley Bills, Principal Broker.

6.2 Management Team

Bill Moss, Chairman and CEO: Bill founded **ABC Consulting** to focus on all aspects of strategic consulting for small and medium enterprises. Bill has a degree in marketing from Harvard, with a minor in finance. Bill has written fifteen books of which two are award-winning books on business planning, and has produced two CDs. His latest work, *Excellence in Planning,* is the manual used in the **ABC Consulting** strategic planning courses. Bill is an adjunct professor at the University of Wisconsin where he is one of four professors chosen to start the new entrepreneurship program at the university. Two of his books are course textbooks in several colleges, and another book was named the number one business planning book in the country by the Small Biz Press and Bizplanningtoday.com in 2001. He is also a frequent guest on radio talk shows throughout the country. He has seventeen years in the business/strategic planning and technology fields.

Bill has been a radio talk show host on the number one station in the Phoenix, AZ market. His show was called "All About Business" and he focused on topics geared towards assisting business owners and managers in running a better organization. Due to family commitments, Bill resigned from producing and airing the show to spend more time with his family on the weekends.

Bill has owned and operated a successful manufacturing and distribution company, which produced the popular Vending Wizard and Vending Mania vending machines. His products were frequently featured on the West Coast Right Game Show as the number one product in the "Technology Today and Forever" catalog; and in three Hollywood movies.

Bill spent four years with Xerox, as a Branch Manager and Regional Director. While at Xerox, Bill received several awards which include: the first ever Outstanding Achievement Award, the Division Managers Award, Marketing Aptitude Award, 120% of Goal Award, Para 100, and the Fast Start Award. As a start-up under Bill's leadership, Xerox Wisconsin was awarded the number one IT Consulting Firm Award in the state of Wisconsin. This was accomplished after only two years in the market.

During the early phases of the Internet, Bill started a Phoenix, AZ-based ISP, which was soon voted the number three ISP in the state of Arizona. He sold his interests in this business.

Bill is the father of six children. He and his lovely wife of sixteen years, Judy, live in Mesa, AZ.

Bob Jones, Chief Operations Officer and Co-Founder: Bob holds a Bachelors Degree in business information systems and is completing an MBA at the University of Phoenix. He has over thirteen years experience in business development and information technology management. Bob is highly qualified and experienced in building development teams for e-Business projects. He has managed several projects involving Web development technologies such as Cold Fusion, script development, database design, overall Web development, and ERP.

The most recent leadership role held by Bob was as a technical manager for Sprint. This management experience lead to a regional professional consulting management position with Sprint Enterprise Network Services. Bob managed the Next Town, WI; Denver, CO; and Las Vegas, NV regions. His previous responsibilities also included analyzing customer IT environments, business requirements, operations, future growth, and determining maturity of operations. His experience aligning IT goals and objectives with business goals has been instrumental in helping Fortune 500 companies gain understanding and control over their environments.

Bob is currently responsible for building customer relationships, partnerships, and business opportunities for **ABC Consulting.** He has worked successfully in a variety of industries including manufacturing, hospital, city emergency services, consulting, information technology, telecommunications, and government. This wide spectrum of experience has given Bob the background necessary to be highly effective in the business and strategic planning arenas.

Sally Thomas, Director of Training and Development: Sally brings six years of successful marketing and advertising expertise to the **ABC Consulting** team. Sally has been personally responsible for marketing seminars and corporate training, which brought in over $2 million in revenue in her previous assignment. She has continued on this same path as she is filling seats with highly qualified prospects for **ABC Consulting.** Her task in 2006 is to market and fill forty-eight seminars, and to drive $958,000 in revenue.

Bradley Bills, President, Mountain West Business Brokers: Bradley has over twenty years business experience in sales, advertising, operations, and real estate.

Board Members are as follows:

Randy Hills was the founder and visionary of what is now known as the Towers at Next Town, WI. This sixty-acre planned commercial development began in 1985 and today consists of class A office space, hotel and guest suites, restaurants, and retail space. The feeling of quality and convenience extends throughout the development with its rich glass twin office towers and the spectacular panoramic views of Next Town. What was once considered green belt property used for livestock is today the fastest-growing freeway commercial property in the state of Wisconsin.

In addition to being one of the most respected commercial real estate developers in Next Town, WI, Randy has been instrumental in syndicating many Wisconsin-based commercial real estate projects and businesses including the Summer Shadows RV Park, St George Ford Automobile dealership, and the Country Inn & Suites. Other syndications include the highly respected and well-established acquisition of Downtown Bank for a disclosed amount of over $250 million.

Randy was also responsible for putting the management team together to form MadTrax Group, LLC, a local bicycle holding company, which today owns over 30 percent of the worldwide bicycle market.

Randy was an S.P in the U.S. Air force and attended four years at the Wisconsin Business College where he majored in building construction.

Jeff Nielsen recently left Zion's First National Bank after twenty-one years of service to join with Downtown Capital. He has extensive banking experience in both the consumer and commercial arena. He was the vice president and branch manager of the Downtown office for the past fifteen years. The Downtown office grew from $2.5 million to $100 million in deposits and $700 thousand to $22 million in loans under his management.

Jeff has also been very active in the community, having served as a charter member of the Downtown Rotary International since 1985 and was the president from 1989 to 1991. He was also a charter member of the Honorary Colonels for the Downtown City Police Department since 1995.

Jeff earned a BS degree at Next Town University in 1980 where he majored in finance and minored in accounting and economics.

Jeff is a Wisconsin native. He was born May 02, 1956 and reared in Orem, Wisconsin. He currently resides in Downtown, Wisconsin, with his wife and five children.

Tom Hills was the founder of DEF Pharmaceuticals, which was recently purchased by a larger pharmaceutical company for $30 million. Tom owns patents on several biomedical products and processes that are currently being used today in many areas. Tom has played an influential role in the development of pain relief products for individuals who cannot take morphine. He is also the president of the American Business Services Michigan Chapter.

6.3 Management Team Gaps

We believe we have a good team for covering the main points of the business plan. The addition of outside professionals is important as a way to cement our fundamental business practices. With the addition of IT, management, legal, and accounting consultants, our management team will be well versed in the complicated issues of running a successful consulting enterprise. We have selected industry professionals with proven track records and exemplary backgrounds.

6.4 Personnel Plan

The Personnel Plan reflects the need to bolster our capabilities to match our positioning. Our total headcount should increase to twelve in year one, thirty-two in year two, forty-eight by year three, and to seventy-two by year four. Detailed monthly projections are included in Table 6.4.

Personnel Plan			
Production Personnel	FY2006	FY2007	FY2008
Operations Executive	$100,000	$110,000	$137,500
Business Consultants	$412,500	$618,750	$773,438
Business Coaches	$275,000	$412,500	$515,625
Bonuses	$0	$41,505	$103,761
Subtotal	$787,500	$1,182,755	$1,530,324
Sales and Marketing Personnel			
Sr. Account Executive	$140,297	$182,386	$227,982
Account Executives	$285,029	$370,537	$463,171
Sales and Marketing Executive	$100,000	$130,000	$162,500
Marketing Assistant	$31,500	$40,950	$51,188
Bonuses	$0	$41,505	$103,761
Subtotal	$556,825	$765,377	$1,008,602
General and Administrative Personnel			
Office Manager	$30,000	$39,000	$50,700
Receptionist	$22,000	$28,600	$37,180
Administrative Assistants	$26,667	$34,667	$45,067
Bonuses	$0	$16,602	$41,505
Subtotal	$78,667	$118,868	$174,451
Other Personnel			
Sr. Executives	$130,000	$286,000	$471,900
HR	$58,000	$127,600	$210,540
Bonuses	$0	$66,407	$166,018
Subtotal	$188,000	$480,007	$848,458
Total Headcount	32	48	72
Total Payroll	$1,610,992	$2,547,007	$3,561,835
Payroll Burden	$241,649	$382,051	$534,275
Total Payroll Expenditures	$1,852,641	$2,929,058	$4,096,110

7.0 Financial Plan

The most important element in the financial plan is the critical need for improving several of the key factors that affect cash flow:

1. We must at any cost emphasize our plans to sell both products and services to our clients and develop better customer service policies than our competition. This should also be a function of the shift in focus toward service revenues to add to the product revenues.

2 We hope to bring the gross margin to 80 percent and the net profit margin to 36 percent by the end of fiscal year 2010. This, too, is related to improving the mix between product and service revenues, because the service revenues offer much better margins.

3. We plan to raise $5 million in equity financing and have commitments to fund an additional $10 million for acquisitions. These amounts seem in line with the balance sheet capabilities.

7.1 Important Assumptions

The financial plan depends on important assumptions. The key underlying assumptions are:

1. We assume a moderate-growth economy, without a major recession.

2. We assume, of course, that there are no unforeseen changes in business and technology to make our products immediately obsolete.

3. We assume access to equity capital and financing sufficient to maintain our financial plan as shown in the accompanying tables.

4. In the sales forecast, the term "other" represents revenue derived from business brokerage, finder's fees, acquisitions, and rental income.

5. Also listed in the sales forecast are the associated **costs** for the products and services in the following manner:

- Consulting 10 percent

- Training and education 25 percent

- Other 5 percent

6. The breakdown of specific lines of business and the **percentage of total revenue** in year 2008 for each area looks like this:

- Consulting 20 percent

- Training and education 54 percent

- Coaching 10 percent

- Other 16 percent

General Assumptions

	FY2006	FY2007	FY2008
Short-term Interest Rate %	10.00%	10.00%	10.00%
Long-term Interest Rate %	10.00%	10.00%	10.00%
Payment Days Estimator	30	30	30
Collection Days Estimator	45	45	45
Inventory Turnover Estimator	4.00	4.00	4.00
Tax Rate %	25.00%	25.00%	25.00%
Expenses in Cash %	10.00%	10.00%	10.00%
Sales on Credit %	75.00%	75.00%	75.00%
Personnel Burden %	15.00%	15.00%	15.00%

7.2 Key Financial Indicators

We are assuming a 20 percent personnel burden for additional items such as vacation, insurance, and sick leave. As far as long-term and/or short-term debt, we have figured in an interest rate of 10 percent. This plan outlines a 25 percent tax burden.

7.3 Break-Even Analysis

For our break-even analysis, we assume monthly running costs of approximately $124,804 per month that includes our full payroll, rent, and utilities, interest, telephone, and an estimation of marketing costs.

Margins are harder to assume. Our overall average of $1,195 per unit sold is based on an average of the workshop and online training prices. However, there are ten primary products and services that **ABC Consulting** sells. We have calculated an average variable cost of 25 percent for each unit sold. We hope to attain a margin that will remain high in the future.

The average cost for five of the primary products and services is approximately $7,066 per unit (for the combined prices of $1,195; $950, $2,500; $395; $25,000 and $12,000). Break-even for this figure is twenty-four units per month sold, or $166,405 in monthly sales.

Break Even Analysis:
Monthly Units Break-even   24
Monthly Sales Break-even $166,405.00

Assumptions:
Average Per-unit Revenue $7,066.67
Average Per-unit Variable Cost $1,751.67
Estimated Monthly Fixed Cost $124,804.00

Break-even Analysis

Monthly Break-even Point

Break-even point = where line intersects with 0

7.4 Projected Profit and Loss

The most important assumption in the projected profit and loss statement is the gross margin, which is estimated to be 61% percent by the end of 2006, 74 percent at the conclusion of 2007, and 81 percent by the end of 2008. Month-by-month assumptions for net profit margin are intended to achieve 4 percent at the conclusion of 2006, 24 percent at the conclusion of 2007, and 36 percent by the end of 2008.

Profit and Loss (Income Statement)

	FY2006	FY2007	FY2008
Sales	$3,182,675	$8,300,900	$18,051,800
Direct Cost of Sales	$336,669	$845,825	$1,742,900
Production Payroll	$787,500	$1,182,755	$1,530,324
Web Development/Email	$37,500	$50,000	$50,000
Design Firm	$20,000	$0	$0
Printing	$43,000	$55,000	$100,000
Infomercial Agency	$0	$0	$0
Total Cost of Sales	$1,224,669	$2,133,580	$3,423,224
Gross Margin	$1,958,006	$6,167,321	$14,628,576
Gross Margin %	61.52%	74.30%	81.04%
Operating expenses:			
Sales and Marketing Expenses			
Sales and Marketing Payroll	$556,825	$765,377	$1,008,602
Advertising/Promotion	$112,500	$281,250	$703,125
Travel	$30,500	$45,750	$68,625
Car Allowance	$7,700	$11,550	$17,325
Royalties	$127,307	$415,045	$902,590
Inventory	$125,000	$187,500	$281,250
Furniture	$44,000	$132,000	$198,000
Postage	$56,000	$168,000	$252,000
Miscellaneous	$12,000	$36,000	$54,000
Total Sales and Marketing Expenses	$1,071,832	$2,042,472	$3,485,517
Sales and Marketing %	33.68%	24.61%	19.31%
General and Administrative Expenses			
General and Administrative Payroll	$78,667	$118,868	$174,451
Payroll Burden	$241,649	$382,051	$534,275
Depreciation	$125	$3,360	$3,360
Leased Equipment	$30,000	$90,000	$180,000
Utilities and phones	$31,500	$67,500	$101,250
Business Insurance	$14,400	$40,000	$60,000
Professional Fees	$27,500	$50,000	$75,000
Rent	$58,800	$176,400	$264,600
Total General and Administrative Expenses	$482,640	$928,180	$1,392,936
General and Administrative %	15.16%	11.18%	7.72%
Other Expenses			
Other Payroll	$188,000	$480,007	$848,458
Total Other Expenses	$188,000	$480,007	$848,458
Other %	5.91%	5.78%	4.70%
Total Operating Expenses	$1,742,473	$3,450,659	$5,726,911
Profit Before Interest and Taxes	$215,534	$2,716,662	$8,901,665
Short-term Interest Expense	$22,463	$23,700	$23,700
Long-term Interest Expense	$21,544	$28,700	$36,167
Taxes Incurred	$42,882	$666,065	$2,210,450
Net Profit	$128,645	$1,998,196	$6,631,349
Net Profit/Sales	4.04%	24.07%	36.74%

7.5 Projected Cash Flow

The cash flow depends on assumptions for projected sales revenue, inventory turnover, payment days, and accounts receivable management. Our projected forty-five-day collection days are critical and also reasonable. We need $5 million in new financing to get through a cash flow dip in the next stages of the business to fund: payroll, rent and utilities, literature costs, and to acquire the necessary inventory as we build up for mid-year sales.

Pro-Forma Cash Flow

	FY2006	FY2007	FY2008
Net Profit	$128,645	$1,998,196	$6,631,349
Plus:			
Depreciation	$125	$3,360	$3,360
Change in Accounts Payable	$120,481	$144,451	$434,380
Current Borrowing (repayment)	$27,000	$0	$0
Increase (decrease) Other Liabilities	$0	$0	$0
Long-Term Borrowing (repayment)	$74,667	$74,667	$74,667
Capital Input	$5,000,000	$0	$0
Subtotal	$5,350,917	$2,220,674	$7,143,755
Less:	FY2006	FY2007	FY2008
Change in Accounts Receivable	$511,116	$995,632	$1,896,812
Change in Inventory	$165,475	($52,735)	($21,559)
Change in Other Short-Term Assets	$0	$0	$0
Capital Expenditure	$0	$1,000,000	$2,500,000
Dividends	$0	$0	$0
Subtotal	$676,591	$1,942,897	$4,375,252
Net Cash Flow	$4,674,327	$277,777	$2,768,503
Cash Balance	$4,699,127	$4,976,904	$7,745,407

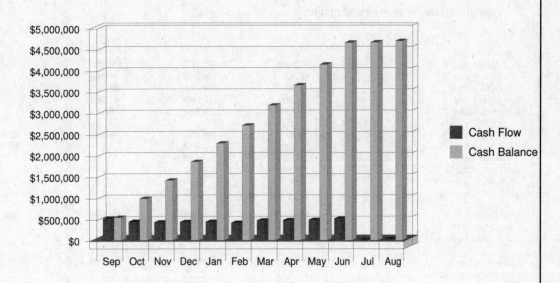

Cash

7.6 Projected Balance Sheet

The projected balance sheet is quite solid. We do not project any real trouble meeting our debt obligations—as long as we can achieve our specific objectives.

Pro Forma Balance Sheet

Assets			
Short-term Assets	FY2006	FY2007	FY2008
Cash	$4,699,127	$4,976,904	$7,745,407
Accounts Receivable	$619,116	$1,614,748	$3,511,559

Inventory	$170,475	$117,740	$96,180
Other Short-term Assets	$350,000	$350,000	$350,000
Total Short-term Assets	$5,838,717	$7,059,391	$11,703,146
Long-term Assets			
Capital Assets	$390,000	$1,390,000	$3,890,000
Accumulated Depreciation	$12,205	$15,565	$18,925
Total Long-term Assets	$377,795	$1,374,435	$3,871,075
Total Assets	$6,216,512	$8,433,826	$15,574,221

Liabilities and Capital			
	FY2006	FY2007	FY2008
Accounts Payable	$182,481	$326,932	$761,312
Short-term Notes	$237,000	$237,000	$237,000
Other Short-term Liabilities	$25,000	$25,000	$25,000
Subtotal Short-term Liabilities	$444,481	$588,932	$1,023,312
Long-term Liabilities	$249,667	$324,333	$399,000
Total Liabilities	$694,147	$913,265	$1,422,312
Paid in Capital	$5,200,000	$5,200,000	$5,200,000
Retained Earnings	$193,720	$322,365	$2,320,561
Earnings	$128,645	$1,998,196	$6,631,349
Total Capital	$5,522,365	$7,520,561	$14,151,910
Total Liabilities and Capital	$6,216,512	$8,433,826	$15,574,221
Net Worth	$5,522,365	$7,520,561	$14,151,910

7.7 Business Ratios

The table illustrates our main business ratios.

Ratio Analysis

Profitability Ratios:	FY2006	FY2007	FY2008	RMA
Gross Margin	61.52%	74.30%	81.04%	0
Net Profit Margin	4.04%	24.07%	36.74%	0
Return on Assets	2.07%	23.69%	42.58%	0
Return on Equity	2.33%	26.57%	46.86%	0
Activity Ratios	FY2006	FY2007	FY2008	RMA
AR Turnover	3.86	3.86	3.86	0
Collection Days	56	65	69	0
Inventory Turnover	13.96	14.81	32.00	0
Accts Payable Turnover	6.74	12.17	12.17	0
Total Asset Turnover	0.51	0.98	1.16	0
Debt Ratios	FY2006	FY2007	FY2008	RMA
Debt to Net Worth	0.13	0.12	0.10	0
Short-term Liabilities to Liabilities	0.64	0.64	0.72	0
Liquidity Ratios	FY2006	FY2007	FY2008	RMA
Current Ratio	13.14	11.99	11.44	0
Quick Ratio	12.75	11.79	11.34	0
Net Working Capital	$5,394,237	$6,470,460	$10,679,835	0
Interest Coverage	4.90	51.84	148.69	0
Additional Ratios	FY2006	FY2007	FY2008	RMA
Assets to Sales	1.95	1.02	0.86	0
Debt/Assets	11%	11%	9%	0
Current Debt/Total Assets	7%	7%	7%	0
Acid Test	11.36	9.05	7.91	0
Asset Turnover	0.51	0.98	1.16	0
Sales/Net Worth	0.58	1.10	1.28	0
Dividend Payout	$0	0.00	0.00	0

8.0 Conclusion

ABC Consulting is a company that provides solid products and services that allow business owners and managers to become more successful, in a much quicker fashion. Our motto is Good Thinking™, and the services and products we offer help to take out the confusion and move things forward. Our executive team is highly capable of achieving the goals and objectives set forth in this business plan. In addition, companies are now able to employ a professional services organization to assist them in planning, design, implementation, and maintenance of their key marketing and financial needs. **ABC Consulting** is that Company, and it is a sound investment.

Artistic Studios

February 2005

Peter Artistic

9001 Thunderbird Street
Lincoln, NE

(555)- 455-9090

Table of Contents

1.0 Executive Summary

Artistic Studios produces better quality reprints of artwork of prominent artists than anyone else. The company was founded in October 1998 by Peter Artistic and for the past seven years has been successful at increasing sales and offerings.

The company has hit a plateau of about $400,000 in annual sales. Artistic Studios is looking to increase sales to become the world leader in quality digital art print works by implementing its company reorganization and three-point marketing plan. To accomplish this, the company is seeking to enter into a consulting management contract with Longstone Consulting to provide a general manager and develop a marketing plan for the company.

The general manager (GM) will handle daily operations not related to production, provide a strategic growth plan for the future, and coordinate the efforts of the sales force. This will allow Peter Artistic the opportunity to focus on production and quality issues as well as recruiting other artists who would be interested in having their work promoted by the studio.

First, the GM will hire and direct the efforts of a sales rep to aggressively market the offerings and capabilities of the company to produce quality art reprints. The sales rep will initially target over 1,500 art galleries nationwide that focus on animal and eclectic offerings, the area in which Jerome Artistic has a strong reputation. Mr. Artistic is a world-renowned artist in the area of wildlife paintings.

Once this is established, another sales rep will be hired to focus on selling the studio printmaking services to high-production clients, publishers, prominent artists, and photographers. As more artists' works are added to the offerings, they will concentrate on other types of art galleries throughout the U.S. and Canada.

Second, aggressively target other reputable artists to add to our list of offerings. Peter will focus on this area with a goal to add one new artist every quarter. These artists will be featured on the website and will be promoted through our sales force. He will also manage the production and quality control issues.

The third is to expand the capabilities of our website to make it the premier art gallery on the web. This will include the capability to do e-Commerce. New artists will pay an initial setup fee and a commission for each sale. Additional or new work by the artist will be added at no cost as an incentive for artists to offer their work through the website. Artists will also agree to have a hyperlink created, if they have their own website, to the Artistic Studios online gallery.

We have carefully expanded the operation over seven years, starting in the basement of the owner's house, moving to the garage, and then to our current location that provides 5,650 square feet of production and office space. The company has recently invested $145,000 in IRIS and Roland printers, which allows it to produce the highest quality prints available on the market today, even surpassing the manufacturer's quality expectations. The printers are only producing at about 10 to 20 percent of capacity, which

3

gives Artistic Studios lots of growth opportunity with little to no investment for capital equipment.

To date, the company has done little to no advertising, relying instead upon word of mouth and the reputation of Jerome Artistic's artistic abilities to promote the company. We have reached a threshold and are ready to move to the next level of production, offerings, and service. To do so, the company is seeking $150,000 in funding to be able to move off the bubble we have been on for the last three years and move sales to $677,206 within two years and over $1.3 million within three years.

Both equity and debt funding are being contemplated with terms for each to be determined by agreement between the parties. The funding will be used to contract for a general manager with Longstone Consulting, provide a base salary and operating expenses for a sales rep, refinance the capital equipment currently owned, and upgrade our website.

1.1 Objectives

1. Develop network of one hundred dealers during 2005.

2. Get to a profitable level by month nine of 2005.

3. Bring in Longstone Consulting to help develop processes and methodologies for administration and marketing for the company.

4. Raise an additional $150,000 for the company by April 2005.

5. Use the proceeds to build the business and hire a solid salesperson.

1.2 Mission

Artistic Studios will consistently strive to be the finest digital printmaker in the world, specializing in producing the highest quality artwork available through use of the latest hardware and software technology. We will provide the most personable service and greatest value for the price. Artistic Studios is known as a fair and honest company; a company operated with integrity and only the best in quality.

1.3 Keys to Success

The keys to this business are leveraging the relationships dealers have with galleries, and giving them the proper tools to be successful. Customer service is an absolute necessity for us to continue to refine and grow.

2.0 Company Summary

Started in 1998, Artistic Studios has become a recognized company among eclectic art dealers and galleries that provides high-quality art with a reputation of excellent customer service.

Revenue for the past three years and for the first month of 2005 has been on a steady growth curve. Revenue streams for the past three years are as follows: 2002—$288,560; 2003—$318,000; and 2004—$276,047. Gross margins for the same operating period are as follows: 2002—66.18 percent; 2003—58.74 percent; and 2004—62.40 percent.

Although 2004 shows a dip in our revenue stream, the gross margins were still kept at a higher level than the previous year. We anticipate revenue and profitability to increase with additional funding and our new marketing plans.

2.1 Company Ownership

Artistic Studios is a limited liability company incorporated in the state of Nebraska. Majority ownership is by Peter Artistic with 70 percent, and Jerome Artistic with 30 percent. Jerome Artistic does not participate in the day-to-day management of the company.

2.2 Company Locations and Facilities

The Company headquarters is located at 9001 Thunderbird Street, Lincoln, Nebraska, in a 4,000 square foot facility. The facility includes a full production area, five office suites, a warehouse, and delivery areas. Artistic Studios is presently leasing the space and does not own the building.

3.0 Products and Services

Artistic Studios provides three main products and a variety of services to the market. We offer over seventy-five different eclectic prints from the famed artist Jerome Artistic in both original art and printed artwork. Our images are printed in two different formats via Roland presses and IRIS presses.

The Roland offers greater longevity over the IRIS due to the use of six pigmented inks verses the four dye-based inks used on the IRIS. This creates prints that should last over a hundred years. The Roland also allows for prints up to 50" wide by almost any length since the media normally comes in rolls.

The media we print on is very important in our process. We use only the finest rag papers such as Arches and Somerset. We are also continually experimenting with new papers to produce the highest quality images possible.

The Somerset was made and sized especially for the IRIS and is one of our favorites. The paper size is 35" x 47", which allows for a 34" x 46" image with 1/2" borders, and is extremely white, producing the highest quality image possible on watercolor paper.

Also one of our favorites is the Ultra Gamut Canvas. This specially coated canvas has the largest color gamut of any fine art material we currently print on.

On the Roland, we have several different choices of canvas and papers to suit your needs and to best complement your artwork and photography.

IRIS · Giclée Printmaking

IRIS prints are often called Giclée (French, meaning "a spray of water," and pronounced, "zhee-clay"). Giclée also refers to the fact that the IRIS printer used to make these prints has been customized to produce longer-lasting, higher-quality images.

The IRIS prints images by spraying one million droplets of ink per second through each of its four nozzles. At a perceived resolution of 1850 dpi, an IRIS print can be applied to nearly any surface or material up to 35" x 47". The drum spins at a speed of 100 to 150 inches per second, and it can take up to eighty minutes to print one 34" x 46" image.

The ink droplets produced by the IRIS printer measure fifteen microns in diameter, approximately the size of a red blood cell. With microscopic accuracy, the printer places anywhere from 0 to 31 of these droplets per color—in whatever CMYK combination is called for by the image data—in a given pixel or dot. In that way, IRIS printers very precisely vary the size of the individual pixels that together form the printed image. Another printer—using a single dot size—would have to place from 1500 to 1800 dots per inch to achieve a resolution comparable to that of an IRIS image. However, no other digital printer can create dots as small or control dots with such microscopic precision as IRIS printers.

Art & Photographic Reproduction

Transparencies are a critical first step when creating fine art prints. Making a "color-correct" transparency is as critical as our scanning it, imaging it, proofing it, and finally printing it. Each step injects its own peculiarities, but the process will be crippled by poor transparencies! Preferably, transparencies should be viewed on a 5000 light box next to the artwork that is also lit at 5000 in order to judge whether the transparency matches the artwork. Otherwise the human eye cannot see color casts and shifts.

When a work of art is reproduced, our normal procedure is to produce four 6" x 8" small proofs to send to the client so they can choose one to print or if further changes and adjustments are desired. When a proof is chosen and returned for our files, the image is ready for printing and editing.

We also have a special custom black and white process especially for photographic reproductions that creates incredibly rich blacks with all the same incredible quality that the IRIS offers. We can also create custom color tones for art and photographic reproductions that can't be accomplished with other methods.

Image Archiving and Printing on Demand

This is an exciting and very attractive feature of IRIS printing, in which an image can be printed on demand. Only a portion of an edition needs be printed. When sales of prints necessitate further printing, the image, which has been stored on a CD, is reprinted.

There is, however, a misconception that results can be duplicated exactly at any time. The factors that contribute to repeatability are numerous and include paper, inks, and even the weather. For example, most of the fine art papers that we use are made in very old European mills on antique machinery, and are subject to minor fluctuations often due to the spring water used by the mills. Winter paper is more consistent than spring and summer paper. Also, the inks that we use are subject to variation. These variations are very minor, although a more apparent change occurs when a huge gain in longevity is established by the introduction of new dyestuffs utilized in the form of new ink sets. This almost always produces a different color gamut from the previous set, so it isn't expected that an image stored on CD at Artistic Studios can be exactly repeated in a year. Changes that affect image repeatability do not occur frequently, and we will give at least sixty days notice prior to any major changes. Any reproofing necessary after a change will be the customer's responsibility.

3.1 Competitive Comparison

The competition that Artistic has faced over the years has been large, national printing firms that specialize in many forms of art. Their scope is broad in nature and does not target the eclectic enthusiast, as does Artistic Studios. A few of our competitors are listed below:

Cumulon Digital Print and Imaging

6532 Clay Ave S.W.

Grand Rapids, MI 49548-7832

Phone: 555-998-0000

Toll-Free: (800) 555-5555

Fax: 555-998-0987

Website: www.cumulondi.com

Tiger Editions

7001 North Fort Avenue

Harrison, FL 33755

Phone: 555-987-5555

Fax: 555-987-6767

Contacts: Steve Carlisle and Philip Langford

Website: www.tigereditions.com

Shone Editions Press, Ltd.

Springs Rd.

P.O. Box 51

Northern Light, VT 05076

Phone: 555-339-5751

Fax: 555-339-6501

Contact: Jon Climate

Website: www.shone-editions.com

Finer Quality Printing

9087 Sexton Avenue

Seattle, WA 91220

Phone: 555-552-9262

Contact: Kristine Smith

Moonlight Productions

90831 S. Via Linda Scarte

New York, NY 90044

Phone: 555-333-1212

Fax: 555-334-8776

Contact: John Dillingham

Eclectic Central Editions

PO Box 9130

Kuning, ME 04333

Phone: 555-234-2802

Fax: 555-234-9720

Contact: Bonnie Bluesmith

Website: www.eclecticcentraleditions.com

3.2 Sales Literature

The company is presently using a full-color, professionally designed catalog with over twenty-five images included. This catalog is sent throughout the world to various art dealers. Plans are to include all available images in the catalog and update it on a regular basis.

In addition, the company offers a full-scale website with plans to offer e-Commerce capabilities for the dealer and art buyer to easily browse the website and choose the prints that are just right for them.

4.0 Market Analysis Summary

Eclectic art is a specialized area of artistic talent that Jerome Artistic is a master of. Jerome Artistic's art is a favorite among many of the dealers and galleries worldwide. However, when it comes to comparing Jerome's art with other eclectic artists, it is very difficult to size up any other artist's work and make a true comparison. For this reason, Artistic Studios digitally prints Jerome Artistic's art that reaches a targeted audience of dealers and buyers. This business plan outlines eclectic dealers in the U.S. and Canada, as well as digital printing firms in the U.S.

4.1 Market Segmentation

Market Analysis Potential Customers	Growth	2005	2006	2007	2008	2009	CAGR
Eclectic Dealers U.S.	3%	1,500	1,545	1,591	1,639	1,688	3.00%
Eclectic Dealers Canada	2%	400	408	416	424	432	1.94%
Printing Firms	2%	200	204	208	212	216	1.94%
Total	2.70%	2,100	2,157	2,215	2,275	2,336	2.70%

Market Analysis (Pie)

■ Wildlife Dealers U.S.
■ Wildlife Dealers Canada
■ Printing Firms

4.2 Target Market Segment Strategy

Our target market is very focused. We offer the highest quality prints and original artwork to a network of eclectic art dealers throughout the U.S. and Canada.

4.3 Industry Analysis

There are approximately 1,500 eclectic dealers in the U.S. and about 500 eclectic dealers in Canada. For this business plan we have also included digital printing firms in the U.S. There are approximately 200 digital printing firms throughout the country.

5.0 Strategy and Implementation Summary

Our main strategy is built on the reliance of dealers throughout the U.S. and Canada to move the products at a quicker pace. As we continue to penetrate the dealer market space, product movement will be dramatically increased. We are presently working with a handful of dealers with plans to increase our dealer network to one hundred by the conclusion of 2005.

5.1 Competitive Edge

The competitive edge that Artistic Studios has over most other print houses is two-fold. We offer:

- **Highest Quality**. We don't settle for "good enough." We've worked hard to make Artistic Studios the best fine art digital printmaking studio in the world.

- **Service**. You'll find friendly, personalized service from people who understand fine art because we're also artists and photographers, and we know how important your work is to you.

- **Quick Turnaround**. We get your work back to you faster, usually within days instead of weeks or months.

- **Competitive Pricing**. In fact, we're one of the least expensive you'll find, but for the quality and service you'll receive, we're the best you'll find anywhere.

5.2 Milestones

Our milestones are listed in the following table:

Milestones					
Milestone	Start Date	End Date	Budget	Manager	Department
Business Plan Completed	2/17/2005	3/15/2005	$0	Peter	Owner

Business Plan to Investor	2/22/2005	tbd	$0	Peter	Owner
Funding Obtained	4/01/2005	tbd	$0	Peter	Owner
General Manager Search/Hire	3/1/2005	4/1/2005	$200	Peter	Owner
Sales Rep Hired	4/1/2005	4/15/2005	$200	GM	Management
Sales Rep Training	4/16/2005	4/30/2005	$500	GM	Management
Sales Rep Out Selling	5/1/2005	indef	$13,500	Sales Rep	Sales
Increasing Dealers	3/1/2005	indef	$14,400	ABC	Department
Totals			$28,800		

6.0 Management Summary

Peter Artistic has over seven years experience in operating a digital printmaking business. He is highly capable of sizing up opportunities for moving products through the dealer and gallery channels. Peter is also very talented in hiring the right personnel for the printmaking business.

6.1 Organizational Structure

Peter Artistic is president and director of operations of Artistic Studios. Jerome Artistic sits on the board of directors, and is the creative consultant for the company.

6.2 Personnel Plan

The Company is moving toward a better-rounded staff as illustrated in the following table:

Personnel Plan

Personnel	2005	2006	2007
General Manager	$36,000	$54,000	$59,400
Production Manager/Peter Artistic	$48,000	$48,000	$52,000
Production Worker/Lead	$13,360	$19,760	$21,840
Production Worker	$16,100	$17,680	$35,360
Production Worker/Part Time	$9,400	$6,760	$13,520
Office/Clerical	$11,760	$16,640	$17,680
Total Payroll	$134,620	$162,840	$199,800
Total Headcount	7	8	10
Payroll Burden	$26,924	$32,568	$39,960
Total Payroll Expenditures	$161,544	$195,408	$239,760

6.3 Management Team

Peter Artistic is the president and founder of Artistic Studios, LLC. He founded the company in 1998 after researching the digital printmaking capabilities of IRIS printers for almost a year. After three years, production required expansion with more equipment, including a second IRIS printer. The following year a new type of printer was introduced on the market, and Peter set out to be the first printmaker on the market with the new Roland printer. After acquiring the first Roland printer anywhere, within weeks he had it producing better prints than the distributor (also a competitor) and manufacturer thought possible.

Artistic Studios started with two customers and now has several hundred artists, photographers, and other clients. Local artists include Chris Young, Jim Norton, and Greg Olsen. National and international clients include Jerome Artistic, Guy Coheleach, and the Valentine Group.

Peter is a founding member of the International Association of Digital Fine Art Printmakers and current member of the board. He studied printmaking at the University of Miami and has spent the past fifteen years creating and selling his own hand-colored etchings and paintings as well as fine-art-related services for other artists through Clearwater Publishing.

<u>Jerome Artistic</u> Lincoln, Nebraska

Education: The University of Nebraska

Jerome Artistic was born and raised in Lincoln, Nebraska, and spent his boyhood admiring artists in the Midwest. Early on, he decided on a career in art, studying at the University of Nebraska. His paintings are rich in detail and muted in tone, true to the remote landscapes he chooses to illustrate. The Indian encampments, eclectic, and hunting subjects portrayed against these magnificent areas are rendered in such a way as to give the viewer a sense of gazing on the past.

Artistic best loves the dusky, grey, misty, muted tones of fall and early winter. His paintings evoke the early 19th century masters of the Hudson River School, artists whom he credits with deeply influencing his art. The mood he captures is that to which all painters of the mystique and power of the tradition and lore of the West aspire.

SELECTED EXHIBITIONS, HONORS, AND AWARDS:

2003 Prix de West Award, National Eclectic Hall of Fame, Oklahoma City, Oklahoma

1998 One-man show, National Hunting Museum, Amsterdam, Netherlands

1999 National Academy of Western Art, Oklahoma City, Oklahoma

Gold Medal Award (Watercolor)

1997 National Academy of Western Art, Oklahoma City, Oklahoma

Silver Medal Award (Oil)

1999 International Eclectic Exposition, Everard Read Gallery, Johannesburg, South Africa

1990 Hubbard Award for Excellence

1991 International Exhibition of Eclectic and Natural History

1997 Hubbard Award for Excellence

1989 One-man show, J.N. Bartfield Gallery, New York

1988 One-man show, J.N. Bartfield Gallery, New York

1986 One-man show, Gerald Peters Gallery, Santa Fe, New Mexico

1985 One-man show, Wunderlich & Co., New York

1985 One-man show, Gerald Peters Gallery, Santa Fe, New Mexico

1984 Museum of Western Art, Denver

1984 One-man show, Wunderlich & Co., New York

1983 Mongerson Gallery, Chicago

1983 Charlie Russell Museum, Great Falls, Montana

1981 Palm Springs Museum, Palm Springs, California

1979 Gold & Silver Medal, Eclectic Hall of Fame, Oklahoma City, Oklahoma

1979 One-man show, Kennedy Galleries, New York

1977 One-man show, Kennedy Galleries, New York

1977 One-man show, Buffalo Bill Historical Center, Cody, Wyoming

1976 One-man show, Kennedy Galleries, New York

PRIVATE AND PUBLIC COLLECTIONS:

Proton International, Lincoln, Nebraska

Gulf States Paper Corporation, Tuscaloosa, Alabama

Texas Commerce Bank, Houston

The White House, Washington, D.C.

Anschutz Collection, Denver

Corning Museum, New York

Buffalo Bill Historical Center, Cody, Wyoming

Charlie Russell Museum, Great Falls, Montana

William Middendorf, Washington, D.C.

Mack Pogue, Dallas

Sports Afield Magazine, New York

Burt Reynolds, Los Angeles

Hal Wallace, Los Angeles

Clint Eastwood, Carmel, California

Los Angeles Athletic Club, Los Angeles

Steven L. Rose, Los Angeles

Stan Kamen, Los Angeles

National Eclectic Art Museum, Jackson Hole, Wyoming

Bill Kerr, Jackson Hole, Wyoming

Ian Cumming, Leucadia Corporation, Salt Lake City

John Huntsman, Huntsman Chemical Company, Salt Lake City

Canadian Embassy

Leaning Tree Museum, Colorado

Long Grass Prairie Preserve, Oklahoma

COMMISSIONS:

1995 National Eclectic Art Museum, Jackson, Wyoming

1985 Boone and Crockett Club, Brown Bear Conservation Stamp

1986 Alaskan Professional Hunters Association, Grizzly Stamp

1987 Alaskan Professional Hunters Association

Hyatt Regency, Aspen, Colorado

Leaning Tree Museum, Colorado

FILMS:

The Romantic Eclectic Landscape of Jerome Artistic, Ian Mandan producer

BIBLIOGRAPHY:

2002 Artists to Watch in '03, *U.S. Art*, December

1996 *Salt Lake City*, November/December

1995 *Southwest Art*, Commemorative Edition

Covering the West: The Best of Southwest Art, July

1992 *Art of the West*, March/April

1992 *Salt Lake City*, January

1990 *Eclectic Art*, November/December

1990 "Top Ten Investments for the 90s," USA Today

1988 *Sporting Classics,* May/June

1987 *Southwest Art*, November

1987 *Sports Afield*, October

1985 *Grays Sporting Journal*, Summer

1984 *American Way*, May

1984 *Sports Afield*, July

1984 *Southwest Art*, January - Cover

1983 *Sports Afield*, April

1978 *Rocky Mountain Magazine*

1977 *Southwest Art*, February

1976 *Ten American Landscape Artists and How They Work*, edited by Susan Meyer, published by Watson Guptill

1975 *American Artist*, January

GALLERY REPRESENTATIONS:

Mongerson Wunderlich Galleries, Chicago, Illinois

Legacy Galleries, Jackson, Wyoming

J.N. Bartfield Galleries, New York, New York

Drummond Gallery, Coeur d'Alene, Idaho

Settlers West Gallery, Tucson, Arizona

Allman Art, Springville, Nebraska

6.4 Management Team Gaps

The current gaps that exist in the management team are in human resources, sales, and finance. The company is pursuing hiring personnel with skills; however, the influx of capital will be required in order to bring on the right people, and hire additional full-time managers.

7.0 Financial Plan

The most important element in the financial plan is the critical need for improving several of the key factors that impact cash flow:

1. We must at any cost emphasize the plan to sell both products and services to our clients and develop better customer service policies than our competition. This should also be a function of the shift in focus toward service revenues to add to the product revenues.

2. We hope to bring the gross margin to 77 percent and the net profit margin to 1.7 percent by the end of fiscal year 2005. This, too, is related to improving the mix between product and service revenues, because the service revenues offer much better margins. Gross margin is anticipated to remain steady for fiscal years 2006 and 2007 at about 72 percent. Net profit margins are anticipated to rise to 11.4 percent in fiscal year 2006 and

to 28.5 percent in fiscal year 2007.

3. We plan to borrow $150,000 in equity financing and have commitments to fund potential acquisitions. The commitment for acquisitions has not yet been determined.

7.1 Important Assumptions

The financial plan depends on important assumptions, most of which are shown in the general assumptions table below. The key underlying assumptions are as follows: We assume a moderate-growth economy, without a major recession. We assume that there are no unforeseen changes in business and technology to make our products immediately obsolete. We assume access to equity capital and financing sufficient to maintain our financial plan as shown in the accompanying tables.

General Assumptions

	2005	2006	2007
Short-term Interest Rate %	10.00%	10.00%	10.00%
Long-term Interest Rate %	10.00%	10.00%	10.00%
Payment Days Estimator	57	57	57
Collection Days Estimator	45	45	45
Inventory Turnover Estimator	3.00	3.00	3.00
Tax Rate %	25.00%	25.00%	25.00%
Expenses in Cash %	10.00%	10.00%	10.00%
Sales on Credit %	95.00%	95.00%	95.00%
Personnel Burden %	20.00%	20.00%	20.00%

7.2 Key Financial Indicators

We are assuming a 20 percent personnel burden for additional items such as vacation, insurance, and sick leave. As far as long-term and/or short-term debt, we have figured in an interest rate of 10 percent. This plan outlines a 25 percent tax burden.

7.3 Break-even Analysis

For our break-even analysis, we assume monthly running costs of approximately $26,000 per month, which includes our full payroll, rent and utilities, interest, telephone, and an estimation of marketing costs. Margins are harder to assume. Our overall average of $1,133 per unit sold is based on an average of the three primary products that the company sells. We have calculated an average of 12.5 percent cost for each unit sold. We hope to attain a margin that will remain high in the future. The chart shows that we need to sell about twenty-three units per month to break even, according to these assumptions.

Break-even Analysis:	
Monthly Units Break-even	23
Monthly Sales Break-even	$26,286
Assumptions:	
Average Per-unit Revenue	$1,133.33

16

Average Per-unit Variable Cost $141.67
Estimated Monthly Fixed Cost $23,000

Break-even Analysis

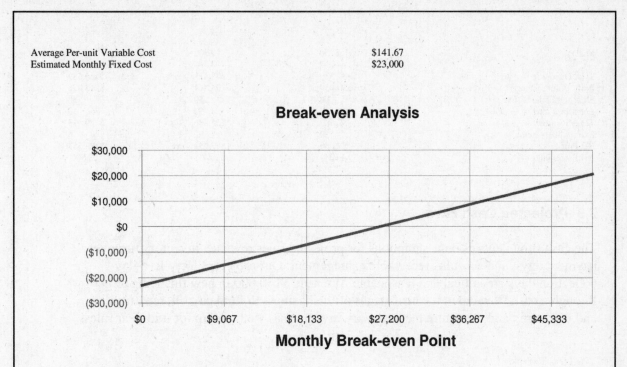

Break-even point = where line intersects with 0

7.4 Projected Profit and Loss

The most important assumption in the projected profit and loss statement is the gross margin, which is estimated to be $347,592 by the end of year one, $488,972 at the conclusion of year two, and $984,765 by the end of year three. Month-by-month assumptions for net profit margin are intended to achieve $7,689 at the conclusion of year one, $77,658 at the conclusion of year two, and $388,557 by the end of year three.

Profit and Loss (Income Statement)

	2005	2006	2007
Sales	$449,048	$677,206	$1,363,509
Direct Cost of Sales	$60,051	$86,654	$174,217
Commissions	$41,405	$101,581	$204,526
	------------	------------	------------
Total Cost of Sales	$101,456	$188,235	$378,743
Gross Margin	$347,592	$488,972	$984,765
Gross Margin %	77.41%	72.20%	72.22%
Operating Expenses:			
Advertising/Promotion	$14,400	$24,000	$38,400
Travel	$18,000	$22,500	$28,125
Miscellaneous	$2,400	$3,600	$5,400
Payroll Expense	$134,620	$162,840	$199,800
Payroll Burden	$26,924	$32,568	$39,960
Depreciation	$7,200	$7,200	$7,200
Leased Equipment	$54,000	$54,000	$54,000
Utilities	$10,015	$12,540	$13,794
Insurance	$3,600	$4,140	$5,175
Legal and Professional Fees	$3,600	$4,140	$5,175
Rent	$32,400	$34,200	$36,000
Contract/Consultants	$22,800	$9,600	$15,000
Website Costs	$5,080	$7,200	$8,400
Entertainment/Sales Rep	$2,050	$6,600	$9,900

Mail	$250	$300	$360
	------------	------------	------------
Total Operating Expenses	$337,339	$385,428	$466,689
Profit Before Interest and Taxes	$10,252	$103,544	$518,076
Short-term Interest Expense	$0	$0	$0
Long-term Interest Expense	$0	$0	$0
Taxes Incurred	$2,563	$25,886	$129,519
Extraordinary Items	$0	$0	$0
Net Profit	$7,689	$77,658	$388,557
Net Profit/Sales	1.71%	11.47%	28.50%

7.5 Projected Cash Flow

The cash flow depends on assumptions for projected sales revenue, inventory turnover, payment days, and accounts receivable management. Our projected forty-five-day collection days are critical and reasonable. We need $150,000 in new financing to get through a cash flow dip in the next stages of the business to fund payroll, rent, utilities, and marketing and to acquire the necessary inventory as we build up for mid-year sales.

Pro-Forma Cash Flow	2005	2006	2007
Net Profit	$7,689	$77,658	$388,557
Plus:			
Depreciation	$7,200	$7,200	$7,200
Change in Accounts Payable	$33,215	($6,420)	$37,381
Current Borrowing (Repayment)	$0	$0	$0
Increase (Decrease) Other Liabilities	$0	$0	$0
Long-term Borrowing (Repayment)	$0	$0	$0
Capital Input	$150,000	$0	$0
Subtotal	$298,104	$78,438	$433,138
Less:	2005	2006	2007
Change in Accounts Receivable	$110,776	$56,600	$170,253
Change in Inventory	$44,139	($6,440)	($2,807)
Change in Other Short-Term Assets	$0	$0	$0
Capital Expenditure	$0	$0	$0
Dividends	$0	$0	$0
Subtotal	$154,914	$50,160	$167,446
Net Cash Flow	$143,190	$28,277	$265,692
Cash Balance	$123,985	$152,262	$417,954

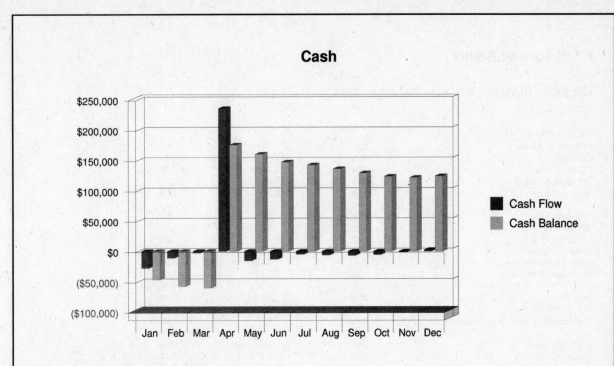

Cash

7.6 Projected Balance Sheet

The projected balance sheet is quite solid. We do not project any real trouble meeting our debt obligations, as long as we can achieve our specific objectives.

Pro Forma Balance Sheet

Assets			
Short-term Assets	2005	2006	2007
Cash	$123,985	$152,262	$417,954
Accounts Receivable	$111,397	$167,997	$338,250
Inventory	$44,139	$37,699	$34,891
Other Short-term Assets	$0	$0	$0
Total Short-term Assets	$279,520	$357,958	$791,096
Long-term Assets			
Capital Assets	$203,000	$203,000	$203,000
Accumulated Depreciation	$136,200	$143,400	$150,600
Total Long-term Assets	$66,800	$59,600	$52,400
Total Assets	$346,320	$417,558	$843,496

Liabilities and Capital			
	2005	2006	2007
Accounts Payable	$44,745	$38,325	$75,706
Short-term Notes	$0	$0	$0
Other Short-term Liabilities	$22,706	$22,706	$22,706
Subtotal Short-term Liabilities	$67,451	$61,031	$98,412
Long-term Liabilities	$0	$0	$0
Total Liabilities	$67,451	$61,031	$98,412
Paid-in-Capital	$270,181	$270,181	$270,181
Retained Earnings-Beginning	$999	$8,688	$86,346
Earnings	$7,689	$77,658	$388,557
Total Capital	$278,869	$356,527	$745,084
Total Liabilities and Capital	$346,320	$417,558	$843,496
Net Worth	$278,869	$356,527	$745,084

19

7.7 Business Ratios

The table illustrates our main business ratios.

Ratio Analysis			
Profitability Ratios:	2005	2006	2007
Gross Margin	77.41%	72.20%	72.22%
Net Profit Margin	1.71%	11.47%	28.50%
Return on Assets	2.22%	18.60%	46.07%
Return on Equity	2.76%	21.78%	52.15%
Activity Ratios	2005	2006	2007
AR Turnover	3.83	3.83	3.83
Collection Days	48	79	71
Inventory Turnover	4.60	4.60	10.44
Accts Payable Turnover	6.37	6.37	6.37
Total Asset Turnover	1.30	1.62	1.62
Debt Ratios	2005	2006	2007
Debt to Net Worth	0.24	0.17	0.13
Short-term Liabilities to Liabilities	1.00	1.00	1.00
Liquidity Ratios	2005	2006	2007
Current Ratio	4.14	5.87	8.04
Quick Ratio	3.49	5.25	7.68
Net Working Capital	$212,069	$296,927	$692,684
Interest Coverage	0.00	0.00	0.00
Additional Ratios	2005	2006	2007
Assets to Sales	0.77	0.62	0.62
Debt/Assets	19%	15%	12%
Current Debt/Total Assets	19%	15%	12%
Acid Test	1.84	2.49	4.25
Asset Turnover	1.30	1.62	1.62
Sales/Net Worth	1.61	1.90	1.83
Dividend Payout	$0	$0	$0

Enviro-Friendly Products
Business Plan

Contact:
Bob Weston
Enviro-Friendly Products
2430 Garamond Rd.
Houston, Texas 56877
(555) 272-5555
bweston@efpofthefuture.com

1.0 Executive Summary

The Company

Enviro-Friendly Products.com is the most comprehensive site for any type of product that benefits the environment or promotes sustainable living. These products consist of energy efficient items, alternative energy, water conservation, recycled materials, organic alternatives, building materials, etc. When one thinks of these products, Enviro-Friendly Products.com is the site they encounter when using a search engine. We will take a 12.5 percent commission for any orders processed on our website, we take the money and pass it on to the manufacturer or distributor who then ships the item or items to the customer. The customer is provided a link to track their order with the manufacturer.

The company is only in the planning phase, and needs to design its logo and website, as well as purchase its domain name. The minimum initial capital necessary to start will be about $15,000 to cover basic expenses for the first year of business. Bob intends to raise the capital from mortgage broker deals, as well as a couple of credit cards. Additional capital will be raised as required through debt, mortgage broker deals, and bringing on new partners or investors by offering them equity. At this stage, Bob Weston is the owner and sole employee. The company will be incorporated before the website is launched.

The Market

As energy prices continue to rise, and global warming and the environment continue to receive attention in the press, the market for environmental or sustainable solutions will grow. This is an inevitable trend, and it would be imperative to be an early mover in this market. From Roper's Green Gauge Report, it appears that at least 15 percent of the U.S. population consider themselves "green" and 31 percent of the U.S. population considers themselves "somewhat green," meaning they will take the environment into consideration on some issues, but on others they will not. According to the *Wall Street Journal,* over 15 percent of appliances sold now have energy star ratings. Many consumers are interested in saving money with investing in renewable or longer lasting, more efficient resources, but may not consider themselves "green." These customers who want to get away from fossil fuels, grid dependency because of costs will also be a big target market.

Marketing Strategy

Sales are generated primarily through search engines that lead people to our website, but we hope to have people hear about us through other avenues as we build up our site. The idea is to cater to the American public's desire for one-stop shopping or informational finding on any subject that relates to the environment, sustainability, green living, or energy.

Products and Services

We will focus primarily on products that can be shipped, that consumers do not need to go to an actual retail location to buy. There is definitely crossover, as some products will be sold primarily through retail locations. We hope to capture a certain percentage of the online customer, which continues to grow as the Internet spreads and makes life more convenient for the typical American who is always on the go juggling their career, family, friends, and various other pursuits.

The products will be broken down into several categories: lighting, water heating, heating, solar, wind, biochemical, water conservation, building materials, etc.

Management

The management consists of Bob Weston, but Enviro-Friendly Products.com hopes to bring aboard some industry veterans to help it grow.

Financial Status

Bob Weston will fund the company primarily through income from his ongoing part-time mortgage business, as well as with debt if necessary with credit cards. Bob hopes to bring on investors or partners with some capital to invest.

Use of Funds

The company plans on paying the basic Web hosting fees, as well as search engine optimization consulting fees in order to keep the website up and running and attracting new customers. The company plans to spend any additional capital possible on advertising to attract new customers from around the U.S. and eventually the rest of the English-speaking globe. The company will have to pay for additional staff as it becomes more profitable.

Financial Data and Exit Strategy

Enviro-Friendly Products.com intends to be acquired within three to five years by one of the giant Internet firms such as Amazon or eBay. This acquisition will settle any debts the company has and hopefully provide a nice return for any investors involved.

1.1 Goals and Objectives

1. Achieve profitability within the first six months.

2. Become the primary website that people go to when thinking of any product or building material that benefits the environment, promotes sustainability, or is "green."

3. Operate an efficient website that pays its manufacturers on time and coordinates shipments on time.

4. Provide an exit strategy for all stakeholders by 2009.

5. Continue to develop relationships with new manufacturers and distributors so that new products can continuously be listed.

6. Achieve a gross profit margin of 20 percent or greater.

7. Achieve projected milestones as outlined in this plan.

8. Create a business that practices what it preaches when it comes to the environment.

9. Create new jobs in the local economy.

1.2 Mission, Vision, and Values

Mission Statement

Enviro-Friendly Products.com aims to provide consumers with the most comprehensive collection of environmental products in the world. We seek to create a work environment that is fun, diverse, and open-minded, as well as honest and fair.

Vision Statement

Enviro-Friendly Products.com strives to promote a sustainable future for our environment and hopes to bring as many new customers to the realization of what role they can play with their own consumption and involvement. We will provide the best quality products we can find and the most cost effective solutions out there for a wide range of clients and consumers. This will help us achieve a successful triple bottom line of economic prosperity, environmental quality, and social justice.

1.3 Keys to Success

1. Staying on top of all the products out there, and being able to translate the return on investment on each product into some sort of energy savings or environmental footprint.

2. Maintaining a decent margin with each manufacturer and a relationship where they will ship for us if we bring them the orders.

3. Developing our name brand into a national household name so that people will think of us if they need to look up an environmental product of any sort.

4. Easy yet attractive user interfaces on our website to retain traffic and bring in more traffic.

Risks

1. We might not be able to get ourselves at the top of all the applicable search engine lists without a lot of capital, and may not be able to develop a good enough relationship with enough manufacturers to have useful referral fee negotiations or margins.

2. A bigger company with bigger pockets may decide to jump into this environmental niche as it grows and smother us in our infancy.

3. The use of advertising on our site might detract from the overall mission of encouraging customers to purchase our products or recommended products.

Contingency Plans

1. We should be able to design our site and pay our top-notch consultants enough money to get to the top of the most common search engine requests such as energy efficiency or low energy or environmental products, to offset our inability to get into all top ten lists where we show up on the first page of the search.

2. We could sell out to the bigger company, or focus resources more on a certain niche that is profitable.

3. We could remove or minimize advertising in the expectation that our revenues will grow from product sales and referrals.

1.4 Use of Proceeds

Year 1:

Legal	$2,000
Consultants	$3,000
Insurance	$2,400
Graphic design	$5,000
Internet hosting	$1,500
Website software	$1,000
Misc. cash requirements	$1,000
Domain name purchase	$1,000

Basic Startup Expense: $16,900

These proceeds will cover the basic requirements to stay in business for the first year. Additional funds will be used primarily for marketing and advertising as the company starts to bring in revenue.

2.0 Company Summary

Enviro-Friendly Products.com not only sells the products, but also provides information on them. Information on environmental products is hard to obtain and no standards are placed on environmental companies to verify claims and make comparable data. It's also hard to find environmental products. The industry is extremely fragmented and it takes a good deal of effort to find out what is out there, and this is the main problem we intend to solve. Consumers benefit from environmental products in two main ways: direct economic savings and environmental benefits.

Direct Economic Savings
A consumer purchasing compact fluorescent bulbs as a replacement to incandescent can expect to save on both replacement and energy costs over the lifetime of the bulb. These types of economic savings through conservation are common in environmentally aware products.

Environmental Benefits
Environmentally sound products are, by definition, champions of environmental betterment. The amount of carbon dioxide you are keeping out of the atmosphere by purchasing wind-generated power, however, is often less clear and measurements of the environmental benefit are seldom provided with environmental products.

Enviro-Friendly Products.com plans to create an Internet portal that sells environmental products, but also provides information on their economic and environmental benefits.

2.1 Company History
The company was created in March of 2006 by Bob Weston.

2.2 Company Locations and Facilities

Enviro-Friendly Products.com plans to start as a home-office based business. As the business expands, increased space and equipment needs will necessitate the expansion of the business from the home office.

3.0 Products and Services
Enviro-Friendly Products.com will provide products that benefit the environment and promote a sustainable solution through conservation, efficiency, or use of alternative energy or substances.

3.1 Product and Service Description
The number of products and services that can and will be listed on our website are unlimited. The following will provide a brief description of some of the products or services.

Portable Solar
Portable solar chargers for small devices such as a cell phone or iPod from manufacturers such as Solio; portable solar panels from such manufacturers as Brunton that can power devices such as stereo systems with larger speakers; backpacks, laptop bags, coolers, tackle boxes, etc, that have solar panels incorporated into the shell from Eclipse Solar Gear and Voltaic Systems

Infrastructure Solar
Solar powered attic fans from Natural Light Energy Systems; solar powered sensor lights; basic water heating systems, and home energy systems

Infrastructure Lighting
Occupancy sensors, especially for rooms that are rarely used except for storage; compact fluorescent bulbs; T8 ballasts for four-foot fluorescent bulbs; skylighting materials; LED lights

Biochemical
Typically from corn or soy, there are thousands of applications for personal beauty, cleaning, protective coatings, paints, BioDiesel fuel, Ethanol fuels, herbicides, and solvents

Water Conservation
Washers, low flow faucets, showers, toilets, composting toilets

Water Heating
Tankless water heaters, pipe insulation, cold water detergents

Building Materials
Fly ash stone siding; fly ash concrete; formaldehyde-free particle board/fiber board made of agricultural waste fiber, post-consumer waste fiber, and recovered wood fiber; bamboo floors; double paned windows; sustainable forest certified wood

Wind Power
Basic wind generators, as well as referrals for larger ones of commercial interest

Organic Foods/Beverages
This is a huge and growing segment, and we do not see any reason to not include this.

Sustainable Fisheries
This is a rapidly growing industry as our oceans run out of fish, and there are several sustainable fisheries out there who can sell through our website, then ship their products.

Miscellaneous
Water-powered calculators and clocks

Information
Return on investments, environmental impacts, where it comes from, and basic info of how to use the product

Advertising

We will provide buttons, columns, and interactive ads for the appropriate advertisers that fit in with our message of environmental responsibility.

4.0 Market Analysis Summary

Seventy percent of Americans are homeowners. These along with homebuilders are our primary market. Our secondary market consists of portable products that do not relate to making one's infrastructure more energy efficient or environmentally friendly. A recent study sponsored by Google concluded that 37 percent of consumers who conduct online searches for various products actually bought them online.

4.1 Market Segmentation

Fifteen percent of the U.S. population will definitely buy green or environmental products according to Roper ASW. This equates to 45 million potential customers, assuming a population of 300 million people in the U.S. If 70 percent of these people are homeowners, then that provides a potential market of 31.5 million people. Assuming that 75 percent of these people have consistent Internet access, and that 37 percent of them will buy online, then you have a market segment of 8,741,250 premier customers.

Thirty-one percent of the U.S. market will sometimes buy environmentally sound products, so this provides a potential market of 46.5 million if you assume that half these people may buy a product based on its environmental impact. Taking that 70 percent of these people are homeowners, you have a market of 32.55 million people. Once you break down those with Internet access who buy online after searching for something, your actual potential market consists of 8,430,450 sometime customers.

Of the remaining U.S. population of 54 percent of 300 million, we can safely assume that at least half of these people will be looking to save money on their utility bills in the coming years as natural gas and electricity prices continue to rise as their supply cannot rise at the rate of growing worldwide demand. If you take the homeowners with Internet who are likely to make an Internet purchase then you can extrapolate a market segment of 15,734,250 occasional customers.

4.2 Target Market Segment Strategy

Provide the "green" consumer with a one-stop shop for all their environmental products. Chase after the marginal consumer who maybe does not really care about the environment but is concerned with saving money on their utility bills.

4.3 Market Trends and Growth

Japan, South Korea, and Europe have very strong environmental tendencies, more than double the level of awareness it seems than U.S. consumers. These marketplaces could provide potential business in the very near future. The English-speaking market worldwide will be served with higher shipping fees initially, and once the revenue streams can justify it, conversions into several languages will be available on the website.

The market of environmentally conscious consumers continues to grow in the U.S., and Enviro-Friendly Products.com will benefit from this early stage growth cycle that will continue to grow for at least the next twenty to forty years in the foreseeable future.

4.4 Competitors

There are no competitors that offer half the products we intend to have on our website, but our biggest and closest competitor at this point is RealGoods.com. RealGoods.com only offers about half the products we intend to sell. GreenFeet.com, GreenProductsAlliance.com, and GreenHome.com sell home products primarily geared to female homemakers. AltEnergyStore.com sells only alternative energy products.

There are several listing websites with links to various manufacturers, of which we hope to put our link on these websites. Some of these websites are GrinningPlanet.com, EcoBusinessLinks.com, EcoMall.com, and GreenPages.com.

There are also several nonprofits and organizations sponsored by government and various donors that have websites that link to various environmental products manufacturers. Some of these include GreenSeal.org, World.org/weo/energy, SolarLiving.org, NRDC.org, GreenBiz.com, and GreenerBuildings.com. We also hope to link to these sites, but these sites do provide a small amount of competition in that they provide ways for the consumer to link directly to the manufacturers or distributor rather than through our site.

5.0 Strategy and Implementation Summary

Our strategy is to line up as many partner manufacturers and distributors as possible, then launch the website. Our revenue streams from purchases and a little advertising will slowly grow, then more rapidly as the public gains exposure to our website through increased advertising and promotion.

5.1 Strategy

Enviro-Friendly Products.com's strategy is to be the biggest provider of environmentally conscious products on the Internet. We aim to do this by focusing on the following practices.

1. Emphasize benefits to consumers

Emphasizing the benefits that consumers will see by purchasing the environmental products we review allows them to make more informed purchases that will conserve the planet's scarce resources for the future.

2. Build strong relationships with manufacturers

Good relationships with the manufacturers of the environmental products are key to the success of Enviro-Friendly Products.com. Providing these manufacturers with fair reviews, quality referrals, and high levels of service will allow us to maintain profitable long-term relationships.

3. Differentiate our service from the competition

The environmental products industry is fragmented and diverse. In order to establish itself as the industry leader, Enviro-Friendly Products.com must provide the highest level of service to both consumers and manufacturers.

4. Provide large quantities of unique information

In order to maintain a competitive advantage over other start-ups, Enviro-Friendly Products.com must provide large quantities of information on its site that is not available elsewhere and is difficult to duplicate.

5.2 Value Proposition

Unique Selling Advantage

Enviro-Friendly Products.com is the only comprehensive site on the Web where consumers can go and quickly access a wide variety of products that benefit the environment in some way. This will lead to more traffic on our site as people become aware of how convenient it is to look up a product that saves them money or makes the environment more sustainable for the immediate future. Also, many people are trying to escape their dependence on fossil fuels, and as this escalates with the coming rise in fossil fuel prices, we will be positioned to capitalize on it.

Value Proposition

We believe that many people have a desire to make environmentally responsible purchases; however, they are not properly educated on the benefits of making these decisions. By making information on these products available and accessible, both consumers and the environment will benefit.

The consumer will be given free reviews and information as we build up our knowledge base. They will also be able to find products that fill their needs in a central location without the effort it currently takes.

Manufacturers will sell more of their products and have to worry less about the obscurity of their products. They will also have a good place to advertise their products—an area heavily visited by those interested in environmentally conscious products or utilizing more efficient or alternative energy.

5.3 Competitive Edge

Currently, the market for environmental products is fragmented and information on available products is difficult to find. By being the first to consolidate the available information and create a portal to all products environmental, we will become the name that is associated with the idea—much like eBay is associated with online auction houses.

By having the most information and the relationships with manufacturers of environmental products, we plan to maintain a competitive advantage that will be hard to reproduce. Much as Consumer Reports maintains a large knowledge bank of product comparisons that is almost irreproducible, we will have a comparisons of products' environmental and economic impacts that will be incredibly difficult to imitate.

5.4 Marketing Strategy

Marketing is central to the overall business strategy. Our success hinges on a few critical behaviors:

- Provide neutral, fact-filled reviews
- Create a Search Engine Optimized (SEO) site that will rank near the top of search results on all search engines
- Build good relationships with suppliers of environmental products

The strategy is to create a site that will drive a good deal of quality traffic and measure the impact that the site is having on suppliers' sales. This information is incredibly valuable for approaching new manufacturers and having them agree to participate in our referral program.

Enviro-Friendly Products.com will also spend money once it has it available on every possible traditional media channel that targets our intended audience to increase awareness of our site.

5.4.1 Pricing Strategy

Advertising

We plan for the pricing of advertisement space on the initial site to be within industry norms. The following table schedules the rates on the different types of ads. We plan to offer discounts to advertisers as they commit to longer advertising contracts.

11

Cost per Thousand Rate	Open Rate	6 Months	12 Months
Tower	$15.00	$10.00	$7.50
Button	$7.50	$5.00	$3.75
Interactive Box	$15.00	$10.00	$7.50

Sales Commissions

Our target pricing for sales through our website will be 12.5 percent of the end purchase price. This assumption is taken from the 20 to 25 percent margins that we found in contacting several potential manufacturers and distributors who were even willing to drop ship for us. The 12.5 percent price of sales commissions would be negotiable on some products.

5.4.2 Promotion Strategy

As an Internet company funded by sales and advertisements, it is imperative that our site has a good deal of traffic. Studies show at least 70 percent of all Internet traffic comes from search engine referrals, so the most important method of promotion for our business model is search engine optimization. We also plan to spend time and money on traditional methods of promotion.

Search Engine Optimization
Optimizing a site for search engines means that you take the HyperText Markup Language (HTML) that makes up the page and make it more accessible to the nongraphic browsers that search engines use to index your site. Search engine spiders are the text-only browsers that search engines use to make their indexes of the World Wide Web. Optimizing the site would be to take an image that said "Products" and put an alternate "tag" in the page so that while the search engine spider can't see the image, it knows that the image says "Products." This makes it easier to determine what the site is about and make it relevant for searches.

Reciprocal Links
Because the services we provide create a good deal of value for the suppliers of environmental products, we plan on leveraging the goodwill created for our promotion. As reviews are written for products, the suppliers of these products will be asked to provide links to our home page on their websites. These links help search engines to know what sites are relevant to ours and boost our ranking in search engine results. Simple link exchanges like this drive traffic to our site, creating revenues.

Traditional Advertising
We plan to place advertisements in magazines whose target market includes consumers of environmental products. These advertisements would help raise the awareness of the site among our targeted audience. We also plan to target radio and TV programs that discuss energy concerns, or environmental concerns.

5.4.3 Marketing Programs

Enviro-Friendly Products.com will take an active role in promoting its services to manufacturers throughout the world. We plan on partnering with 10x Marketing to help us fill our Internet marketing needs. 10x Marketing is an Internet marketing firm that specializes in search engine and other forms of online marketing, 10x Marketing has helped companies of all sizes and in all industries benefit from the Internet.

5.5 Sales Strategy

Initially our sales strategy is to drive eyeballs to our website and entice them to actually click through and purchase our products. The more people that visit our site, the more potential sales we generate.

Sales forecasts are on the last two pages of this plan.

5.6 Strategic Alliances

Enviro-Friendly Products.com will have strategic alliances with any website that is willing to provide links to it, specifically those geared toward the environment, energy efficiency, or organic foods.

5.7 Milestones

July 2006: achieve $1,000 in total sales
May 2007: achieve $100,000 in total sales
June 2010: achieve over $500,000 in sales for the year

Enviro-Friendly Products.com is hoping to expand at an exponential rate that ramps up four to ten times faster than the above milestones, but this is the bare minimum it hopes to make.

6.0 Management Summary

6.1 Organizational Structure

Bob Weston is the owner and sole employee.

6.2 Management Team

Bob Weston is currently a first-year student in the MBA program at the University of Texas. He will be looking to add additional people to the management team in the near future.

6.3 Management Team Gaps

Bob Weston does not have any real experience working in the dot-com world other than helping set up his own website for his mortgage business. He will need to bring aboard someone with some technical experience and overall dot-com marketing and logistics experience. In the meantime, he plans on using consultants to help him with the basics.

6.4 Personnel Plan

Eventually we will need a Web administrator and an inside sales person to develop more relationships with manufacturers, distributors, and potential advertisers. A full-time marketing manager will be required to help get the name out there once the inside sales person starts to become overwhelmed. Much of the work initially can be outsourced to Internet consultants, Web designers, attorneys, and marketing firms.

7.0 Financial Plan

The break-even point for Enviro-Friendly Products.com is forecast for October 2006 to recover the total minimum costs of $16,900 as outlined in the use of proceeds section earlier. If more money is required to launch and maintain the site, then it could break even in the end of 2006 or beginning of 2007.

Since the only personnel will consist of Bob Weston for the foreseeable future, profit and loss statements are not included since this a relatively simple one-man operation. Please see the sales forecasts, as well as the breakdown of startup costs if more capital is available.

In the year 2007, the plan will be reevaluated, and if it looks like a successful venture, more capital will be invested or the plug will be pulled altogether.

Global Wholesale

Global Wholesale LLC
1452 North Foxglove Road
St. Louis, Missouri. 84025
801-673-3529
ryanJamison@comcast.net

Confidentiality Agreement

The undersigned reader acknowledges that the information provided by
_____ in this business plan is confidential; therefore, reader agrees not to
disclose it without the express written permission of _____.

It is acknowledged by reader that information to be furnished in this business plan is in
all respects confidential in nature, other than information which is in the public domain
through other means and that any disclosure or use of same by reader, may cause serious
harm or damage to _____.

Upon request, this document is to be immediately returned to _____.

_____
Signature

_____
Name (typed or printed)

_____
Date

This is a business plan. It does not imply an offering of securities.

Table of Contents

1. Executive Summary

Global Wholesale LLC, in St. Louis, Missouri, is a start-up company created for the purpose of selling items online for us and for small businesses that are unable to do it for themselves.

Our service focuses on giving small local businesses the opportunity to reach millions of customers instead of only thousands. It gives them a storefront that is a lot less expensive than one they have to rent. They have no employees to pay to sit around and wait for sales to happen. We only get paid when the products sell and we take care of delivering them to the customers. We know that our service is good, because we are successfully using it to financially support the start of Global Wholesale. Other small businesses will certainly find it profitable as well.

There are many small businesses that need our service. Currently there is almost no competition in this industry. Because of our first mover advantage we feel that we can secure this segment of the market in this area.

1.1. Objectives

1. Get one of the partners working full time on Global Wholesale LLC. This will allow us to grow faster. We will be able to hire employees and turn over our inventory at our target rate.

2. Move into a warehouse and have six part-time employees listing inventory on eBay, Amazon, Overstock, and our own personal website.

3. Have over $25,000 of our own inventory.

4. Have ten business clients who use us to sell online for them.

1.2. Mission

Global Wholesale LLC will enable our clients to have a reasonable online selling environment. We will have flexible work hours and a profit sharing system that rewards employees for their own personal results. We believe that both working smart and working hard are critical for our clients and ourselves.

1.3. Keys to Success

1. Appropriately pricing and managing our service, allowing us to gain more customers

2. Keep costs as low as possible so that our profit margins are maximized

2. Company Summary

Global Wholesale LLC has been resurrected from a sole-proprietor company that stopped running two years ago. This company sold cell phones, satellite equipment, and computers on eBay. The company had not understood the necessity of growing, having employees, and being disciplined in money management issues. These issues are the reason for this business plan. With renewed focus, Global Wholesale LLC will be able to grow and remain stable.

2.1. Company Ownership

Global Wholesale LLC is a limited liability corporation (LLC). The members include Ryan Jamison with a 51 percent share, Gary Thayne with a 29 percent share and James Gibson with the remaining 20 percent share. The company has chosen to be taxed like a partnership. Mr. Jamison has an MBA and contributed start-up cash and some of his home for an initial start-up office and warehouse space. Mr. Gibson the previous owner of the company is bringing industry technical expertise, he has also contributed start-up funds. Mr. Thayne is bringing start-up funds, industry expertise and has the ability to dedicate over 40+ hours a week to the success of Global Wholesale. Mr. Jamison and Mr. Gibson are choosing to remain fully employed by other companies until Global Wholesale has enough revenue.

2.2. Start-up Summary

Our start-up costs come to $10,450. The majority of the costs come from getting or having inventory. The small legal and other miscellaneous start-up fees are negligible.

Start-up	
Requirements	
Start-up Expenses	
Legal	$100
Insurance	$0
Software	$50
Other	$0
Total Start-up Expenses	$150
Start-up Assets	
Cash Required	$4,000
Start-up Inventory	$6,000
Other Current Assets	$300
Long-term Assets	$0
Total Assets	$10,300
Total Requirements	$10,450

3. Products and Services

Global Wholesale LLC sells products and services. The company has expertise in online sales. Global Wholesale is currently able to sell tens of thousands of dollars a month of computer, satellite and cell phone equipment on eBay. The products that it sells are to online customers. The service that Global Wholesale provides to small companies is consignment selling of their items online. Many small businesses are unable to afford to hire a qualified expert in online sales and do not possess the knowledge to do it themselves. We provide them the opportunity to sell online.

4. Market Analysis Summary

We service 2 distinctly different markets. 1 market is the people that we sell products to online. This market is huge, literally hundreds of millions of people throughout the world. The other market is our small business customers. This market is small compared to the other, but is still sizeable enough to pursue. We will target small retail companies with less than 20 employees that do not have any online sales experience. We will also target larger companies that are not into retail that need to sell their old assets (ie a Hospital that needs to get rid of hospital beds and wants to make some money on them). Our marketing analysis will focus on our small business customers.

4.1. Market Segmentation

Based on the 1997 Economic Census, Davis county had 241 wholesale companies and 582 retail companies. Because of the growth in the county over the last 9 years, I'm sure that number has grown. All of these companies are potential clients, even if they are currently handling their own internet sales. The first round of clients that we will attempt to acquire will be small companies. These companies may only be self employed people with very few or no employees. Computers, cell phones, clothes and antiques sell the best online and we will target those segments as well. Based on the 1997 Census about 40 percent of wholesale and retail companies sell something that tends to perform well online (Computers, cell phones, antiques etc.). The first segment that we will pursue is the computer and cell phone segments. As we grow we will then pursue clothes and antiques.

Market Analysis							
Potential Customers	Growth	Year 1	Year 2	Year 3	Year 4	Year 5	CAGR
Retail Companies	50%	10	15	23	35	53	51.73%
High asset turnover companies	50%	2	3	5	8	12	56.51%
Wholesale Companies	50%	4	6	9	14	21	51.37%
Other	0%	0	0	0	0	0	0.00%
Total	52.26%	16	24	37	57	86	52.26%

4.2. Target Market Segment Strategy

The reason we will focus on computers and cell phone retailers and wholesalers to start is for two reasons. The first is that the members of Global Wholesale LLC are very familiar with these industries. The second is that it is easier to sell mid to high priced electronics online than anything else.

4.3. Service Business Analysis

In a way we are competing with our customers. Much like ADP (who offers human resources, benefits and payroll administration), we offer a service that companies could provide for themselves. Because we have expertise we can provide this service to them cheaper than they can do it for themselves. I have looked hard and have not found any companies that provide our specific service. There are a lot of companies that provide a similar service to the regular public but do not yet target small businesses. I hope to have a first mover advantage over these companies.

4.3.1. Competition and Buying Patterns

Clients will purchase our service if we can sell more of their product faster and by taking a smaller percent than competitors or themselves. Once we develop a clientele, we can use the numbers from their success to help us gain more customers.

5. Strategy and Implementation Summary

Global Wholesale has all of the resources it needs to succeed. The partners in the LLC have funded the company well enough to get it started. As long as we can remain attractive to our clientele we will succeed. Our main priority is to establish our own product selling and gain our initial clients.

5.1. SWOT Analysis

We provide a rare service. We have the expertise to do it well. We have years or experience and connections that make our strategy possible. As a new company we don't currently have a lot of clients or a lot of start-up capital. Even with these few weaknesses the opportunity is large. There are many small businesses and many who don't have a strong online presence. I know that eventually most small companies will find it more profitable to use us to sell than to try and do their own sales.

5.1.1. Strengths

Our strength is in our knowledge of our industry and service and in our organizational structure. We have years of experience selling online. We are currently our own customers and we like our service. We purchase computers and satellite equipment in bulk at low prices and resell them. We have an extremely organized inventory that would allow anyone we hire to be taught to sell and ship our products within a short time. We plan on hiring a lot of part time help, targeting mostly housewives looking for extra income.

Most people believe that these sellers would need a high level of computer knowledge to perform this work, we feel that with they way we have things organized we could teach the necessary job skills in a few weeks. By working our employees under 20 hours a week (allowing these housewives and mothers to work while their children are at school), we have a large pool of inexpensive labor that doesn't need some very expensive benefits like insurance.

5.1.2. Weaknesses

The biggest weakness that we have is that we are new and small. As a new company we have very few clients and the work from these clients can be sporadic. We also need a better way to sell our service. Currently our only clients are friends of members of the company. We hope that our sales strategy will be sufficient to generate new clients as quickly as we can handle them.

5.1.3. Opportunities

The opportunities that exist in the market involve certain clients. Most large retailers already have on online presence. It would be difficult but if we could average a better return on their money than they could, we could win their business. There are other large companies that have high asset turnover, like IHC or the LDS Church. Both of those groups don't sell retail or wholesale, but have a lot of equipment that they use and once it is used need to either resell it or throw it away. Having a contract like that would also be very lucrative. Even having a lot of smaller business clients would work very well.

5.1.4. Threats

There will be two threats to our business. The first is direct competition. So far, I have not been able to find any online resellers that target small businesses. The second is our clients themselves may feel that they can do this themselves. We need to show them that we can do this better and cheaper than they can do it for themselves.

5.2. Competitive Edge

Our competitive edge comes from our focus on servicing small businesses. We are targetting this niche and feel it to be very lucrative. Our flexible structure will allow us to grow with our company.

5.3. Marketing Strategy

Our strategy is to position ourselves as a means for small companies to increase sales or see some return on used assets that they would normally have to throw away. Word of mouth advertising will be huge for us, as well as a savvy sales staff that knows how the techniques needed to sell to small business owners.

5.4. Sales Strategy

We are going to have a salesperson to directly contact the businesses we want as clients and make our offer. We will compensate our salesperson with a 20 percent commission on our profits from the clients. As long as the salesman is still with the company and as long as we still have there clients, they will continue to get their commission.

5.4.1. Sales Forecast

We feel that we have two very realistic expectations from our sales forecast. The first is that we will add a new business customer every month and a half. The other is that we can grow our own individual sales 20 percent per month until we double our original sales numbers and we level off. I'm not forecasting more because we don't have the resources to grow any faster.

Sales Forecast			
	Year 1	Year 2	Year 3
Unit Sales			
Clients	42	84	126
Our own Products	3,887	8,000	15,000
Total Unit Sales	3,929	8,084	15,126
Unit Prices	Year 1	Year 2	Year 3
Clients	$2,000.00	$2,000.00	$2,000.00
Our own Products	$55.00	$55.00	$55.00
Sales			
Clients	$84,000	$168,000	$252,000
Our own Products	$213,767	$440,000	$825,000
Total Sales	$297,767	$608,000	$1,077,000
Direct Unit Costs	Year 1	Year 2	Year 3
Clients	$500.00	$500.00	$500.00
Our own Products	$44.00	$44.00	$44.00
Direct Cost of Sales			
Clients	$21,000	$42,000	$63,000
Our own Products	$171,014	$352,000	$660,000
Subtotal Direct Cost of Sales	$192,014	$394,000	$723,000

5.5. Milestones

We are small and are bootstrapping our financing. After becoming incorporated, getting an EIN and allow the state and local paperwork done, all of our milestones will be small. One of the company partners will start working fulltime. We have enough start-up money to fund our own eBay selling. We want to increase our sales units from 200 a month to 200 a week. We can do this once we have a fulltime lister. After a few months we will have enough cash to move into a warehouse. When we move into a warehouse it will be time to hire a part time lister and a part time shipper. It is our goal to have at least one customer by then, but it won't be necessary for our success, because of our own selling opportunities.

Milestones

Milestone	Start Date	End Date	Budget	Manager	Department
Get Incorporated	5/3/2006	6/2/2006	$100	Ryan	Administration
Gary goes fulltime	5/3/2006	6/2/2006	$0	Gary	Listing
Get first customer	5/3/2006	6/2/2006	$100	Ryan and James	Administration
Get Warehouse	8/1/2006	8/31/2006	$1,000	Ryan	Administration
Hire shipper	8/31/2006	9/30/2006	$0	Gary and Ryan	Shipping
Hire Lister	8/31/2006	9/30/2006	$0	Gary and Ryan	Listing
Totals			$1,200		

6. Web Plan Summary

Most of our online sales will be done via eBay, Amazon.com and Overstock.com. We will also have our own site that we can do online sales directly to the customer.

6.1. Website Marketing Strategy

If we can get more people to buy from our online store than from eBay, we will earn more per sale. The way that we will get our online customers to come to our site is by having links to our site from our eBay ads and to pack advertisements with our shipments.

6.2. Development Requirements

Our front end will need to be sales friendly. We will list our recurring items from our small business clients. We would just need to pay an e-commerce hosting site to manage the specifics of the back end.

7. Management Summary

Currently there are only three people in the company. Ryan Jamison will manage shipping and administration. James Gibson and Gary Thayne will handle listing responsibilities. Gary will eventually be handling the day to day operations of the company and oversee employees.

Our insurance needs will be handled by Dan Springer. Dan has over 20 years of experience and operates from St. Louis, Missouri. We hope to have our accounting handled by Hillberg, Burnett and Thorpe of St. Louis. One of the partners in Global Wholesale is friends with Ross Junto a partner in HBT. For legal counsel we are planning on McPhie and Pingree, LLC of St. Louis.

7.1. Personnel Plan

Personnel will be inexpensive because no one requires a large salary while we start up. We assume that Gary's day to day work and James' part time work will be enough to finance everything easily. Both Gary and James are being paid for their efforts. Ryan is not being paid.

Personnel Plan			
	Year 1	Year 2	Year 3
CEO	$12	$12,000	$24,000
General Manager	$24,000	$26,000	$28,000
Listing Manager	$4,800	$6,000	$8,000
Total People	5	5	5
Total Payroll	$28,812	$44,000	$60,000

8. Financial Plan

Our business should grow at about a 30 percent rate per month for about the first half year. Then the growth will slowly level off. Because Global Wholesale will almost instantly be profitable, we will fund our growth by our own sales.

8.1. Start-up Funding

Only needing about 10,000 dollars for start-up cash is really a small amount. We plan on bootstrapping our company and don't want any help to get going. Most of our money is going to go to inventory. Some of the cell phones and electronic equipment can become expensive when buying in the quantities that we need. We expect to be able to turn over about 15,000 dollars in inventory a week from 1 full time lister. Most of the money made from sales will come back into the company for additional inventory.

Start-up Funding	
Start-up Expenses to Fund	$150
Start-up Assets to Fund	$10,300
Total Funding Required	$10,450
Assets	
Non-cash Assets from Start-up	$6,300
Cash Requirements from Start-up	$4,000
Additional Cash Raised	$2,050
Cash Balance on Starting Date	$6,050
Total Assets	$12,350
Liabilities and Capital	
Liabilities	
Current Borrowing	$0
Long-term Liabilities	$0
Accounts Payable (Outstanding Bills)	$0
Other Current Liabilities (Interest Free)	$0
Total Liabilities	$0
Capital	
Planned Investment	
Ryan	$6,000
Gary	$3,000
James	$3,500
Additional Investment Requirement	$0
Total Planned Investment	$12,500
Loss at Start-up (Start-up Expenses)	($150)
Total Capital	$12,350
Total Capital and Liabilities	$12,350
Total Funding	$12,500

8.2. Important Assumptions

We assume that there will not be a major recession or catastrophe in the next five years.

8.3. Break-even Analysis

The chart says it all. We need to sell about 163 items to break even. We feel that we can sell four times that in a month.

Break-even Analysis	
Monthly Units Break-even	163
Monthly Revenue Break-even	$12,350
Assumptions:	
Average Per-unit Revenue	$75.79
Average Per-unit Variable Cost	$48.87
Estimated Monthly Fixed Cost	$4,386

8.4. Projected Profit and Loss

We have a high turnover of our inventory. We can buy $10,000 of inventory and sell it for $13,000 in a week. We can hopefully dedicate $12,000 to purchase more inventory to sell the next week. Salaries are the major part of our non-COGS expenses.

Pro Forma Profit and Loss			
	Year 1	Year 2	Year 3
Sales	$297,767	$608,000	$1,077,000
Direct Costs of Goods	$192,014	$394,000	$723,000
Other Costs of Goods	$0	$0	$0
	------------	------------	------------
Cost of Goods Sold	$192,014	$394,000	$723,000
Gross Margin	$105,753	$214,000	$354,000
Gross Margin %	35.52%	35.20%	32.87%
Expenses			
Payroll	$28,812	$44,000	$60,000
Marketing/Promotion	$300	$600	$1,000
Depreciation	$0	$0	$0
Rent	$12,000	$12,000	$12,000
Utilities	$1,200	$1,300	$1,400
Insurance	$4,800	$5,000	$5,200
Payroll Taxes	$4,322	$6,600	$9,000
Other	$1,200	$1,500	$1,800
	------------	------------	------------
Total Operating Expenses	$52,634	$71,000	$90,400
Profit Before Interest and Taxes	$53,120	$143,000	$263,600
EBITDA	$53,120	$143,000	$263,600
Interest Expense	$0	$0	$0
Taxes Incurred	$15,936	$42,900	$79,080
Net Profit	$37,184	$100,100	$184,520
Net Profit/Sales	12.49%	16.46%	17.13%

8.5.   Projected Cash Flow

We have pooled together about $10,000 in start-up cash and saleable assets. With this base and our high inventory turnover, we will only experience a short period of negative cash flow. Since we are bootstrapping this company, we can't afford to be in the red for long.

Pro Forma Cash Flow

	Year 1	Year 2	Year 3
Cash Received			
Cash from Operations			
Cash Sales	$297,767	$608,000	$1,077,000
Subtotal Cash from Operations	$297,767	$608,000	$1,077,000
Additional Cash Received			
Sales Tax, VAT, HST/GST Received	$0	$0	$0
New Current Borrowing	$0	$0	$0
New Other Liabilities (Interest Free)	$0	$0	$0
New Long-term Liabilities	$0	$0	$0
Sales of Other Current Assets	$0	$0	$0
Sales of Long-term Assets	$0	$0	$0
New Investment Received	$0	$0	$0
Subtotal Cash Received	$297,767	$608,000	$1,077,000
Expenditures	Year 1	Year 2	Year 3
Expenditures from Operations			
Cash Spending	$28,812	$49,700	$63,279
Bill Payments	$221,925	$464,875	$832,883
Subtotal Spent on Operations	$250,737	$514,575	$896,162
Additional Cash Spent			
Sales Tax, VAT, HST/GST Paid Out	$0	$0	$0
Principal Repayment of Current Borrowing	$0	$0	$0
Other Liabilities Principal Repayment	$0	$0	$0
Long-term Liabilities Principal Repayment	$0	$0	$0
Purchase Other Current Assets	$0	$0	$0
Purchase Long-term Assets	$0	$0	$0
Dividends	$0	$0	$0
Subtotal Cash Spent	$250,737	$514,575	$896,162
Net Cash Flow	$47,030	$93,425	$180,838
Cash Balance	$53,080	$146,505.	$327,343

8.6. Projected Balance Sheet

We currently have about enough cash and assets to get going. We expect to put another small sum of money in the company soon. The numbers in the chart look good and the net worth of the company looks to steadily improve.

Pro Forma Balance Sheet

	Year 1	Year 2	Year 3
Assets			
Current Assets			
Cash	$53,080	$146,505	$327,343
Inventory	$20,600	$42,270	$77,566
Other Current Assets	$300	$300	$300
Total Current Assets	$73,980	$189,075	$405,209
Long-term Assets			
Long-term Assets	$0	$0	$0
Accumulated Depreciation	$0	$0	$0
Total Long-term Assets	$0	$0	$0
Total Assets	$73,980	$189,075	$405,209
Liabilities and Capital	Year 1	Year 2	Year 3
Current Liabilities			
Accounts Payable	$24,446	$39,441	$71,055
Current Borrowing	$0	$0	$0
Other Current Liabilities	$0	$0	$0
Subtotal Current Liabilities	$24,446	$39,441	$71,055
Long-term Liabilities	$0	$0	$0
Total Liabilities	$24,446	$39,441	$71,055
Paid-in Capital	$12,500	$12,500	$12,500
Retained Earnings	($150)	$37,034	$137,134
Earnings	$37,184	$100,100	$184,520
Total Capital	$49,534	$149,634	$334,154
Total Liabilities and Capital	$73,980	$189,075	$405,209

Jeff Miller Landscapes, LLC

Jeff Miller Landscapes, LLC
11743 Amber Stone Drive
South Jordan, Utah. 84095
801-783-5386
866-643-9571
jeff@jmlandscapes.com

Confidentiality Agreement

The undersigned reader acknowledges that the information provided by _____ in this business plan is confidential; therefore, reader agrees not to disclose it without the express written permission of _____.

It is acknowledged by reader that information to be furnished in this business plan is in all respects confidential in nature, other than information which is in the public domain through other means and that any disclosure or use of same by reader, may cause serious harm or damage to _____.

Upon request, this document is to be immediately returned to _____.

_____
Signature

_____
Name (typed or printed)

_____
Date

This is a business plan. It does not imply an offering of securities.

Table of Contents

Jeff Miller Landscapes, LLC

1.0 Executive Summary

Introduction

Jeff Miller Landscapes, LLC is a full service landscape contractor. We specialize in creating custom outdoor living spaces for our clients. Our goal is to provide our clients with excellent landscaping service, at a price that is fair and reasonable. As a company, we feel that it is our duty to provide exceptional service to our clients, as well as nurture good relationships with our employees. Our desire is to become an important contributor to our community through honest, reliable work ethic. We are located in South Jordan, Utah. The purpose of this business plan is to familiarize the reader with the intricate workings of our business.

The Company

We were formed in January, 2003. The company has experienced constant growth since then, to the point where we now have three out of our five employees have been with the company for more than two years. In 2005, our gross revenues were $328,000. In addition to our five employees, we also have two managing members. We are in a great position for expanding, and anticipate much growth over the next three years.

Our Services

Jeff Miller Landscapes, LLC is a licensed S330 Landscape Contractor in the state of Utah. We specialize on installing landscapes on new residential homes. Often, retaining wall work is needed before the landscaping can be completed. In this case, we build rock retaining walls, as well as any shaping or grading that needs to take place in order to prepare the home for landscaping. We install sprinkler systems, topsoil, trees and shrubs, bark mulch, and sod.

The Market

We are located in the heart of the Utah building boom. Three out of the five fastest growing cities in the state are within less than a mile of our headquarters. For the past three years, we have worked closely with new home owners and home builders in meeting their landscaping needs. We intend to continue new home landscaping, and we are working on building more relationships with local area home builders in order to increase our market share. Last year alone, more than 3,000 new homes were built in our area. Although competition is high, we are confident that we will be able to capitalize on a portion of that growth.

Future Plans

We intend to continue a steady growth process over the next three years. We have worked hard to maintain a good relationship with our current employees, and feel that they are ready to expand and to take on additional responsibility in order to help the company grow. We do not intend to seek outside financial assistance. We feel that our growth can be financed internally. We hope that by the year 2008, our gross revenues can be in excess of $750,000. We feel that this goal is reasonable and will be achieved through steady, focused effort on our part.

Jeff Miller Landscapes, LLC

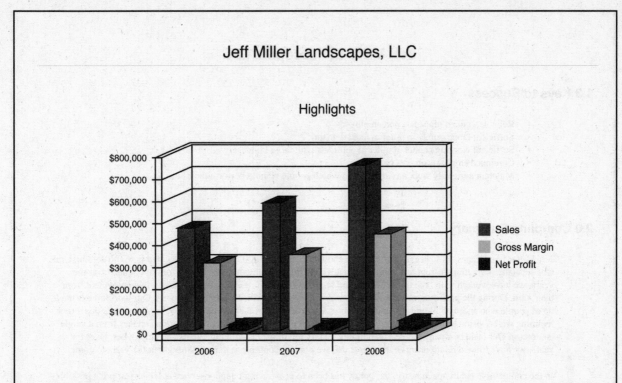

Highlights

1.1 Objectives

1. Achieve 100% customer friendship and satisfaction.
2. Hire only high caliber employees who are capable of providing quality service.
3. Continue company growth by making $60,000 net profit in 2006.
4. Create constant business throughout the winter of 2006.
5. Establish contracts with four major builders in our area by April 2006.
6. Establish lease or financing for new machine by April 2006.

1.2 Mission

The mission of Jeff Miller Landscapes, LLC (JML) is to become the most reliable and profitable landscape construction company in the Salt Lake Valley. JML knows its two greatest assets are its employees and its customers. Through unique recognition programs, JML will continue to build relationships based on mutual trust with its employees. Through excellent customer service, JML will continue to build high quality relationships with current and future customers in order to achieve its mission. JML will also put emphasis on building relationships with our suppliers in order to obtain the best prices and highest quality services, which will result in less stress for our employees and lower prices for our clients. Through these three objectives, JML will continue to work towards its mission of becoming the most reliable and profitable landscape construction company in the Salt Lake Valley.

Jeff Miller Landscapes, LLC

1.3 Keys to Success

- Reliable, trained managers and employees
- Sufficient labor supply in order to meet demand
- Sufficient working capital in order to contracts with large builders
- Continued emphasis on cost control
- Maintain a friendly work environment in which people want to perform their best

2.0 Company Summary

Jeff Miller Landscapes, LLC began as a two-man show in January of 2003. We are now located in South Jordan, Utah. Our specialty is creating custom residential landscapes and quality outdoor living spaces for our clients. Over the years, we have worked with both home owners and home builders in order to get the most possible enjoyment from their yard. During the peak summer months, we employ up to eight skilled landscape laborers. Our workforce is made up of people who enojoy building custom landscapes and take pride in their work. In 2005, we formally added a rock retaining wall division to further enhance our ability to offer complete landscape construction services from a single contractor. Our main company focus is on building quality relationships with our clients and employees. Over the years, we have formed relationships with clients that we hope to continue to nurture throughout the years to come.

In the competitive landscape industry, our policy has been to provide high quality service at the lowest price possible. We are dedicated to continuing our low cost operations, and to passing those cost savings on to our clients.

Our team of core employees consists of seven dedicated employees. Jeff Miller, who takes care of sales and operations, has six years of experience in the landscape construction industry. Brandon Andersen is the company's general foreman, and has five years experience in the industry. The company's two landscape foremen both have more than two years in the industry. Jessica Miller, a former marketing consultant for a reknowned Utah company, joined us last year to assist in our marketing and efficiency improvement efforts.

With this team in place, we look to the future and we are excited about building relationships with future clients, as well as nurturing those relationships that we have formed along the way.

2.1 Company Ownership

Jeff Miller Landscapes, LLC is a privately owned limited liability company. It was formed in April of 2004. The company has three members. Jeff Miller is the founder and managing partner, with 50% ownership. Jessica Miller has 45% part ownership. Recently, it became necessary to add a third parter. This parter, Chris Theurer, will has 5% ownership as well as the ability to hire and fire employees and give direction in other necessary business functions.

2.2 Company History

In our first year, we did $200,000 in total revenue with a profit margin of about 10%. In 2005, the company grew to $300,000 in revenue with a profit margin of 20%. We attribute this significant gain in profit margin to employee retention and more efficient systems. However, we attribute the increased margin in 2005 to the fact that this was the first year in which we employed a full-time retaining wall division. Retaining walls generally give a much higher return than landscaping.

Jeff Miller Landscapes, LLC

Table: Past Performance

Past Performance			
	2003	2004	2005
Sales	$202,700	$291,108	$328,450
Gross Margin	$20,008	$25,866	$65,211
Gross Margin %	9.87%	8.89%	19.85%
Operating Expenses	$0	$0	$111,489
Collection Period (days)	0	0	5

Balance Sheet			
	2003	2004	2005
Current Assets			
Cash	$3,000	$8,000	$10,000
Accounts Receivable	$0	$0	$4,000
Other Current Assets	$0	$0	$8,000
Total Current Assets	$3,000	$8,000	$22,000
Long-term Assets			
Capital Assets	$0	$0	$48,000
Accumulated Depreciation	$0	$0	$24,000
Total Long-term Assets	$0	$0	$24,000
Total Assets	$3,000	$8,000	$46,000
Current Liabilities			
Accounts Payable	$0	$0	$5,000
Current Borrowing	$0	$0	$38,000
Other Current Liabilities (interest free)	$0	$0	$0
Total Current Liabilities	$0	$0	$43,000
Long-term Liabilities	$0	$0	$0
Total Liabilities	$0	$0	$43,000
Paid-in Capital	$0	$0	$7,000
Retained Earnings	$3,000	$8,000	($69,211)
Earnings	$0	$0	$65,211
Total Capital	$3,000	$8,000	$3,000
Total Capital and Liabilities	$3,000	$8,000	$46,000
Other Inputs			
Payment Days	0	0	15
Sales on Credit	$0	$0	$150,000
Receivables Turnover	0.00	0.00	37.50

Jeff Miller Landscapes, LLC

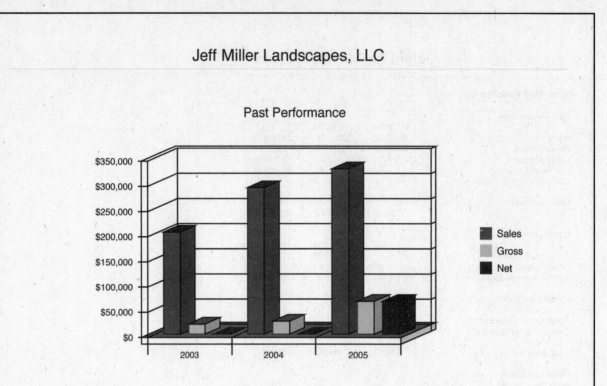

3.0 Services

We provide full landscape construction services. This includes everything from finish grading a new home to laying the sod or planting the seed at the end of the project. We also provide retaining wall construction service. We build retaining walls out of both rock and block. We take great pride in providing top quality parts and installation at a cost that is competitive with companies of a lesser quality.

4.0 Market Analysis Summary

Our target market at the current time can be split into two different groups. The first group are owners of recently built residential homes. The second group consists of the builders of new residential homes. Our target geographical area is focused on the southwest corner of the Salt Lake Valley. We are focusing on this area for the following reasons.

- Our business is located in the area.
- 3 out of the state's 5 highest growing cities are located in our target area.
- New, high volume residential developments such as "Daybreak" and "Rosecrest" require landscaping to be completed before the permit of occupation can be issued.

According to research conducted by the University of Utah's Bureau of Economic and Business Research, in 2005 our target area alone saw over 3,000 new residential dwellings built. Therefore, our intentions are to continue to acquire new customers through direct mail, word of mouth incentives, and creating alliances with local home builders who are in need of landscaping contractors.

Jeff Miller Landscapes, LLC

4.1 Market Segmentation

The market for residential landscaping can be divided into three categories.

The first segment consists of local home builders who build homes in developments that require landscaping to be installed before the home buyer can move in. Demand in this area is high, but so is competition. Landscape contractors who target contractors as customers have the ability to do many, usually smaller homes for a low price and in a short amount of time. Landscapers in this area must be highly efficient in order to make a profit. The advantages to having these types of customers is that they provide a constant source of work, as well as the advantage of not having an actual homeowner to deal with. The landscaper deals directly with the contractor before the homeowner moves in. Currently, 50% of our business comes from this segment.

The second segment consists of people who have recently purchased a new or existing home which does not have landscaping installed. This category usually consists of larger homes than the first category, and so they also require much more customization and contact with the client. The advantages of targeting this market are higher profit margins and little or no float time on getting paid. The disadvantages of this market include more customer service issues do to the more customized yard, as well as less labor efficiency due to the highly varying type of work. Currently, about 45% of our business comes from this segment.

The third segment consists of home owners in home with existing landscaping who desire to remodel their yard. The advantages of this segment are higher possible profit margins due to the difficulty of the work. However, these types of projects are very difficult to estimate, which can result in under bidding. This segment currently makes up about 5% of our business.

Table: Market Analysis

Market Analysis Potential Customers	Growth	2006	2007	2008	2009	2010	CAGR
New residential home construction	13%	3,500	3,959	4,478	5,065	5,729	13.11%
Other	5%	250	263	276	290	305	5.10%
Total	12.63%	3,750	4,222	4,754	5,355	6,034	12.63%

Market Analysis (Pie)

■ New residential home construction
■ Other

Jeff Miller Landscapes, LLC

4.2 Target Market Segment Strategy

Currently, Jeff Miller Landscapes finds itself with the perfect opportunity to grow and acquire new clients. Most of the company's employees have been with the company for more than two years, and we are ready to expand and give more responsibility to these individuals. Also, we find ourselves located in the middle of one of the fastest growing areas in the state, and we feel that it is time to capitalize on the growth and establish new relationships with more home builders. Also, with so many homes being built that are not required to have landscaping installed, we find ourselves in a situation where it is possible to acquire new residential customers as well.

4.3 Service Business Analysis

We are in the landscape contracting business. That means that we install landscaping, from sprinkler systems to sod, trees, and shrubs. The exact size of the landscaping industry is unknown. However, in our geographical area there are many, many landscape contractors. Generally, when a homeowner is in need of landscaping services, they will ask their neighbors who did their yard, or they will look in the yellow pages to try and find a landscaper. Most homeowners solicit at least two or three estimates from different companies, and then make a decision on which landscaper to use.

4.3.1 Competition and Buying Patterns

In the residential landscaping market, competitors come from all walks of life. Most companies compete on price. However, there are a few that compete on quality and curb appeal. There are many companies who operate illegally, without an official state contractors license. Clients in less expensive homes usually are looking for a low quality, low price job that just gets grass on the ground and nothing more. Clients in more expensive homes usually want more than just a basic landscape, and are willing to pay more for something that will set them apart from their neighbors. As previously mentioned, home builders who are in need of landscapers often want just-enough-to-get-by quality, at a low price.

5.0 Strategy and Implementation Summary

Jeff Miller Landscapes strives to provide top quality landscaping services. In order to maintain growth expectations, we must focus on developing employee core competencies and provide them with managerial experience. Also, we must develop relationships with home builders who are in need of landscaping contractors in order to insure constant growth. Growth will be financed internally, expect in the case of equipment or vehicle purchases. This strategy is essential in order for us to meet our goals.

5.1 Competitive Edge

Our competitive edge consists of our ability to form lasting relationships with our customers and employees. As a company, we understand that people and relationships are our strongest assets. Many companies don't take relationships as seriously as we do, which we feel gives us a competitive advantage that will last as long as our relationships do.

Jeff Miller Landscapes, LLC

5.2 Marketing Strategy

At Jeff Miller Landscapes, we feel that our marketing strategy revolves around our reputation in the community and the relationships that we have with our clients. However, we also understand that in order to gain more business and to grow, we must have a plan for making ourselves known in the community and to our target market. We intend to do this in the following ways:

- Direct mail advertising to residents of our target market
- Word-of-mouth incentives to our existing clients
- Create new relationships with area home builders through referrals

5.3 Sales Strategy

Jeff Miller is currently the only salesperson that the company employs. We would like to hire on a full-time salesman, but the company is still not ready to handle the kind of work volume that a full-timer could bring in. Jeff considers sales the most important part of his job description, and dedicates the most part of his days to performing sales functions. Due to the fact that we are selling a highly customized service, the sales process is usually very long and drawn-out. It can take weeks and many meetings in order to close one sale and be ready to begin the service.

5.3.1 Sales Forecast

Our sales forecast reflects our goal for constant, steady growth. We are assuming constant growth in the new residential home building market, or in other words, constant demand. We do not plan on rapid expansion, but rather constant growth in order to build a solid foundation of well trained employees and good clientele.

Table: Sales Forecast

Sales Forecast	2006	2007	2008
Sales			
Residential landscaping	$340,000	$400,000	$500,000
Rock retaining walls	$125,000	$180,000	$250,000
Total Sales	$465,000	$580,000	$750,000
Direct Cost of Sales	2006	2007	2008
Residential Landscaping - COGS	$103,000	$150,000	$200,000
Rock retaining wall - COGS	$47,000	$75,000	$100,000
Subtotal Direct Cost of Sales	$150,000	$225,000	$300,000

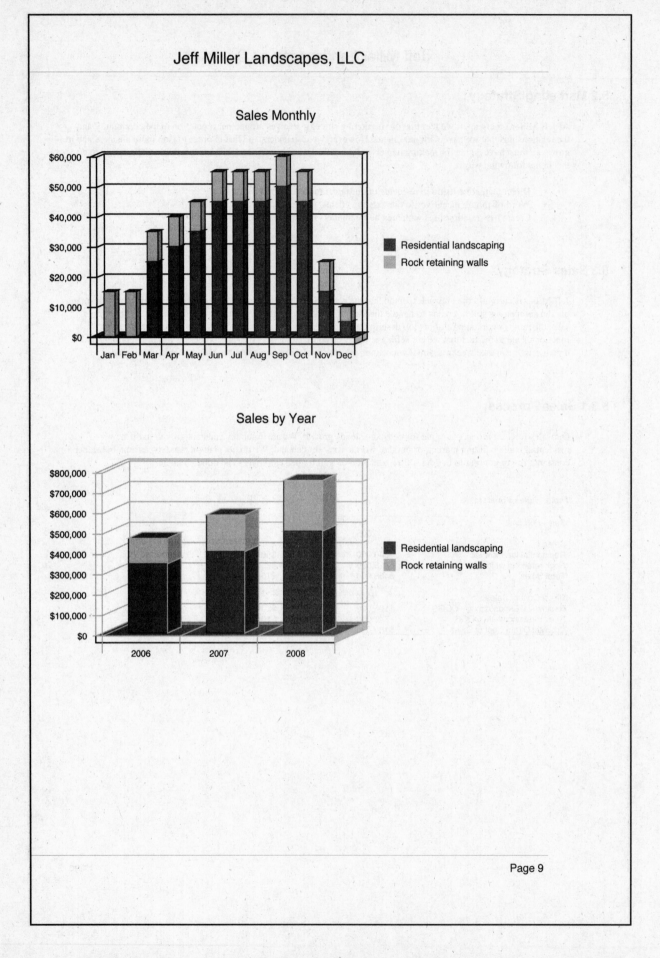

Jeff Miller Landscapes, LLC

Sales Monthly

Residential landscaping
Rock retaining walls

Sales by Year

Residential landscaping
Rock retaining walls

Jeff Miller Landscapes, LLC

5.4 Milestones

- Web site design and implementation we wish to have online by May 11th, 2006. Brandon Andersen is in charge of the website creation. In order for the task to be completed, details concerning the website must be ironed out. Also, pictures for the portfolio section of the website need to be taken and prepared for insertion into the web page. The domain name has already been purchased.
- Equipment purchase options are to be analyzed and presented to the managers by Jeff Miller. This task must be completed by no later than May 6th, 2006. This option should take top priority and be taken very seriously. In order for the company to maintain profitability and stick with current strategy, the company must either decide to purchase or lease a mini track hoe for building rock retaining walls. For the past two years, the company has been renting machines, which has ended up costing us tens of thousands of dollars with nothing to show for it. We feel this is foolishness and need to make a decision towards ownership.
- The company must have a fully functional office by no later than May 1st, 2006. The office is currently running at 75% capacity, with just a few more odds and ends to tye up and get organized. These items include employee paperwork and training videos. Also, a telephone answering system must be established in order to minimize calls to the manager's mobile telephones.
- The company's accounting software, Quickbooks, needs to be audited and corrected before the company can complete its 2005 tax return. Currently, the balance sheet is incorrect and must be fixed. This item is of utmost importance and must be addressed immediately by Jeff Miller and our accountant.
- As soon as the company financial statements are corrected, taxes must be filed and paid. This is to be done as soon as possible by Jeff Miller and our accountant.
- It was advised to our company that it would be wise to establish a corporate agreement with our lawyer. This item needs to be taken care of by Jeff Miller and our lawyer before May 1st, 2006.
- We currently operate one landscaping group, but would like to divide the group sometime in mid-summer. This task is to be worked on jointly by Brandon Andersen and Jeff Miller.

Table: Milestones

Milestones

Milestone	Start Date	End Date	Budget	Manager	Department
Web site	5/29/2006	7/18/2006	$150	BA	Marketing
Equipment purchase options	5/29/2006	7/13/2006	unknown	JM	Operations
Fully functional office	5/29/2006	7/8/2006	$100	JTM	Accounting
Quickbooks updated	5/29/2006	6/8/2006	$0	JM	Accounting
Taxes filed	5/29/2006	6/13/2006	$50	JM	Accounting
Corporate Agreement	5/29/2006	7/8/2006	$75	JM	Corporate
Group division	5/29/2006	9/6/2006	$0	JM	Operations
Totals			$375		

Jeff Miller Landscapes, LLC

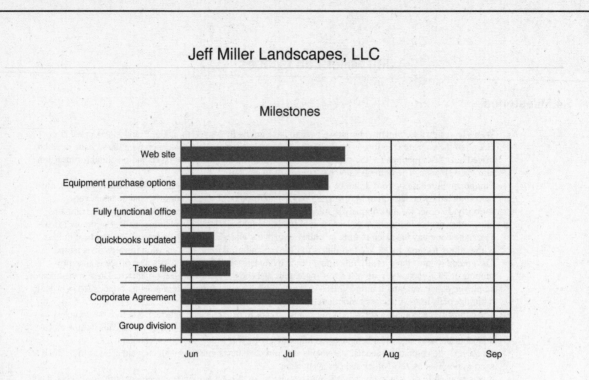

Milestones

6.0 Management Summary

Jeff Miller Landscapes, LLC has five employees, and two managing partners.

Jeff Miller is the founder, and has been in the landscaping business since May 2001.

Jessica Miller is a managing partner, and recently joined the company in August 2005.

Brandon Andersen is the landscaping manager, and has been working with Jeff since Jun 2001.

The company has four other employees. They are, in order of seniority, Sebastian H. Martinez, Mauricio Zaragoza A., Javier Zaragoza A., and Rogelio Hernandez.

This is Sebastian and Mauricio's third year with the company, Javier's second, and Rogelio's first.

6.1 Personnel Plan

We are planning on the managing members, Jeff and Jessica Miller, to take a combined average salary of $60,000 per year for the next three years. We are estimating that with the employee's salary amounts will vary depending on demand. Hence, in the summer months payroll expense is much greater than in the spring, winter, and fall months when demand isn't as high. The company may find it necessary to hire temporary laborers in the months with higher demand.

Jeff Miller Landscapes, LLC

Table: Personnel

Personnel Plan			
	2006	2007	2008
Managing Members	$60,000	$60,000	$60,000
Employees	$81,600	$100,000	$125,000
Total People	0	0	0
Total Payroll	$141,600	$160,000	$185,000

7.0 Financial Plan

The business is expected to maintain a constant growth rate of about 15% per year over the next three years. We intend to finance growth with mostly internal funds. However, some external financing may be required for equipment purchases. As our company and employees mature, we should be able to maintain constant growth in both revenue and profit margin.

7.1 Important Assumptions

The current interest rate is what our company pays for it's short term bank notes to purchase equipment. This rate is currently at 8%. The long term rate is the rate the company pays for vehicles, which is currently at 6%. The company's tax rate varies depending on many factors, but is at an average of 30%.

7.2 Break-even Analysis

The break-even analysis is a very useful tool in order to know how much work needs to be done in order to begin making money. However, the difficult implication of this tool in our case is the fact that we are a seasonal business. In essence, our break-even analysis needs to become a rolling analysis. That is, the surplus from January needs to be added to February and so forth. We don't expect to break even until the first parts of June or July, weather depending.

Table: Break-even Analysis

Break-even Analysis	
Monthly Revenue Break-even	$32,764
Assumptions:	
Average Percent Variable Cost	32%
Estimated Monthly Fixed Cost	$22,195

Jeff Miller Landscapes, LLC

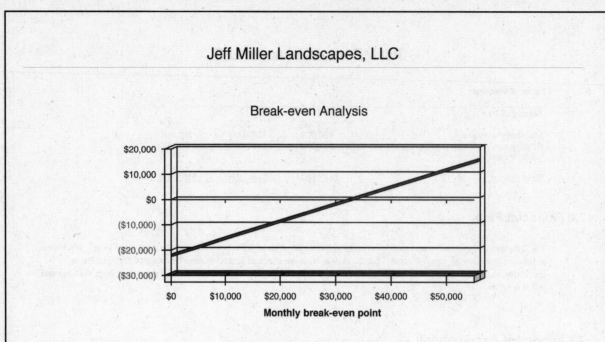

Break-even point = where line intersects with 0

7.3 Projected Profit and Loss

The most important point about these profit and loss projections is the sales forecast. It is vital, and absolutely feasible, that the company maintain sales growth in order to achieve positive margins. The items that may need to be modified are insurance, taxes, and payroll costs. It is unknown at this time how many more employees the company will have to hire in order to obtain these sales figures. However, we understand and realize that this type of growth will take planning and great attention to detail in order to maintain profitability.

Jeff Miller Landscapes, LLC

Table: Profit and Loss

Pro Forma Profit and Loss	2006	2007	2008
Sales	$465,000	$580,000	$750,000
Direct Cost of Sales	$150,000	$225,000	$300,000
Other Costs of Sales	$8,000	$10,000	$12,000
	-------------	-------------	-------------
Total Cost of Sales	$158,000	$235,000	$312,000
Gross Margin	$307,000	$345,000	$438,000
Gross Margin %	66.02%	59.48%	58.40%
Expenses			
Payroll	$141,600	$160,000	$185,000
Marketing/Promotion	$1,200	$2,200	$3,000
Depreciation	$3,000	$5,000	$5,000
Debt service	$10,800	$13,000	$15,000
Gasoline/diesel	$16,500	$20,000	$25,000
Insurance	$12,000	$8,500	$10,000
Payroll Taxes	$21,240	$24,000	$27,750
Other	$60,000	$80,000	$100,000
	-------------	-------------	-------------
Total Operating Expenses	$266,340	$312,700	$370,750
Profit Before Interest and Taxes	$40,660	$32,300	$67,250
EBITDA	$43,660	$37,300	$72,250
Interest Expense	$3,040	$3,040	$3,040
Taxes Incurred	$11,286	$8,778	$19,263
Net Profit	$26,334	$20,482	$44,947
Net Profit/Sales	5.66%	3.53%	5.99%

Profit Monthly

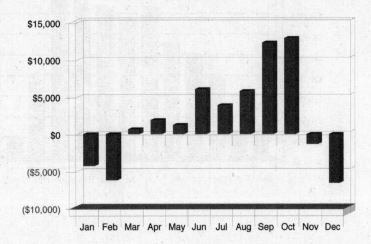

Jeff Miller Landscapes, LLC

Profit Yearly

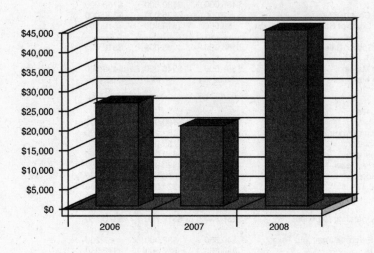

Gross Margin Monthly

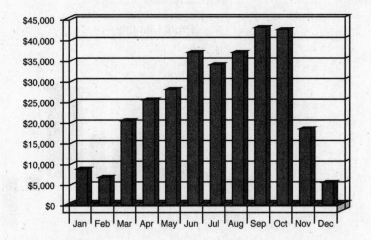

Jeff Miller Landscapes, LLC

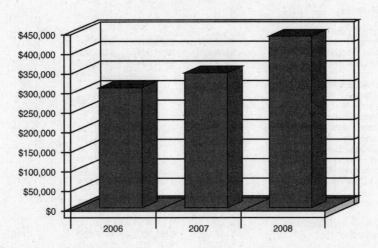

7.4 Projected Cash Flow

The key to our cash flow analysis is to keep in mind that our business is cyclical. You can see that throughout the year we are adding to our cash balance, only to decrease it slightly during the slower winter months. The good news is that we have managed to keep our debt service payments to a minimum, as well as build up enough reserve cash just in case the weather inhibits work for a long period of time.

Jeff Miller Landscapes, LLC

Table: Cash Flow

Pro Forma Cash Flow			
Cash Received	2006	2007	2008
Cash from Operations			
Cash Sales	$279,000	$348,000	$450,000
Cash from Receivables	$186,133	$231,044	$298,586
Subtotal Cash from Operations	$465,133	$579,044	$748,586
Additional Cash Received			
Sales Tax, VAT, HST/GST Received	$0	$0	$0
New Current Borrowing	$0	$0	$0
New Other Liabilities (interest-free)	$0	$0	$0
New Long-term Liabilities	$0	$0	$0
Sales of Other Current Assets	$0	$0	$0
Sales of Long-term Assets	$0	$0	$0
New Investment Received	$0	$0	$0
Subtotal Cash Received	$465,133	$579,044	$748,586
Expenditures	2006	2007	2008
Expenditures from Operations			
Cash Spending	$141,600	$160,000	$185,000
Bill Payments	$288,905	$372,253	$505,146
Subtotal Spent on Operations	$430,505	$532,253	$690,146
Additional Cash Spent			
Sales Tax, VAT, HST/GST Paid Out	$0	$0	$0
Principal Repayment of Current Borrowing	$0	$0	$0
Other Liabilities Principal Repayment	$0	$0	$0
Long-term Liabilities Principal Repayment	$0	$0	$0
Purchase Other Current Assets	$0	$0	$0
Purchase Long-term Assets	$0	$0	$0
Dividends	$0	$0	$0
Subtotal Cash Spent	$430,505	$532,253	$690,146
Net Cash Flow	$34,628	$46,791	$58,440
Cash Balance	$44,628	$91,419	$149,860

Jeff Miller Landscapes, LLC

Cash

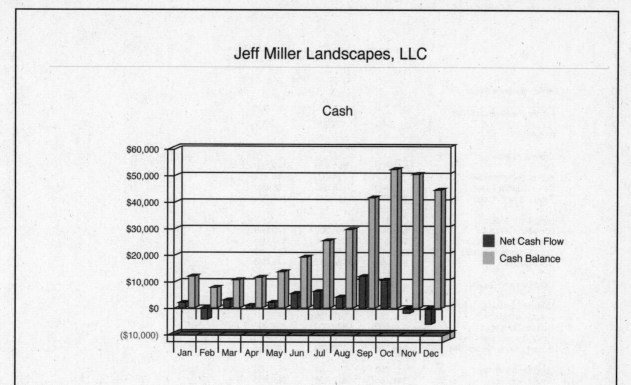

7.5 Projected Balance Sheet

Our balance sheet appears to be quite stable. Net worth is increasing, and we do not foresee any problems in meeting our future debt obligations.

Jeff Miller Landscapes, LLC

Table: Balance Sheet

Pro Forma Balance Sheet	2006	2007	2008
Assets			
Current Assets			
Cash	$44,628	$91,419	$149,860
Accounts Receivable	$3,867	$4,823	$6,237
Other Current Assets	$8,000	$8,000	$8,000
Total Current Assets	$56,495	$104,242	$164,096
Long-term Assets			
Long-term Assets	$48,000	$48,000	$48,000
Accumulated Depreciation	$27,000	$32,000	$37,000
Total Long-term Assets	$21,000	$16,000	$11,000
Total Assets	$77,495	$120,242	$175,096
Liabilities and Capital	2006	2007	2008
Current Liabilities			
Accounts Payable	$10,161	$32,426	$42,333
Current Borrowing	$38,000	$38,000	$38,000
Other Current Liabilities	$0	$0	$0
Subtotal Current Liabilities	$48,161	$70,426	$80,333
Long-term Liabilities	$0	$0	$0
Total Liabilities	$48,161	$70,426	$80,333
Paid-in Capital	$7,000	$7,000	$7,000
Retained Earnings	($4,000)	$22,334	$42,816
Earnings	$26,334	$20,482	$44,947
Total Capital	$29,334	$49,816	$94,763
Total Liabilities and Capital	$77,495	$120,242	$175,096
Net Worth	$29,334	$49,816	$94,763

7.6 Business Ratios

The following table contains our business ratios for your convenience.

Jeff Miller Landscapes, LLC

Table: Ratios

Ratio Analysis

	2006	2007	2008	Industry Profile
Sales Growth	41.57%	24.73%	29.31%	0.00%
Percent of Total Assets				
Accounts Receivable	4.99%	4.01%	3.56%	0.00%
Other Current Assets	10.32%	6.65%	4.57%	100.00%
Total Current Assets	72.90%	86.69%	93.72%	100.00%
Long-term Assets	27.10%	13.31%	6.28%	0.00%
Total Assets	100.00%	100.00%	100.00%	100.00%
Current Liabilities	62.15%	58.57%	45.88%	0.00%
Long-term Liabilities	0.00%	0.00%	0.00%	0.00%
Total Liabilities	62.15%	58.57%	45.88%	0.00%
Net Worth	37.85%	41.43%	54.12%	100.00%
Percent of Sales				
Sales	100.00%	100.00%	100.00%	100.00%
Gross Margin	66.02%	59.48%	58.40%	0.00%
Selling, General & Administrative Expenses	60.36%	55.95%	52.41%	0.00%
Advertising Expenses	0.00%	0.00%	0.00%	0.00%
Profit Before Interest and Taxes	8.74%	5.57%	8.97%	0.00%
Main Ratios				
Current	1.17	1.48	2.04	0.00
Quick	1.17	1.48	2.04	0.00
Total Debt to Total Assets	62.15%	58.57%	45.88%	0.00%
Pre-tax Return on Net Worth	128.25%	58.74%	67.76%	0.00%
Pre-tax Return on Assets	48.55%	24.33%	36.67%	0.00%

Additional Ratios	2006	2007	2008	
Net Profit Margin	5.66%	3.53%	5.99%	n.a
Return on Equity	89.77%	41.12%	47.43%	n.a
Activity Ratios				
Accounts Receivable Turnover	48.10	48.10	48.10	n.a
Collection Days	29	7	7	n.a
Accounts Payable Turnover	28.94	12.17	12.17	n.a
Payment Days	28	20	26	n.a
Total Asset Turnover	6.00	4.82	4.28	n.a
Debt Ratios				
Debt to Net Worth	1.64	1.41	0.85	n.a
Current Liab. to Liab.	1.00	1.00	1.00	n.a
Liquidity Ratios				
Net Working Capital	$8,334	$33,816	$83,763	n.a
Interest Coverage	13.38	10.63	22.12	n.a
Additional Ratios				
Assets to Sales	0.17	0.21	0.23	n.a
Current Debt/Total Assets	62%	59%	46%	n.a
Acid Test	1.09	1.41	1.97	n.a
Sales/Net Worth	15.85	11.64	7.91	n.a
Dividend Payout	0.00	0.00	0.00	n.a

Appendix

Appendix Table: Sales Forecast

Sales Forecast

		Jan	Feb	Mar	Apr	May	Jun	Jul	Aug	Sep	Oct	Nov	Dec
Sales													
Residential landscaping	0%	$15,000	$15,000	$25,000	$30,000	$35,000	$45,000	$45,000	$45,000	$50,000	$45,000	$15,000	$5,000
Rock retaining walls	0%	$0	$10,000	$10,000	$10,000	$10,000	$10,000	$10,000	$10,000	$10,000	$10,000	$10,000	$5,000
Total Sales		$15,000	$25,000	$35,000	$40,000	$45,000	$55,000	$55,000	$55,000	$60,000	$55,000	$25,000	$10,000

	Jan	Feb	Mar	Apr	May	Jun	Jul	Aug	Sep	Oct	Nov	Dec
Direct Cost of Sales												
Residential Landscaping - COGS	$3,000	$5,000	$10,000	$10,000	$12,000	$12,000	$15,000	$12,000	$12,000	$8,000	$3,000	$1,000
Rock retaining wall - COGS	$3,000	$3,000	$4,000	$4,000	$4,000	$5,000	$5,000	$5,000	$4,000	$4,000	$3,000	$3,000
Subtotal Direct Cost of Sales	$6,000	$8,000	$14,000	$14,000	$16,000	$17,000	$20,000	$17,000	$16,000	$12,000	$6,000	$4,000

Appendix

Appendix Table: Personnel

Personnel Plan		Jan	Feb	Mar	Apr	May	Jun	Jul	Aug	Sep	Oct	Nov	Dec
Managing Members	0%	$5,000	$5,000	$5,000	$5,000	$5,000	$5,000	$5,000	$5,000	$5,000	$5,000	$5,000	$5,000
Employees	0%	$800	$1,000	$4,000	$7,000	$10,000	$12,000	$12,000	$12,000	$9,000	$8,000	$5,000	$800
Total People		0	0	0	0	0	0	0	0	0	0	0	0
Total Payroll		$5,800	$6,000	$9,000	$12,000	$15,000	$17,000	$17,000	$17,000	$14,000	$13,000	$10,000	$5,800

Appendix

Appendix Table: Profit and Loss

Pro Forma Profit and Loss

	Jan	Feb	Mar	Apr	May	Jun	Jul	Aug	Sep	Oct	Nov	Dec
Sales	$15,000	$15,000	$35,000	$40,000	$45,000	$55,000	$55,000	$55,000	$60,000	$55,000	$25,000	$10,000
Direct Cost of Sales	$6,000	$8,000	$14,000	$16,000	$16,000	$20,000	$20,000	$17,000	$16,000	$12,000	$6,000	$4,000
Other Costs of Sales	$250	$250	$500	$500	$1,000	$1,000	$1,000	$1,000	$1,000	$500	$500	$500
Total Cost of Sales	$6,250	$8,250	$14,500	$14,500	$17,000	$18,000	$21,000	$18,000	$17,000	$12,500	$6,500	$4,500
Gross Margin	$8,750	$6,750	$20,500	$25,500	$28,000	$37,000	$34,000	$37,000	$43,000	$42,500	$18,500	$5,500
Gross Margin %	58.33%	45.00%	58.57%	63.75%	62.22%	67.27%	61.82%	67.27%	71.67%	77.27%	74.00%	55.00%
Expenses												
Payroll	$5,800	$6,000	$9,000	$12,000	$15,000	$17,000	$17,000	$17,000	$14,000	$13,000	$10,000	$5,800
Marketing/Promotion	$100	$100	$100	$100	$100	$100	$100	$100	$100	$100	$100	$100
Depreciation	$250	$250	$250	$250	$250	$250	$250	$250	$250	$250	$250	$250
Debt service	$900	$900	$900	$900	$900	$900	$900	$900	$900	$900	$900	$900
Gasoline/diesel	$700	$1,200	$1,700	$1,500	$1,500	$1,300	$1,400	$1,700	$1,800	$1,600	$1,400	$700
Insurance	$1,000	$1,000	$1,000	$1,000	$1,000	$1,000	$1,000	$1,000	$1,000	$1,000	$1,000	$1,000
Payroll Taxes (15%)	$870	$900	$1,350	$1,800	$2,250	$2,550	$2,550	$2,550	$2,100	$1,950	$1,500	$870
Other	$5,000	$5,000	$5,000	$5,000	$5,000	$5,000	$5,000	$5,000	$5,000	$5,000	$5,000	$5,000
Total Operating Expenses	$14,620	$15,350	$19,300	$22,550	$26,000	$28,100	$28,200	$28,500	$25,150	$23,800	$20,150	$14,620
Profit Before Interest and Taxes	($5,870)	($8,600)	$1,200	$2,950	$2,000	$8,900	$5,800	$8,500	$17,850	$18,700	($1,650)	($9,120)
EBITDA	($5,620)	($8,350)	$1,450	$3,200	$2,250	$9,150	$6,050	$8,750	$18,100	$18,950	($1,400)	($8,870)
Interest Expense	$253	$253	$253	$253	$253	$253	$253	$253	$253	$253	$253	$253
Taxes Incurred	($1,837)	($2,656)	$284	$809	$524	$2,594	$1,664	$2,474	$5,279	$5,534	($571)	($2,812)
Net Profit	($4,286)	($6,197)	$663	$1,888	$1,223	$6,053	$3,883	$5,773	$12,318	$12,913	($1,332)	($6,561)
Net Profit/Sales	-28.58%	-41.32%	1.89%	4.72%	2.72%	11.00%	7.06%	10.50%	20.53%	23.48%	-5.33%	-65.61%

Appendix

Appendix Table: Cash Flow

Pro Forma Cash Flow

		Jan	Feb	Mar	Apr	May	Jun	Jul	Aug	Sep	Oct	Nov	Dec
Cash Received													
Cash from Operations													
Cash Sales		$9,000	$9,000	$21,000	$24,000	$27,000	$33,000	$33,000	$33,000	$36,000	$33,000	$15,000	$6,000
Cash from Receivables		$4,200	$6,000	$6,267	$14,067	$16,067	$18,133	$22,000	$22,000	$22,067	$23,933	$21,600	$9,800
Subtotal Cash from Operations		$13,200	$15,000	$27,267	$38,067	$43,067	$51,133	$55,000	$55,000	$58,067	$56,933	$36,600	$15,800
Additional Cash Received													
Sales Tax, VAT, HST/GST Received	0.00%	$0	$0	$0	$0	$0	$0	$0	$0	$0	$0	$0	$0
New Current Borrowing		$0	$0	$0	$0	$0	$0	$0	$0	$0	$0	$0	$0
New Other Liabilities (interest-free)		$0	$0	$0	$0	$0	$0	$0	$0	$0	$0	$0	$0
New Long-term Liabilities		$0	$0	$0	$0	$0	$0	$0	$0	$0	$0	$0	$0
Sales of Other Current Assets		$0	$0	$0	$0	$0	$0	$0	$0	$0	$0	$0	$0
Sales of Long-term Assets		$0	$0	$0	$0	$0	$0	$0	$0	$0	$0	$0	$0
New Investment Received		$0	$0	$0	$0	$0	$0	$0	$0	$0	$0	$0	$0
Subtotal Cash Received		$13,200	$15,000	$27,267	$38,067	$43,067	$51,133	$55,000	$55,000	$58,067	$56,933	$36,600	$15,800
Expenditures		Jan	Feb	Mar	Apr	May	Jun	Jul	Aug	Sep	Oct	Nov	Dec
Expenditures from Operations													
Cash Spending		$5,800	$6,000	$9,000	$12,000	$15,000	$17,000	$17,000	$17,000	$14,000	$13,000	$10,000	$5,800
Bill Payments		$5,441	$13,293	$15,285	$25,113	$25,951	$28,633	$31,770	$33,804	$32,026	$33,279	$28,412	$15,897
Subtotal Spent on Operations		$11,241	$19,293	$24,285	$37,113	$40,951	$45,633	$48,770	$50,804	$46,026	$46,279	$38,412	$21,697
Additional Cash Spent													
Sales Tax, VAT, HST/GST Paid Out		$0	$0	$0	$0	$0	$0	$0	$0	$0	$0	$0	$0
Principal Repayment of Current Borrowing		$0	$0	$0	$0	$0	$0	$0	$0	$0	$0	$0	$0
Other Liabilities Principal Repayment		$0	$0	$0	$0	$0	$0	$0	$0	$0	$0	$0	$0
Long-term Liabilities Principal Repayment		$0	$0	$0	$0	$0	$0	$0	$0	$0	$0	$0	$0
Purchase Other Current Assets		$0	$0	$0	$0	$0	$0	$0	$0	$0	$0	$0	$0
Purchase Long-term Assets		$0	$0	$0	$0	$0	$0	$0	$0	$0	$0	$0	$0
Dividends		$0	$0	$0	$0	$0	$0	$0	$0	$0	$0	$0	$0
Subtotal Cash Spent		$11,241	$19,293	$24,285	$37,113	$40,951	$45,633	$48,770	$50,804	$46,026	$46,279	$38,412	$21,697
Net Cash Flow		$1,959	($4,293)	$2,981	$954	$2,116	$5,500	$6,230	$4,196	$12,041	$10,654	($1,812)	($5,897)
Cash Balance		$11,959	$7,665	$10,647	$11,600	$13,716	$19,216	$25,446	$29,642	$41,683	$52,337	$50,525	$44,628

Appendix

Appendix Table: Balance Sheet

Pro Forma Balance Sheet

	Starting Balances	Jan	Feb	Mar	Apr	May	Jun	Jul	Aug	Sep	Oct	Nov	Dec
Assets													
Current Assets													
Cash	$10,000	$11,959	$7,665	$10,647	$11,600	$13,716	$19,216	$25,446	$29,642	$41,683	$52,337	$50,525	$44,628
Accounts Receivable	$4,000	$5,800	$5,800	$13,533	$15,467	$17,400	$21,267	$21,267	$21,267	$23,200	$21,267	$9,667	$3,867
Other Current Assets	$8,000	$8,000	$8,000	$8,000	$8,000	$8,000	$8,000	$8,000	$8,000	$8,000	$8,000	$8,000	$8,000
Total Current Assets	$22,000	$25,759	$21,465	$32,180	$35,067	$39,116	$48,483	$54,713	$58,909	$72,883	$81,604	$68,192	$56,495
Long-term Assets													
Long-term Assets	$48,000	$48,000	$48,000	$48,000	$48,000	$48,000	$48,000	$48,000	$48,000	$48,000	$48,000	$48,000	$48,000
Accumulated Depreciation	$24,000	$24,250	$24,500	$24,750	$25,000	$25,250	$25,500	$25,750	$26,000	$26,250	$26,500	$26,750	$27,000
Total Long-term Assets	$24,000	$23,750	$23,500	$23,250	$23,000	$22,750	$22,500	$22,250	$22,000	$21,750	$21,500	$21,250	$21,000
Total Assets	$46,000	$49,509	$44,965	$55,430	$58,067	$61,866	$70,983	$76,963	$80,909	$94,633	$103,104	$89,442	$77,495
Liabilities and Capital	Jan	Feb	Mar	Apr	May	Jun	Jul	Aug	Sep	Oct	Nov	Dec	
Current Liabilities													
Accounts Payable	$5,000	$12,795	$14,449	$24,251	$25,000	$27,576	$30,641	$32,738	$30,911	$32,318	$27,876	$15,546	$10,161
Current Borrowing	$38,000	$38,000	$38,000	$38,000	$38,000	$38,000	$38,000	$38,000	$38,000	$38,000	$38,000	$38,000	$38,000
Other Current Liabilities	$0	$0	$0	$0	$0	$0	$0	$0	$0	$0	$0	$0	$0
Subtotal Current Liabilities	$43,000	$50,795	$52,449	$62,251	$63,000	$65,576	$68,641	$70,738	$68,911	$70,318	$65,876	$53,546	$48,161
Long-term Liabilities	$0	$0	$0	$0	$0	$0	$0	$0	$0	$0	$0	$0	$0
Total Liabilities	$43,000	$50,795	$52,449	$62,251	$63,000	$65,576	$68,641	$70,738	$68,911	$70,318	$65,876	$53,546	$48,161
Paid-in Capital	$7,000	$7,000	$7,000	$7,000	$7,000	$7,000	$7,000	$7,000	$7,000	$7,000	$7,000	$7,000	$7,000
Retained Earnings	($69,211)	($4,000)	($4,000)	($4,000)	($4,000)	($4,000)	($4,000)	($4,000)	($4,000)	($4,000)	($4,000)	($4,000)	($4,000)
Earnings	$65,211	($4,286)	($10,484)	($9,821)	($7,933)	($6,711)	($658)	$3,225	$8,997	$21,315	$34,228	$32,895	$26,334
Total Capital	$3,000	($1,286)	($7,484)	($6,821)	($4,933)	($3,711)	$2,342	$6,225	$11,997	$24,315	$37,228	$35,895	$29,334
Total Liabilities and Capital	$46,000	$49,509	$44,965	$55,430	$58,067	$61,866	$70,983	$76,963	$80,909	$94,633	$103,104	$89,442	$77,495
Net Worth	$3,000	($1,286)	($7,484)	($6,821)	($4,933)	($3,711)	$2,342	$6,225	$11,997	$24,315	$37,228	$35,895	$29,334

MacuGen, Inc.

Mobile Macular Degeneration Screening Service

Tom Compton, PhD
2756 Greenway
Charlotte, NC 28232
704-364-3795
704-303-1701
tcompton245678@hotmail.com

Confidentiality Agreement

The undersigned reader acknowledges that the information provided by _____ in this business plan is confidential; therefore, reader agrees not to disclose it without the express written permission of _____.

It is acknowledged by reader that information to be furnished in this business plan is in all respects confidential in nature, other than information which is in the public domain through other means and that any disclosure or use of same by reader, may cause serious harm or damage to _____.

Upon request, this document is to be immediately returned to _____.

_____
Signature

_____
Name (typed or printed)

_____
Date

This is a business plan. It does not imply an offering of securities.

Table of Contents

1. Executive Summary

MacuGen, Inc., headquartered in Charlotte, North Carolina, is a start-up company founded for the purpose of creating an eye health screening service with the long-term goal of reducing the incidence of AMD among the senior citizens it screens.

Our solution focuses on meeting the AMD screening need of senior citizens by providing convenience in coming to the patient and by providing a service affordable to those on a fixed income.

Our service will come to locations that are easily accessible to many senior citizens such as senior centers and retirement community clubhouses and test customers efficiently and accurately. Such an eye health screening service is not yet available anywhere in North Carolina, and we intend to dominate this segment.

Highlights

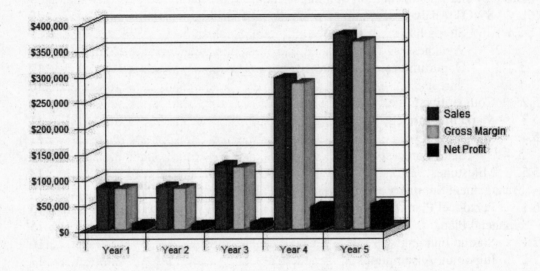

1.1. Objectives

The goals and objectives for the proposed macular degeneration screening service over the next five years:

- Provide a convenient, low-cost, and effective method for helping reduce the risk of age-related macular degeneration in the U.S. population over sixty-five years of age
- Expand this business to all of Washington County by 2008
- Expand this business to Fayetteville, Park City, and St. Anderson by 2009
- Develop and nurture relationships with North Carolina senior centers, retirement community management, and eventually retirement homes

Short-term milestones:

- Successful leasing of screening machine by August 2006
- One paying customer by September 2006
- Break even in month 3
- Hire first employee September 2007
- Leasing of two more screening machines by August 2009

1.2. Mission

MacuGen's purpose is to provide an accurate, convenient, and low-cost means to help reduce risk for macular degeneration, the leading cause of blindness for people over age sixty-five. We seek to screen, educate, and to provide options to those tested with the end goal of improving the quality of life for senior citizens as they grow older. We believe in providing maximum value to our customers while holding ourselves to the highest standards of honesty and fairness.

1.3. Keys to Success

Keys to Success

- Successful leasing of screening machine (manufacturer prefers to sell to eye professionals)
- Successful advertising campaign to elicit appropriate demand for screening service and product
- Mutually beneficial relationship with North Carolina's senior centers, retirement communities' management, and retirement homes.
- A local well-known ophthalmologist to act as a consultant.

2. Company Summary

MacuGen, Inc., provides a macular degeneration screening service designed to assess one of the major risks for blindness in the elderly population of North Carolina.

2.1. Company Ownership

MacuGen, Inc., is a privately held C Corporation wholly owned by Tom I. Compton.

2.2. Start-up Summary

Our start-up costs come to $8,630, which is mostly equipment lease, stationery, legal costs, and expenses associated with making sure that there is three months of money for these items. The start-up costs are to be financed by direct owner investment. The assumptions are shown in Table 1 and Illustration 2.

Start-up

Requirements

Start-up Expenses

Legal	$1,000
Stationery etc.	$100
Insurance	$1,000
MacuScope lease	$350
Incorporation costs—North Carolina	$500
MacuScope repairs	$100
Gasoline and automobile use	$180
Total start-up expenses	$3,230

Start-up Assets

Cash required	$4,400
Other current assets	$1,000
Long-term assets	$0
Total assets	$5,400

Total Requirements	**$8,630**

Start-up

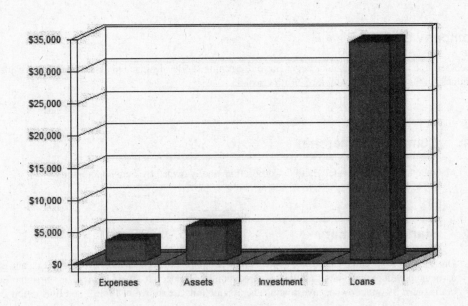

3. Services

MacuGen, Inc., provides a macular degeneration screening service designed to assess one of the major risks for blindness in the elderly population of North Carolina (people of at least sixty-five years of age).

The company's services are distributed by shuttling a macular degeneration machine in an automobile to various North Carolina senior centers, retirement communities, and eventually retirement homes. The company generates its revenues by collecting twenty dollars per screen (both eyes) per customer for a thirty-minute screen and assessment.

4. Market Analysis Summary

The prime market for MacuGen, Inc., is the elderly population over age sixty-five initially in Washington County and eventually in three different counties in North Carolina having significant numbers of senior citizens who generate a fixed income of at least $40,000 and who are willing to pay for a mobile macular degeneration examination.

North Carolina contains about 390,000 people age 65 or older (www.census.gov) and of these, approximately 37 percent live in nursing homes, or 70,300 (Nursing Home Residents 65 Years Old and Over, by Selected Characteristics: 1995,2004 LexisNexis Academic & Library Solutions). The remaining 119,700 individuals likely live in their own homes and may frequent local senior centers. In addition, there are those elderly who live in nonrestrictive retirement communities who likely frequent their communities clubhouse. We would like to target these individuals since if they lose their eyesight, they will not be able to drive or read. In this case, they may have to opt for higher-priced and more restrictive elderly housing arrangements (e.g., visiting caregivers, nursing homes) (Fong DS, American Family Physician (2000) vol. 61 no. 10). Initially, we will target the 72,768 customers in Washington County.

4.1. Market Segmentation

As mentioned previously, our target market will be the elderly population over the age of 65 who live in residential homes or retirement communities in North Carolina. The U.S. population without a relative with the disease has a 12 percent lifetime risk of developing age-related macular degeneration (AMD). If a family member does have AMD, this risk increases four-fold (http://www.answers.com/topic/macular-degeneration?method=22). Hence, in North Carolina, initially the elderly population will be targeted followed by the identification and testing family members of those afflicted.

Market Analysis							
Potential Customers	Growth	Year 1	Year 2	Year 3	Year 4	Year 5	CAGR
Elderly who go to senior centers	1%	36,300	36,663	37,030	37,400	37,774	1.00%
Elderly in retirement communities	1%	36,300	36,663	37,030	37,400	37,774	1.00%
Total	1.00%	72,600	73,326	74,060	74,800	75,548	1.00%

Market Analysis (Pie)

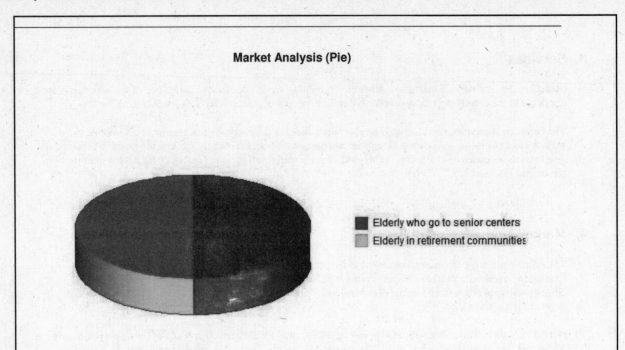

Elderly who go to senior centers
Elderly in retirement communities

4.2. Target Market Segment Strategy

We will not be successful waiting for the customer to come to us. Instead, we must focus on going to and the selling to senior citizens over the age of 65 who require convenience and inexpensive costs for our services. We will develop our message, communicate it primarily through newspaper advertising, and fulfill our commitment to excellence.

4.3. Service Business Analysis

Macular degeneration is the leading cause of blindness and its onset is correlated to lowered levels of two pigments in the retina of the eye: lutein and zeaxanthin. Currently the only way to reduce the risk for macular degeneration is to supplement one's diet with these two pigments. The business idea is to screen customers with an FDA-approved device that measures these pigment levels in their eyes and to use this information to encourage them to see an ophthalmologist. Revenues would be secured only from the scan itself. Since eye vitamin supplement sales would be logical for those found at risk by screening, the projected revenues for such sales is less than 10 percent of the revenues generated from screenings. Hence, vitamin sales will not be pursued for the at-risk customers at this time.

4.3.1. Competition and Buying Patterns

While there is no direct competitor for the FDA-approved machine we will use for screening (www.macuscope.com), the competition is from substitutes, namely optometrists and ophthalmologists who use traditional ophthalmoscopes which are hard to move. These machines detect drusen, a biomarker for early onset age-related macular degeneration.

In addition, for this business, there is a very low barrier for entry since all that is required is a MacuScope lease.

5. Strategy and Implementation Summary

1. **Convenience.** We will differentiate ourselves from our competitors by offering a convenient means for the elderly to be regularly tested for AMD.
2. **Cost.** A traditional complete eye exam is not only uncomfortable, but can be expensive. We provide a service that is affordable for senior citizens who are on a fixed income.
3. **Speed.** As we screen more individuals, managerial know-how and learning curve advantages will allow us to dramatically increase our throughput of patients. These improvements will significantly shorten the time needed for testing.

5.1. SWOT Analysis

The following SWOT analysis provides a succinct listing of MacuGen's strengths, weaknesses, opportunities, and threats.

MacuGen's strengths include: access to the MacuScope; relationships nurtured with senior centers and retirement communities; and first-move advantage. Weaknesses that must be overcome are: possible difficulty in obtaining MacuScope and use of state-of-the-art equipment as it becomes available; our firm is new to this arena of business and our inexperience will pose a significant challenge in the short term; we currently have no relationship with any significant senior citizen population and we need to develop this relationship from scratch.

MacuGen's strengths will help it capitalize on emerging opportunities. These opportunities include, but are not limited to, a growing population of senior citizens, the need for a low-cost and convenient means for senior citizens to assess their risk for AMD, and that very few eye professionals have access to this rapid screening device. Threats that MacuGen should be aware of include withdrawal of the supplier, emerging local competitors, the possibility of being locked into using obsolete screening technologies, and the desire for seniors to be properly diagnosed instead of just a rapid screen.

5.1.1. Strengths

1. **State-of-the art equipment.** MacuGen uses the only currently marketed device approved by the FDA for screening for increased risk of macular degeneration (MacuScope).
2. **Convenience.** MacuGen comes to a location near its customers to regularly assess their risk for AMD. This information is important since the sooner they know if they are at risk, the sooner something can be done about preserving their vision in the long term.
3. **Cost.** Those customers who need to be screened the most are senior citizens on a fixed budget. Our service is affordable, costing only twenty dollars. This is a small price to pay to decrease the risk of age-related macular degeneration and blindness in the future.

Blindness prevents driving and reading and may force some senior citizens to pay for costly in-home or senior residence home care.

5.1.2. Weaknesses

1. **Education of customer base will be important.** It is likely that many senior citizens do not know what AMD is and the gravity of the disease. Therefore, a fair amount of customer education through seminars and educational literature may be required to realize significant demand.
2. **Screening device is psychophysical in nature.** MacuGen screens with the Macuscope, which relies on customer feedback with different visual stimuli. As such, the screening is partially subjective in nature and repeated measurements may be more variable than objective methods that are currently being developed.
3. **Screening device only for one specific eye disease.** While our screening service provides key information for the customer to assess their risk of age-related macular degeneration, it does not replace diagnosis by a licensed eye professional for all eye diseases.
4. **Screening may be too costly for some senior citizens.**

5.1.3. Opportunities

1. **Growing senior citizen population.** The number of people in the baby boomer generation is aging and will increasingly enter the population of people at risk for AMD.
2. **There is currently no affordable mobile eye health screening service present.** Senior citizens are typically less mobile and have a fixed income. For this reason, there is a need for a service that is convenient and low cost for seniors to assess their risk for this eye disease. The reasons AMD risk must be tested with regularity are its possible rapid onset, its harmful reduction on seniors' quality of life, and that the risk substantially increases with age.
3. **Few eye professionals have this device.** The MacuScope has been recently approved by the FDA and therefore, it is not popular yet with eye professionals. Hence, our service would provide a rare service.

5.1.4. Threats

- **There is a threat of suppliers.** The manufacturer of the MacuScope is recalcitrant to sell to non-eye professionals. Therefore, there may be significant initial resistance in obtaining the device.
- **The manufacturer of the MacuScope requires a five-year leasing plan contract.** Since there are new objective technologies for AMD screening in development, there is a strong possibility that we will be locked into a situation whereby we are required to use these obsolete devices for a span of two to three years.
- **There is a low barrier to entry for entering this industry.** Once competitors see the possible revenues, they just need to lease a MacuScope, advertise effectively, and travel to the senior citizen gathering sites by car.

- **There is a constant threat of substitutes.** The key substitute is eye professionals with ophthalmoscopes who can diagnose a patient (as opposed to our service which can only serve as a prerequisite for diagnosis).

5.2. Competitive Edge

MacuGen's competitive advantage will be derived from the following factors.

1. **State-of-the art equipment.** MacuGen expects to be one of few non-eye professionals with access to the MacuScope, the only FDA-approved device that uses an accepted method for assessing risk for AMD.
2. **Convenience.** MacuGen comes to a location near its customers to regularly assess their risk for age-related macular degeneration.
3. **Cost.** We expect to charge a rate that any senior on a fixed income can afford.
4. **Relationships**. We expect to forge long-term relationships with senior centers and retirement communities so that trust in our ability is formed.

5.3. Marketing Strategy

Our marketing strategy is three-fold: the first part is based on word-of-mouth. We plan to develop relationships with senior centers and retirement communities in our target markets so that we can come and test people on a regular basis. Within these settings, demand will be sparked by word-of-mouth from management in each setting. The second part is based on exploiting the inheritability of the disease: since there is a genetic basis for AMD, family members of those at high risk or are suffering from AMD will be contacted for screening. The final part is based on conventional advertising. Initially, our services will be advertised using local Sunday newspapers. If this mode of advertising is successful, we plan to advertise in local magazines as well.

5.4. Sales Strategy

MacuGen, Inc., introduces its unique screening service and eye supplements through two routes: fliers at local senior centers, retirement community clubhouses, and other retirement homes. In addition, a newspaper advertisement (two column inches) will be placed in both of North Carolina's largest newspapers.

Initially we will be selling to individual senior citizens. In the long term, our goal is to establish relationships with retirement community and retirement home management so that we can sell them an ongoing package for testing their tenants.

5.4.1. Sales Forecast

For the first and second years of the company's existence, the company will have only one employee (it is expected two years will be needed to establish a reputation and brand). In the third year, a second employee will be hired and our throughput will increase by 50 percent. In year four, we plan to set up two more one-person teams who will service the Anderson and Spartanville areas. Again, assuming all else is equal, total throughput will increase almost four-fold from year one. In year five, a second person will be added to the one-person teams where their throughput should increase 50 percent and our total throughput will increase more than four-fold from year one.

Clearly, two more Screening machines must be leased at 350 dollars/month as well as the salaries of each employee ($35,000 base pay + $11,500 in benefits).

Sales Forecast	Year 1	Year 2	Year 3	Year 4	Year 5
Unit sales					
Screening service	2,796	2,800	4,200	9,800	12,600
	0	0	0	0	0
Total unit sales	2,796	2,800	4,200	9,800	12,600
Unit prices	Year 1	Year 2	Year 3	Year 4	Year 5
Screening service	$30.00	$30.00	$30.00	$30.00	$30.00
	$0.00	$0.00	$0.00	$0.00	$0.00
Sales					
Screening service	$83,880	$84,000	$126,000	$294,000	$378,000
	$0	$0	$0	$0	$0
Total sales	$83,880	$84,000	$126,000	$294,000	$378,000
Direct unit costs	Year 1	Year 2	Year 3	Year 4	Year 5
Screening service	$0.99	$0.99	$0.99	$0.99	$0.99
	$0.00	$0.00	$0.00	$0.00	$0.00
Direct cost of sales					
Screening service	$2,768	$2,772	$4,158	$9,702	$12,474
	$0	$0	$0	$0	$0
Subtotal direct cost of sales	$2,768	$2,772	$4,158	$9,702	$12,474

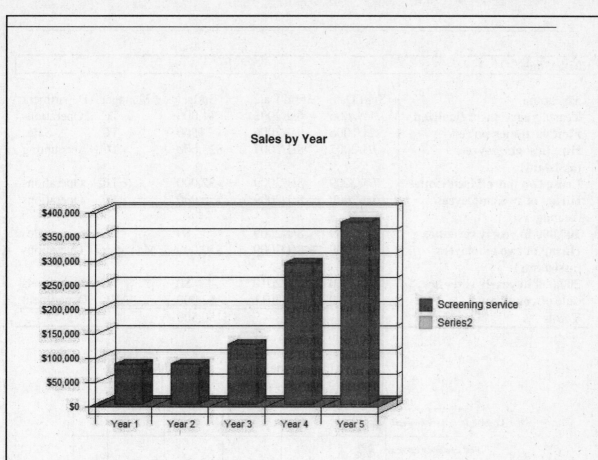

Sales by Year

5.5. Milestones

The following table lists important program milestones, with dates and managers in charge, and budgets for each. The milestone schedule indicates our emphasis on planning for implementation.

Milestones

Milestone	Start Date	End Date	Budget	Manager	Department
Leasing agreement finalized	3/12/2006	6/2/2006	$1,000	TC	Operations
First customer served	6/11/2006	9/2/2006	$500	TC	Sales
Hire first employee (assistant)	7/1/2007	8/1/2007	$25,000	TC	Accounting
Lease two more MacuScopes	7/1/2009	8/1/2009	$2,000	TC	Operations
Hiring of two employees (managers)	6/1/2009	8/1/2009	$70,000	TC	Operations
100,000 in yearly revenues	1/1/2009	8/1/2009	$0	TC	Sales
Hiring of two employees (assistants)	7/1/2009	8/1/2009	$50,000	Managers	Operations
200,000 in yearly revenues	1/1/2010	8/1/2010	$0	TC	Operations
Sale of company	8/1/2010	8/1/2011	$2,000	ABC	Department
Totals			**$150,500**		

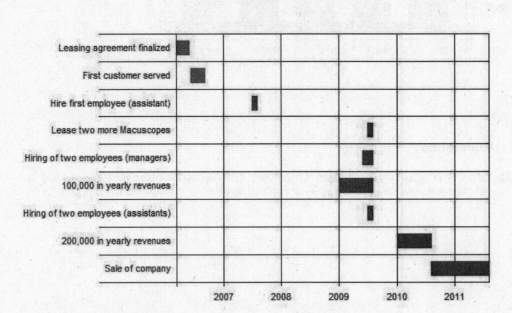

Milestones

6. Management Summary

MacuGen, Inc., management is comprised of one person at this point, but will expand by one person each time a new MacuScope is purchased. Currently, our management team consists of the owner only (Dr. Tom Compton), who will handle all business activities for years one and three. When the next two MacuScopes are purchased, a vice president of sales as well as a vice president of marketing will be hired (each will have at least two years' experience in these areas).

The largest gap in management will be in ophthalmological affairs and in operations. To this end, we will have, in the short term, a well-known local ophthalmologist on our board of advisors (Dr. Paul Bern from the Suxton Eye Center at the University of North Carolina), as well as a current director of operations for a local benefits firm (Ms. Amelia Jones of National Benefit Alliance). Mr. Brian Hansen, a local successful entrepreneur, will also be invited to be on the board.

6.1.   Personnel Plan

The total head count in the first two years is one (Dr. Tom Compton). It is expected that the first two years will be needed for establishment of a reputation for excellent service. In the third year, it is expected that demand will increase to the point that an additional employee (an assistant) will need to be added so that all of Washington County can be serviced. In year four, two more managers of individual MacuScopes will be hired, each with sales or marketing experience and who will service either northern North Carolina (Washington City and Anderson) or southern North Carolina (Spartanville). The primary responsibilities of each manager will be to log customers into the company's database, prepare patient questionnaires, and test customers with MacuScope. In addition, the manager must collect fees from the customer.

After each manager is successful at managing the operation of an individual MacuScope, an assistant will be hired who handles logging in, questionnaires, and collecting fees.

Assuming employee benefits are 33 percent of his or her base salary, managers will be paid a total of $46,550 (base salary $35,000) and assistants $33,250 (base salary $25,000).

Personnel Plan					
	Year 1	Year 2	Year 3	Year 4	Year 5
Sales	$46,550	$46,550	$46,550	$139,650	$139,650
Marketing	$0	$0	$33,250	$33,250	$99,750
Total people	1	1	2	4	6
Total payroll	$46,550	$46,550	$79,800	$172,900	$239,400

7. Financial Plan

Our start-up costs come to $8,630, which is mostly equipment lease, stationery, legal costs, and expenses associated with making sure that there are three months of money for these items. The start-up costs are to be financed by direct owner investment.

We will achieve profitability in the first year. Net profits will exceed $12,000, which will be reinvested into the company. We expect to have six employees with total revenues of $378,000 and net profits of $49,555 dollars by year five.

7.1. Start-up Funding

Owner

Tom Compton will invest $5,000 in cash, benefits, and labor to the start-up.

Investors

Friends and family will contribute the remaining $3,670 required to finance the business venture.

Start-up Funding	
Start-up Expenses to Fund	$3,230
Start-up Assets to Fund	$5,400
Total Funding Required	$8,630
Assets	
Non-cash Assets from Start-up	$1,000
Cash Requirements from Start-up	$4,400
Additional Cash Raised	$25,370
Cash Balance on Starting Date	$29,770
Total Assets	$30,770
Liabilities and Capital	
Liabilities	
Current Borrowing	$0
Long-term Liabilities	$0
Accounts Payable (Outstanding Bills)	$0
Other Current Liabilities (Interest Free)	$34,000
Total Liabilities	$34,000
Capital	
Planned Investment	
Owner	$0
Investor	$0
Additional Investment Requirement	$0
Total Planned Investment	$0
Loss at Start-up (Start-up Expenses)	($3,230)
Total Capital	($3,230)
Total Capital and Liabilities	$30,770
Total Funding	$34,000

7.2. Important Assumptions

NOTES FOR PROJECTIONS FOR YEARS ONE THROUGH FIVE

Revenues will come from screening services. In the first year, it is expected that maximum throughput will be two patients per hour or sixteen patients a day. If MacuGen is open for business 350 days a year and charges twenty dollars per screen, the predicted revenues from screening services are $112,000. (Vitamin sales will not be pursued at this time as an add-on product to screening since projected revenues are approximately 1 percent of screening revenues. How this conclusion was reached is described as follows: only those individuals at high risk for AMD from our screen would be potential customers for our vitamins. Since 15 percent of the population is at high risk for AMD, then 15 percent of sixteen customers/day or about one person per day would be a potential vitamin buyer. Since competitor prices for vitamins are $14.99 for a four-month supply or $3.75 dollars/month, it is expected that 360 customers will buy the vitamin for revenue of $1,350 dollars.)

In year two, customer throughput is expected to remain stable but grow toward the end of the year. In year three, customer throughput is expected to increase by 50 percent due to higher brand popularity and from learning curve advantages and managerial know-how. We plan to hire an assistant to help in handling the additional customers. The grand total revenue for year three will be $84,000. In year four, two more machines and two more managers each with $46,500 of salary and benefits combined (benefits are assumed to be 33 percent of salary). Total revenues are expected to increase to $196,000. For year five, the two new managers will obtain their own assistant as well as gain learning curve advantages and managerial know-how. It is expected revenues will increase to $252,000.

7.3.   Break-even Analysis

For our break-even analysis, we assume running costs (i.e., monthly total operating expenses) of approximately $5,200 per month in the first two years, which increases to approximately about $8,000/month in year three when an assistant is added. Running costs increase to $17,400/month in year four when two more managers are added. Finally, running costs increase to about $23,000/month in year five when two assistants are hired for the new managers. These costs include our full payroll with benefits, business insurance, screening device lease, travel to each site, and weekly newspaper advertising.

At maximal throughput at year five, the total number of customers who can be serviced totals 25,200, or 21 percent of the total market.

Break-even Analysis	
Monthly Units Break-even	179
Monthly Revenue Break-even	$5,385
Assumptions:	
Average Per-unit Revenue	$30.00
Average Per-unit Variable Cost	$0.99
Estimated Monthly Fixed Cost	$5,207

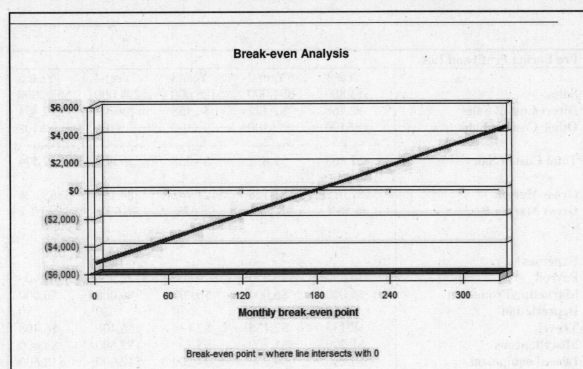

Break-even Analysis

Break-even point = where line intersects with 0

7.4. Projected Profit and Loss

Based on the realistic sales projections and efficient cost control measures in place, MacuGen plans to be profitable after its first year. Since this company needs few assets to generate revenue, initial spending will be low. The biggest expense in the first two years will be the salary of the owner at $35,000 (T. Compton) plus employee benefits, leasing cost of MacuScope screening device, and travel expenses. Indeed, gross profit increases substantially to over 15 percent of revenues in year four due to improved managerial know-how and learning curve advantages. The third year profit percentage will decrease from years one and two due to hiring an assistant.

Pro Forma Profit and Loss

	Year 1	Year 2	Year 3	Year 4	Year 5
Sales	$83,880	$84,000	$126,000	$294,000	$378,000
Direct Cost of Sales	$2,768	$2,772	$4,158	$9,702	$12,474
Other Costs of Sales	$100	$100	$100	$100	$100
Total Cost of Sales	$2,868	$2,872	$4,258	$9,802	$12,574
Gross Margin	$81,012	$81,128	$121,742	$284,198	$365,426
Gross Margin %	96.58%	96.58%	96.62%	96.67%	96.67%
Expenses					
Payroll	$46,550	$46,550	$79,800	$172,900	$239,400
Marketing/Promotion	$6,000	$6,000	$6,000	$6,000	$6,000
Depreciation	$0	$0	$0	$0	$0
Travel	$2,136	$2,136	$2,136	$6,408	$6,408
Miscellaneous	$1,200	$1,200	$1,200	$3,600	$3,600
Leased equipment	$4,200	$4,200	$4,200	$12,600	$12,600
Business Insurance	$2,400	$2,400	$2,400	$7,200	$7,200
Total Operating Expenses	$62,486	$62,486	$95,736	$208,708	$275,208
Profit Before Interest and Taxes	$18,526	$18,642	$26,006	$75,490	$90,218
EBITDA	$18,526	$18,642	$26,006	$75,490	$90,218
Interest Expense	$1,138	$3,150	$5,775	$11,025	$19,425
Taxes Incurred	$5,217	$4,648	$6,069	$19,340	$21,238
Net Profit	$12,172	$10,844	$14,162	$45,126	$49,555
Net Profit/Sales	14.51%	12.91%	11.24%	15.35%	13.11%

Profit Yearly

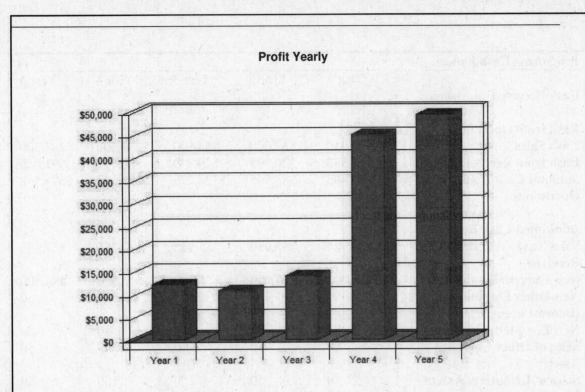

7.5.   Projected Cash Flow

MacuGen has calculated its financial plan so that it will have enough cash from investors to survive until a positive cash flow is realized in 2007. The amount of credit that we need to cover customers' credit and/or check payments totals three months of expenses plus expected profits (for example: in year one, 84,000/4 or $21,000 is the expected sales for one three-month span).

Pro Forma Cash Flow

	Year 1	Year 2	Year 3	Year 4	Year 5
Cash Received					
Cash from Operations					
Cash Sales	$62,910	$63,000	$94,500	$220,500	$283,500
Cash from Receivables	$17,533	$20,995	$29,779	$66,617	$91,058
Subtotal Cash from Operations	$80,443	$83,995	$124,279	$287,117	$374,558
Additional Cash Received					
Sales Tax, VAT, HST/GST Received	$3,984	$3,990	$5,985	$13,965	$17,955
New Current Borrowing	$21,000	$21,000	$31,500	$73,500	$94,500
New Other Liabilities (Interest Free)	$0	$0	$0	$0	$0
New Long-term Liabilities	$0	$0	$0	$0	$0
Sales of Other Current Assets	$0	$0	$0	$0	$0
Sales of Long-term Assets	$0	$0	$0	$0	$0
New Investment Received	$0	$0	$0	$0	$0
Subtotal Cash Received	$105,428	$108,985	$161,764	$374,582	$487,013
Expenditures	Year 1	Year 2	Year 3	Year 4	Year 5
Expenditures from Operations					
Cash Spending	$46,550	$46,550	$79,800	$172,900	$239,400
Bill Payments	$22,077	$26,499	$31,592	$72,364	$87,970
Subtotal Spent on Operations	$68,627	$73,049	$111,392	$245,264	$327,370
Additional Cash Spent					
Sales Tax, VAT, HST/GST Paid Out	$3,990	$3,990	$5,985	$13,965	$17,955
Principal Repayment of Current Borrowing	$0	$0	$0	$0	$0
Other Liabilities Principal Repayment	$0	$0	$0	$0	$0
Long-term Liabilities Principal Repayment	$0	$0	$0	$0	$0
Purchase Other Current Assets	$0	$0	$0	$0	$0
Purchase Long-term Assets	$0	$0	$0	$0	$0
Dividends	$0	$0	$0	$0	$0
Subtotal Cash Spent	$72,617	$77,039	$117,377	$259,229	$345,325

Net Cash Flow	$32,810	$31,946	$44,387	$115,353	$141,688
Cash Balance	$62,580	$94,526	$138,913	$254,266	$395,954

7.6.   Projected Balance Sheet

Our projected balance sheet shows we will not have any difficulty with meeting any debt obligations as long as our revenue projections are met.

Pro Forma Balance Sheet

	Year 1	Year 2	Year 3	Year 4	Year 5
Assets					
Current Assets					
Cash	$62,580	$94,526	$138,913	$254,266	$395,954
Accounts Receivable	$3,437	$3,442	$5,163	$12,046	$15,488
Other Current Assets	$0	$0	$0	$0	$0
Total Current Assets	$66,017	$97,967	$144,076	$266,312	$411,442
Long-term Assets					
Long-term Assets	$0	$0	$0	$0	$0
Accumulated Depreciation	$0	$0	$0	$0	$0
Total Long-term Assets	$0	$0	$0	$0	$0
Total Assets	$66,017	$97,967	$144,076	$266,312	$411,442
Liabilities and Capital	Year 1	Year 2	Year 3	Year 4	Year 5
Current Liabilities					
Accounts Payable	$2,081	$2,187	$2,633	$6,244	$7,319
Current Borrowing	$21,000	$42,000	$73,500	$147,000	$241,500
Other Current Liabilities	$33,994	$33,994	$33,994	$33,994	$33,994
Subtotal Current Liabilities	$57,075	$78,181	$110,128	$187,239	$282,813
Long-term Liabilities	$0	$0	$0	$0	$0
Total Liabilities	$57,075	$78,181	$110,128	$187,239	$282,813
Paid-in Capital	$0	$0	$0	$0	$0
Retained Earnings	($3,230)	$8,942	$19,786	$33,948	$79,074
Earnings	$12,172	$10,844	$14,162	$45,126	$49,555
Total Capital	$8,942	$19,786	$33,948	$79,074	$128,629
Total Liabilities and Capital	$66,017	$97,967	$144,076	$266,312	$411,442

Moore Pharmacy

Moore Pharmacy
1553 E. Barcon Rd.
Boise, Idaho 84117
(555) 272-5555
Moore.Jeff@getmynewemail.com

Confidentiality Agreement

The undersigned reader acknowledges that the information provided by
_____ in this business plan is confidential; therefore, reader agrees not to
disclose it without the express written permission of _____.

It is acknowledged by reader that information to be furnished in this business plan is in
all respects confidential in nature, other than information which is in the public domain
through other means and that any disclosure or use of same by reader, may cause serious
harm or damage to _____.

Upon request, this document is to be immediately returned to _____.

_____
Signature

_____
Name (typed or printed)

_____
Date

This is a business plan. It does not imply an offering of securities.

Table of Contents

Moore Pharmacy

1. Executive Summary

Moore Pharmacy is a start-up enterprise focused on establishing a presence in small town markets in the western U.S. The primary focus to establish a store is in communities that have under 25,000 residents.

Moore Pharmacy is a retail pharmacy with a strong focus on creating efficiencies in the mail-order market. Upon commencement of operations, Moore Pharmacy will sell prescription only medication to the general public. A focused marketing effort will be on establishing relationships with those patients that need to fill prescriptions on an on-going consistent basis, and are sensitive to price increases. Patients who have diabetes, heart conditions, or high blood pressure will be our main focus. Moore Pharmacy will capitalize on the owners' experience in working in and running a retail pharmacy and of basic business tools knowledge.

Highlights

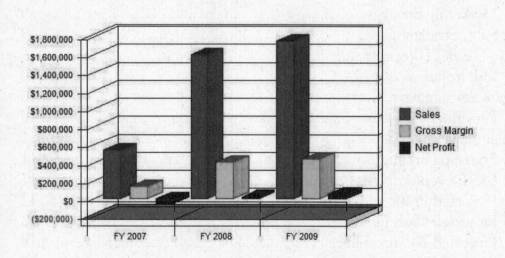

1.1. Objectives

The objectives of Moore Pharmacy are to:

1. Provide affordable and reliable prescription drug medication in an easy and convenient manner
2. Change the way pharmaceuticals are sold to the general public by allowing orders online
3. Establish beneficial business relationships with suppliers, vendors, and strategic partners
4. Provide counseling services to customers to help them understand any risks, side effects, and dangers in regards to the medicine prescribed

Moore Pharmacy

5. Earn the loyalty of our customers by providing exceptional customer service, fast response times, and quality products
6. Share company profits with the employees to keep morale high and retention of key employees

1.2. Mission

Moore Pharmacy's mission is to provide an alternative to the high cost with little personalization in the prescription drug industry. We will accomplish this by developing and cultivating relationships with suppliers so we can pass those savings on to customers. Our promise is to exhibit the highest standards of integrity, provide exceptional customer service/counseling, affordable prices, all with the convenience of home delivery.

1.3. Keys to Success

The keys to success for the Moore Pharmacy are:

1. Offering high quality prescription drugs, both generic and brand name, in a timely, efficient, and affordable manner
2. Develop and maintain a reputation of superior customer service
3. Reliable and timely deliveries; Moore Pharmacy must make good on its next day delivery promises
4. A reliable administration that is ready to serve customers, prepare accurate billing, follow up on orders and other documentation, and maintain a close watch on expenses and collection of accounts receivable from insurance companies and Medicaid

2. Company Summary

2.1. Company Ownership

The Moore Pharmacy will be a limited liability corporation. All membership shares initially will be owned by Jeff and April Moore. As the pharmacy grows, a portion of the shares of the pharmacy will be earmarked for key employees. We will be generous with the ownership units to retain key pharmacists and staff in the long term.

2.2. Start-up Summary

Like any other new company, Moore Pharmacy will have some start-up costs associated with it before opening its doors for business. Management would like to minimize these costs as much as possible. Some expenses cannot be avoided, however. In regards to these expenses, management has estimated as best as possible what these costs will be.

To ensure we are in compliance with laws and regulations, there will be some legal fees and consulting fees prior to opening. The legal fees will be designed to separate business risks from personal assets while the consulting fees will be more specifically focused on pharmacy-designed objectives. As this is a highly regulated industry, there are additional business licenses required.

Moore Pharmacy

In order to dispense and inventory controlled substances, the DEA must examine the pharmacy and perform an audit of its control procedures. The DEA will not issue a license to a business if the business is based in the home. A separate building must be used in order to inventory the drugs. Because of this law, a building space must be rented. Other basic start-up costs are listed below and are included in the "Other" category to include unexpected expenses that may arise prior to opening.

The purpose of this business plan is to determine the feasibility of opening this business. Many of the numbers are best guesses on the true start-up costs associated with opening a mail-order pharmacy. As we open new pharmacies, management will examine the costs and expenses associated with opening a new business, and weigh it against projected sales and net income. The outcome of these estimates will help to decide whether to undertake this adventure of opening another retail pharmacy in a very competitive market.

Start-up	
Requirements	
Start-up Expenses	
Legal Fees	$500
Stationery, etc.	$500
Insurance	$1,000
Rent	$1,800
Computer	$500
Business License	$500
Other	$500
Total Start-up Expenses	$5,300
Start-up Assets	
Cash Required	$8,000
Other Current Assets	$1,000
Long-term Assets	$10,000
Total Assets	$19,000
Total Requirements	$24,300

Moore Pharmacy

Start-up

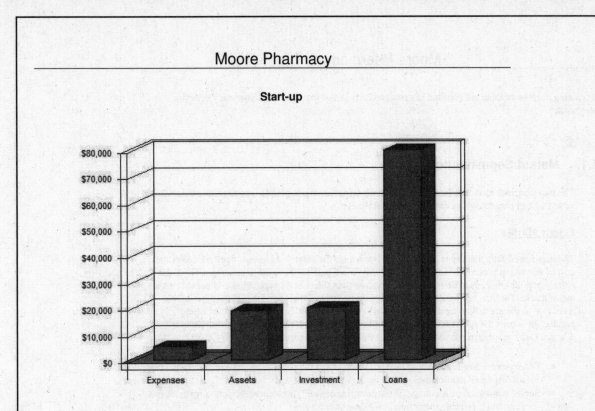

3. Products

Moore Pharmacy offers a variety of prescription drug medications. We offer both generic and name brand medications. Because our business strategy focuses on the mail-order market, we will have a limited supply of OTC drugs and natural herbal medications. Most drugs we will carry will be for the treatment of chronic illness, like diabetes, high blood pressure, and heart conditions.

4. Market Analysis Summary

The main users of mail service pharmacy today are women over the age of 65. The next largest group, and far behind in terms of numbers, consists of men over the age of 65. A major factor in the rising cost of health care relates to the aging of the population. The frequency and intensity of health-care utilization increases sharply with age. People are living longer, and the over-65 age population is increasing. Thus, the size of the elderly population will continue to drive the increase in health-care expenditures—in particular, prescription drug expenditures. Beyond 2010, the aging of the population will have a significant impact on health-care spending. Those people age 65 and over account for about 13 percent of the population and 34 percent of health expenditures. However, as baby boomers enter their seventies and eighties, the share of the population ages 65 and over will exceed 20 percent. Extended life expectancy is frequently accompanied by increasing health problems whose treatment creates the potential for drug therapy problems.

An increasing number of Americans are being diagnosed and treated with medications for chronic conditions such as high blood pressure, elevated cholesterol, and diabetes. This is a result of the new focus on early detection and treatment of chronic conditions, improved diagnosis, and an increasing number of pharmaceutical breakthroughs that address chronic conditions. A substantial number of patients under the age of 65 who have chronic conditions have prescription drug coverage, and an

Moore Pharmacy

increasing number of them are enrolled in managed care and/or managed care pharmacy benefits programs.

4.1. Market Segmentation

The two principal markets Moore Pharmacy will target are those people who are older than 60 years old and patients with a chronic recurrent illness.

Elderly Market

The expense of drug therapy is an enormous burden on the elderly. Medicare does not cover the cost of outpatient prescription drugs, and few Medicare patients have other coverage. Thus, the elderly population tends to be more price-sensitive than the general population and constitutes a major market for mail service pharmacy. The convenience of mail service is also of particular relevance to the aged, who tend to have limited mobility. Approximately 70 percent of the population is over the age of 65—about 24 million people—and suffers from cardiovascular disease. Demographic trends indicate that this number could exceed 50 million by 2050.

- Older Americans, representing nearly 13 percent of the population, take nearly 34 percent of all dispensed medications.
- Senior women take an average of six prescriptions and three nonprescription medications concurrently, creating the potential for drug interactions
- Adverse drug reactions account for an estimated 17 percent of all hospitalization among senior citizens—nearly six times more than the general population
- One out of six older Americans is using drugs generally considered unsuitable for their age group

Maintenance Drug Market

Maintenance and chronic drugs represent the mainstay of the mail service pharmacy business. By definition, they are consumed for the long term and in predictable quantities. Furthermore, patients who take them do not typically require recurrent counseling by a pharmacist. Maintenance and chronic drugs represent a high and rising share of the pharmaceutical market. Industry executives estimate that these drugs make up 75 percent of the total pharmaceutical market. Drugs such as cardiovascular drugs and insulin typically account for 70 percent of the prescription drug expense of a large employer or a managed care organization.

Moore Pharmacy

Market Analysis

Potential Customers	Growth	2006	2007	2008	2009	2010	CAGR
Under Age 65	0%	249,815,000	250,814,260	251,817,517	252,824,787	253,836,086	0.40%
Over Age 65	3%	36,166,000	37,287,146	38,443,048	39,634,782	40,863,460	3.10%
Other	0%	0	0	0	0	0	0.00%
Total	**0.75%**	**285,981,000**	**288,101,406**	**290,260,565**	**292,459,569**	**294,699,546**	**0.75%**

Market Analysis (Pie)

Legend:
- Under Age 65
- Over Age 65
- Other

4.2. Target Market Segment Strategy

We will focus on two main markets: the elderly and those who suffer from chronic illnesses. With the baby boomers increasing in numbers and people living longer, our initial focus will be on the elderly market. This is a huge and growing market. But, long term, the chronically ill market is where we would eventually like to specialize.

Moore Pharmacy

5. Strategy and Implementation Summary

Moore Pharmacy will target the Wasatch Front geographic area. Sales will be driven from phone orders by doctors and patients. A strong focus will be on developing relationships with health care professionals.

5.1. Competitive Edge

Moore Pharmacy's competitive edge is simple. Moore Pharmacy provides a high quality product at a competitive price with the ease and convenience of home delivery. Our local presence in a mail-order retail pharmacy brings comfort to our customers and their loyalty in return.

5.2. Marketing Strategy

Our marketing strategy will focus heavily on advertising in local newspapers, direct mail campaigns, and direct sales to medical professionals. As our target market is people over the age of 65 and people who suffer from chronic illnesses, we will use direct marketing campaigns to focus our efforts. Our marketing budget will start off at a higher percentage of sales in the first years, and then taper off to a more consistent amount by year five.

• The marketing budget will not exceed 5 percent of our gross annual sales by year five.

• Our promotions will always stay in tune with our company objectives and mission statement.

5.3. Sales Strategy

Initially, our sales strategy will be to rely on customers calling in prescriptions over the phone. We will run adds in the local newspaper, hand out flyers, and send direct mailers to our target market. We will take phone calls and fill prescriptions over the phone. There will be a storefront where customers can drop off and pick-up prescriptions, but the focus of the business will be in the mail-order prescriptions. Because phone orders will be our main source of clients, we will spend the majority of our marketing budget on getting our name out to the public by ways of advertising. By our second year in business, we will have a website which will allow for refilling orders.

There will be strong marketing efforts by management to contact doctors to let them know who we are. Eventually, there may be a full-time position for somebody to go out and solicit business from doctors and other professionals who write prescriptions for patients. We believe the doctor can play a major influence on patients and where they choose to fill their prescription. This will be a focus from the very beginning, but will be performed by management or by a part-time employee.

Moore Pharmacy

5.3.1. Sales Forecast

The following table and chart give a highlight on forecasted sales. We expect sales to start off conservatively and increase extensively as awareness of the pharmacy becomes better known to the public.

The average independent pharmacy fills 59,432 prescriptions annually, or around 5,000 per month for total average sales of $3.28 million. The average cost per prescription is $55.19. We have used very conservative numbers to project the first three years of business, not only in the number of prescriptions filled per month, but also the average cost per prescription. These numbers could very easily be greater than those shown.

Sales Forecast			
	FY 2007	FY 2008	FY 2009
Unit Sales			
Prescription Drugs	10,718	32,000	35,000
Total Unit Sales	10,718	32,000	35,000
Unit Prices	FY 2007	FY 2008	FY 2009
Prescription Drugs	$50.00	$50.00	$50.00
Sales			
Prescription Drugs	$535,900	$1,600,000	$1,750,000
Total Sales	$535,900	$1,600,000	$1,750,000
Direct Unit Costs	FY 2007	FY 2008	FY 2009
Prescription Drugs	$37.50	$37.50	$37.50
Direct Cost of Sales			
Prescription Drugs	$401,925	$1,200,000	$1,312,500
Subtotal Direct Cost of Sales	$401,925	$1,200,000	$1,312,500

Moore Pharmacy

Sales by Year

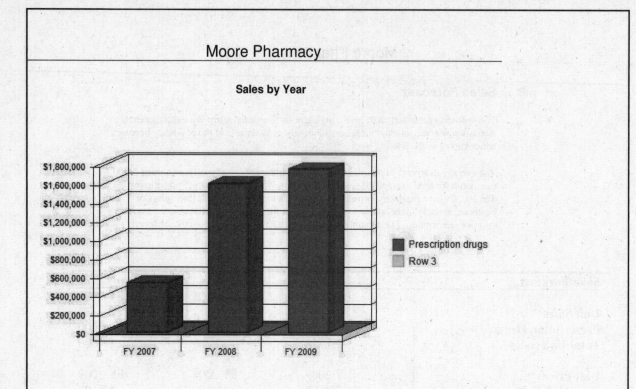

5.4. Milestones

The following table lists important milestones, with dates and persons primarily responsible for planning, as well as budgets where applicable. Mentioned by first name in the table are a few persons whose expertise in their field of work is required to make The Moore Pharmacy a reality. This schedule reflects our strong commitment to organization and detail.

Moore Pharmacy

Milestones

Milestone	Start Date	End Date	Budget	Manager	Department
Business License	9/1/2006	10/31/2006	$500	Jeff	Department
Create Legal Entity	9/1/2006	10/31/2006	$500	Josh Foukas	Department
Find a Building	9/1/2006	10/31/2006	$2,000	Jeff	Department
Sign Contract with Suppliers	9/1/2006	10/31/2006	$10,000	Jeff	Department
Open Doors for Business	11/1/2006	Ongoing	$20,000		Department
Complete Marketing Plan	9/1/2006	10/31/2006	$5,000	Jeff & Dick	Department
Send out Flyers	11/1/2006	Ongoing	$2,000		Department
Ads in the Paper	11/1/2006	Ongoing	$2,000	Jeff	Department
Hire a Technician	3/1/2007	5/1/2007	$1,000	April	Department
Hire 2 More Technicians	11/1/2007	1/1/2008	$1,000	April	Department
Hire 1 More Pharmacist	11/1/2007	1/1/2008	$1,000	April	Department
Totals			**$45,000**		

6. Management Summary

The Moore Pharmacy will be owned by Jeff and April Moore. April is a licensed pharmacist and has worked in the retail pharmacy industry for over five years. Her experience working as an intern and a pharmacist for Kroger Foods is invaluable knowledge and expertise. She will be responsible for the operational side of the business. April will run the daily operations of the business including the filling of prescriptions and counseling with patients. Jeff is an MBA with seven years of experience in business and finance. His education and experience has prepared him to run the accounting and marketing side of things. Jeff will keep track of the books and do the billing, marketing, and sales. Many of these functions will be delegated out as the pharmacy grows and additional staff can be hired.

Josh Brown is an attorney for Williams & Brown, will be retained to handle all legal issues, including consulting, setting up the LLC, and making sure we are in compliance with all laws and regulations.

Robert Johnson will be in charge of marketing ideas. His thirty years of experience in marketing will be useful in focusing our marketing dollars to our specific target market.

6.1. Personnel Plan

The personnel plan is included in the following table. Initially, there will be one full-time pharmacist (April) and one full-time pharmacist technician. Jeff will not draw a salary the first year. The technician will be paid $18.75 per hour. Additional technicians and pharmacists will be hired in year two as needed. All employees will benefit from a one-day paid holiday on their respective birthdays and one week of paid vacation after twelve months of employment.

Moore Pharmacy

At this time medical benefits will not be offered to employees. As profits increase in the future, medical benefits will be offered to all employees.

Personnel Plan	FY 2007	FY 2008	FY 2009
Pharmacist	$90,000	$180,000	$180,000
Technicians	$36,000	$108,000	$108,000
CPA	$900	$900	$900
Marketing Professional	$960	$1,000	$1,000
Attorney	$900	$1,000	$1,000
Total People	3	5	7
Total Payroll	$128,760	$290,900	$290,900

7. Financial Plan

The growth of Moore Pharmacy will be moderate and the cash balance will always be positive. Being a retail environment we will not be selling on credit. We will accept cash, checks, and all major credit cards. A majority of our billings will be to medical insurance companies. Marketing and advertising will remain at or below 5 percent of sales. We will continue to reinvest residual profits into company expansion and personnel.

7.1. Start-up Funding

Moore Pharmacy's start-up funds are summarized as follows and as shown in the table below:

- $60,000 SBA loan
- $20,000 short-term/credit card
- $20,000 owner investment

The additional capital is needed to fund salaries, inventory lags, and other costs during the first months of the business year.

Moore Pharmacy

Start-up Funding	
Start-up Expenses to Fund	$5,300
Start-up Assets to Fund	$19,000
Total Funding Required	$24,300
Assets	
Non-cash Assets from Start-up	$11,000
Cash Requirements from Start-up	$8,000
Additional Cash Raised	$75,700
Cash Balance on Starting Date	$83,700
Total Assets	$94,700
Liabilities and Capital	
Liabilities	
Current Borrowing	$20,000
Long-term Liabilities	$60,000
Other Current Liabilities (Interest Free)	$0
Total Liabilities	$80,000
Capital	
Planned Investment	
Owner	$20,000
Investor	$0
Additional Investment Requirement	$0
Total Planned Investment	$20,000
Loss at Start-up (Start-up Expenses)	($5,300)
Total Capital	$14,700
Total Capital and Liabilities	$94,700
Total Funding	$100,000

Moore Pharmacy

7.2. Break-even Analysis

Break-even Analysis	
Monthly Units Break-even	1,209
Monthly Revenue Break-even	$60,458
Assumptions:	
Average Per-unit Revenue	$50.00
Average Per-unit Variable Cost	$37.50
Estimated Monthly Fixed Cost	$15,115

Break-even Analysis

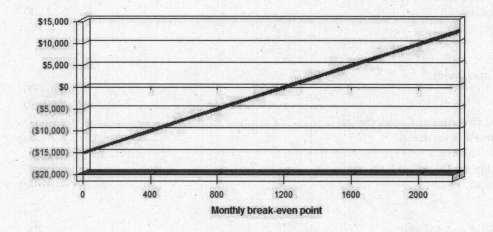

Break-even point = where line intersects with 0

Moore Pharmacy

7.3. Projected Profit and Loss

Pro Forma Profit and Loss			
	FY 2007	FY 2008	FY 2009
Sales	$535,900	$1,600,000	$1,750,000
Direct Costs of Goods	$401,925	$1,200,000	$1,312,500
Other Costs of Goods	$0	$0	$0
Cost of Goods Sold	$401,925	$1,200,000	$1,312,500
Gross Margin	$133,975	$400,000	$437,500
Gross Margin %	25.00%	25.00%	25.00%
Expenses			
Payroll	$128,760	$290,900	$290,900
Marketing/Promotion	$7,500	$10,000	$15,000
Depreciation	$0	$0	$0
Rent	$18,000	$18,000	$18,000
Utilities	$4,800	$4,800	$4,800
Insurance	$3,000	$3,000	$3,000
Payroll Taxes	$19,314	$43,635	$43,635
Other	$0	$0	$0
Total Operating Expenses	$181,374	$370,335	$375,335
Profit Before Interest and Taxes	($47,399)	$29,665	$62,165
EBITDA	($47,399)	$29,665	$62,165
Interest Expense	$8,000	$8,000	$8,000
Taxes Incurred	$0	$0	$0
Net Profit	($55,399)	$21,665	$54,165
Net Profit/Sales	-10.34%	1.35%	3.10%

Moore Pharmacy

Profit Monthly – Year One

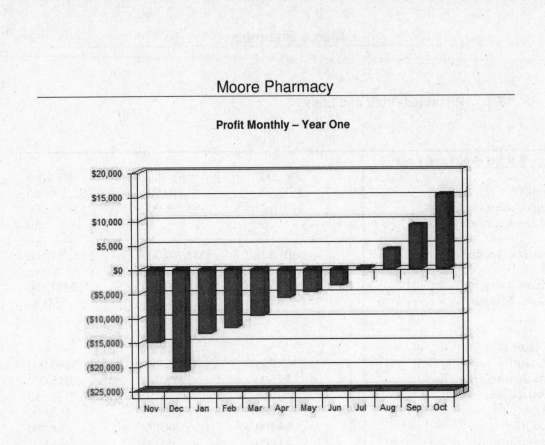

Profit Yearly

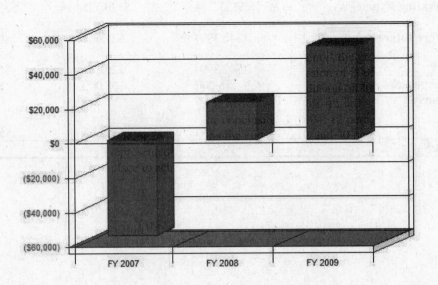

Moore Pharmacy

Gross Margin Monthly – Year One

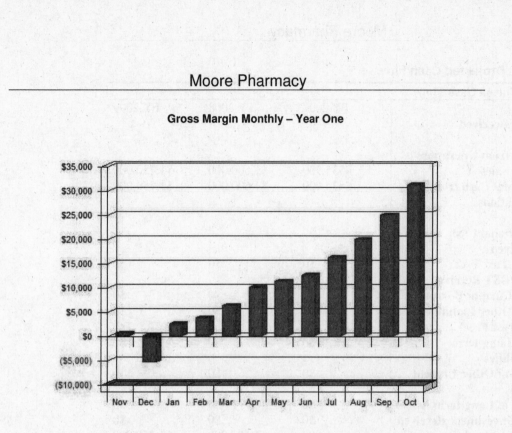

Gross Margin Yearly

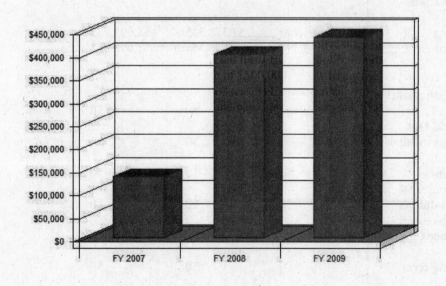

Moore Pharmacy

7.4. Projected Cash Flow

Pro Forma Cash Flow			
	FY 2007	FY 2008	FY 2009
Cash Received			
Cash from Operations			
Cash Sales	$535,900	$1,600,000	$1,750,000
Subtotal Cash from Operations	$535,900	$1,600,000	$1,750,000
Additional Cash Received			
Sales Tax, VAT, HST/GST Received	$0	$0	$0
New Current Borrowing	$0	$0	$0
New Other Liabilities (Interest Free)	$0	$0	$0
New Long-term Liabilities	$0	$0	$0
Sales of Other Current Assets	$0	$0	$0
Sales of Long-term Assets	$0	$0	$0
New Investment Received	$0	$0	$0
Subtotal Cash Received	$535,900	$1,600,000	$1,750,000
Expenditures	FY 2007	FY 2008	FY 2009
Expenditures from Operations			
Cash Spending	$591,299	$1,578,335	$1,695,835
Subtotal Spent on Operations	$591,299	$1,578,335	$1,695,835
Additional Cash Spent			
Sales Tax, VAT, HST/GST Paid Out	$0	$0	$0
Principal Repayment of Current Borrowing	$0	$0	$0
Other Liabilities Principal Repayment	$0	$0	$0
Long-term Liabilities Principal Repayment	$0	$0	$0
Purchase Other Current Assets	$0	$0	$0
Purchase Long-term Assets	$0	$0	$0

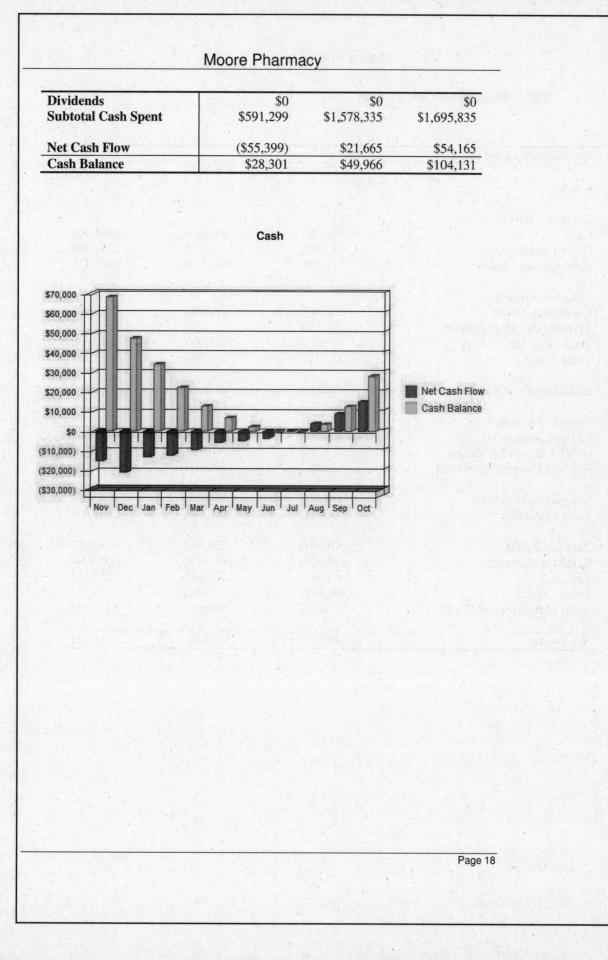

Moore Pharmacy

Dividends	$0	$0	$0
Subtotal Cash Spent	$591,299	$1,578,335	$1,695,835
Net Cash Flow	($55,399)	$21,665	$54,165
Cash Balance	$28,301	$49,966	$104,131

Moore Pharmacy

7.5. Projected Balance Sheet

Pro Forma Balance Sheet

	FY 2007	FY 2008	FY 2009
Assets			
Current Assets			
Cash	$28,301	$49,966	$104,131
Other Current Assets	$1,000	$1,000	$1,000
Total Current Assets	$29,301	$50,966	$105,131
Long-term Assets			
Long-term Assets	$10,000	$10,000	$10,000
Accumulated Depreciation	$0	$0	$0
Total Long-term Assets	$10,000	$10,000	$10,000
Total Assets	$39,301	$60,966	$115,131
Liabilities and Capital	FY 2007	FY 2008	FY 2009
Current Liabilities			
Current Borrowing	$20,000	$20,000	$20,000
Other Current Liabilities	$0	$0	$0
Subtotal Current Liabilities	$20,000	$20,000	$20,000
Long-term Liabilities	$60,000	$60,000	$60,000
Total Liabilities	$80,000	$80,000	$80,000
Paid-in Capital	$20,000	$20,000	$20,000
Retained Earnings	($5,300)	($60,699)	($39,034)
Earnings	($55,399)	$21,665	$54,165
Total Capital	($40,699)	($19,034)	$35,131
Total Liabilities and Capital	$39,301	$60,966	$115,131
Net Worth	($40,699)	($19,034)	$35,131

Moore Pharmacy

7.6. Business Ratios

Ratio Analysis

	FY 2007	FY 2008	FY 2009	Industry Profile
Sales Growth	0.00%	198.56%	9.38%	0.00%
Percent of Total Assets				
Other Current Assets	2.54%	1.64%	0.87%	100.00%
Total Current Assets	74.56%	83.60%	91.31%	100.00%
Long-term Assets	25.44%	16.40%	8.69%	0.00%
Total Assets	100.00%	100.00%	100.00%	100.00%
Current Liabilities	50.89%	32.81%	17.37%	0.00%
Long-term Liabilities	152.67%	98.42%	52.11%	0.00%
Total Liabilities	203.56%	131.22%	69.49%	0.00%
Net Worth	-103.56%	-31.22%	30.51%	100.00%
Percent of Sales				
Sales	100.00%	100.00%	100.00%	100.00%
Gross Margin	25.00%	25.00%	25.00%	0.00%
Selling, General & Administrative Expenses	35.34%	23.65%	21.90%	0.00%
Advertising Expenses	0.00%	0.00%	0.00%	0.00%
Profit Before Interest and Taxes	-8.84%	1.85%	3.55%	0.00%
Main Ratios				
Current	1.47	2.55	5.26	0.00
Quick	1.47	2.55	5.26	0.00
Total Debt to Total Assets	203.56%	131.22%	69.49%	0.00%
Pre-tax Return on Net Worth	136.12%	-113.82%	154.18%	0.00%
Pre-tax Return on Assets	-140.96%	35.54%	47.05%	0.00%
Additional Ratios	FY 2007	FY 2008	FY 2009	
Net Profit Margin	-10.34%	1.35%	3.10%	n.a
Return on Equity	0.00%	0.00%	154.18%	n.a
Activity Ratios				
Accounts Payable Turnover	4.34	12.17	12.17	n.a
Total Asset Turnover	13.64	26.24	15.20	n.a

Moore Pharmacy

Debt Ratios				
Debt to Net Worth	0.00	0.00	2.28	n.a
Current Liab. to Liab.	0.25	0.25	0.25	n.a
Liquidity Ratios				
Net Working Capital	$9,301	$30,966	$85,131	n.a
Interest Coverage	-5.92	3.71	7.77	n.a
Additional Ratios				
Assets to Sales	0.07	0.04	0.07	n.a
Current Debt/Total Assets	51%	33%	17%	n.a
Acid Test	1.47	2.55	5.26	n.a
Sales/Net Worth	0.00	0.00	49.81	n.a
Dividend Payout	0.00	0.00	0.00	n.a

Sales Forecast – Year One

		Nov	Dec	Jan	Feb	Mar	Apr	May	Jun	Jul	Aug	Sep	Oct
Unit Sales													
Prescription Drugs	0%	50	(432)	200	300	500	800	900	1,000	1,300	1,600	2,000	2,500
Row 3	0%	0	0	0	0	0	0	0	0	0	0	0	0
Total Unit Sales		50	(432)	200	300	500	800	900	1,000	1,300	1,600	2,000	2,500
Unit Prices		Nov	Dec	Jan	Feb	Mar	Apr	May	Jun	Jul	Aug	Sep	Oct
Prescription Drugs		$50.00	$50.00	$50.00	$50.00	$50.00	$50.00	$50.00	$50.00	$50.00	$50.00	$50.00	$50.00
Row 3		$0.00	$0.00	$0.00	$0.00	$0.00	$0.00	$0.00	$0.00	$0.00	$0.00	$0.00	$0.00
Sales													
Prescription Drugs		$2,500	($21,600)	$10,000	$15,000	$25,000	$40,000	$45,000	$50,000	$65,000	$80,000	$100,000	$125,000
Row 3		$0	$0	$0	$0	$0	$0	$0	$0	$0	$0	$0	$0
Total Sales		$2,500	($21,600)	$10,000	$15,000	$25,000	$40,000	$45,000	$50,000	$65,000	$80,000	$100,000	$125,000
Direct Unit Costs		Nov	Dec	Jan	Feb	Mar	Apr	May	Jun	Jul	Aug	Sep	Oct
Prescription Drugs	75.00%	$37.50	$37.50	$37.50	$37.50	$37.50	$37.50	$37.50	$37.50	$37.50	$37.50	$37.50	$37.50
Row 3	0.00%	$0.00	$0.00	$0.00	$0.00	$0.00	$0.00	$0.00	$0.00	$0.00	$0.00	$0.00	$0.00
Direct Cost of Sales													
Prescription Drugs		$1,875	($16,200)	$7,500	$11,250	$18,750	$30,000	$33,750	$37,500	$48,750	$60,000	$75,000	$93,750
Subtotal Direct Cost of Sales		$1,875	($16,200)	$7,500	$11,250	$18,750	$30,000	$33,750	$37,500	$48,750	$60,000	$75,000	$93,750

Personnel Plan – Year One

		Nov	Dec	Jan	Feb	Mar	Apr	May	Jun	Jul	Aug	Sep	Oct
Pharmacist	0%	$7,500	$7,500	$7,500	$7,500	$7,500	$7,500	$7,500	$7,500	$7,500	$7,500	$7,500	$7,500
Technicians	0%	$3,000	$3,000	$3,000	$3,000	$3,000	$3,000	$3,000	$3,000	$3,000	$3,000	$3,000	$3,000
CPA	0%	$75	$75	$75	$75	$75	$75	$75	$75	$75	$75	$75	$75
Marketing Professional	0%	$80	$80	$80	$80	$80	$80	$80	$80	$80	$80	$80	$80
Attorney	0%	$75	$75	$75	$75	$75	$75	$75	$75	$75	$75	$75	$75
Total People		3	3	3	3	3	3	3	3	3	3	3	3
Total Payroll		$10,730	$10,730	$10,730	$10,730	$10,730	$10,730	$10,730	$10,730	$10,730	$10,730	$10,730	$10,730

Pro Forma Profit and Loss – Year One

	Nov	Dec	Jan	Feb	Mar	Apr	May	Jun	Jul	Aug	Sep	Oct
Sales	$2,500	($21,600)	$10,000	$15,000	$25,000	$40,000	$45,000	$50,000	$65,000	$80,000	$100,000	$125,000
Direct Costs of Goods	$1,875	($16,200)	$7,500	$11,250	$18,750	$30,000	$33,750	$37,500	$48,750	$60,000	$75,000	$93,750
Other Costs of Goods	$0	$0	$0	$0	$0	$0	$0	$0	$0	$0	$0	$0
Cost of Goods Sold	$1,875	($16,200)	$7,500	$11,250	$18,750	$30,000	$33,750	$37,500	$48,750	$60,000	$75,000	$93,750
Gross Margin	$625	($5,400)	$2,500	$3,750	$6,250	$10,000	$11,250	$12,500	$16,250	$20,000	$25,000	$31,250
Gross Margin %	25.00%	25.00%	25.00%	25.00%	25.00%	25.00%	25.00%	25.00%	25.00%	25.00%	25.00%	25.00%
Expenses												
Payroll	$10,730	$10,730	$10,730	$10,730	$10,730	$10,730	$10,730	$10,730	$10,730	$10,730	$10,730	$10,730
Marketing/Promotion	$500	$500	$500	$600	$600	$600	$700	$700	$700	$700	$700	$700
Depreciation	$0	$0	$0	$0	$0	$0	$0	$0	$0	$0	$0	$0
Rent	$1,500	$1,500	$1,500	$1,500	$1,500	$1,500	$1,500	$1,500	$1,500	$1,500	$1,500	$1,500
Utilities	$400	$400	$400	$400	$400	$400	$400	$400	$400	$400	$400	$400
Insurance	$250	$250	$250	$250	$250	$250	$250	$250	$250	$250	$250	$250
Payroll Taxes 15%	$1,610	$1,610	$1,610	$1,610	$1,610	$1,610	$1,610	$1,610	$1,610	$1,610	$1,610	$1,610
Other	$0	$0	$0	$0	$0	$0	$0	$0	$0	$0	$0	$0
Total Operating Expenses	$14,990	$14,990	$14,990	$15,090	$15,090	$15,090	$15,190	$15,190	$15,190	$15,190	$15,190	$15,190
Profit Before Interest and Taxes	($14,365)	($20,390)	($12,490)	($11,340)	($8,840)	($5,090)	($3,940)	($2,690)	$1,061	$4,811	$9,811	$16,061
EBITDA	($14,365)	($20,390)	($12,490)	($11,340)	($8,840)	($5,090)	($3,940)	($2,690)	$1,061	$4,811	$9,811	$16,061
Interest Expense	$667	$667	$667	$667	$667	$667	$667	$667	$667	$667	$667	$667
Taxes Incurred	$0	$0	$0	$0	$0	$0	$0	$0	$0	$0	$0	$0
Net Profit	($15,031)	($21,056)	($13,156)	($12,006)	($9,506)	($5,756)	($4,606)	($3,356)	$394	$4,144	$9,144	$15,394
Net Profit/Sales	-601.25%	97.48%	-131.56%	-80.04%	-38.02%	-14.39%	-10.24%	-6.71%	0.61%	5.18%	9.14%	12.32%

Pro Forma Cash Flow – Year One

		Nov	Dec	Jan	Feb	Mar	Apr	May	Jun	Jul	Aug	Sep	Oct
Cash Received													
Cash from Operations													
Cash Sales		$2,500	($21,600)	$10,000	$15,000	$25,000	$40,000	$45,000	$50,000	$65,000	$80,000	$100,000	$125,000
Subtotal Cash from Operations		$2,500	($21,600)	$10,000	$15,000	$25,000	$40,000	$45,000	$50,000	$65,000	$80,000	$100,000	$125,000
Additional Cash Received													
Sales Tax, VAT, HST/GST Received	0.00%	$0	$0	$0	$0	$0	$0	$0	$0	$0	$0	$0	$0
New Current Borrowing		$0	$0	$0	$0	$0	$0	$0	$0	$0	$0	$0	$0
New Other Liabilities (Interest Free)		$0	$0	$0	$0	$0	$0	$0	$0	$0	$0	$0	$0
New Long-term Liabilities		$0	$0	$0	$0	$0	$0	$0	$0	$0	$0	$0	$0
Sales of Other Current Assets		$0	$0	$0	$0	$0	$0	$0	$0	$0	$0	$0	$0
Sales of Long-term Assets		$0	$0	$0	$0	$0	$0	$0	$0	$0	$0	$0	$0
New Investment Received		$0	$0	$0	$0	$0	$0	$0	$0	$0	$0	$0	$0

	Nov	Dec	Jan	Feb	Mar	Apr	May	Jun	Jul	Aug	Sep	Oct
Subtotal Cash Received	$2,500	($21,600)	$10,000	$15,000	$25,000	$40,000	$45,000	$50,000	$65,000	$80,000	$100,000	$125,000
Expenditures												
Expenditures from Operations												
Cash Spending	$17,531	($544)	$23,156	$27,006	$34,506	$45,756	$49,606	$53,356	$64,606	$75,856	$90,856	$109,606
Subtotal Spent on Operations	$17,531	($544)	$23,156	$27,006	$34,506	$45,756	$49,606	$53,356	$64,606	$75,856	$90,856	$109,606
Additional Cash Spent												
Sales Tax, VAT, HST/GST Paid Out	$0	$0	$0	$0	$0	$0	$0	$0	$0	$0	$0	$0
Principal Repayment of Current Borrowing	$0	$0	$0	$0	$0	$0	$0	$0	$0	$0	$0	$0
Other Liabilities Principal Repayment	$0	$0	$0	$0	$0	$0	$0	$0	$0	$0	$0	$0
Long-term Liabilities Principal Repayment	$0	$0	$0	$0	$0	$0	$0	$0	$0	$0	$0	$0
Purchase Other Current Assets	$0	$0	$0	$0	$0	$0	$0	$0	$0	$0	$0	$0
Purchase Long-term Assets	$0	$0	$0	$0	$0	$0	$0	$0	$0	$0	$0	$0
Dividends	$0	$0	$0	$0	$0	$0	$0	$0	$0	$0	$0	$0
Subtotal	$17,531	($544)	$23,156	$27,006	$34,506	$45,756	$49,606	$53,356	$64,606	$75,856	$90,856	$109,606

Cash Spent											
Net Cash Flow	($15,031)	($21,056)	($13,156)	($12,006)	($9,506)	($5,756)	($4,606)	($3,356)	$394	$4,144	$9,144	$15,394
Cash Balance	$68,669	$47,613	$34,457	$22,450	$12,944	$7,188	$2,582	($774)	($380)	$3,763	$12,907	$28,301

Pro Forma Balance Sheet – Year One

	Starting Balances	Nov	Dec	Jan	Feb	Mar	Apr	May	Jun	Jul	Aug	Sep	Oct
Assets													
Current Assets													
Cash	$83,700	$68,669	$47,613	$34,457	$22,450	$12,944	$7,188	$2,582	($774)	($380)	$3,763	$12,907	$28,301
Other Current Assets	$1,000	$1,000	$1,000	$1,000	$1,000	$1,000	$1,000	$1,000	$1,000	$1,000	$1,000	$1,000	$1,000
Total Current Assets	$84,700	$69,669	$48,613	$35,457	$23,450	$13,944	$8,188	$3,582	$226	$620	$4,763	$13,907	$29,301
Long-term Assets													
Long-term Assets	$10,000	$10,000	$10,000	$10,000	$10,000	$10,000	$10,000	$10,000	$10,000	$10,000	$10,000	$10,000	$10,000
Accumulated Depreciation	$0	$0	$0	$0	$0	$0	$0	$0	$0	$0	$0	$0	$0
Total Long-term Assets	$10,000	$10,000	$10,000	$10,000	$10,000	$10,000	$10,000	$10,000	$10,000	$10,000	$10,000	$10,000	$10,000
Total Assets	$94,700	$79,669	$58,613	$45,457	$33,450	$23,944	$18,188	$13,582	$10,226	$10,620	$14,763	$23,907	$39,301
Liabilities and Capital		Nov	Dec	Jan	Feb	Mar	Apr	May	Jun	Jul	Aug	Sep	Oct
Current Liabilities													
Current Borrowing	$20,000	$20,000	$20,000	$20,000	$20,000	$20,000	$20,000	$20,000	$20,000	$20,000	$20,000	$20,000	$20,000
Other Current Liabilities	$0	$0	$0	$0	$0	$0	$0	$0	$0	$0	$0	$0	$0
Subtotal Current Liabilities	$20,000	$20,000	$20,000	$20,000	$20,000	$20,000	$20,000	$20,000	$20,000	$20,000	$20,000	$20,000	$20,000

Long-term Liabilities	$60,000	$60,000	$60,000	$60,000	$60,000	$60,000	$60,000	$60,000	$60,000	$60,000	$60,000	$60,000	$60,000
Total Liabilities	$80,000	$80,000	$80,000	$80,000	$80,000	$80,000	$80,000	$80,000	$80,000	$80,000	$80,000	$80,000	$80,000
Paid-in Capital	$20,000	$20,000	$20,000	$20,000	$20,000	$20,000	$20,000	$20,000	$20,000	$20,000	$20,000	$20,000	$20,000
Retained Earnings	($5,300)	($5,300)	($5,300)	($5,300)	($5,300)	($5,300)	($5,300)	($5,300)	($5,300)	($5,300)	($5,300)	($5,300)	($5,300)
Earnings	$0	($15,031)	($36,087)	($49,244)	($61,250)	($70,756)	($76,512)	($81,118)	($84,474)	($84,081)	($79,937)	($70,793)	($55,399)
Total Capital	$14,700	($331)	($21,387)	($34,544)	($46,550)	($56,056)	($61,812)	($66,418)	($69,774)	($69,381)	($65,237)	($56,093)	($40,699)
Total Liabilities and Capital	$94,700	$79,669	$58,613	$45,457	$33,450	$23,944	$18,188	$13,582	$10,226	$10,620	$14,763	$23,907	$39,301
Net Worth	$14,700	($331)	($21,387)	($34,544)	($46,550)	($56,056)	($61,812)	($66,418)	($69,774)	($69,381)	($65,237)	($56,093)	($40,699)

PRODUCT MANUFACTURING COMPANY

December 2004

Provided by:
Brad Justin
Product Manufacturing
P.O. Box 1
Nogales, AZ 85555
Telephone: (888) 555-5555
Fax: (480) 555-5555
www.productmanufacturingconogaz1.com

THIS IS A BUSINESS PLAN FOR REVIEW AND DOES NOT IMPLY AN OFFERING OF SECURITIES

1.0 Executive Summary

The Company: Product Manufacturing Company (PMC) is the original manufacturer of a multi-line of widgets. Developed in 1993, the original widget was sold door to door as a gadget. Today the original design has expanded into a multi-line of products that range from super widgets to super gadgets.

The Company is in its second round of funding and wishes to raise capital in the amount of $500,000 for the following purposes: 1) For marketing costs, 2) For raw goods, 3) To establish a retail line for the products, 4) To expand the existing manufacturing facility, 5) To increase inventory, and 6) To hire key personnel.

Product Manufacturing needs additional capital to fund growth and to roll out new products that have been developed. The past ten years have been successful building years for the Company. The products that have been developed are in high demand—with a 70-plus percent retention ratio. We are currently marketing and selling fourteen product lines and will be launching a nationwide television ad campaign in December 2004 that is anticipated to reach about 100 million households.

Product Manufacturing Company has been in operation since 1993. The product was previously manufactured under the XYZ product name (since 1982). Manufacturing was moved from South Dakota to the present Arizona facility. Today, the Company has over 10,000 customers. During the past twenty-four months, many positive things have happened that have spurred on new ideas in adding to the product line. New distributors from around the world have purchased larger than normal orders. The word is rapidly getting out that PMC products live up to the promises made by the Company. Developing a retail line of products was a highly necessary step in capturing additional market share.

The corporate strategic focus has been enhanced by these events and the Company is highly motivated to meet the demand. The recent market tests for retail giants such as Big Big Stores, Simple Food Marts, Home Shopping Stores, Ohio Valley Marts, and Super Giant Mega Stores have increased our brand identity. However, the demand has also created the need for additional financing in order to meet demand.

The Market: The widget market is estimated to be $6 billion at end user value in Q1 2004. This market is expected to grow at 4 percent annually according to professional forecasts published in *Media Research Reports*. Well-known products accounted for the majority of the market penetration; however, they do not offer the same handmade widgets as do our products.

Widget B is used by over 25 million Americans, Widget C helps over 67 million Americans, and Widget D is utilized in over 5 million offices every year. The international market represents well over three times as many individuals that use the same widgets in the United States. Our products are marketed directly to these customers who require these types of products.

Marketing Strategy: Management has streamlined the Company to market and sell a multi-line of products through a combination of distributor sales, Web-based marketing and retail outlets. Specifically, sales are being generated through targeted email campaigns, direct mail exclusive offerings, and product displays located in retail stores, hardware sections of regional stores, and at hospitals and doctors' offices. The Company will showcase four of its products in 210 markets nationwide through Triple ZZZ Shopping Network beginning in December 2004.

The foundation of the products is built upon the unique design of each product. The customer base is already intact, the manufacturing lines are in production, the marketing strategy is accelerated, and with the ownership of the original design, PMC will be a streamlined business with a bright future.

Products and Services: There are variations of the main products in size and packaging, but the following represents PMC's tangible products line *1) Widget A, 2) Widget B, 3) Widget C, 4) Widget D, 5) Widget AA, 6) Widget BB, 7) Widget CC, and 8) A combination of all widgets.*

A list of the products with pricing and pictures is included in Section 3 as well as in the Appendix.

The intangible products of the Company consist of consulting contracts that are under negotiation with distributors around the world to set up manufacturing and labeling stations for distribution in certain countries.

Management: The management team brings with them many industry best practices and combined experience of over one hundred years in manufacturing, banking, strategic planning, management, sales, general business management, and information technology-based applications. This is a solid team of professionals with experience.

Financial Status: The Company has been funded to date by Mr. Brad Justin and bank loans. Although this has been a necessary step to get the business off the ground for the first phases of operation, capital resources are needed to meet the demands of growth and expansion. With the additional funding, the Company hopes to reach over $1 million in revenue for fiscal year 2004 and over $19 million for fiscal 2008.

Use of Funds: The Company plans to borrow up to $500,000 to fund growth, including manufacturing equipment, further develop its distributor network, purchase raw goods to meet the demand of new product introductions, expand its employee and distributor base, and provide marketing capital for the new products.

Financial Data and Exit Strategy: The Company intends to repay any loans in the time frame agreed to, or be acquired sometime after year five of this business plan. PMC may even opt to purchase back the shares of any outside shareholders if applicable. Any one of these options is intended to provide a remuneration event for the stakeholders and personnel who built the Company. Bank loans are intended to be paid off by year 2005, or sooner. In addition, the Company intends to be actively involved in mergers and acquisitions in year 2007. This will require additional capital if this is to occur.

Name and Company Logo: Product Manufacturing's trademarked logo is an original, proprietary design used on all the widgets.

1.1 Goals and Objectives

1. Achieve a 10 percent response rate on direct mail and email campaigns

2. Convert 10 percent of the responses for the first six months after funding, and bump this number to 12 percent thereafter

3. Operate a highly successful enterprise that continues to provide superior products

4. Achieve the sales projections previously outlined

5. Borrow $500,000 for the expansion of the enterprise and new products, as well as have commitments for capital for acquisitions

6. Provide an exit strategy for any stakeholders after 2008

7. Continue to develop new products that enhance the lifestyle of our customers

8. Build a successful distributor channel with worldwide presence

9. Achieve a Gross Profit Margin of 65 percent or greater

10. Achieve projected milestones, as outlined in this business plan

11. Have the products in 5,000 retail outlets by year five of this business plan

12. Create jobs in rural areas close to the manufacturing and sales facilities (personnel plan)

1.2 Mission and Vision

Mission Statement

Product Manufacturing Company is dedicated to the manufacturing and distribution of superior products, as we provide the most effective products at a price that is affordable. We seek to create and nurture a healthy, creative, respectful, and fun working environment in which our employees are fairly compensated and encouraged to respect the customer and the quality of the product we produce. Our guiding principles are to exercise integrity in everything we do.

Vision Statement

Product Manufacturing Company will always exercise integrity in its business dealings and strive to provide the finest products and services available for our customers. We will continually recognize our employees and customers as the lifeblood to the success of our operations and will treat each of them with respect and dignity. By so doing, this will enable Product Manufacturing Company to be a successful and profitable enterprise for our employees, customers, and our financial stakeholders.

1.3 Keys to Success

The keys to success in this business are:

1. Uncompromising commitment to the quality of the products: Quality components, efficient production, cost-effective packaging, and on-time delivery
2. Successful niche marketing: Locate the quality-conscious customer in the right channels and make sure that customer can easily find us
3. A desire that all customers should have an enjoyable experience interacting with employees and technology of the Company when ordering products
4. A high degree of product quality and consistency
5. Management: Products and services delivered on time, costs controlled, marketing budgets managed; remove the temptation to fix on growth at the expense of profits

In today's market, individuals do not have the expertise to decipher what products are the best for themselves and their family. They simply want relief from the things that plague them. More often than not, consumers settle for the recognizable name of a product due to the marketing efforts of global conglomerates that saturate the airwaves with advertisements of grandeur. However, the products delivered generally have undesired side effects and may not provide the relief that consumers are hoping for. Individuals are searching for products that provide relief but do not compromise on quality. PMC provides these products.

With eight mainstream products specifically geared to the challenge-relief markets, we offer a wide variety of challenge-relief solutions to individuals who suffer from discomfort and challenge.

Risks

Every business faces risks in today's economy, and the products and consulting services provided are no exception. There are three areas that are especially risky. The first is putting too much trust into one area of the business that is intended to drive revenue. If we do not have a solid mix of products and services, we may be vulnerable to market downturns and individual spending cuts.

The second area that represents a risk is allocating the right amount of capital to the development and marketing of all of the products. Management and investment sources must continue to provide the necessary capital to expand production and to expand into new markets.

The Company has balanced its revenue streams by offering a broad base of products and services. In the past, the Company has generated a majority of its revenues from the salve and material products. This heavy reliance on one product line is no longer the case. Management has taken into account past experiences and has adjusted for sales variations, by basing its sales forecasts for expansion and growth with a balanced mix of products and services.

Contingency Plans

Management has developed contingency plans to mitigate the risks that were described in the last section. By providing a balanced mix of products, these risks should be reduced. Distributor channel, retail sales, and home shopping network sales are intended to make up a solid mixture of product offerings. Additionally, PMC will expand its sales efforts to increase the number of distributors in its core business to offset the time required to enter this market and generate revenue.

1.4 Use of Proceeds

Legal	$ 2,500		
Marketing & Advertising*	$ 80,500	***Marketing & Advertising Mix**	
Travel	$ 48,000	Radio	$ 38,500
Raw Goods	$ 75,000	Literature	$ 4,500
Insurance	$ 10,400	Print Ads	$ 15,000
Free up Line of Credit	$ 40,000	Direct Mail	$ 15,000
Total Expansion Expenses	**$256,400**	Email	$ 5,500
		Web Design	$ 2,000
		Total	**$ 80,500**

Expansion Assets Needed	
Additional Inventory	$ 70,000
Other Short-term Assets	$ 20,000
Total Short-term Assets	**$ 90,000**
Long-term Assets	$ 0
Total Assets	**$ 90,000**
Total Requirements:	**$346,400**

NOTE: These figures do not include landing a large national account.

2.0 Company Summary

The Company has experienced steady growth in customer acquisition and is currently expanding its sales internationally. The products are well received among contractors and homeowners. The Company continues to add new customers and distributors. With the expansion of international markets, the development of retail sales, and the product introduction to the television shopping networks, the Company is expected to grow at a more rapid pace.

2.1 Company Ownership

Product Manufacturing Company is an Arizona-based limited liability company, currently owned by Brad Justin (75 percent) and Bob Smith (25 percent).

2.2 Company History

The company was founded in 1993 by Brad Justin and officially incorporated as a C Corporation in June 1994. PMC licenses the original and highly guarded design of the products from Widget Company. Operating history for the product has been steady, except for fiscal year 2002, when sales dropped 13 percent due to a very sluggish economy. The following table and chart illustrate the Company's growth.

Table: Past Performance

Past Performance	1999	2000	2001	2002	2003
Sales	$336,737	$408,034	$406,310	353,696	469,335
Gross Margin	$214,041	$279,253	$323,044	122,025	358,889
Gross Margin %	71.91%	68.44%	79.51%	34.05%	70.00%
Operating Expenses	$92,696	$128,781	$83,266	231,671	345,315
Inventory Turnover	12.00	12.00	12.00	6.00	12.00
Earnings	$56,776	$42,844	$48,887	55,949	(106,741)
Other Inputs	1999	2000	2001	2002	2003
Payment Days	30	30	45	15	30
Sales on Credit	$43,674	$40,803	$40,631	$35,050	51,350

2.3 Company Locations and Facilities

The company is located in Nogales, AZ and operates in a 7,500-square-foot building. The building is close to the Nogales International Airport. The facility includes: office space, shipping area, stock area, ingredient-mixing area, and fill-line area.

The manufacturing area has an automated manufacturing line; fluid steel mixer, including a cooling tunnel; and inventory equipment for shipping and receiving purposes. There are computer workstations running on an internal LAN system and a Meridian phone system for data and voice communication. PMC also has specialty software for shipping and financial accounting.

The fluid-steel mixing area of the facility can accommodate a 32,000 gallon heated tank (2500 degrees), which will be supplied by Steelco, USA.

The capacity of the line (per one eight-hour shift) is dependent upon product cooling capacity. Currently, our company can fill 7,000 orders per day of its popular widgets. This equates to approximately 210,000 orders per month for one shift, operating seven days per week. The current fill line has the ability to run three shifts per day when necessary.

PMC also maintains a sales and marketing office in Ajo, AZ.

3.0 Products and Services

Product Manufacturing Company offers superior quality widgets designed to effectively reduce costs.

3.1 Product and Service Description

Widget A
Reduces costs in every department

Widget B
Works with all types of mechanical devices

Widget C
Keeps engines running smoothly

Widget D
Speeds up the production process of copiers

Widget AA
Increases cell phone range

Widget BB™
Patented design to eliminate door squeaks

Widget CC™
Increases the length of a long haul for semi trucks

Widget DD™
A multipurpose widget used primarily for cleaning automobiles

Consulting Services

PMC will continue to provide production consulting to distributors in other countries outside of the United States. This is a lucrative and steady market that exists for start-up and ongoing manufacturing and distribution consulting. With a mixture of consulting, strategic planning and production training, our company plans to become a key partner with several distributors who rely on a strategic focus from the manufacturer to assist them in their manufacturing processes.

3.2 Competitive Comparison

Plans are to continue to differentiate PMC as a business partner with the vision of a company that wishes to be a strategic ally. Company products and consulting must continue to offer real value.

PMC benefits include many intangibles including superior products, vision, confidence, strategic direction, reliability, high-end product knowledge base, and the knowledge that someone will be there to answer questions and help at the important times.

Competing products to our company's products are listed below:

- AAB209
- Complete 2523
- Breezee
- W2X4J
- KPLO22
- 332211
- Buttons3939
- Star558899
- Table3ONL
- 91573XXJU

These competing products are well-known names in the industry. The power of marketing and advertising has created billions of dollars in sales for these products. At a glance, the following chart shows the ingredients of a few of the competing products. Note that none of the competing products have a special design.

Product Manufacturing	Complete 2523	W2X4J	332211	Table3ONL
Dynamic Design	Static Design	Static Design	Static Design	Static Design
Titanium	Titanium	Steel	Brass	Nickel
Polished Aluminum	Aluminum	Copper	Tin	Tin
Gold Sprocket	Plastic Sprocket	Plastic Sprocket	Plastic Sprocket	Plastic Sprocket
Chrome Chain				

3.3 Sales Literature

Product Manufacturing Company has developed sales literature that illustrates a highly professional organization with vision. Company literature also illustrates how the products enhance the way that other widgets work together. There will always be additional pieces of literature that need to be developed. To accomplish this, our company is constantly refining its marketing mix through a number of different literature packets. These include:

- Direct mail with an introduction letter and product price sheet
- Corporate brochures
- Product information brochures
- Press releases

- New product information literature
- Email marketing campaigns
- Website content
- Television advertisements

(Other copies of Product Manufacturing advertisements and sales literature are attached in the Appendix at the end of this document.)

3.4 Sourcing

Our company manufacturers its own products, using mostly local and regional vendors of materials and services.

- Gold: Argentina
- Boxes/Plastic Containers: Colorado
- Containers/Jars: Utah
- Copper: Utah
- Steel: Arizona
- Labels: Utah
- Packing Material: Florida
- Shipping: UPS and USPS

The cost of goods sold (COGS) usually runs the company about 30 percent. However, a more detailed cost per item is listed in the following table:

PRODUCT	SIZE	COST	WHOLESALE
Widget A	6 in dia.	$.91	$2.98
Widget B	8 in dia.	$4.22	$10.45
Widget C	10 in dia.	$19.44	$71.48
Widget D	12 in dia.	$29.41	$79.90
Widget AA	14 in dia.	$39.76	$81.59
Widget BB	16 in dia.	$49.30	$91.05
Widget CC	18 in dia.	$59.76	$101.59
Widget DD	24 in. dia.	$71.60	$115.49

3.5 Technology

Product Manufacturing Company technology management involves processes and activities that will establish standards and monitor the direction in all areas of our distributed computing environment. The further establishment of company standards and direction include operating systems, network LAN/WAN topologies, hardware, applications, and network protocols.

Technology is currently not as critical for the overall operation. However, as the Company continues to expand and grow, these areas will be of mission-critical importance.

4.0 Market Analysis Summary

The widget market is worth an estimated $4 billion at end-user value in 2003 and is projected to grow at 4 percent per year, according to professional forecasts published by Media Research, Inc., New York, NY.

Of this $4 billion, the United States' leading brands for challenge relief topical solution including AAB209, W2X4J, and Star558899 account for $2 billion of the market. The market is still large enough and fragmented enough to bear additional competition. Currently Star558899 and 91573XXJU are heavily marketing their products via television and radio. Other such industry leaders include multi-level marketing (MLM) companies such as Sell a Lot, Next Sell a Lot, and Keep It Coming.

Source: Market research is from Media Research, Inc., New York, NY

4.1 Market Segmentation

PMC products cater to a variety of consumers that belong to several different market segments. Market research has shown the following market/industry classifications:

- Chronic pain: 6.7 percent growth in the total market place with potential customers reaching over 25,000,000. Chronic pain in the United States (figures from the National Chronic pain Foundation):
  - One-third of the entire population suffers from chronic pain.
  - 2.5 million Americans are afflicted with rheumatoid chronic pain.
  - Juvenile chronic pain affects 71,000.
  - Over one million Americans have been diagnosed with gout.

- Lactose Intolerance: 4.2 percent growth in the total marketplace, with potential customers exceeding 39,000,000.

- Back Aches: 3.3 percent growth in the total marketplace with potential customers exceeding 28,000,000.

- Sports Injury: 2.5 percent growth in the total marketplace with potential customers exceeding 5,000,000.

- Diabetes: 2.5 percent growth. Every year about 800,000 people learn they have diabetes. Over 25 million people in the United States, Canada, and Mexico have diabetes.

- Camping and Hiking: 2.0 percent growth. Kampgrounds of America (KOA) has over 500 campsites, and an estimated 8.5 million people go camping and hiking every year.

*Sources: Media Research, Inc., New York, NY

Market Analysis (Pie)

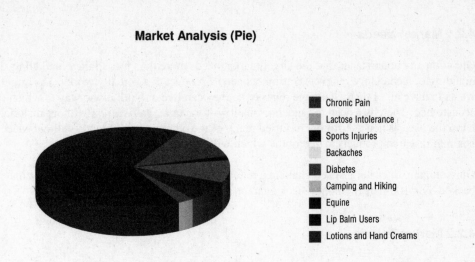

- Chronic Pain
- Lactose Intolerance
- Sports Injuries
- Backaches
- Diabetes
- Camping and Hiking
- Equine
- Lip Balm Users
- Lotions and Hand Creams

Table: Market Analysis

Market Analysis

Potential Customers	Growth	2003	2004	2005	2006	2007	CAGR
Chronic Pain	6.7%	25,000,000	26,675,000	28,462,225	30,369,194	32,403,930	6.70%
Lactose Intolerance	4.2%	39,000,000	40,638,000	42,344,796	44,123,277	45,976,455	4.20%
Sports Injuries	2.5%	5,000,000	5,125,000	5,253,125	5,384,453	5,519,064	2.50%
Backaches	3.3%	28,000,000	28,924,000	29,878,492	30,864,482	31,883,010	3.30%
Diabetes	2.5%	25,000,000	25,625,000	26,265,625	26,922,266	27,595,323	2.50%
Camping and Hiking	2.0%	8,500,000	8,670,000	8,843,400	9,020,268	9,200,673	2.00%
Total	3.90%	130,502,003	135,659,004	141,049,668	146,685,946	152,580,462	3.90%

4.2 Target Market Segment Strategy

PMC is not advocating that it replace widgets intended for multiple uses, rather only for those who are demanding quality widgets that actually work. Our products are of higher quality, last longer, and are effective for a lower price than competitive national brands. PMC addresses the needs of the customer who has been unsuccessful in finding solutions using other well-known brands of challenge relief products.

Within our market, there are many buyers who have tried several national brands without finding relief from their challenges. In documented studies, seven out of ten people found that our products relieve their challenges and will continue to purchase the product for many years, becoming very brand specific loyal. These people also become walking testimonials who share their positive attitude about the PMC products with others; they even share their purchases with other challenge sufferers.

4.2.1 Market Needs

Our company understands that the target market needs more than just a fancy marketing slogan or branding of a challenge reliever; consumers need a product that actually works. The target customer wants to have all of their challenge relieved so they can live or work in the way to which they are accustomed. There is a need for superior quality—for *challenge relievers* without materials that can harm the user. When a customer has tried many of the other national brands without success, they begin to research products to determine which will best relieve their challenges.

Our company does not just sell challenge relief; it sells challenge relief with superior materials, and is backed by a 100-percent money-back guarantee.

4.2.2 Market Trends

The market has grown to recognize what works and what does not. Consumers are constantly looking for products that relieve challenges. The products developed by PMC cater to all types of users, and particularly those that experience the need to be better at what they do. PMC serves a trend toward customers who desire additional products offering the same features. For this reason, our company has formulated a widget with the highest blend of desired attributes.

4.2.3 Market Growth

According to Media Research, Inc., the market for Widget A is growing at a 6.7 percent rate; the market for Widget B is growing at a 4.2 percent rate; the market for Widget C is growing at a 3.3 percent rate; and the market for Widget D is growing at a 2.5 percent rate.

The market for Widget A should grow to 97,000,000 customers in the United States by 2010, which again is a projected growth rate of 2.5 percent to 6.7 percent.

The international market is about three times larger than the U.S. market.

*Market research is from Media Research, Inc.

4.3 Industry Analysis

The Widget A industry has undergone a great deal of change in the past decade. The introduction of new products found in the marketplace seems to be taking market share away from the dominant national brand such as 91573XXJU in the Widget A market; 332211 in the Widget B market; and Buttons3939 in the Widget C market. Star558899 produces relatively expensive widgets with fewer materials compared to our products. Table3ONL and 91573XXJU are in the same price range, but do not contain as many challenge reducing features.

Since our company caters to several different markets as outlined in the market analysis table, there are multiple areas of focus. The primary focus is to cater to markets that have a need for challenge relief products. Each one of the markets that our company sells to may have specific needs, yet the products fulfill those needs.

4.3.1 Distribution Patterns

The main volume in the industry is now concentrated in the national brands already mentioned, all of which compete for retail sales through all major retail chain stores.

Designs are similar and quite competitive. Costs and cost control is critical; channel management and channel marketing is the key to these corporations' continued success.

There are also some smaller manufacturers still making highly specialized challenge relief products for small niche markets such as figure skaters, sports photographers, and catering company owners. Most of these are small companies, with one member in their product family.

4.3.2 Competition and Buying Patterns

The primary manufacturers are selling directly to the chain stores and hardware distribution markets. This accounts for their main volume of distribution. The challenge relief customer seems to be growing more comfortable with purchasing new or improved products that might relieve their challenges, rather than keeping their challenge and staying brand loyal.

The major corporate purchases are still made directly with manufacturers. Although this is still a major channel for some of the more traditional manufacturers, it is essentially closed to new competition. The direct channel is dominated by a few manufacturers and many distributors.

- The cost of marketing a new product is becoming a serious barrier to entry. Major retailers usually do not accept a new product without major advertising and promotion expenses.
- Brand names carry more weight. The channels are dominated by existing brands. Retailers don't have to experiment when they carry name brands.

Through experience, management has found that 90 percent of the total sales volume in the market goes through the retail channel. Most of this is through major national or regional chains. About 7 percent goes through the direct sales channel although, in this case, direct sales include sales by distributors who are buying from small manufacturers. Most of the remainder—3 percent—is sold directly to buyers through catalogs, direct mail, and the Internet.

4.3.3 Main Competitors

In the mainstream business, channels are critical to volume. The manufacturers with impact in the national sales are going to win display space in the store, and most buyers seem content to purchase their product from the store sales floor. Price is critical, because the channels take significant margins. Buyers are willing to settle for brand name recognition, but are starting to become more aware of product components.

The primary competitors are outlined for the following markets:

Category	Product	Product	Product	Product	Product	Product
Chronic pain	Competitor A	Competitor B	Competitor C	Competitor D	Competitor E	Competitor F
Lactose Intolerance	Competitor A	Competitor C	Competitor F	Competitor H	Competitor I	
Sports Injuries	Competitor A	Competitor B	Competitor C	Competitor D	Competitor E	
Back Aches	Competitor A	Competitor B	Competitor C	Competitor D	Competitor E	
Diabetes	Competitor C	Competitor G	Competitor J	Competitor K	Competitor L	Competitor M
Camping/Hiking	Competitor B	Competitor D	Competitor F	Competitor H	Competitor J	Competitor M
Equine	Competitor W	Competitor X	Competitor Y	Competitor Z	Competitor S	
Lip Balm	Competitor S	Competitor T	Competitor U	Competitor V	Competitor W	Competitor X
Lotions and Hand Cream	Competitor A	Competitor G	Competitor I	Competitor M	Competitor N	Competitor O

There is still a lot of room for new products and new companies outside the main design types.

- In the main design types, marketing and advertising generates more market share. Table3ONL, for example, is not the best challenge reliever, but it is the market leader. Consumer perception is that it is a better product than any other challenge relief material. Most importantly, retailers carry this product, and it continues to dominate in the market. Despite the existence of better products, it is the most recognizable choice for the buyer.

- Buyers migrate to the products that are heavily marketed and perceived to be a brand name. Quality of challenge relief products is difficult to measure. Brand names do not always ensure superior quality. However, brand names only operate in mainstream product types; there is plenty of room for smaller names with specific solutions or multipurpose solution products that appeal to buyers, driven by results.

- Depending on the age of buyers, consumers may be willing to pay higher prices for a challenge relief material that works. While competitors chip away at market leaders with lower prices, the leaders continue to command high prices with less product effectiveness.

- Channels discount heavily. Brand name, packaged challenge reliever formulas become a commodity and are bought on price.

- Distribution channels are clogged. Lack of channels is a serious barrier to industry growth. Chain stores and food retailers are insufficient for the wealth of products available and the constant flood of new products.

5.0 Strategy and Implementation Summary

Product Manufacturing Company focuses on a few practices that are in place to help maintain healthy growth. These are:

1. Emphasize service and support.

Continue to differentiate the products from the canned presentation and box pushers. We need to establish our business offering as a clear and viable alternative for our target markets, to the price-only kind of buying.

2. Build a relationship-oriented business.

Build long-term relationships with customers, not single-transaction deals. Become their challenge relief partner, not just a vendor. Help them understand the value of the relationship.

3. Focus on target markets.

PMC focuses on product offerings to individuals who experience challenges and are seeking relief with superior products. Our company values superior products, excellent customer service, and distributor support and knowledge.

4. Differentiate and fulfill the promise.

PMC does not just market and sell products. The Company must continue to actually deliver the very best products the market has to offer, and ensure that the products are superior and meet the claims made by the Company.

5. Market products that no one else offers.

The product mix for our company is unique in that each product caters to a specific need. With the use of the mix of products, PMC can provide challenge relief options to all kinds of consumers from all walks of life.

6. Provide the consumer with more offers and give them the opportunity to buy additional products.

Known as "back-end selling," this concept is where the real revenue is generated from repeat customers and could mean an increase of millions of dollars to the Company.

7. Total quality management for the entire line of products produced by PMC.

Since the Company is producing several products, rather than one individual product, manufacturing must keep up with the demands. This is another reason the additional capital is so crucial to the further growth of our company. If demand is created as anticipated with sales and marketing efforts, a larger facility and multiple manufacturing lines will be required.

5.1 Strategy Pyramids

The strategy for selling PMC products and consulting services includes the multi-pronged approach previously outlined.

Our main strategy has been to sell through a network of distributors, which helps place emphasis on service and support. The specific programs for developing the distributor network include direct calls, mailers and educational seminars. Specific programs for retail sales include direct contact with key buyers within the retail enterprises. For getting to the right decision makers, our company initiates direct mail marketing and follow-up phone calls to meet with these key buyers.

The second strategy is emphasizing relationships. Through strategic alliance partners, PMC has developed new business opportunities, where partners initially opened doors. These have turned into very good engagements for the Company. Therefore, the tactics are marketing the Company (instead of just the products), more regular contacts with the customers, and increasing sales per customer. Programs for marketing the Company include new sales literature, revised ad strategies, email campaigns, and direct mail. Programs for more regular contacts include callbacks after consultation, direct mail, and sales management. Programs for increasing sales per customer include upgraded mailings and sales training.

5.2 Value Proposition

Unique Selling Advantage

Our company's unique selling advantage is that the design of each of our products is inspected three times for quality prior to shipping. Product pricing is also highly affordable and very competitive. The Company offers a 100 percent money-back guarantee if the customer is not satisfied. During the past ten years, no one has returned a single widget due to dissatisfaction of the product. The products are multi-use and they have an immediate effect on challenge relief. With five essential materials in every product, PMC has the most key challenge relief ingredients on the market today—all-inclusive within each product. Competing products only have one to two essential materials.

Value Proposition

We offer uniquely premium goods and services that are easily adaptable to all forms of challenge relief. The products and services that the Company sells meet the needs of many different market segments, particularly in the areas of challenges. The Company offers simple products and services. In addition to simplicity, product and service offerings cover several different levels of pricing specifically designed to meet the needs of consumers and contractor professionals.

5.3 Competitive Edge

Our company promotes products that are highly effective and provide relief in many areas for a variety of aches and challenges. We offer a 100 percent money-back guarantee if the consumer is dissatisfied with the product for any reason. Repeat customers are the best advertisements because they purchase more products than they use, in order to give a jar of relief to their friends.

The PMC products contain more usual ingredients and higher percentages of challenge relieving agents than the competition: Our competitive edge can be illustrated in three ways. First, the product superiority is far above the competition. Second, the experience of the management team is based on a solid foundation of know-how. The management team has been through some very tough and very rewarding times. The learning curve is drastically reduced. Third, the products are in high demand and needed in the market. By building a business based on long-standing relationships with satisfied clients, PMC simultaneously builds defenses against the competition by improving customer loyalty.

5.4 Marketing Strategy

The marketing strategy is the core of the Company's main business strategy:

1. Emphasize service and support.

2. Build a relationship-oriented business.

3. Focus on building the distributor network with a balance of developing a solid line of retail sales.

4. Keep the company's unique brand names in front of customers through a comprehensive marketing mix.

5. Strengthen existing relationships and build new relationships with strategic alliance partners.

6. Provide a broad mix of products and consulting that can be spread out to reduce risk.

7. Work with many customers to reduce any risk of too much business in one area that may be vulnerable.

8. Assist international distributors to improve the quality of production and distribution processes.

The strategy, moving forward, is to emphasize the products that have been, and are being, sold to the market. In addition to this, PMC will continue to focus on strategic alliances with outside partners that will increase revenue streams from both the Company and the distributors.

Management has streamlined the Company to market and sell the product line through a combination of Web-based marketing, the distributor network, retail outlets and television. This is accomplished specifically through targeted email campaigns, direct mail exclusive offerings, trade shows, and product displays located in retail stores. This strategy of the marketing mix caters specifically to the massive consumer market.

The second strategy focuses on rapidly building the international distributor network. This includes onsite training for the establishment of manufacturing facilities and education on distribution of the products.

International Sales

The Company is currently selling its products in Western Europe, Canada, Africa, and India. Negotiations are taking place to enter such markets as Brazil, China, many South American countries, Australia, and Southeast Asia.

Wholesale orders of $30,000 are becoming more and more common with these international markets. As the Company sells pre-packaged products to its distributors overseas, the margins are not as good as they could be. PMC must move quickly into promoting manufacturing in the overseas market through bulk sales of the products and a consulting package for the establishment of a manufacturing/fulfillment facility within a country for production and distribution. This is anticipated to be a lucrative area for both our company and its distributor network.

5.4.1 Pricing Strategy

PMC will maintain its current pricing position and offer the most effective challenge relieving ingredients for a mid-range priced challenge-relieving product. The strategy going forward does not call for any significant changes in pricing; except maybe in shipping and handling charges. The current pricing structure suggests superior quality and value at a reasonable price. The market has been quite capable of bearing the pricing strategy currently in place. (Please refer to the product and pricing sheet in the Appendix.)

5.4.2 Promotion Strategies

In the past, the most effective vehicles for sales promotion have been direct sales to the current customer base and sales through the distributor network. These strategies will continue for the Company along with other strategies.

1. Management is currently working with many retail chains throughout the country to get the products into the retail distribution channel. The products have been received with a favorable reaction from most of the buyers, and several retail chains are placing regular orders.

2. International marketing and distribution is listed in this business plan as a significant contributor to the flow of revenue, beginning in the fourth quarter of 2004. Our company is currently engaged in international distribution of its products, and the Company is currently exploring several options to opening up new distribution channels into several countries. Specifically, PMC is in negotiations with Ghana, Nigeria, South Africa, Mali, Burkina Faso, and Benin in the African continent. Much interest for the products has been shown throughout Asia and South America. Several countries have also requested that the Company set up a manufacturing facility in their respective countries.

3. Contractor magazines are an untapped market that the Company is focusing on as well. The American Contractor Club produces a highly successful magazine, and has recently conducted a test with 5,000 of its readers for two of our products: Widget A and Widget D. The purpose of these tests is to review the viability of the products. The test has been completed and we have received the Contractor Tested Seal of Approval. With an overall approval rating of 90 percent, PMC joins the ranks of the upper echelon of companies to receive such a high rating. We will also receive a four-color, ¼ page ad in the magazine for three issues. *The American Contractor* magazine has 500,000 subscribers and is produced twelve times annually.

4. PMC will also continue to exhibit at trade shows throughout the country. Trade shows in the past have been mostly favorable for the Company, and international trade shows will be targeted once the funding is in place.

5. Private labeling is becoming a popular method of manufacturing and distribution of the products. Our company is working with large retailers and private organizations to private label three primary products: 1) Widget A, 2) Widget B, and 3) Widget C.

6. We will continue to sell to retail home improvement stores, contractor associations, and athletic teams throughout the country. This campaign is just underway, and seems to be a solid market for Widget A and Widget B.

7. A campaign for acquiring new distributors will be introduced in the winter of 2004 via a massive email campaign. Contractor and subcontractor professionals such as generals, plumbers, framers, and landscapers will be targeted.

8. The equestrian industry has been very popular for many years in the United States. Internationally, this industry has been an important mainstay for thousands of years. Currently there are over 4 million quarter horses in the world. PMC's Widget DD™ is manufactured specifically for horses. Since it has been approved by the Center for Veterinary Medicine, it is currently being marketed to equestrian parks and retail stores that supply products to this industry.

9. Finally, every six months, our company offers a case lot special, which generates a substantial amount of reorders to the existing customer base. Customers favorably respond to these specials and take the opportunity to stock up on the products.

5.4.3 Marketing Programs

PMC will also be active in promoting its products to distributors throughout the world. Soon, the Company will unveil a promotion strategy by adding profitability incentives for distributors on their initial orders. Distributors will also receive free samples with their initial orders so they can distribute these samples to their potential customers.

Additional marketing programs that are anticipated to begin in Q2 2005 are contracting with a contractor marketing company such as the Contractor Marketing Group (Superior, MN), which specializes in marketing to the contractor niche. They will present a plan, and actual implementations for the PMC Widget DD product, marketing to all different contracting areas. Management feels this is an important segment since building challenges are one of the fastest growing markets in the construction field. The product, if used before and after a project, can reduce the chance of pulled challenges.

5.5 Sales Strategy

Product Manufacturing Company products have been marketed on a very limited budget; yet, in the past, the majority of the sales have been by word of mouth. Statistical data for the past four years indicate that this translates into 50 new customers and two new retail stores per week.

For 2005, the Company will continue to focus on distributor sales and increase retail sales and direct sales through the marketing campaigns previously outlined.

The work with distributors has been promising. Management hopes to continue building and strengthening relationships with distributors selling directly to larger corporations, even though this takes working capital to support receivables and requires increasing international exposure.

Management recognizes the need to generate additional distribution. This is one of the key elements of success during the next twelve months. The products need to be displayed in retail outlets with multiple locations. The Company will also foster the relationships with current distributors who sell to smaller dealers.

The company will continue to sell to its current customer base and broaden its sales territory to international markets. As vertical markets are segmented, the strategy is to attack each market individually. For example, email campaigns will require a robust website, e-Commerce for online purchasing, and proper follow-up. Consulting services require one-on-one selling to distributors and proper positioning of the product line and timely follow-up.

5.5.1 Sales Forecast

The important elements of the sales forecast are shown in the following table that outlines estimated revenue streams and gross profit margins. The line item marked as "Int'l. Consulting" represents anticipated international contracts for consulting to set up manufacturing facilities that license the PMC designs.

Table: Sales Forecast

Sales Forecast

Sales	FY2004	FY2005	FY2006	FY2007	FY2008
Distributor Sales	$400,710	$601,065	$751,331	$939,164	$1,173,954
Retail Sales	$184,112	$736,449	$1,841,122	$4,602,805	$11,507,013
Home Shopping Networks	$357,294	$500,000	$875,000	$1,312,500	$1,968,750
International Sales	$48,600	$500,000	$1,200,000	$2,000,000	$3,500,000
Int'l. Consulting	$150,000	$300,000	$400,000	$600,000	$1,000,000
Total Sales	$1,140,716	$2,637,514	$5,067,453	$9,454,469	$19,149,717

Direct Cost of Sales	FY2004	FY2005	FY2006	FY2007	FY2008
Distributor Sales	$120,213	$180,319	$225,399	$281,749	$352,186
Retail Sales	$55,234	$220,935	$552,337	$1,380,842	$3,452,104
Home Shopping Networks	$140,381	$196,450	$343,788	$515,681	$773,522
International Sales	$29,160	$300,000	$720,000	$1,200,000	$2,100,000
Int'l. Consulting	$4,500	$9,000	$12,000	$18,000	$30,000
Subtotal Cost of Sales	$349,487	$906,704	$1,853,523	$3,396,272	$6,707,812

Sales Monthly

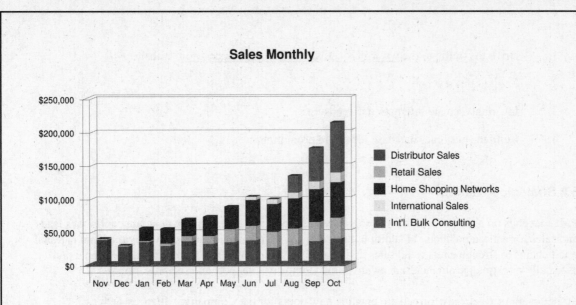

5.5.2 Sales Programs

Direct mail: PMC intends to continue to use direct mail to invite consumers to try the products. Direct mail will also be used as a medium for special offers. Plans are to send out 5,000 mailers each month to a targeted list.

Internet: The Internet is a tool that allows us to reach millions of potential clients with minimal costs. It helps build brand awareness through direct marketing via email. Increasingly companies are testing the direct marketing model, sending complex emails to highly targeted lists of prospects. This technique works much the same way as offline direct marketing campaigns: PMC has built a database of email addresses by enticing customers to register on the website in exchange for information or access to a special offer.

Face-to-face visits: Of course, Company representatives will continue to visit with customers one on one. Owners of the Company and sales executives will call on buyers to explain the Company strategic objectives and products.

Television: Everything in the marketing mix is intended to create greater awareness of other products and services that PMC offers. By selling the products through the television airways, the intent is to drive sales and to create more brand awareness. The company is aggressively pursuing this marketing medium with Network of Consumers Who Buy Products over the Television. The commercials begin airing December 22, 2004 in 310 markets in the United States. The total potential households to be reached are 135,000,000. The cable networks that will carry the commercials are ESPN, ESPN News, CNN, and Fox News.

Print Ads: Plans are to run display ads in the *American Contractor* magazine, *Lovin' Contracting,* and *Building New Commercial Dreams* magazine.

Each one of the promotions—from television to print ads, and even the email campaigns—must be intertwined with driving traffic to the PMC website or a call to action to pick up the phone and order products. This marketing mix is intended to accomplish four things:

1.   Drive the traffic to the www.productmanufacturingcompany.com website

2.   Create sales revenue

3.   Invariably, create international exposure

4.   Build the customer database for future promotions

5.6 Strategic Alliances

PMC depends on alliances with distributors, retailers, and loyal customers to generate continuous leads and sales for add-on products. In addition, the Company is forming alliances with regional and national retail chains to strengthen its retail sales division. Management will make certain that personnel and especially our strategic alliances are aware of the Company's support and reciprocation.

Strategic alliances already formed are opening new doors for the Company. Alliances such as:

- JIJ—Casper, Wyoming
- LOMJ—Salt Lake City, UT
- KOPPL—Bentonville, AK
- BRING IT ON NETWORK—Pompano Beach, FL
- Big Time Pharmacy—Uganda Africa
- Your Partner, Inc.—Salt Lake City, UT
- Business Council—Cheyenne, WY
- U.S. Commercial Service—Denver, CO
- New and Improved Products USA—Washington, D.C.
- Big Time Growth Industries USA—Washington, D.C.
- BLI—South Africa
- World Wide Contracting—Panama
- Independent Contracting Distributors—Branson, MO
- Linkside to the Beach Marketing—Tampa, FL
- Mr. Goodbar's—Mexico
- Big East and West Distribution—Memphis, TN
- Webb Distribution—Yuma, AZ
- Blue Star Laboratories—England
- Over 10,000 loyal customers

5.7 Milestones

The accompanying table lists important program milestones, with dates and managers in charge, and budgets for each. The milestone schedule indicates the Company's emphasis on planning and implementation.

Table: Milestones (Planned)

Milestones

Milestone	Start Date	End Date	Budget	Manager	Department
Update Business Plan	11/1/2004	Ongoing	$2,500	Brad	Operations
Complete Funding	10/25/2004	2/15/05	$2,500	Bob	Operations
Hire Sales Personnel	1/15/2005	4/15/2005	$5,000	Bob	Sales
First 100 Retail Stores	8/15/2004	9/1/2005	$25,000	Bob	Sales
First 1,000 Retail Stores	8/15/2004	9/1/2006	$75,000	Bob	Sales
First 5,000 Retail Stores	8/15/2004	1/1/2009	$250,000	Bob	Sales
Add'nl Manufacturing Lines	7/15/2005	1/1/2006	$100,000	Brad	Operations
International Expansion	8/15/2004	Ongoing	$100,000	Team	Marketing/Sales
First Consulting Contract	4/15/2005	10/1/2005	$3,500	Team	Marketing/Sales
Achieve $5 Million in Revenue	4/15/2004	12/15/2006	$125,000	Team	Marketing/Sales

6.0 Management and Personnel Summary

PMC develops and manufacturers a line of products focused on challenge relief through topical application. These products are manufactured and marketed by an experienced management team that has a good track record and has worked out many of the inherent problems that comes with manufacturing and distribution.

6.1 Organizational Structure

Brad Justin is the president of Product Manufacturing Company. The Company also relies on outside advisors to assist in the further growth and development of the enterprise. The Company organization chart is presented here:

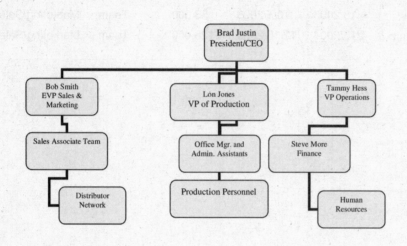

6.2 Management Team

The management team has over one hundred years combined experience in banking, finance, operations, manufacturing, sales, and marketing. The outside advisors to the Company have provided valuable insight to the further development and expansion of markets. The Company plans to continue working with its current outside advisors as valuable resources to drive the success of the enterprise.

Brad Justin, President

- Twenty years contracting experience
- CEO of Regional Contracting Association
- Successful franchise operator
- Successful small business owner
- Solid experience in manufacturing in a multi-line environment

Bob Smith, VP Sales and Marketing

- Twenty-one years in operations and international contracting consulting
- Started and operated other successful small businesses
- Developed and produced *The Ultimate Contractor's Guide for Building Homes*
- Manufactured and marketed the popular widget machines on a national, as well as an international, scale
- Regional director of Fortune 50 Conglomerate; increased sales from $500,000 to $5 million in three years
- Board member of:
  - AZTec—Arizona Entrepreneur Center
  - Jones Business Innovation Center, Ajo Community College
  - Arizona Entrepreneur Challenge—business plan competition for all colleges in the state of Arizona
  - Superstition High School Community Council—Higley, Arizona

Tom Dansell, Plant Manager (joining upon funding)

- Highly skilled in the art of multi-line product production
- Over twenty years experience in manufacturing and production at Big Time Bottling
- Twenty-five years as a machinist
- Fifteen years as a plant foreman
- Eight years as a plant manager

Linda Johnson, Office Manager

- Worked in the office environment for over fifteen years
- Executive assistant to C-level executives
- Highly skilled in management of a distributor network

James Ellings, Board of Advisors

- Senior editor, Big Time Law Review, 1977–1978
- Tucson Board of Adjustment and Planning Commission, 1979–1980
- Secretary, Arizona Environmental Quality Council, 1985–1987
- U.S. Marshall, 1991–1999
- Member, Arizona Judicial Commission, 1992–1996
- Advisory Committee on Rules, Arizona Supreme Court, 1999–2002
- Fellow, American Academy of Appellate Lawyers

Steve More, Board of Advisors

- Twenty-eight years experience as a CPA
- Sr. Partner in Howe, Much & More, P.C.
- Trusted advisor to several small businesses and major corporations

6.3 Management Team Gaps

PMC has a solid team for covering the main points of the business plan. The addition of outside professionals is important as a way to cement our fundamental business practices. With the addition of legal and accounting consultants, the management team will be well versed in the complicated issues of running a successful consulting enterprise. Industry professionals have been selected with proven track records and exemplary backgrounds.

6.4 Personnel Plan

The personnel plan reflects the need to bolster capabilities to match positioning. Total headcount should increase to 17 by end of year 2004, 26 in 2005, 41 by 2006, 70 by 2007, and to an estimated 132 employees by 2008. Detailed monthly projections are included in table 6.4.

Table: Personnel

Personnel Plan	FY2004	FY2005	FY2006	FY2007	FY2008
Executive Personnel					
Executives	$150,300	$225,000	$258,750	$297,563	$342,197
Executive Assistants	$6,000	$26,000	$57,200	$94,380	$103,818
Other	$0	$0	$0	$0	$0
Subtotal	$156,300	$251,000	$315,950	$391,943	$446,015
Sales and Marketing Personnel					
Sales Associates	$77,403	$159,501	$256,698	$450,179	$873,989
Marketing Assistants	$10,500	$24,000	$72,000	$108,000	$162,000
Other	$0	$0	$0	$0	$0
Subtotal	$87,903	$183,501	$328,698	$558,179	$1,035,989
General and Administrative Personnel					
Office Manager	$27,000	$29,700	$32,670	$35,937	$39,531
Administrative Support	$7,500	$19,800	$43,560	$47,916	$95,832
Finance	$7,500	$48,000	$52,800	$58,080	$63,888
International	$40,000	$121,200	$152,024	$283,634	$574,492
Subtotal	$82,000	$218,700	$281,054	$425,567	$773,742
Production Personnel					
Production Manager	$29,167	$55,000	$60,500	$66,550	$73,205
Production Personnel	$32,000	$108,160	$156,160	$252,160	$444,160
Distribution	$6,667	$45,000	$49,500	$54,450	$59,895
Other	$0	$0	$0	$0	$0
Subtotal	$67,833	$208,160	$266,160	$373,160	$577,260
Total Headcount	17	26	41	70	132
Total Payroll	$394,036	$861,361	$1,191,862	$1,748,848	$2,833,006
Payroll Burden	$59,105	$129,204	$178,779	$262,327	$424,951
Total Payroll Expenditures	$453,142	$990,565	$1,370,641	$2,011,176	$3,257,957

7.0 Internet Strategy

The Corporate website is currently an information site that provides general information about the Company's products and services. Customers are able to order online at the present time through an e-Commerce solution. The site still needs to be upgraded with new options and menus for our clients to receive real-time information and have the capabilities of viewing an online demonstration of the products offered.

The strategy is to develop a dynamic, robust site that has real streaming video capabilities to show how our solution works. This will be a four- to five-minute overview of the products and services with a call to action. The call to action will provide the prospect or client with the opportunity to choose three options:

- Register and send their information via the Internet to receive a response call
- Sign up for our newsletter
- Purchase products

As we continue to develop strategic alliances with well-known industry names, a further strategy is to place a link from our site to the strategic partner's site, thus creating a portal of general health information for our customers and prospects.

In order to properly disseminate the information to the general public, the corporate website will need to be upgraded using the latest in Flash and video streaming technology. The initial programming will be outsourced to a competent Web design firm. This will save the expense of not having a full-time Web developer on staff in the beginning.

Since there will be a database developed that will be used for ongoing marketing and customer support, the programming will be required to be fully compatible with technology issues such as bandwidth, software, and support.

8.0 Financial Plan

The most important element in the financial plan is the critical need for improving several of the key factors that impact cash flow:

1. The Company must, at any cost, emphasize its plans to sell both products and services to clients and to develop better customer service policies than the competition. This should also be a function of the shift in focus toward service revenues to add to the product revenues.

2. Management hopes to bring the gross margin to 61 percent and the net profit margin to 30 percent by the end of fiscal year 2008. This, too, is related to improving the mix between product and service revenues, because the service revenues offer much better margins.

3. The Company plans to borrow $500,000 in financing and have commitments to fund future acquisitions. These amounts seem in line with the balance sheet capabilities.

8.1 Important Assumptions

The financial plan depends on important assumptions, most of which are shown in Table 6. The key underlying assumptions are:

1. The Company assumes a moderate-growth economy, without a major recession.

2. The Company assumes, of course, that there are no unforeseen changes in business and technology to make its products immediately obsolete.

3. The Company assumes access to equity capital and financing sufficient to maintain the financial plan as shown in the accompanying tables.

4. In the sales forecast, the term "consulting" represents international opportunities to establish manufacturing and distribution facilities whereby PMC will charge a fee for startup operations and training.

5. Bulk products represent products shipped to international distributors in 55-gallon drums for the further packaging of the product. The international distributors will, in turn, package and label the product in their respective countries.

6. Also listed in the sales forecast are the associated costs of goods sold (COGS) for the products and services in the following manner:

   - Distributor sales—24 percent
   - Retail sales—30 percent
   - Home shopping sales—30 percent
   - Bulk products—35 percent
   - Consulting fees—3 percent

7. The breakdown of the specific lines of business and the anticipated percentage of total revenue in year 2004 is listed first, and the anticipated percentages are listed for each area in 2008 in the next column:

Sales	2004 Percentage	2008 Percentage
Distributor Sales	35%	6%
Retail Sales	16%	60%
Home Shopping Networks	31%	10%
International Sales	4%	18%
Int'l. Bulk Consulting	13%	5%

Table: General Assumptions

General Assumptions

	FY2004	FY2005	FY2006	FY2007	FY2008
Short-term Interest Rate %	10.00%	10.00%	10.00%	10.00%	10.00%
Long-term Interest Rate %	10.00%	10.00%	10.00%	10.00%	10.00%
Payment Days Estimator	50	50	50	50	50
Collection Days Estimator	45	45	45	45	45
Inventory Turnover Estimator	6.00	6.00	6.00	6.00	6.00
Tax Rate %	25.00%	25.00%	25.00%	25.00%	25.00%
Expenses in Cash %	10.00%	10.00%	10.00%	10.00%	10.00%
Sales on Credit %	10.00%	10.00%	10.00%	10.00%	10.00%
Personnel Burden %	15.00%	15.00%	15.00%	15.00%	15.00%

8.2 Key Financial Indicators

The plan shows an assumption of a 15 percent personnel burden for additional items such as vacation, insurance, and sick leave. As far as long-term and/or short-term debt, the Company has figured in an interest rate of 10 percent. This plan outlines a 25 percent tax burden.

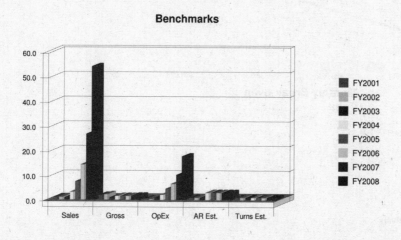

Benchmarks

8.3 Break-even Analysis

For the Break-even Analysis, the plan assumes monthly operating costs of approximately $41,000 in month six of 2004, which includes our full payroll, rent, and utilities, interest, telephone, and an estimation of marketing costs.

Margins are harder to assume. The overall average of $32.76 per order sold is based on an average of the retail/distributor orders. Calculated in this plan is an average variable cost of 30 percent for each unit sold. The Company hopes to attain a margin that will remain high in the future.

The break-even per month is 1,800 units per month sold, which means that the Company will need to generate in excess of $59,000 per month to break even.

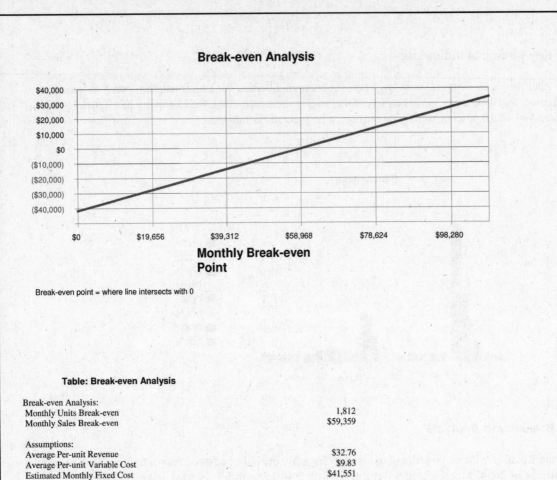

Break-even Analysis

Monthly Break-even Point

Break-even point = where line intersects with 0

Table: Break-even Analysis

Break-even Analysis:	
Monthly Units Break-even	1,812
Monthly Sales Break-even	$59,359
Assumptions:	
Average Per-unit Revenue	$32.76
Average Per-unit Variable Cost	$9.83
Estimated Monthly Fixed Cost	$41,551

8.4 Projected Profit and Loss

The most important assumption in the projected profit and loss statement is the gross margin, which is estimated to be 55 percent by the end of 2004, 55 percent at the conclusion of 2005, 56 percent by the end of 2006, 59 percent by the end of 2007, and 51 percent at the conclusion of 2008.

We hope to achieve 7 percent net profit margin at the conclusion of 2004; 12 percent at the conclusion of 2005; 20 percent by the end of 2006; 26 percent by the end of 2007; and 30 percent at the conclusion of 2008. The figures represented in these profit and loss assumptions are based on having the proper amount of funding in place to achieve growth.

Table: Profit and Loss
Profit and Loss (Income Statement)

	FY2004	FY2005	FY2006	FY2007	FY2008
Sales	$1,140,716	$2,637,514	$5,067,453	$9,454,469	$19,149,717
Direct Cost of Sales	$349,487	$906,704	$1,853,523	$3,396,272	$6,707,812
Executive Payroll	$156,300	$251,000	$315,950	$391,943	$446,015
Other	$0	$21,100	$45,607	$85,090	$191,497

Total Cost of Sales	$505,787	$1,178,804	$2,215,080	$3,873,305	$7,345,324
Gross Margin	$634,928	$1,458,709	$2,852,372	$5,581,164	$11,804,393
Gross Margin %	55.66%	55.31%	56.29%	59.03%	61.64%
Operating Expenses:					
Sales and Marketing Expenses					
Sales and Marketing Payroll	$87,903	$183,501	$328,698	$558,179	$1,035,989
Advertising/Promotion	$84,000	$92,313	$202,698	$378,179	$765,989
Internet and Phones	$9,500	$14,400	$18,000	$24,000	$42,000
Travel	$24,500	$45,000	$70,000	$100,000	$150,000
Miscellaneous	$4,300	$5,375	$6,719	$8,398	$10,498
Total Sales and Marketing Expenses	$210,203	$340,589	$626,115	$1,068,756	$2,004,475
Sales and Marketing %	18.43%	12.91%	12.36%	11.30%	10.47%
General and Administrative Expenses					
General and Administrative Payroll	$82,000	$218,700	$281,054	$425,567	$773,742
Payroll Burden	$59,105	$129,204	$178,779	$262,327	$424,951
Depreciation	$5,000	$10,800	$13,500	$16,875	$21,094
Leased Equipment	$46,500	$60,000	$60,000	$90,000	$135,000
Utilities	$6,000	$6,600	$13,200	$14,520	$17,424
Business Insurance	$2,400	$3,600	$3,960	$4,356	$4,792
Rent	$24,000	$54,000	$66,000	$84,000	$96,000
Total General and Administrative Expenses	$225,005	$482,904	$616,493	$897,645	$1,473,002
General and Administrative %	19.72%	18.31%	12.17%	9.49%	7.69%
Production Expenses					
Production Payroll	$67,833	$208,160	$266,160	$373,160	$577,260
Professional/Consultants	$7,500	$25,000	$25,000	$25,000	$50,000
Total Production Expenses	$75,333	$233,160	$291,160	$398,160	$627,260
Production %	6.60%	8.84%	5.75%	4.21%	3.28%
Total Operating Expenses	$510,542	$1,056,653	$1,533,768	$2,364,561	$4,104,738
Profit Before Interest and Taxes	$124,387	$402,057	$1,318,605	$3,216,603	$7,699,655
Short-term Interest Expense	$5,475	$10,200	$18,000	$25,800	$33,600
Long-term Interest Expense	$0	$0	$0	$0	$0
Taxes Incurred	$29,728	$97,964	$325,151	$797,701	$1,916,514
Charitable Contributions	$0	$15,000	$25,000	$50,000	$100,000
Net Profit	$89,184	$308,893	$1,000,453	$2,443,102	$5,849,541
Net Profit/Sales	7.82%	11.71%	19.74%	25.84%	30.55%

8.5 Projected Cash Flow

The cash flow depends on assumptions for projected sales revenue, inventory turnover, payment days, and accounts receivable management. The projected forty-five-day collection days are critical, and it is also reasonable. The Company needs a minimum of $500,000 in new financing: 1) Fund marketing costs, 2) Meet the demands of the ordering of products, 3) Establish retail sales, 4) Build the additional manufacturing facilities required for anticipated increased product demand, 5) Purchase raw goods and inventory, and 6) Fund operations activities.

Cash

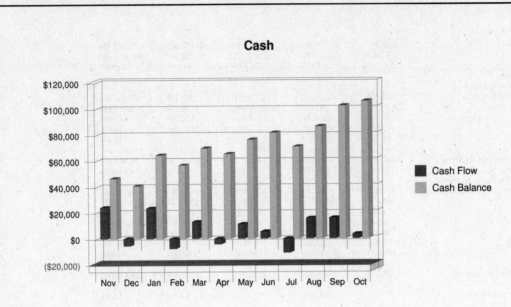

Table: Cash Flow

Pro Forma Cash Flow

	FY2004	FY2005	FY2006	FY2007	FY2008
Net Profit	$89,184	$308,893	$1,000,453	$2,443,102	$5,849,541
Plus:					
Depreciation	$5,000	$10,800	$13,500	$16,875	$21,094
Change in Accounts Payable	$76,819	$96,201	$174,269	$297,560	$670,201
Current Borrowing (Repayment)	$18,000	$78,000	$78,000	$78,000	$78,000
Increase (Decrease) Other Liabilities	$0	$0	$0	$0	$0
Long-term Borrowing (Repayment)	$0	$0	$0	$0	$0
Capital Input	$0	$0	$0	$0	$0
Subtotal	$189,003	$493,894	$1,266,223	$2,835,537	$6,618,836
Less:	FY2004	FY2005	FY2006	FY2007	FY2008
Change in Accounts Receivable	$16,259	$39,705	$64,458	$116,372	$257,181
Change in Inventory	$89,130	$84,831	$109,811	$160,861	$338,477
Change in Other Short-term Assets	$0	$0	$0	$0	$0
Capital Expenditure	$0	$0	$0	$0	$0
Dividends	$0	$30,889	$100,045	$244,310	$584,954
Subtotal	$105,390	$155,425	$274,314	$521,543	$1,180,612
Net Cash Flow	$83,613	$338,469	$991,909	$2,313,993	$5,438,224
Cash Balance	$105,804	$444,274	$1,436,182	$3,750,175	$9,188,399

8.6 Projected Balance Sheet

The projected balance sheet is quite solid. The Company does not project any real trouble meeting its debt obligations—as long as it can achieve the funding requirements and meet specific objectives.

Table: Balance Sheet

Pro-forma Balance Sheet

Assets

Short-term Assets	FY2004	FY2005	FY2006	FY2007	FY2008
Cash	$105,804	$444,274	$1,436,182	$3,750,175	$9,188,399
Accounts Receivable	$30,259	$69,964	$134,422	$250,794	$507,974
Inventory	$107,020	$191,851	$301,662	$462,523	$801,001
Other Short-term Assets	$15,000	$15,000	$15,000	$15,000	$15,000
Total Short-term Assets	$258,084	$721,089	$1,887,266	$4,478,492	$10,512,374
Long-term Assets					
Capital Assets	$65,000	$65,000	$65,000	$65,000	$65,000
Accumulated Depreciation	$11,500	$22,300	$35,800	$52,675	$73,769
Total Long-term Assets	$53,500	$42,700	$29,200	$12,325	($8,769)
Total Assets	$311,584	$763,789	$1,916,466	$4,490,817	$10,503,605

Liabilities and Capital

	FY2004	FY2005	FY2006	FY2007	FY2008
Accounts Payable	$84,819	$181,020	$355,290	$652,849	$1,323,050
Short-term Notes	$63,000	$141,000	$219,000	$297,000	$375,000
Other Short-term Liabilities	$0	$0	$0	$0	$0
Subtotal Short-term Liabilities	$147,819	$322,020	$574,290	$949,849	$1,698,050
Long-term Liabilities	$0	$0	$0	$0	$0
Total Liabilities	$147,819	$322,020	$574,290	$949,849	$1,698,050
Paid in Capital	$0	$0	$0	$0	$0
Retained Earnings	$74,581	$132,876	$341,723	$1,097,866	$2,956,014
Earnings	$89,184	$308,893	$1,000,453	$2,443,102	$5,849,541
Total Capital	$163,765	$441,768	$1,342,176	$3,540,968	$8,805,555
Total Liabilities and Capital	$311,584	$763,789	$1,916,466	$4,490,817	$10,503,605
Net Worth	$163,765	$441,768	$1,342,176	$3,540,968	$8,805,555

8.7 Business Ratios

Ratio Analysis

Profitability Ratios:	FY2004	FY2005	FY2006	FY2007	FY2008
Gross Margin	55.66%	55.31%	56.29%	59.03%	61.64%
Net Profit Margin	7.82%	11.71%	19.74%	25.84%	30.55%
Return on Assets	28.62%	40.44%	52.20%	54.40%	55.69%
Return on Equity	54.46%	69.92%	74.54%	69.00%	66.43%

Activity Ratios	FY2004	FY2005	FY2006	FY2007	FY2008
AR Turnover	3.77	3.77	3.77	3.77	3.77
Collection Days	71	69	74	74	72
Inventory Turnover	8.10	7.89	8.98	10.14	11.63
Accts Payable Turnover	7.24	7.24	7.24	7.24	7.24
Total Asset Turnover	3.66	3.45	2.64	2.11	1.82

Debt Ratios	FY2004	FY2005	FY2006	FY2007	FY2008
Debt to Net Worth	0.90	0.73	0.43	0.27	0.19
Short-term Liab. to Liab.	1.00	1.00	1.00	1.00	1.00

Liquidity Ratios	FY2004	FY2005	FY2006	FY2007	FY2008
Current Ratio	1.75	2.24	3.29	4.71	6.19
Quick Ratio	1.02	1.64	2.76	4.23	5.72
Net Working Capital	$110,265	$399,068	$1,312,976	$3,528,643	$8,814,324
Interest Coverage	22.72	39.42	73.26	124.67	229.16

Additional Ratios	FY2004	FY2005	FY2006	FY2007	FY2008
Assets to Sales	0.27	0.29	0.38	0.47	0.55
Debt/Assets	47%	42%	30%	21%	16%
Current Debt/Total Assets	47%	42%	30%	21%	16%
Acid Test	0.82	1.43	2.53	3.96	5.42
Asset Turnover	3.66	3.45	2.64	2.11	1.82
Sales/Net Worth	6.97	5.97	3.78	2.67	2.17
Dividend Payout	$0	$0	$0	$0	$0

8.8 Conclusion

PMC is a company that provides superior products and consulting that far exceed what is in the market today. Our executive team is highly capable of achieving the goals and objectives set forth in this business plan. In addition, our products provide much needed relief from challenge. PMC is a progressive company and is expanding to new heights. The products are in demand and the new product designs are being well accepted.

With the advent of retail sales and television shopping networks, the sales will increase over previous years. In order to meet the demands that these two divisions are anticipated to generate, investment into the growth of the Company will need to occur.

APPENDIX

- Testimonials
- Month-by-Month Financial Projections
- Marketing Materials (in printed and bound version of the business plan)

NOTES

TRM LLC

TRM LLC
1631 Raintree Way
Pueblo, Colorado. 84054
(555) 981-0000
17689TRM@yahoo.com

Confidentiality Agreement

The undersigned reader acknowledges that the information provided by Thomas Williams in this business plan is confidential; therefore, reader agrees not to disclose it without the express written permission of Thomas Williams.

It is acknowledged by reader that information to be furnished in this business plan is in all respects confidential in nature, other than information which is in the public domain through other means and that any disclosure or use of same by reader, may cause serious harm or damage to Thomas Williams.

Upon request, this document is to be immediately returned to Thomas Williams.

_____
Signature

_____
Name (typed or printed)

_____
Date

This is a business plan. It does not imply an offering of securities.

Table of Contents

TRM LLC

1. Executive Summary

GENERAL

TRM LLC will be an Internet retailer run from Pueblo, Colorado, that will sell creatively designed T-shirts to the youth market at a premium price. This plan constitutes a blueprint that will guide TRM through setup, implementation, and operation of its business, as well as provide a future growth strategy.

The company will receive orders through its website, which will use a PayPal application to ensure immediate payment and avoid uncollected payment scenarios. It will then send data to its printing supplier (who will also provide the T-shirts). The print shop will print and ship the finished product directly to the customer, thus causing TRM to avoid inventory-holding costs.

MARKET

TRM's products will not only fill a utilitarian need, but also, more importantly, address the youth market's need to express their individuality through creative and innovative design. By involving a highly creative designer as well as gaining valuable feedback from the target audience through its website, TRM will keep its pulse on the needs and wants of its target market and position itself for growth.

The Internet T-shirt industry is a growing market with excellent margins. The market for T-shirt printing is estimated to be 20 billion dollars. TRM will specifically target young men and young women in the 15–24 age range, segmented into two distinct groups: 15–17 and 18–24. This target market was comprised of approximately 41 million individuals in the United States in 2002 and was expected to grow 17.1 percent by 2007. Market research has shown that individuals in this age range place a high importance on and consequently spend the most on apparel—more than 10 billion annually. TRM intends to capitalize on this growing and lucrative market.

ADVERTISING

Key to TRM's success will be sufficient marketing and advertising to drive a sufficient number of potential customers to its website and convert as large a percentage of these visitors to sales as possible. TRM will continually work with its Web designer to optimize its website to increase sales. It will further engage in CRM efforts to retain existing customers and promote word of mouth advertising from loyal customers. Advertising will consist primarily of Internet banners, higher returns on search engines, press releases, corporate blog, strategic partnerships with companies that market their products to the same target market, and word of mouth. TRM will have increased advertising in Pueblo and will engage junior and senior high schools.

FINANCIAL

TRM will be funded with a short-term loan and further backed by an investment from its owner. It is estimated that no further debt will be necessary, regardless of growth due to its business model. We anticipate a positive net worth after the first six months of operation. We further expect to achieve over $70,000 in gross sales by end of year three.

- Growth will be moderate.

- Marketing will remain between 10 to 15 percent of sales.

- The Company will invest residual profits into new design efforts and Web services.

TRM LLC

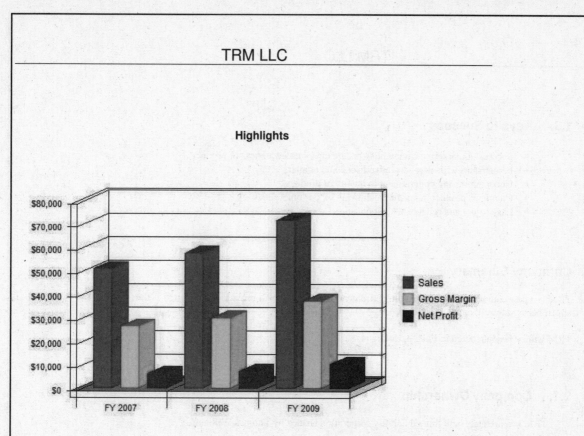

Highlights

1.1. Objectives

1. Convert at least 15 percent of website visitors to sales

2. Achieve at least 15 percent sales growth year over year

4. Sustain 40 percent operating profit margin

5. Use CRM initiatives to ensure at least 20 percent repeat customers

6. Expand product line

7. Be in a position to be acquired by the end of year five

1.2. Mission

TRM LLC is dedicated to the idea of Internet apparel e-Commerce for the youth market. TRM will provide easy-to-use tools and fun, creative, and cutting-edge ideas. We constantly strive to create an environment where innovation, creativity, and humor are encouraged and rewarded. We also endeavor to give our consumers new and exciting means to demonstrate their individuality. Our guiding principles are to exercise integrity and good judgment in everything we do and to respect the values of others without infringing on our own.

TRM LLC

1.3. Keys to Success

- Successful marketing campaign to ensure customer awareness of product
- Partnerships with suppliers, advertisers, and retailers
- Uncompromising commitment to quality of products
- Continued product innovation—drawing on customer feedback
- Easy-to-use and reliable Web application

2. Company Summary

TRM is a new company, which upon commencement of operations will provide cutting-edge T-shirt apparel geared toward the youth market.

TRM will be headquartered in Pueblo, Colorado.

2.1. Company Ownership

TRM is a privately held limited liability corporation headed by Thomas Williams.

2.2. Start-up Summary

Start-up expenses will include legal fees associated with creating the company and registering a company name. It will also include insurance for the business. The most expensive start-up expense will be creating the Web page that the business will be primarily run through, followed by a business computer.

Assets that we will need before the company starts include trademark phrases and names that will be included on merchandise.

Financing for start-up expenses and initial assets will be funded with a short-term loan and by the owner, Thomas Williams.

TRM LLC

Start-up

Requirements

Start-up Expenses	
Legal	$300
Insurance	$300
Web Design	$8,500
Business Computer	$2,000
Other	$200
Total Start-up Expenses	**$11,300**

Start-up Assets	
Cash Required	$1,000
Other Current Assets	$300
Long-term Assets	$0
Total Assets	**$1,300**

Total Requirements	**$12,600**

Start-up

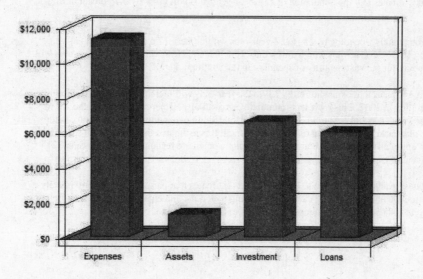

TRM LLC

3. Products

TRM will sell high quality T-shirts designed specifically for the youth market. This will be done through its Internet site. It will accomplish its purpose through key partnerships with T-shirt and graphic design suppliers to meet customer needs. It will also use its Web tool to gain valuable customer feedback on new product ideas. After the initial T-shirt introduction, TRM will consider moving into other related product lines.

4. Market Analysis Summary

TRM will market to the youth market in the United States. The youth market is defined as those between the ages of 15 and 24. According to Packaged Facts (a division of MarketResearch.com), there are approximately 41 million individuals in the U.S. youth market (as of 2002). The youth market is highly diverse and many live with their parents.

The latest available data from the U.S. Census Bureau indicate that 15- to 24-year olds have an average income of $12,479 and generate an aggregate annual income in excess of $350 billion. Young men in the 18- to 24-year-old group have the highest average income and account for the majority of aggregate income in the youth population

According to Packaged Facts, the youth population enjoys shopping, is less driven by bargains, spends the most on apparel, is driven by fashion, and spends more than $10 billion on apparel.

Packaged Facts goes on to say that growth in the youth population will outpace that of the population as a whole between 2002 and 2007. While the U.S. population is expected to increase by 4.7 percent, Packaged Facts estimates that the population of 15- to 24-year-olds will grow by 5.1 percent during this period.

From 2002 through 2007, spending by 15- to 17-year-olds will increase 17.1 percent, while expenditures by 18- to 24-year-olds will grow by only 16.5 percent. However, 18- to 24-year-olds will continue to account for the vast majority of spending in the youth market.

Packaged Facts estimates that expenditures by 15- to 24-year-olds will increase from $466 billion in 2002 to $546 billion in 2007. This represents cumulative growth of 17.1 percent. Those in the 15- to 17-year-old age group account for around 10 percent of total youth expenditures ($47 billion), while 18- to 24-year-olds make up 90 percent of the youth market. It is estimated that young men spend $252 billion (54 percent of all youth expenditures), while young women are responsible for spending $215 billion (46 percent of expenditures).

Based on the latest available USDA data, Packaged Facts estimates that parents spend approximately $54 billion on food, clothing, personal-care items, reading materials, and entertainment for children in the 15- to 17-year-old age group. Clothing expenditures exceed $10 billion.

I.T. Strategies estimates that the US market for T-shirt printing is about $20 billion.

4.1. Market Segmentation

TRM will target the youth population—those between the ages of 15 and 24. It will target both young men and young women equally. Potential customers will be those who reside within the

TRM LLC

United States. It will market to two separate groups within the youth market—one to the 15- to 17-year-olds and the other to the 18- to 24-year-olds.

Market Analysis							
Potential Customers	Growth	2006	2007	2008	2009	2010	CAGR
Age 15–17	5%	12,118,000	12,736,018	13,385,555	14,068,218	14,785,697	5.10%
Age 18–24	4%	27,830,000	28,831,880	29,869,828	30,945,142	32,059,167	3.60%
Other	0%	0	0	0	0	0	0.00%
Total	4.06%	39,948,000	41,567,898	43,255,383	45,013,360	46,844,864	4.06%

Market Analysis (Pie)

- 15 - 17 Year Olds
- 18 - 24 Year Olds
- Other

4.2. Target Market Segment Strategy

The youth population enjoys shopping, is less driven by bargains, spends the most on apparel, is driven by fashion, and spends more than $10 billion annually on apparel.

Compared to the adult population as a whole, young men and women are significantly more likely to say that they like to make a unique fashion statement and that they try to keep up with changes in fashion. They are far more likely to "really enjoy" clothes shopping, to spend more than they can afford on clothes, and to buy new clothes each season.

TRM LLC

Under-25 consumer units allocate an above-average portion of their budgets to apparel. Single young women are especially likely to place a relatively high priority on buying clothes— spending 7 percent of their budgets on apparel, significantly more than the 4.4 percent spent by consumer units as a whole.

Those within the 15–17 age range are a prime target market as they live with their parents and receive clothing from their parents, who have more disposable income. TRM will market to both young men and young women equally within this market segment.

Those within the 18–24 age range are also a prime target market as they work full-time and as they spend a disproportionate amount of money on apparel. Those that attend college are also key customers as this is the time that brand loyalty creation can carry through life. TRM will market to both young men and young women equally.

4.3. Industry Analysis

INTERNET

The Internet T-shirt industry is expanding faster than ever. With over 1,500 websites now selling T-shirts, they are capturing an ever-growing portion of the estimated 20 billion dollar U.S. T-shirt market. Exceptional margins and low overhead costs make this an attractive industry. Mix in the ease of Internet use and one has a winning combination.

RETAIL

The T-shirt market is also important to most retail chains across the country that target the youth market. Retail chains add the one thing that the Internet cannot offer, the ability to handle and try on the apparel prior to purchase. Retail chains also provide a showcase for companies that hope to gain increased market share due to brand awareness.

4.3.1. Competition and Buying Patterns

Consumers purchase T-shirts for one of three reasons: 1) Brand, 2) Originality, and 3) Humor. The youth market is a highly diverse market that branches over all the above-mentioned categories. TRM intends to create a desirable brand, consistently innovate to produce original products, and to infuse a number of the product lines with witty humor. We feel that in this way TRM will be able to build brand awareness across the diverse youth market that will allow it to command premium pricing in the T-shirt market. TRM's website will provide an easy way for customers to search for and purchase from its various category lines.

5. Strategy and Implementation Summary

TRM will pursue a differentiation strategy by offering a specific line of young men's and young women's shirts over the Internet. TRM will target the youth segment (ages 15–24). We expect that along the way we will find niche markets within this segment that we can cater to. Overall, we expect to increase sales at least 10 to 15 percent year over year.

TRM LLC

5.1. SWOT Analysis

The SWOT analysis provides us with an opportunity to examine the internal strengths and weaknesses TRM must address. It also allows us to examine the opportunities presented to TRM as well as potential threats.

TRM has a valuable inventory of **strengths** that will help it succeed. These strengths include: original and creative designs and wording, a fun and easy-to-use website, a 100 percent money back guarantee, strong relationships with suppliers and advertisers, and careful CRM initiatives designed to promote repeat buying.

Strengths are valuable, but it is also important to realize the **weaknesses** TRM must address. These weaknesses include: a limited advertising budget, wait time for customers to receive their product, and an owner who is new to online business. TRM's strengths will help it capitalize on emerging opportunities.

These **opportunities** include, but are not limited to, an increasing expansion of Internet T-shirt companies, a youth market that is increasingly comfortable with and dependent on technology, a target market that spends the largest amount of their income on apparel, and strategic alliances with key companies like Yearbook Interactive and Gray Whale CD Exchange.

Threats that TRM should be aware of include, existing retailers, existing Internet T-shirt companies, imitators, and the importance of properly identifying with the target market.

5.1.1. Strengths

1. **Original and creative designs** based on a modernized form of graffiti art coupled with fun, witty, and humorous sayings

2. **Fun and easy-to-use website** that not only allows customers to see and order products, but also enlists their feedback on upcoming designs and wording concepts

3. **100 percent money back guarantee**

4. **CRM initiatives** that look to build a relationship with customers to improve customer satisfaction and increase the likelihood of repeat buying

5. **Strong relationship with key suppliers** to improve delivery time

TRM LLC

5.1.2. Weaknesses

1. Limited advertising budget—could lessen impact of sales initially

2. Product is not immediately available and the customer will have to wait for printing and shipping

3. Owner new to online business model

5.1.3. Opportunities

1. The Internet T-shirt business has grown rapidly in the past few years. The Internet has become a common shopping place for T-shirts and its acceptance has grown substantially in recent years.

2. The youth market is increasingly using and depending on technology. The youth market today grew up with computers and the Internet and is completely at ease with purchasing items through the Internet.

3. The youth market has and uses a disproportionate amount of their disposable income on apparel; in fact, they spend the most on apparel. They thoroughly enjoy shopping and are less influenced by bargains.

4. Key strategic alliances. The younger end of the youth market is heavily tied to yearbooks. There has been a growing trend in CD-ROM yearbooks that reflects this target market's acceptance of technology. TRM will leverage a strategic alliance with Yearbook Interactive to gain access to the 15- to 18-year-old market. This alliance will allow for quick and reliable penetration into the younger end of the youth market and help build brand recognition and acceptance, which will carry into the next market segment. The youth market is also highly tied to and spends a great deal of money on music. TRM will also forge a strategic alliance with Gray Whale CD Exchange to gain additional exposure to the youth market.

5.1.4. Threats

1. Existing Retailers. Existing retailers pose a threat as they offer the tangibility that the Internet experience cannot duplicate. Customers may prefer to do business with a company where they can see, handle, and try on the products they are considering purchasing. TRM feels, however, that its target market's comfort with and use of the Internet for purchases will help offset this threat.

2. Existing and Upcoming Internet T-shirt Companies. There are a growing number of Internet T-shirt companies. As the number of these types of companies grows, it may become increasingly difficult to differentiate TRM's products. Proper advertising and marketing will be critical to band recognition. Further, this industry thrives on creativity. If TRM can continually produce innovative designs and sayings, it has the potential to maintain visibility in an ever-growing sea of competitors.

3. Imitators. Companies that imitate TRM's graphic style and wording concepts could take business away from TRM. TRM will attempt to mitigate this threat by gaining

TRM LLC

trademarks on key wording combinations that it feels will be popular with the target market.

4. Failure to identify with target market. If TRM's brand fails to identify with the target market, sales will suffer. TRM will use focus groups to gauge design and wording popularity as well as gain new ideas for upcoming products. It will also use its website to gain valuable customer feedback that it can apply to ongoing operations.

5.2. Competitive Edge

TRM's competitive edge is simple: TRM has the ability to create unique and innovative product designs and wording that lend themselves to brand desirability. Further, TRM will deploy CRM practices that will engage their customers and obtain their feedback on future product designs/wording so it can continually keep pace with changes.

5.3. Marketing Strategy

Our marketing strategy will focus heavily on driving potential customers to its website. This will occur through the following mechanisms:

- Advertising budget between 10 and 15 percent of gross annual sales
- Strategic alliances with Yearbook Interactive and Gray Whale CD Exchange to better engage target market
- Advertising on key college campuses
- Enlisting services that will cause TRM to return toward the top of key Internet search engines
- Sending custom bumper stickers that promote TRM's website with each new customer's product
- Listing TRM's Web address in a visible area on each T-shirt
- Sending a quarterly e-newsletter that will encourage customer loyalty and increase repeat sales to its existing customer base; and offer special promotions to existing customers
- Increasing advertising and special promotions to coincide with seasonality peaks
- In future years, as TRM's advertising budget grows, it will advertise in key magazines for the target population (automotive for men and fashion magazines for women)
- Promotions and advertising will always stay in tune with TRM's company objectives and mission statement

5.4. Sales Strategy

Because TRM is a new entity, we understand that we will have to prove our company's worth to consumers in order to earn their respect and business and in order to grow.

Key to this effort is a properly designed website that has a good balance between utility and aesthetics geared toward the target market. Sales will be facilitated through a PayPal application. TRM will offer a thirty-day money back guarantee to back the brand.

TRM LLC

TRM will also maintain a comprehensive customer database that it will use in later direct marketing campaigns focusing on repeat customers.

5.4.1. Sales Forecast

The following table and chart give an estimate on forecasted sales. We expect sales in the 15- to 17-year-old range to grow 10 percent in year two and 15 percent in year three. This contrasts with the expected growth of the 18-to 24-year-old market, which we believe will grow 15 percent in year two and 20 percent in year three. We expect the older group to grow faster due to the following: 1) there are more members of this population than the younger population and 2) this group has more disposable income. We believe that as the brand gains increased name recognition, sales in subsequent years will increase.

The sales forecast also takes some seasonality into consideration. We expect to have higher sales in the spring and summer months as well as in December. We anticipate that sales in the non-peak months to be smaller, but stable.

The sales forecast will be contingent upon sufficient marketing efforts driving enough people to the website as well as a favorable response from the target market. All T-shirts were priced equally ($18.95—includes shipping and handling) for the first two years of the sales forecast. In the third year, the T-shirt price will increase to $19.95 to cover cost of living increases.

TRM LLC

Sales Forecast

	FY 2007	FY 2008	FY 2009
Unit Sales			
TRM T-shirts (15- to 17-year-old market)	896	986	1,133
TRM T-shirts (18- 24-year-old market)	1,792	2,061	2,473
Total Unit Sales	2,688	3,047	3,606
Unit Prices	FY 2007	FY 2008	FY 2009
TRM T-shirts (15- to 17-year-old market)	$18.95	$18.95	$19.95
TRM T-shirts (18- 24-year-old market)	$18.95	$18.95	$19.95
Sales			
TRM T-shirts (15- to 17-year-old market)	$16,979	$18,685	$22,603
TRM T-shirts (18- 24-year-old market)	$33,958	$39,056	$49,336
Total Sales	$50,938	$57,741	$71,940
Direct Unit Costs	FY 2007	FY 2008	FY 2009
TRM T-shirts (15- to 17-year-old market)	$9.10	$9.10	$9.58
TRM T-shirts (18- 24-year-old market)	$9.10	$9.10	$9.58
Direct Cost of Sales			
TRM T-shirts (15- to 17-year-old market)	$8,150	$8,969	$10,850
TRM T-shirts (18- 24-year-old market)	$16,300	$18,747	$23,681
Subtotal Direct Cost of Sales	$24,450	$27,716	$34,531

TRM LLC

Sales Monthly – FY 2007

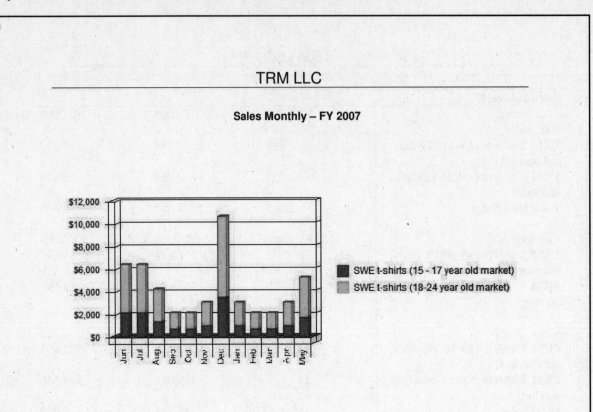

Sales by Year

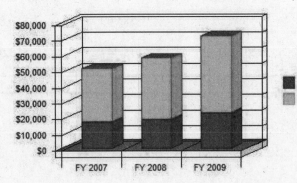

TRM LLC

5.5. Milestones

The accompanying milestone chart highlights TRM's plan with specific dates. This schedule reflects our strong commitment to organization and detail.

Milestones

Milestone	Start Date	End Date	Budget	Manager	Department
Update Business Plan	3/19/2006	Ongoing	$50	Thomas	Operations
Freelance Artwork	4/1/2006	4/15/2006	$300	Vedranna	Operations
Have T-shirt Demos Created	4/15/2006	4/30/2006	$300	Thomas	Operations
Acquire Initial Trademarks	3/19/2006	6/1/2006	$738	Thomas	Operations
Design / Setup Website	3/19/2006	6/1/2006	$8,500	Thomas / Shad	Marketing
Strategic Alliance with Yearbook Interactive	5/1/2006	Ongoing	$1,000	Thomas / John L.	Marketing
Strategic Alliance with Gray Whale CD Exchange	5/1/2006	Ongoing	$1,000	Thomas / John T.	Marketing
Achieve Gross Sales of $100,000 by the end of year two	6/1/2006	12/31/2009	$15,000	Thomas	Sales
Totals			**$26,888**		

6. Web Plan Summary

TRM's business model is exclusively driven by e-Commerce. TRM will work with Lunawebs, a local Web developer/host, to create a youth-oriented website that will showcase its products and promote sales activity. The website will be www.s-w-e.com and will utilize a PayPal application for easy purchase. Data will be gathered on each customer transaction that takes place as well as other visitor activity. Reports will be generated and provided to the owner, who will then regularly coordinate with Lunawebs to optimize the website. TRM will also utilize the data gathered on its website to provide customers with a quarterly e-newsletter that will give them exclusive previews of new products as well as discounts on purchases. Newsletters will coincide with expected seasonal sales spikes. The website will also conduct visitor surveys on new product graphics/wording to better assess which ones are most promising.

TRM will also provide advertising for its key strategic partners (Yearbook Interactive and Gray Whale CD Exchange) on its website. It will also provide cutting-edge music that is aimed at its target market to make the site more desirable.

TRM will also host a blog page where visitors can post comments. This will foster a sense of belonging to those who visit the site and will likely promote the site.

Due to the supreme importance of TRM's website, it will constantly be reviewed and modified to maximize sales.

TRM LLC

6.1. Website Marketing Strategy

TRM's marketing strategy will be to drive potential customers within its target segment to its website. This will be accomplished through a number of advertising efforts as well as through strategic alliances with companies that will advertise and promote the website.

General Advertising:

- Purchasing targeted key word searches
- Obtaining banner advertising
- Publishing news releases announcing the new website
- Advertising the Web address on the product itself
- Sending bumper stickers with Web address on them to new customers
- Word of mouth

Strategic Advertising Alliances:

- Yearbook Interactive (I am a personal friend of the CEO)
- Gray Whale CD Exchange (I am a good friend of one of the partners that owns the company)

6.2. Development Requirements

TRM will utilize Lunawebs to design and host its website. Vlad Schick, president of Lunawebs and Thomas Williams, owner of TRM, will develop it. Maintenance will be an ongoing partnership between Thomas Williams and Vlad Schick. Key elements of the website are listed below:

Website Design

- Youth friendly aesthetic design
- High quality product photos
- Target market specific background music—promoting Gray Whale CD Exchange
- e-Commerce package (includes extensive data gathering, analysis, reporting and CRM applications)
- PayPal component for quick and easy payment
- Various surveys to gather customer feedback
- Corporate blog page
- Quarterly newsletter creation

Ongoing Costs

- Initial Web design fee: $8,500 (includes website name registration fee)
- Yearly ongoing design fee: $300
- Monthly Web hosting fee: $30

TRM LLC

7. Management Summary

The management of TRM is made up of the owner, Thomas Williams and the graphic design artist, Vedranna Inc.. Thomas will concentrate primarily on maximizing sales as well as on the daily operations of the business. Verna will concentrate on the creative design process. Thomas has worked as an operations manager, a senior business manager, and a senior client services manager. Further, Thomas has key contacts that will propel the business forward. Verna is an accomplished artist with a unique and creative style that we anticipate will be very desirable to the target market.

TRM will also draw on key individuals in its external management team. These individuals have expertise in their fields that can be leveraged to TRM's benefit. These individuals are:

- John Simmons—CEO of Yearbook Interactive (strong sales/marketing experience a well as general small business ownership experience)
- Susan Jackson—Allstate Insurance (extensive general management experience)
- Bill Hannson—Attorney

TRM still needs to acquire an individual with intellectual property expertise for its external management team.

7.1. Personnel Plan

TRM is intended to be a part-time business that provides a creative outlet for the employees and creates some additional revenue in the process. Monthly salaries will be based on sales. TRM will take 70 percent of the total profit from sales and put this toward the two key individual's monthly salaries. The owner will receive 60 percent of the salary while the creative manager will receive 40 percent of the salary. As such, the profit each individual receives will vary by month and will be subject to seasonality. As a part-time business, other benefits will not be necessary.

Personnel Plan	FY 2007	FY 2008	FY 2009
Thomas Williams	$6,837	$7,749	$9,173
Vedranna Inc.	$4,562	$5,166	$6,116
Total People	2	2	2
Total Payroll	$11,399	$12,915	$15,289

8. Financial Plan

It is assumed that the only outside funding that TRM will need is for start-up fees. Growth is expected to be between 10 and 15 percent per year and can easily be maintained without additional debt due to the business setup.

TRM LLC

8.1. Start-up Funding

TRM's start-up funds are summarized in the following table:

- $6,000 short-term/credit card
- $6,200 owner investment

TRM LLC

Start-up Funding	
Start-up Expenses to Fund	$11,300
Start-up Assets to Fund	$1,300
Total Funding Required	$12,600
Assets	
Non-cash Assets from Start-up	$300
Cash Requirements from Start-up	$1,000
Additional Cash Raised	$0
Cash Balance on Starting Date	$1,000
Total Assets	$1,300
Liabilities and Capital	
Liabilities	
Current Borrowing	$6,000
Long-term Liabilities	$0
Accounts Payable (Outstanding Bills)	$0
Other Current Liabilities (Interest Free)	$0
Total Liabilities	$6,000
Capital	
Planned Investment	
Owner	$6,600
Investor	$0
Additional Investment Requirement	$0
Total Planned Investment	$6,600
Loss at Startup (Start-up Expenses)	($11,300)
Total Capital	($4,700)
Total Capital and Liabilities	$1,300
Total Funding	$12,600

8.2. Important Assumptions

We do not sell anything on credit. The personnel burden is very low because benefits are not paid to part-timers. The short-term loan for the business is minimal and is estimated to carry a 10 percent interest rate. Salaries are paid on a commission only basis and are paid out as a percentage of sales profit.

TRM LLC

8.3. Break-even Analysis

TRM's break-even analysis is summarized by the following chart and table.

Break-even Analysis	
Monthly Units Break-even	138
Monthly Revenue Break-even	$2,618
Assumptions:	
Average Per-unit Revenue	$18.95
Average Per-unit Variable Cost	$9.10
Estimated Monthly Fixed Cost	$1,362

Break-even Analysis

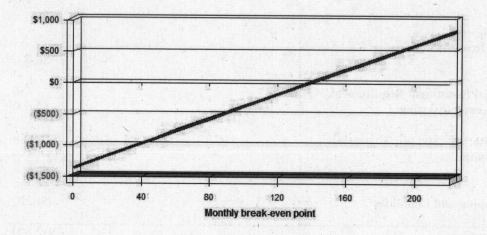

Break-even point = where line intersects with 0

8.4. Projected Profit and Loss

TRM's marketing and advertising budget is estimated to be between 10 and 15 percent of the total projected gross sales profit, which is expected to fluctuate with the seasonality of the market. Payroll expenses are also a factor of projected gross sales profit, with 70 percent of gross profit

TRM LLC

sales being divided between the owner and the creative design artist (60 and 40 percent respectively).

The only other notable expense is related to continued Web design updates and Web hosting fees.

Pro Forma Profit and Loss	FY 2007	FY 2008	FY 2009
Sales	$50,938	$57,741	$71,940
Direct Costs of Goods	$24,450	$27,716	$34,531
Other Costs of Goods	$0	$0	$0
	------------	------------	------------
Cost of Goods Sold	$24,450	$27,716	$34,531
Gross Margin	$26,488	$30,025	$37,409
Gross Margin %	52.00%	52.00%	52.00%
Expenses			
Payroll	$11,399	$12,915	$15,289
Marketing/Promotion	$3,680	$4,167	$4,934
Depreciation	$0	$0	$0
Web Maintenance	$660	$660	$660
Other	$600	$600	$600
	------------	------------	------------
Total Operating Expenses	$16,339	$18,342	$21,483
Profit Before Interest and Taxes	$10,149	$11,683	$15,926
EBITDA	$10,149	$11,683	$15,926
Interest Expense	$1,200	$1,200	$1,200
Taxes Incurred	$2,685	$3,145	$4,418
Net Profit	$6,264	$7,338	$10,308
Net Profit/Sales	12.30%	12.71%	14.33%

TRM LLC

Profit Monthly – FY 2007

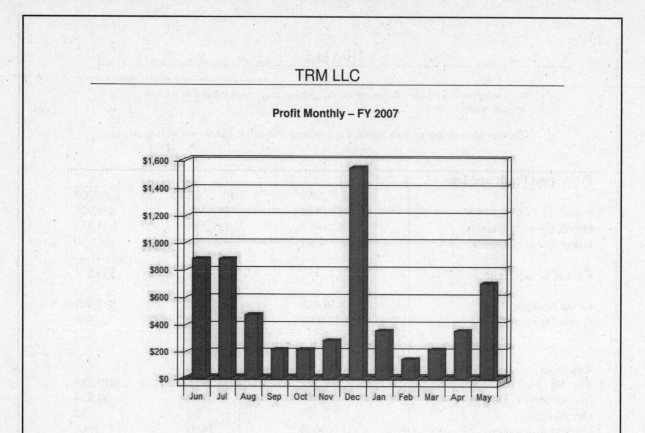

Profit Yearly

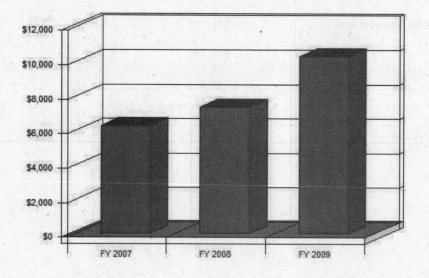

TRM LLC

Gross Margin Monthly – FY 2007

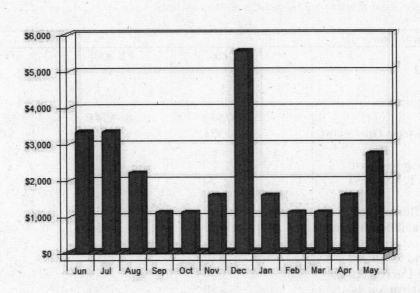

Gross Margin Yearly

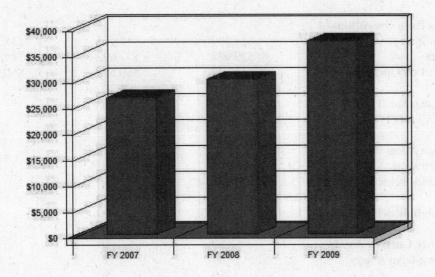

TRM LLC

8.5. Projected Cash Flow

Our projected cash flow is outlined in the following chart and table.

Pro Forma Cash Flow			
	FY 2007	FY 2008	FY 2009
Cash Received			
Cash from Operations			
Cash Sales	$50,938	$57,741	$71,940
Subtotal Cash from Operations	$50,938	$57,741	$71,940
Additional Cash Received			
Sales Tax, VAT, HST/GST Received	$0	$0	$0
New Current Borrowing	$6,000	$0	$0
New Other Liabilities (Interest free)	$0	$0	$0
New Long-term Liabilities	$0	$0	$0
Sales of Other Current Assets	$0	$0	$0
Sales of Long-term Assets	$0	$0	$0
New Investment Received	$0	$0	$0
Subtotal Cash Received	$56,938	$57,741	$71,940
Expenditures	FY 2007	FY 2008	FY 2009
Expenditures from Operations			
Cash Spending	$11,399	$12,915	$15,289
Bill Payments	$29,988	$37,693	$45,615
Subtotal Spent on Operations	$41,387	$50,608	$60,904
Additional Cash Spent			
Sales Tax, VAT, HST/GST Paid Out	$0	$0	$0
Principal Repayment of Current Borrowing	$0	$0	$0
Other Liabilities Principal Repayment	$0	$0	$0
Long-term Liabilities Principal Repayment	$0	$0	$0
Purchase Other Current Assets	$0	$0	$0
Purchase Long-term Assets	$0	$0	$0
Dividends	$0	$0	$0
Subtotal Cash Spent	$41,387	$50,608	$60,904
Net Cash Flow	$15,551	$7,133	$11,036
Cash Balance	$16,551	$23,683	$34,719

TRM LLC

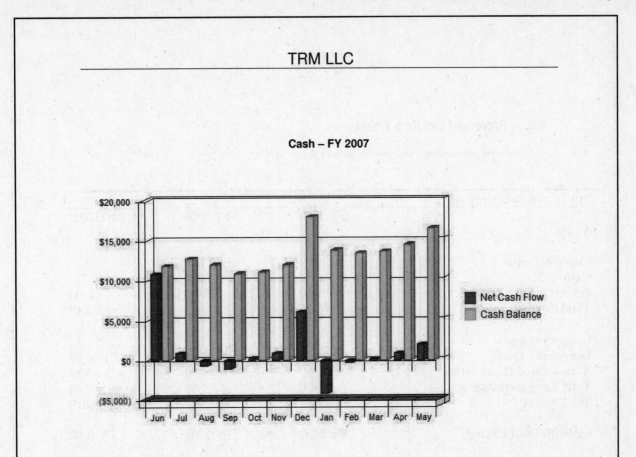

Cash – FY 2007

Net Cash Flow
Cash Balance

TRM LLC

8.6. Projected Balance Sheet

The table below outlines the projected balance sheet.

Pro Forma Balance Sheet			
Assets	FY 2007	FY 2008	FY 2009
Current Assets			
Cash	$16,551	$23,683	$34,719
Other Current Assets	$300	$300	$300
Total Current Assets	$16,851	$23,983	$35,019
Long-term Assets			
Long-term Assets	$0	$0	$0
Accumulated Depreciation	$0	$0	$0
Total Long-term Assets	$0	$0	$0
Total Assets	$16,851	$23,983	$35,019
Liabilities and Capital	FY 2007	FY 2008	FY 2009
Current Liabilities			
Accounts Payable	$3,287	$3,081	$3,809
Current Borrowing	$12,000	$12,000	$12,000
Other Current Liabilities	$0	$0	$0
Subtotal Current Liabilities	$15,287	$15,081	$15,809
Long-term Liabilities	$0	$0	$0
Total Liabilities	$15,287	$15,081	$15,809
Paid-in Capital	$6,600	$6,600	$6,600
Retained Earnings	($11,300)	($5,036)	$2,302
Earnings	$6,264	$7,338	$10,308
Total Capital	$1,564	$8,902	$19,210
Total Liabilities and Capital	$16,851	$23,983	$35,019
Net Worth	$1,564	$8,902	$19,210

TRM LLC

8.7. Business Ratios

Business ratios for the years of this plan are shown below. Industry profile ratios based on the Standard Industrial Classification (SIC) code 2329, for Men's & Boys' Clothing

TRM LLC

Ratio Analysis

	FY 2007	FY 2008	FY 2009	Industry Profile
Sales Growth	0.00%	13.36%	24.59%	-6.49%
Percent of Total Assets				
Other Current Assets	1.78%	1.25%	0.86%	22.63%
Total Current Assets	100.00%	100.00%	100.00%	89.20%
Long-term Assets	0.00%	0.00%	0.00%	10.80%
Total Assets	100.00%	100.00%	100.00%	100.00%
Current Liabilities	90.72%	62.88%	45.14%	30.58%
Long-term Liabilities	0.00%	0.00%	0.00%	20.63%
Total Liabilities	90.72%	62.88%	45.14%	51.21%
Net Worth	9.28%	37.12%	54.86%	48.79%
Percent of Sales				
Sales	100.00%	100.00%	100.00%	100.00%
Gross Margin	52.00%	52.00%	52.00%	22.54%
Selling, General & Administrative Expenses	39.70%	39.29%	37.67%	11.39%
Advertising Expenses	0.00%	0.00%	0.00%	0.38%
Profit Before Interest and Taxes	19.92%	20.23%	22.14%	1.14%
Main Ratios				
Current	1.10	1.59	2.22	2.64
Quick	1.10	1.59	2.22	1.00
Total Debt to Total Assets	90.72%	62.88%	45.14%	54.29%
Pre-tax Return on Net Worth	572.16%	117.76%	76.66%	3.72%
Pre-tax Return on Assets	53.11%	43.71%	42.05%	8.13%
Additional Ratios	FY 2007	FY 2008	FY 2009	
Net Profit Margin	12.30%	12.71%	14.33%	NA
Return on Equity	400.51%	82.43%	53.66%	NA
Activity Ratios				
Accounts Payable Turnover	10.12	12.17	12.17	NA
Payment Days	27	31	27	NA
Total Asset Turnover	3.02	2.41	2.05	NA
Debt Ratios				
Debt to Net Worth	9.77	1.69	0.82	NA
Current Liab. to Liab.	1.00	1.00	1.00	NA
Liquidity Ratios				

TRM LLC

Net Working Capital	$1,564	$8,902	$19,210	NA
Interest Coverage	8.46	9.74	13.27	NA
Additional Ratios				
Assets to Sales	0.33	0.42	0.49	NA
Current Debt/Total Assets	91%	63%	45%	NA
Acid Test	1.10	1.59	2.22	NA
Sales/Net Worth	32.57	6.49	3.74	NA
Dividend Payout	0.00	0.00	0.00	NA

Sales Forecast – FY 2007

		Jun	Jul	Aug	Sep	Oct	Nov	Dec	Jan	Feb	Mar	Apr	May
Unit Sales													
TRM T-shirts (15- to 17-year-old market)	0%	113	113	75	38	38	54	188	54	38	38	54	93
TRM T-shirts (18-24-year-old market)	0%	226	226	150	76	76	108	376	108	76	76	108	186
Total Unit Sales		339	339	225	114	114	162	564	162	114	114	162	279
Unit Prices													
TRM T-shirts (15- to 17-year-old market)	$18.95	$18.95	$18.95	$18.95	$18.95	$18.95	$18.95	$18.95	$18.95	$18.95	$18.95	$18.95
TRM T-shirts (18-24-year-old market)	$18.95	$18.95	$18.95	$18.95	$18.95	$18.95	$18.95	$18.95	$18.95	$18.95	$18.95	$18.95
Sales													
TRM T-shirts (15- to 17-year-old market)	$2,141	$2,141	$1,421	$720	$720	$1,023	$3,563	$1,023	$720	$720	$1,023	$1,762
TRM T-shirts (18-24-year-old market)	$4,283	$4,283	$2,843	$1,440	$1,440	$2,047	$7,125	$2,047	$1,440	$1,440	$2,047	$3,525
Total Sales	$6,424	$6,424	$4,264	$2,160	$2,160	$3,070	$10,688	$3,070	$2,160	$2,160	$3,070	$5,287

		Jun	Jul	Aug	Sep	Oct	Nov	Dec	Jan	Feb	Mar	Apr	May
Direct Unit Costs													
TRM T-shirts (15- to 17-year-old market)	48.00%	$9.10	$9.10	$9.10	$9.10	$9.10	$9.10	$9.10	$9.10	$9.10	$9.10	$9.10	$9.10
TRM T-shirts (18-24-year-old market)	48.00%	$9.10	$9.10	$9.10	$9.10	$9.10	$9.10	$9.10	$9.10	$9.10	$9.10	$9.10	$9.10
Direct Cost of Sales													
TRM T-shirts (15- to 17-year-old market)		$1,028	$1,028	$682	$346	$346	$491	$1,710	$491	$346	$346	$491	$846
TRM T-shirts (18-24-year-old market)		$2,056	$2,056	$1,364	$691	$691	$982	$3,420	$982	$691	$691	$982	$1,692
Subtotal Direct Cost of Sales		$3,084	$3,084	$2,047	$1,037	$1,037	$1,474	$5,130	$1,474	$1,037	$1,037	$1,474	$2,538

		Jun	Jul	Aug	Sep	Oct	Nov	Dec	Jan	Feb	Mar	Apr	May
Direct Unit Costs													
TRM T-shirts (15- to 17-year-old market)	48.00%	$9.10	$9.10	$9.10	$9.10	$9.10	$9.10	$9.10	$9.10	$9.10	$9.10	$9.10	$9.10
TRM T-shirts (18-24-year-old market)	48.00%	$9.10	$9.10	$9.10	$9.10	$9.10	$9.10	$9.10	$9.10	$9.10	$9.10	$9.10	$9.10
Direct Cost of Sales													
TRM T-shirts (15- to 17-year-old market)		$1,028	$1,028	$682	$346	$346	$491	$1,710	$491	$346	$346	$491	$846
TRM T-shirts (18-24-year-old market)		$2,056	$2,056	$1,364	$691	$691	$982	$3,420	$982	$691	$691	$982	$1,692
Subtotal Direct Cost of Sales		$3,084	$3,084	$2,047	$1,037	$1,037	$1,474	$5,130	$1,474	$1,037	$1,037	$1,474	$2,538

Personnel Plan – FY 2007		Jun	Jul	Aug	Sep	Oct	Nov	Dec	Jan	Feb	Mar	Apr	May
Thomas Williams	0%	$862	$862	$575	$287	$287	$414	$1,436	$414	$287	$287	$414	$712
Vedranna Inc.	0%	$575	$575	$383	$192	$192	$276	$958	$276	$192	$192	$276	$475
Total People		2	2	2	2	2	2	2	2	2	2	2	2
Total Payroll		$1,437	$1,437	$958	$479	$479	$690	$2,394	$690	$479	$479	$690	$1,187

Pro Forma Profit and Loss – FY 2007

	Jun	Jul	Aug	Sep	Oct	Nov	Dec	Jan	Feb	Mar	Apr	May
Sales	$6,424	$6,424	$4,264	$2,160	$2,160	$3,070	$10,688	$3,070	$2,160	$2,160	$3,070	$5,287
Direct Costs of Goods	$3,084	$3,084	$2,047	$1,037	$1,037	$1,474	$5,130	$1,474	$1,037	$1,037	$1,474	$2,538
Other Costs of Goods	$0	$0	$0	$0	$0	$0	$0	$0	$0	$0	$0	$0
Cost of Goods Sold	$3,084	$3,084	$2,047	$1,037	$1,037	$1,474	$5,130	$1,474	$1,037	$1,037	$1,474	$2,538
Gross Margin	$3,341	$3,341	$2,217	$1,123	$1,123	$1,596	$5,558	$1,596	$1,123	$1,123	$1,596	$2,749
Gross Margin %	52.00%	52.00%	52.00%	52.00%	52.00%	52.00%	52.00%	52.00%	52.00%	52.00%	52.00%	52.00%
Expenses												
Payroll	$1,437	$1,437	$958	$479	$479	$690	$2,394	$690	$479	$479	$690	$1,187
Marketing/Promotion	$464	$464	$308	$156	$156	$222	$772	$222	$156	$156	$222	$382
Depreciation	$0	$0	$0	$0	$0	$0	$0	$0	$0	$0	$0	$0
Web Maintenance	$30	$30	$130	$30	$30	$130	$30	$30	$130	$30	$30	$30
Other	$50	$50	$50	$50	$50	$50	$50	$50	$50	$50	$50	$50
Total Operating Expenses	$1,981	$1,981	$1,446	$715	$715	$1,092	$3,246	$992	$815	$715	$992	$1,649
Profit Before Interest and Taxes	$1,360	$1,360	$771	$408	$408	$504	$2,312	$604	$308	$408	$604	$1,100
EBITDA	$1,360	$1,360	$771	$408	$408	$504	$2,312	$604	$308	$408	$604	$1,100
Interest Expense	$100	$100	$100	$100	$100	$100	$100	$100	$100	$100	$100	$100
Taxes Incurred	$378	$378	$201	$93	$93	$121	$663	$151	$63	$93	$151	$300
Net Profit	$882	$882	$470	$216	$216	$283	$1,548	$353	$146	$216	$353	$700
Net Profit/Sales	13.72%	13.72%	11.02%	9.99%	9.99%	9.22%	14.49%	11.50%	6.75%	9.99%	11.50%	13.24%

Pro Forma Cash Flow – FY 2007

		Jun	Jul	Aug	Sep	Oct	Nov	Dec	Jan	Feb	Mar	Apr	May
Cash Received													
Cash from Operations													
Cash Sales		$6,424	$6,424	$4,264	$2,160	$2,160	$3,070	$10,688	$3,070	$2,160	$2,160	$3,070	$5,287
Subtotal Cash from Operations		$6,424	$6,424	$4,264	$2,160	$2,160	$3,070	$10,688	$3,070	$2,160	$2,160	$3,070	$5,287
Additional Cash Received													
Sales Tax, VAT, HST/GST Received	0.00%	$0	$0	$0	$0	$0	$0	$0	$0	$0	$0	$0	$0
New Current Borrowing		$6,000	$0	$0	$0	$0	$0	$0	$0	$0	$0	$0	$0
New Other Liabilities (Interest Free)		$0	$0	$0	$0	$0	$0	$0	$0	$0	$0	$0	$0
New Long-term Liabilities		$0	$0	$0	$0	$0	$0	$0	$0	$0	$0	$0	$0
Sales of Other Current Assets		$0	$0	$0	$0	$0	$0	$0	$0	$0	$0	$0	$0
Sales of Long-term		$0	$0	$0	$0	$0	$0	$0	$0	$0	$0	$0	$0

Long-term Liabilities Principal Repayment	$0	$0	$0	$0	$0	$0	$0	$0	$0	$0	$0	$0
Purchase Other Current Assets	$0	$0	$0	$0	$0	$0	$0	$0	$0	$0	$0	$0
Purchase Long-term Assets	$0	$0	$0	$0	$0	$0	$0	$0	$0	$0	$0	$0
Dividends	$0	$0	$0	$0	$0	$0	$0	$0	$0	$0	$0	$0
Subtotal Cash Spent	$1,574	$5,542	$5,021	$3,269	$1,944	$2,176	$4,646	$7,278	$2,489	$2,012	$2,174	$3,260
Net Cash Flow	$10,850	$882	($757)	($1,109)	$216	$893	$6,042	($4,208)	($329)	$148	$896	$2,027
Cash Balance	$11,850	$12,732	$11,975	$10,866	$11,081	$11,975	$18,017	$13,808	$13,479	$13,627	$14,523	$16,551

Pro Forma Balance Sheet – FY 2007

Assets	Starting Balances	Jun	Jul	Aug	Sep	Oct	Nov	Dec	Jan	Feb	Mar	Apr	May
Current Assets													
Cash	$1,000	$11,850	$12,732	$11,975	$10,866	$11,081	$11,975	$18,017	$13,808	$13,479	$13,627	$14,523	$16,551
Other Current Assets	$300	$300	$300	$300	$300	$300	$300	$300	$300	$300	$300	$300	$300
Total Current Assets	$1,300	$12,150	$13,032	$12,275	$11,166	$11,381	$12,275	$18,317	$14,108	$13,779	$13,927	$14,823	$16,851
Long-term Assets													
Long-term Assets	$0	$0	$0	$0	$0	$0	$0	$0	$0	$0	$0	$0	$0
Accumulated Depreciation	$0	$0	$0	$0	$0	$0	$0	$0	$0	$0	$0	$0	$0
Total Long-term Assets	$0	$0	$0	$0	$0	$0	$0	$0	$0	$0	$0	$0	$0
Total Assets	$1,300	$12,150	$13,032	$12,275	$11,166	$11,381	$12,275	$18,317	$14,108	$13,779	$13,927	$14,823	$16,851

Liabilities and Capital		Jun	Jul	Aug	Sep	Oct	Nov	Dec	Jan	Feb	Mar	Apr	May
Current Liabilities													
Accounts Payable	$0	$3,969	$3,969	$2,741	$1,417	$1,417	$2,027	$6,521	$1,959	$1,484	$1,417	$1,959	$3,287
Current Borrowing	$6,000	$12,000	$12,000	$12,000	$12,000	$12,000	$12,000	$12,000	$12,000	$12,000	$12,000	$12,000	$12,000
Other Current Liabilities	$0	$0	$0	$0	$0	$0	$0	$0	$0	$0	$0	$0	$0
Subtotal Current Liabilities	$6,000	$15,969	$15,969	$14,741	$13,417	$13,417	$14,027	$18,521	$13,959	$13,484	$13,417	$13,959	$15,287

Long-term Liabilities	$0	$0	$0	$0	$0	$0	$0	$0	$0	$0	$0	$0	$0
Total Liabilities	$6,000	$15,969	$15,969	$14,741	$13,417	$13,417	$14,027	$18,521	$13,959	$13,484	$13,417	$13,959	$15,287
Paid-in Capital	$6,600	$6,600	$6,600	$6,600	$6,600	$6,600	$6,600	$6,600	$6,600	$6,600	$6,600	$6,600	$6,600
Retained Earnings	($11,300)	($11,300)	($11,300)	($11,300)	($11,300)	($11,300)	($11,300)	($11,300)	($11,300)	($11,300)	($11,300)	($11,300)	($11,300)
Earnings	$0	$882	$1,763	$2,233	$2,449	$2,665	$2,948	$4,496	$4,849	$4,995	$5,211	$5,564	$6,264
Total Capital	($4,700)	($3,818)	($2,937)	($2,467)	($2,251)	($2,035)	($1,752)	($204)	$149	$295	$511	$864	$1,564
Total Liabilities and Capital	$1,300	$12,150	$13,032	$12,275	$11,166	$11,381	$12,275	$18,317	$14,108	$13,779	$13,927	$14,823	$16,851
Net Worth	($4,700)	($3,818)	($2,937)	($2,467)	($2,251)	($2,035)	($1,752)	($204)	$149	$295	$511	$864	$1,564

Market Analysis

XYZ Consulting Co., LLC

1234 Arctic Parkway
Bldg. C-2
Potter County, PA 04020

December 17, 2004

Provided by:
XYZ Consulting Co.
1234 Arctic Parkway, Bldg. C-2
Potter County, PA 04020
Telephone: (555) 723-3545
Fax: (555) 723-3408
www.XYZconsultingcompany.com

Published by
XYZ Consulting Co.
Statement of Confidentiality

*The information in this proposal is confidential and proprietary. It has been made available to
_____ solely for its consideration in evaluation of this proposal. In no event shall all or
any portion of this proposal be copied without the express written permission of XYZ Consulting Co.*

Table of Contents

1. Opening Statement

XYZ Consulting Co. was contracted to perform a market analysis for the property located at 123 North and Peak Parkway. XYZ Consulting Co.'s methodology for conducting such an analysis is part of the strategic planning process that it utilizes in its business practices. This process is outlined in Appendix A.

The research for this market analysis was conducted using resources including the Internet, local chambers of commerce, city and county governments, on-site and local direct observations, and targeted research. The following is the findings of this research.

2. Property Value

During the past twenty-four months, retail land prices have been offered at $10.00 – $14.50 per square foot along the 123 North east of I-515 corridor. David Early recently closed a build to suit requirement for Excellent Burger for a pad site at approximately 500 East 123 North with the land priced at $14.50 per square foot. Quick and Fast Lube has also recently acquired a small pad with high visibility frontage priced at approximately $13.00 per square foot. Land prices will vary in the aforementioned range depending on size, frontage, and visibility.

Based upon property valuations for the surrounding areas, Four Peaks Realty suggests a current average value of land at 123 North and Peak Parkway to be approximately $12.00 a square foot. Given that value, one acre of land is worth approximately $522,720.00. Therefore, the combined property totaling 18.46 acres at 123 North and Peak Parkway is worth approximately $9,649,411.00. This is not an official appraisal for the purpose of securing a bank loan. This estimation of the value of the property is based upon surrounding land values. Parcel #1 is worth approximately $1,907,928.00, parcel #2 is worth approximately $3,998,808.00 and parcel #3 is worth approximately $3,742,655.00. The projection of land valuation according to Four Peaks is expected to remain steady for the next twelve months. Given the current trend of real estate values in this area of the Grand Valley, a prediction of the approximate value for undeveloped land in three years is anticipated to increase 4 to 6 percent per year. Of course, there may be extenuating circumstances that could change this value that may not be in anyone's control.

3. Demographics

Potter County land area is comprised of 80.2 square miles. The demographics for the Potter County area are as follows:

3.1 General Demographics

3.1.1 Income Levels

Income levels have been on the rise in the Potter County area since the late 1980s. The 2000 U.S. Census Bureau shows Potter County, PA as having the second highest median household income in Pennsylvania at $56,400 per year. The average household income is reported at $60,700.

3.1.2 Population

The total population as reported by the U.S. Census Bureau for 2000 in the Potter County, PA area is 25,220 with the median age being 28.6 years. In comparison, the population for 1990 was 5,350 and in 1997 grew to 19,004. A more detailed population breakdown is as follows:

Sex

Male	14,248
Female	10,972

Age

Under 5 years of age	2,640
5 to 9 years	2,340
10 to 14	1,959
15 to 19	1,807
20 to 24	2,150
25 to 34	5,173
35 to 44	4,498
45 to 54	2,525
55 to 59	707
60 to 64	495
65 to 74	556
75 to 84	271
Over 85 years of age	99

Race

Caucasian	23,013
African American	384
Hispanic	1,469
American Indian	189
Asian	329
Pacific Islander	92
Other race not mentioned	684
Two or more races	529

Housing and Household by Type

Total households	6,305
Married with children	5,426
Married couples	3,449
Single mom	351
Householder living alone	879

Average home price	$252,190
Average family size	3.69
Vacant housing units	283
Owner occupied	5,285
Rental occupied	1,020

3.2 Municipal Information

The following information is provided to assist in understanding the make-up of municipal government officers and services available for the property outlined in this market analysis.

The current Potter County city mayor is Paul Jones (D). Potter County's city council is comprised of six members:

Doug Bedke (R)
Bill Colbert (D)
Paul Edwards (R)
Paul McCarty (D)
John Shakula (D)
Melanie Dansi (R)

The city manager is Thomas Julian.

Potter County city offers several city services including:
- Administrative
- Community development, including the building and planning commission
- Judicial
- Finance
- Engineering, which recently updated and is implementing a new storm drain master plan, water system master plan, and traffic transportation master plan for Potter County. Potter County engineering has also received funding for various projects in the city including PTA trails along 1300 East, 124 North to 138 North, two bridges crossing the East Jackson Canal at 190 North and 120 North, Jackson River Tri-City Parkway.
- Parks and recreation
- City recorder
- Public safety

Public safety in Potter County is a high priority as evidenced by the history and structure of the public safety departments. Fire department services are provided by the Grand County Fire Department. The fire department operates seventeen full-time and three volunteer stations and employs 300 full-time and 100 part-time employees. One such full-time station is located on 123 North just East of the Lone Peak Parkway area. Fire and medical response from this station to Lone Peak Parkway would be under five minutes. The fire department utilizes a four-person engine company where most communities of equal size only operate a three-person engine. This increases efficiency by at least 35 percent.

Police services for Potter County city is provided by the Grand County Sheriff's Office. Although there has been an increase in the number of calls from 9,848 in 1997 to 14,433 in 2003, a spokesman for the sheriff's department explained the number of violent crimes has gone down. The reason for the increase of overall calls is due to an extremely fast growth of local population.

A strategic priority of the Potter County city council is to:

- Establish a plan for appropriate facilities for Potter County city operations and cultural arts.

- Public opinion poll (March 2004) stated that:

  o 98 percent said it is important that citizens of all ages feel safe, have places to gather,

December 17, 2004

Market Analysis Study

and enjoy traditions, events and culture

o 99 percent said it is important that Potter County is clean, pleasant, pastoral, has a small-town feeling and sense of identity

Potter County's Mission Statement

Mission
Potter County is a community that preserves its unique identity and heritage, and provides protection and services for its citizens.

Values
Unity
Neighbors work together to build a strong community.
Respect
Citizens have tolerance, understanding, and sensitivity to one another's differences.
Quality of Life
Citizens of all ages feel safe, have places to gather, and enjoy traditions, events and culture.
Environment
Potter County is clean, pleasant, pastoral, has a small-town feeling and sense of identity.
Pride
Citizens are proud to call Potter County "home," and are involved in community well being.

Adopted by Resolution No. 99-12, April 6, 1900

Climate and Weather

Potter County average annual snowfall is 64.5 inches per year.
The average low temperature is 40 degrees F.
The average high temperature is 64 degrees F.

History and History Related Items

Potter County history: Potter County was first called North Willow Creek. Ebenezer Brown, Phoebe (his wife), and their five children are acknowledged as the first settlers of Potter County in 1749. They farmed the land and raised cattle to sell to emigrants going to the gold fields in the West. The name of their home was Potter County Fort. When a post office was established there, aboPA1754, the name was changed to Potter Countyville Post Office, then to just Potter County later. The name was for William Potter County, who was the first presiding elder of the Religious Church at that time. The winter of 1755–56 found the settlers in Fort Potter County and then in the spring, they left the safety of the fort to build homes and irrigation systems, and further establish the community. The city was incorporated on 22 February 1778.

3.3 Education

There are a number of kindergarten through 12th grade schools in the Potter County area. The breakdown of schools is as follows:

Elementary Schools:
- Potter County Elementary   1080 East 122 North
- North Mountain Elementary   900 East Park School Road

Middle Schools
- Crescent View Middle School   110 North 300 Road

High Schools
- Stone High School   115 North 1000 East Highway
- River View High School   120 North 200 Westerton

Private Schools
- Sacket Catholic Center   300 East 100 North

3.4 Quality of Life Study

Given the higher average sales price for homes in the Potter County area—coupled with the average salary, Potter County enjoys a certain affluential distinction. The neighborhoods are kept clean and the majority of homeowners maintain a well-groomed yard. Several business parks have been developed with additional business parks under construction. The percentage of building occupancy is currently 68 percent. This is due to the number of newly completed buildings for lease. Building owners are confident that with the steady shifting of the businesses to the north valley, they will fill all the available space.

To measure the current climate of business, the American Chamber of Commerce Research Association (ACCRA) gives a rating based on a national average of 100 representing the baseline. **Potter County was given an ACCRA score of 106.5.** This shows that Potter County is scoring above the national average.

3.5 Location of Potter County

Potter County is located the following distances from other major cities:

- 18 miles north of Pittsburgh
- 28 miles north of Altaview
- 411 miles from Washington, D.C.
- 512 miles from New York City
- 637 miles from Buffalo
- 673 miles from Atlanta

4. Psychographics

Potter County is comprised of many different individuals from all walks of life. This is evident with the demographics previously outlined. The businesses that have located in Potter County cater to a wide variety of consumer interests, and there exists a good mix of businesses in the area. Indications are that the mix of goods and services in the area serve the population well. There are many businesses that seem to be doing very well and they continue to increase business, or at a minimum stay in business.

The buying patterns for the area justify a higher standard of living and thus provide for a good economic base for businesses to thrive.

5. Transportation

There are four existing interchanges on Interstate 15 in the Potter County area. The first is located at State Street, the second at 123 North, the third at 146 North, and the fourth at Bostonian Highway. The PDOT and Potter County city master plan shows a planned interchange at 114 North.

The Grand International Airport is located twenty-one miles from Potter County. The Pennsylvania Transit Authority (PTA) has assigned several bus routes to and from Potter County to the Pittsburgh and Altaview areas. Future PTA light rail line connections to downtown Grand are planned. No completion date has been announced.

6. Traffic Flow

123rd North

Current UDOT traffic counts for 123 North and I-515 is an average of 28,674 cars per day. The busiest times are from 7:00 a.m. to 9:00 p.m. with 9,761 cars traveling on the road, and from 4:00 p.m. to 6:00 p.m. with 10,574 cars on average. The remainder of the car counts is over the remaining twenty-four hours not included in the UDOT peak travel study.

I-95 North and South bound

Although traffic varies from day to day, the average number of cars that pass over the 123 North I-595 interchange on a daily basis is 472,360.

Lone Peak Parkway

The figures for the 123 North and 300 West areas are not yet available.

7. Businesses within a Three-Mile Radius

<u>Regional</u>

– North Town Centre	106 North 100 West	Nordstrom, May Company and Mervyns
– Target	102 North State Street	
– Wal-Mart	104 North State Street	

– Factory Stores of America 121 North Factory Outlet Dr.

Community Shopping Centers		Anchor Tenants
– Hidden Valley	1300 East Potter County Pkway	Albertsons, Rite Aid, and Kmart
– Potter County Crossing	123 North 150 East	Smiths, T.J. Maxx, and GreenDollar
– Potter County Plaza	114 North State Street	Albertsons

Business Parks

– Potter County Business Park	123 S. Lone Peak Parkway	330,000 Square Feet
– Water Corporate Center	120 S. Lone Peak Parkway	311,000 Square Feet
– Potter County Business Park N.	117 S. Lone Peak Parkway	262,000 Square Feet
– Southtown Business Park	137 S. Minute Dr	120,000 Square Feet

Gas Stations/Convenience Stores

– Albertsons Gas Station	114 S. State Street
– Costco Gas Station	114 S. State Street
– Chevron	126 S. 1700 W.
– Holiday Oil	126 S. 1300 W.
– Phillips Kicks 66	126 S. 1300 W.
– Flying J	123 S. 100 E.
– Texaco	123 S. 100 E.
– Holiday Oil	123 S. 300 E.
– Maverick	104 S. 1300W
– Chevron	106 S. 1300 E.
– Amoco	106 S. 700 E.
– Amoco	126 S. 1300 W.

Hotels

– Country Inn and Suites	104 S. Jackson Gateway (North Jackson)
– Sleep Inn and Suites	106 S. 300 W. (North Jackson)
– Best Western	106 S. Automall Dr. (Rocky Port)
– Hampton Inn	107 S. Holiday Park Dr. (Rocky Port)
– Courtyard by Marriott	107 S. Holiday Park Dr. (Rocky Port)
– Extended Stay America	107 S. Automall Dr. (Rocky Port)
– Holiday Inn Express	120 S. Factory Outlet Dr. (Potter County)
– Ramada Inn	126 S. 100 E. (Potter County)

Banks

– Zion's Bank	123 S. 100 E.
– University of Pennsylvania CU	123 S. 100 E.

– Key Bank	123 S. 400 E.	
– Wells Fargo	123 S. 322 E.	
– Jackson Credit Union	123 S. 400 E.	
– Zion's Bank	123 S. 200 E.	
– Wells Fargo	126 S. 1700 W.	
– Mountain America	126 S. 2000 W.	
– Wells Fargo	110 S. State Street	
– Wells Fargo	106 S. 1300 E.	
– Mountain America	106 S. State Street	
– US Bank	106 S. State Street	
– Zion's	106 S. 200 W.	
– Beehive Credit Union	103 S. 1300 E.	
– US Bank	103 S. 1300 E.	
– Zion's	103 S. 1300 E.	

Movie Theaters

– Carmike	910 S. Oakwood Road	8 Theaters
– Northtown Cinema	106 S. 282 W.	Closed / Downsize
– Rocky Port Starship 4	940 S. 800 E.	4 Theaters
– Potter Commons	940 S. State Street	17 Theaters
– Jackson Landing	750 S. Boomtown Highway	24 Theaters

Sit Down Style Restaurants

– Ruby Tuesday	120 S. Frontage Road
– Fazioles	126 S. 100 E.
– Wingers	126 S. 100 E.
– Cowboy Grub	123 S. 400 E.
– Giovanni's	104 S. Jackson Gateway
– Chili's	104 S. State Street
– Black Angus	104 S. State Street
– IHOP	112 S. State Street
– Dos Amigo's	107 S. State Street
– Bennett's	104 S. 108 W.
– TGI Friday's	106 S. 103 W.
– Village Inn	106 S. 105 W.
– Home Town Buffet	103 S. State Street
– Gecko's	106 S. 1100 W.
– Maddox	106 S. 1100 W.
– Carvers	107 S. Holiday Park Dr.
– Tony Roma's	102 S. State Street
– Sweet Tomatoes	100 S. State Street
– Fuddruckers	103 S. State Street
– Olive Garden	106 S. State Street (new)

8. Surrounding Business Climate

Business buildings are continuing to be constructed in the North Jackson Gateway area, and just North of Potter County in the Lewiston area. There is some concern among commercial real estate brokers that with the number of new buildings recently constructed and in progress of being constructed, there may be a surplus of office space for the foreseeable future.

According to NEI Mortgage in Potter County, there is approximately 4,000,000 sq. ft. of unleased office space in the Gemstone Valley. However, the population of the study area is continuing to grow and new businesses are moving to the Potter County area on a regular basis. All economic indicators for the Potter County and the surrounding areas are showing continued growth for the next several years.

9. Highest and Best Use of the Property

As the parcel consists of approximately 743 feet of visible frontage on the north side of the property, and with the current construction of the road through the property, there are a few options to consider for the highest and best use of the three parcels. The following options are recommendations derived from a thorough analysis of the surrounding businesses, demographics, and psychographics of the area, and the area of 18.46 acres to work with.

Option A

Movie theater as an anchor tenant on Parcels #2 and #3 with a strip mall attached. The anchor tenant could be located in the middle of the strip mall. One suggestion is to consider a movie complex in the area. The closest movie theaters are approximately six miles away.

Jackson Commons and Jackson Landing have been successful in their operations as a larger, master-planned community.

This parcel is just slightly smaller than the parcels for each of these successful venues. A third example for this type of use of property is located in Layton, UT. It is located on the frontage road to I-15 with no obstructions from freeway view. It boasts three multi-theater complexes and at least twelve name brand, sit-down style restaurants. This particular property has been highly successful for all of the businesses located in the complex.

Parcel #1 could also have a gas station with a convenience store/food mart, and possibly an indoor fast food restaurant. The venue should also face 123 North. Also located on this parcel could be a sit-down style restaurant for couples to frequent prior to viewing a movie.

Parking for this parcel could be under the large electric poles located on the east side of the property.

There are several considerations for a sit-down restaurant; however, some strong possibilities could be Applebees, Alberto's, Potter's Sports Grill, Sizzler, Ruby River, Diamond Joe's.

A consideration could also be made for constructing a banking facility on this property. American Credit Union, Bank of American Culture, US Bank, Bank One, and possibly Zion's Bank might be good options for negotiating a pad on the parcel.

Option B

Keep the same theme with a main anchor and a strip mall, a gas station/convenience store, and one sit-down restaurant. Add in two or three fast food restaurants that are stand alone buildings, with a few additional fast food types that are located in the strip mall. These could cater to the three business parks close by (Potter County Business Park, Oghean Corp. Center, and Potter County Business Park North).

The main anchor could be a Harmon's or Food 4 Less grocery tenant.

Another option is to have a furniture store as the main anchor like RC Willey or Granite Furniture. Or, for a more upscale furniture tenant, a consideration may be given to Drexel Heritage or Ethan Allen to add a nice variety to the local area.

Still another option is to invite Office Depot to be the main anchor. They have two stores in Grand Valley located at 200 North 300 West, and one at 700 North and Red Lion Rd. Office Max boasts nine locations in and along the Oghean Front with the closest store located at 1900 North and State Street. Staples has fours stores in the valley with the closest store located at 1300 North and State Street.

Add in a Hotel on Parcel #1 and consider Crystal Inn, Days Inn, Fairfield Inn, Red Roof Inn, La Quinta, Hilton, or a Marriott Hotel.

Option C

Create Parcels #2 and #3 into a medical park that would house doctors, dentists, chiropractors, physical therapists, hospice care, etc. This could be an extension of the medical facilities for America's Health Care, the University of Pennsylvania, and the University of Columbia.

A freestanding building for medical supplies could also be on the property located on Parcel #1.

This theme could also lend a nice effect for a mattress store, and even a spa and fitness center—staying with the health theme.

Option D

Assisted living is a booming business in the Grand Valley as there are thirty-five of these facilities in the Valley. The closest facilities to the property are located on 100 North 700 East, 100 North 700 East, 100 North 2000 East, 465 East and Lily Drive (10000 North), 100 North 1600 West, 1000 North 1600 West, and 1300 East 900 North. This theme could be located on Parcels #2 and #3.

Build freestanding facilities for medical offices to cater to the patrons and medical personnel at the assisted living facility.

Keep the idea of a hotel on Parcel #1 with a gas station/convenience store.

10. Appendix A

10.1 References

- Potter County Chamber of Commerce
- Potter County City
- Pennsylvania Department of Transportation
- Grand Chamber of Commerce
- Four Peaks Real Estate
- Grand County Fire Department
- Grand County Sheriff Department
- North Jackson City
- Rocky Port City
- U.S. Census Bureau (1990 and 2000)

10.2 Next Steps

There are a few steps that should be taken in order to make this property a "shining star" in the North Valley. These steps are necessary in order to continue growth and to provide quality education, real estate at affordable prices, and safety infrastructure.

The next steps moving forward are as follows:

- Develop a workable 90-day rolling business plan

- Finalize the strategic plan for 2005

- Start on the development of a disaster recovery plan

- Finalize on the real estate and zoning plan for noticeable properties along the 123rd Corridor

10.2.1 Business Plan

The first step is to determine the highest and best use of the property, and then begin to prepare a comprehensive business plan. The business plan would outline several areas that will be required to assist potential lessees or buyers of parcels of land when securing financing.

More importantly, however, the business plan will assist you in clearly understanding how to proceed with this business proposition, and how to realize the maximum return on your investment. XYZ Consulting Co. offers business planning services to its clients, and it principals have over eighteen years experience in developing business plans for many uses. This can be outlined in another proposal if you would like to see what this all entails. Joseph Greenberg has also written four best selling books on business planning.

10.2.2 Marketing Team

Next, a consideration should be made on how to assemble the team that will market the property to the right companies, and that will make a good fit for the area. This team should be experienced in sizing up the right mix of tenants, negotiating contracts, and working with city officials.

This is also a part of the business planning process; XYZ Consulting goes far beyond and must require the best communication between the property owners and the team.

XYZ Consulting Co. also offers these property management consulting services to its clients, and its principals have over twenty-five years experience in development of commercial properties. This can be outlined in another proposal if you would like to see the details for this type of service offering.

10.3 XYZ Consulting Co. Planning Model and Process

Our planning model is a simple, graphical representation of the proper flow of planning, and is the foundation of our business planning and strategic planning methodologies.

This process in developing a solid strategic plan should be followed to a science and allow the internal strategic planning team to research and strategize a successful organization.

INDEX

D

E

F

G

H

I

M

W

About the Authors

Joseph A. Covello is the founder of The Covello Group, a professional firm specializing in business planning and finance located in Clearwater, Florida, and serving the greater Tampa Bay area. His firm services small- and medium-size clients in various industries including manufacturing, distribution, service, and retail.

Joe holds a Masters of Business Administration degree in Finance from Fairleigh Dickinson University and he has a Bachelor of Arts degree in Accounting from William Paterson University. He has coauthored two books, *Your First Business Plan* and *The Complete Book of Business Plans*, and in addition he has written several notable papers on business related subjects.

He has been a radio talk show cohost with Brian Hazelgren on the number one station in the Phoenix, Arizona, market. The show was called "All About Business" and the focus topics were geared toward assisting business owners and managers in creating business efficiencies in management, sales, marketing, production, and finance.

In addition, Joe served as an adjunct faculty member for the State of Arizona Community College District were he taught classes in Sales, Marketing, Management, Human Relations, and Business Planning. He was instrumental in creating, developing, and presenting the course on business planning to the College District Board where it was approved and implemented as an official course to be used throughout the College District.

Over his twenty-six year career, he has been hired into several key management positions for the primary purpose to spearhead business start-ups, turnarounds, and expansions. During his tenure, each business enterprise achieved higher sales levels, increased employee moral and productivity, and a more profitable bottom line.

Brian J. Hazelgren is Managing Partner of Business Training Camp and is a globally recognized expert in business planning, strategic planning, infrastructure development, training, sales, and operations.

Brian has written and cowritten seven books and has produced Business Game Plan Collection CDs for entrepreneurs. Three of his books have received prestigious awards, and are course textbooks in several colleges. Brian is also a frequent guest on radio talk shows and conventions throughout the country.

During the past twenty-two years, Brian has been consulting with many companies on a local, national, and international scale where he has developed strategies and tactical programs to increase sales by 400 percent to over 4,000 percent. His techniques of sales, marketing, logistics, and operations have spanned small business, large enterprises, nonprofit organizations, and government. He has owned several successful businesses in manufacturing and consulting, and also manufactured and distributed the popular Gumball Wizard vending machines.

Brian is an Adjunct Professor at the University of Utah in the Entrepreneurship Program for graduates and undergraduates. He has a degree in Marketing from Western International University, with a minor in Finance where he graduated Summa Cum Laude. He has developed the teaching curriculum for several courses in the Entrepreneurship Program for the University of Utah and has been a judge for several years for the statewide business planning competition, The Entrepreneur Challenge, for all universities and colleges.

Brian has been a radio talk show cohost with Joe Covello on the number one station in the Phoenix, Arizona, market KFYI AM. The talk show was called "All About Business" and the focus of topics were geared towards assisting entrepreneurs and managers in running a better organization.

As a member of the BYU National Championship Football Team in 1984, Brian played defensive back and kick return specialist. He was a two-sport All American, and four-sport All State athlete in high school. As a sprinter in track and field, Brian has held five records in the State of Utah.

Brian and his wife, Ann, have six children and live in Riverton, Utah.